NCLB at the Crossroads

REEXAMINING THE FEDERAL EFFORT TO CLOSE THE ACHIEVEMENT GAP

NCLB
at the
Crossroads

- - - - - - - - - - - - -

REEXAMINING THE FEDERAL EFFORT
TO CLOSE THE ACHIEVEMENT GAP

Michael A. Rebell
Jessica R. Wolff
------ *Editors* ------

Teachers College, Columbia University
New York and London

Published by Teachers College Press, 1234 Amsterdam Avenue, New York, NY 10027

Library of Congress Cataloging-in-Publication Data

NCLB at the crossroads : reexamining the federal effort to close the achievement gap / Michael A. Rebell, Jessica R. Wolff, editors.
   p. cm.
     ISBN 978-0-8077-4944-9 (hardcover : alk. paper)
     1. Educational accountability–United States. 2. Educational equalization–United States. 3. Academic achievement–United States. 4. United States. No Child Left Behind Act of 2001. I. Rebell, Michael A. II. Wolff, Jessica R.
   LB2806.22.N4   2009
   379.1'580973–dc22   2008054826

ISBN 978-0-8077-4944-9 (hardcover)

Printed on acid-free paper
Manufactured in the United States of America

16   15   14   13   12   11   10   09   8   7   6   5   4   3   2   1

Contents

Acknowledgments

The general theme of this volume developed during the planning for the Campaign for Educational Equity's second annual Equity Symposium, "Examining America's Commitment to Closing Achievement Gaps: NCLB and Its Alternatives," held in November 2006 at Teachers College, Columbia University. Many of the chapters began as papers commissioned for that event. We are grateful to the authors who, in their symposium presentations and in their chapters in this volume, very thoughtfully tackled some of the most difficult questions presented by current federal education policy. The many discussants and moderators who participated contributed importantly to making the symposium a success. Congressman Charles Rangel, Mayor Cory Booker of Newark, and New York City Council Member Robert Jackson also lent vital support to the event.

We extend our thanks to the Laurie M. Tisch Foundation for sponsoring the symposium and especially to Laurie Tisch for her personal interest in and foundational support for the Campaign for Educational Equity. In addition, we thank Teachers College president Susan Fuhrman for her support and her insightful contributions to the symposium, and we are truly appreciative of Dr. Fuhrman and the trustees of Teachers College for their ongoing support of the Equity Campaign.

The following people at Teachers College played very important roles in planning and running the symposium, and we appreciate their advice and their efforts: Amy Stuart Wells, Edmund Gordon, Tom Sobol, Erica Walker, Jeff Henig, Elisabeth Thurston, Joe Levine, Janice Robinson, Mark Noizumi, and Chandra Cates. We were also lucky to have the help of student volunteers too numerous to mention.

We thank Carole Saltz and the staff at Teachers College Press for their encouragement and assistance in assembling this volume. Finally, we are very grateful to Anna Douthat for her gracious and capable editorial assistance.

Michael A. Rebell
Jessica R. Wolff

Introduction

The promise that federal policymakers made to the American public when they enacted the No Child Left Behind Act (NCLB) in 2002 was that this law would take our nation a step closer to educational equity through its focus on the needs of African American, Latino, special education, and low-income students. By requiring that public schools ensure that all students are proficient in math and reading by 2014, NCLB has put a great deal of pressure on educators to pay more attention to the achievement of traditionally neglected or underserved students. However, today, at the midpoint of the law's timeline for full proficiency and in the midst of uncertainly about its re-authorization, faith in the law is flagging. NCLB is significantly behind schedule in meeting its goals for student performance, teacher quality, academic standards, and other key school improvement measures. Furthermore, there is little evidence to date that the law has made much headway in closing the achievement gap between the nation's wealthier, predominantly white students and those from poor and minority backgrounds. The number of schools identified as needing improvement under the law has continued to grow each year, and it is expected to balloon as 2014 nears and schools in many states are required to make ever-greater leaps toward full proficiency.

One of the important questions President Barack Obama and his administration now need to raise is why NCLB—ostensibly enacted to further the mission of the original Elementary and Secondary Education Act of 1965, the first federal policy to target much-needed resources to our country's most disadvantaged students—is not achieving its vital aims. To help provide answers, the Campaign for Educational Equity at Teachers College, Columbia University, invited a number of the nation's foremost experts on different components of NCLB to consider the following questions: What does the evidence suggest about our public educational system's ability to help all children achieve at high levels by 2014? What would it *really* take—which policies, practices, and resources—to close our nation's academic achievement gaps? To what extent does NCLB actually move us toward these policies, practices, and resources?

The result is this collection of cutting-edge analyses of the various components of the law written by some of the leading researchers and thinkers in the field of educational equity. Each chapter of this book addresses a specific aspect of the challenges of closing our national achievement gaps and assesses NCLB's contribution to these challenges in the years since its enactment. Collectively, these essays lay out the scope of the national challenge to reduce the inequities that have caused and perpetuate academic achievement gaps and the actual potential of NCLB to effect change. Written for a broad audience of policymakers, practitioners, and researchers, they provide a range of provocative critiques of NCLB that go well beyond what has already been said on the subject. Unlike many books on NCLB, this volume tackles the truly difficult questions about how to ensure meaningful educational opportunities for all children, rather than shirking such questions in favor of discussion of politically palatable issues or quick-fix solutions. It speaks not only to current debates during NCLB's reauthorization period, but also to discussions about the future direction of U.S. education research, policy, and practice that will continue as our nation is forced in the near future to come to grips with the obstacles to universal school quality and student proficiency.

Many of the essays in the volume began as papers commissioned for the Campaign for Educational Equity's second annual Equity Symposium, "Examining America's Commitment to Closing Achievement Gaps: NCLB and Its Alternatives," held in November 2006 at Teachers College. A companion book to this volume, *Moving Every Child Ahead: From NCLB Hype to Meaningful Educational Opportunities* by Michael A. Rebell and Jessica R. Wolff (2008), was also inspired by the 2006 Equity Symposium; it provides a detailed set of policy recommendations for revising NCLB, which draws on many of the chapters in this book.

Sociologist Amy Stuart Wells's seminal chapter, "'Our Children's Burden': A History of Federal Education Policies That Ask (Now Require) Our Public Schools to Solve Societal Inequality," opens the volume by placing the achievement gap issue and the difficulties of overcoming those gaps in an important broader context of poverty, inequality, segregation, and U.S. social welfare policies. She raises the critical question of whether schools alone can be expected to overcome student performance gaps. Wells argues that, since World War II, the bulk of the burden of solving social and economic inequality in the United States has been "laid at the schoolhouse door." As other industrialized countries built comprehensive social welfare systems—subsidizing income, health care, pensions, and housing to create more equality among their citizens—the United States saw the public schools as the central means of improving the lives of the poor and disadvantaged. This heavy burden is all the more problematic in the current accountability era and at a time when the United States is experiencing growing income inequality, a downsizing of welfare, and an influx of poor immigrant children. Schools matter, Wells argues, but schools alone cannot solve societal inequalities that are replicated inside their doors: A more comprehensive set of policies is needed to solve the comprehensive inequalities that many children in our public schools confront daily. Without broader social policies that attempt to equalize lives in terms of income, access to health care, and social services, she contends, NCLB may actually punish the students it purports to help.

The next set of chapters by Michael Nettles and his colleagues; Eugene García; and Margaret McLaughlin and her colleagues closely examines NCLB in light of the special needs of specific groups of students traditionally neglected by our schools. Each of these chapters asks the important preliminary question about what these children really need for success and then evaluates the extent to which NCLB is responding to these needs. As advocates for these students, the authors support the provisions of the law that require schools to account for the success of all students; however, they all highlight limitations in the law's mechanisms actually to effect change on these students' behalf.

In Chapter 2, "The Challenge and Opportunity of African American Educational Achievement," Michael Nettles, Catherine Millett, and Hyeyoung Oh of the Educational Testing Service's Policy Evaluation and Research Center tackle the persistent academic achievement gaps between African American and white students in this country. Though the gap between black and white students is the largest and seemingly most intractable, Nettles and his colleagues argue that it provides the "best target of opportunity for the nation to realize the greatest overall gains in achievement and return on investment." They applaud NCLB as historic in its explicit focus both on measuring and understanding black-white achievement gaps and on "making a national imperative of academic gains for everyone and closing gaps among people of various race/ethnic groups and social classes." As our nation weighs options for revising NCLB to accomplish its goal of closing these gaps, the authors ground the debate in an exploration of the human, institutional, and societal elements of African American underachievement. They examine the plausibility of some of the recurring explanations of African American achievement gaps: oppositional culture, racism, socioeconomic factors, family- and community-based factors, and school-based factors. Recognizing the challenge of persuading the public that it is in the national interest to invest in raising the achievement of each race/ethnic group and social class, they nevertheless argue that the unique characteristics and challenges of African American students need to be taken into account in shaping policies directed toward their progress. They outline some practical recommendations for doing so.

Chapter 3, "Educational Policy for Linguistically and Culturally Diverse Students: Foundation or Barrier?" by Eugene E. García of Arizona

State University, confronts the challenge for school systems throughout the United States of educating children from non-English-speaking families. The achievement gaps between these language-minority students and their peers continue to be wide and, as this population expands, ever more critical an issue for our country. Unfortunately, as García argues, today's education policies are largely out of sync with emerging practices that can assist in the reduction of the achievement gap for language-minority students. To provide an important backdrop for revising NCLB to benefit these children, García first discusses the complex range of issues that must be addressed to meet the needs of the nation's linguistically and culturally diverse students. He then evaluates the effect of recent federal, state, and local policy changes on English language learners (ELLs). NCLB's requirements for assessing the progress of ELLs, in particular, create a Catch-22 for schools. Under NCLB, all ELLs, like all other subgroups of students, must be proficient in challenging state standards by 2014, in spite of the obvious contradiction that this subgroup is made up of an ever-changing collection of students defined by their limited English proficiency and inability to meet standards—and in spite of evidence that current methods cannot accurately assess these students' learning. García also decries the trend toward English-only policies and away from support for multiple languages and literacies. He argues that federal education policy, and the state policies it drives, must be more responsive to the needs of ELLs, both in designing the assessments that drive accountability for the achievement of these students and in fostering capacity building among schools and districts to engage experientially diverse students in learning successfully. In particular, García argues for an asset-oriented pedagogical approach in which diversity is perceived as a resource for teaching and learning instead of a problem.

In Chapter 4, "Standards, Assessments, and Accountability for Students with Disabilities: An Evolving Meaning of a 'Free and Appropriate Public Education,'" Margaret McLaughlin, Meredith Miceli, and Amanda Hoffman of the University of Maryland provide a thorough analysis of NCLB's effectiveness in promoting the narrowing of achievement gaps for students with disabilities and their peers. They tackle the thorny problem of the inherent tension between the two policies that shape the education of children with disabilities, NCLB, which is rooted in standards-based reform and creating uniform requirements for all students, and the Individuals with Disabilities Education Act (IDEA), which takes an individualized approach to meeting students' academic needs. Their findings suggest that NCLB may not be closing the achievement gap for students with disabilities, but, nevertheless, it is having a profound effect on the field of special education. The future of special education, McLaughlin and her colleagues suggest, may be in its past; pressures imposed by NCLB may lead us back to treating as "special" only those students with severe disabilities, as opposed to the current practice of providing "compensatory services for students whose only 'disability' has been poor or insufficient general education."

A key question for the reauthorization of NCLB is whether its powerful equity objectives are truly supported by effective educational reform mechanisms. Much of the equity muscle in NCLB comes from its emphasis on outcomes and its demand that positive academic results be demonstrated for all racial/ethnic, language, and economic groups. But, as the next grouping of chapters in this volume by Richard Rothstein and colleagues; Robert Linn; and Robert Schwartz argues, in a number of particular ways, the emphasis on outcomes has become counterproductive.

The adequate yearly progress (AYP) targets that schools must meet are calibrated from NCLB's mandate that all students—100%—be proficient in challenging state standards by 2014. As we approach 2014, it is becoming increasingly clear that this mandated goal cannot be met. In Chapter 5, "'Proficiency for All'—An Oxymoron," Richard Rothstein, a researcher with the Economic Policy Institute and the Campaign for Educational Equity, and his colleagues Rebecca Jacobsen and Tamara Wilder argue that the NCLB goal of 100% proficiency is technically impossible. There is *no date* by which all (or even nearly all) students in any subgroup, even middle-class white students, can achieve proficiency. The authors argue that proficiency for all is an oxymoron because no goal can be simultaneously challenging to and achievable by all students across the entire achievement distribution. NCLB's goal of closing the achievement gap can only sensibly be understood to mean that the range of achievement for groups of disadvantaged and for groups of middle-class children should be more similar. "Proficiency for all," which implies the elimination of variation *within* socioeconomic groups, is inconceivable. Closing the achievement gap, which implies elimination of variation *between* socioeconomic groups, is an extraordinarily difficult but ultimately achievable aim. To reach this goal, Rothstein and colleagues propose a comprehensive 19-year program that includes prenatal care, pre-K, high-quality teaching, preventive health care, and after-school programs for bringing a birth cohort of children to maturity with high levels of performance.

Further, as a result of setting the 100% goal, NCLB requires rates of progress that no school system worldwide has ever achieved and the feasibility of which has never been demonstrated. The law, in part, reflects a business motivational perspective that assumes that, once clear goals and expectations have been set, industrious managers and workers can meet them. In the educational sector, however, there is as yet no definitive understanding of how even the most highly motivated educators can achieve consistently positive results with students with widely differing educational needs. There is also no clear agreement about how educational results should best be assessed.

According to Robert L. Linn of the University of Colorado at Boulder, "some of the specific NCLB accountability requirements are unrealistic or counterproductive and threaten to undermine the praiseworthy aspects of the law." In Chapter 6, "Improving the Accountability Provisions of NCLB," Linn recommends a number of key revisions to the NCLB accountability system. He agrees with Rothstein and colleagues that the law's current expectations for student performance, including AYP targets, are unobtainable; he argues for more realistic goals based on past data on exemplary gains. He believes, in addition, that proficiency is so poorly defined and varies so much from state to state that the concept is nearly meaningless. In addition, he argues for an improved NCLB accountability system that would give schools credit for student learning gains as well as for meeting absolute performance targets and that would use multiple sources of information about student achievement instead of relying on test scores in a limited number of subjects. Finally, for a system that is fairer to schools with multiple subgroups and more reliable in its identification of low-performing schools, Linn argues that a revised accountability system should allow for high performance in one area to compensate to some degree for lower performance in another area.

The reliance on states to define proficiency goals for their state standards and to develop assessments in the absence of any federal standards or benchmarks has created a huge loophole that may be leading to a race to the bottom, as the number of schools in need of improvement increases and pressures mount to meet AYP targets in the next few years. Moreover, few of the state tests used to measure AYP are valid and reliable in accordance with established psychometric standards, and most state tests are not fully aligned with the state's academic standards.

As Robert Schwartz of Harvard University writes in Chapter 7, "Standards, Tests, and NCLB: What Might Come Next," "[t]he 'adequate yearly progress' provisions of the law have brought to the surface the absurdity of attempting to impose a federal accountability template on 50 states after each state has developed its own standards, adopted its own assessments, and set its own definition of proficiency." How did we reach this point and how might we recover? From an insider's perspective, Schwartz reviews the history of the standards movement and its important equity goals. Almost from the beginning, the movement has struggled to find a balance between the need for nationwide consistency and the need for states to retain local control over education policy. The quality control methods attempted to date have not been successful, and, as a result, the quality of state standards and state proficiency definitions varies enormously. Schwartz introduces a number of innovative recommendations for remedying this problem, including a greater reliance on the National Assessment of Educational Progress (NAEP) tests, an end to the imposition of federal AYP requirements on districts and schools, and a proposal for a "national" rather than "federal" set of strategies to ensure all students the right to be taught to comparably high standards. Implementation of these strategies would enlist several national organizations to create aligned systems of standards, tests, and curricula for use by the states or to encourage states to band together voluntarily to benchmark and align their standards and assessments.

The theory of action behind NCLB was that increased resources for education essentials would be provided in return for increased accountability. Although funding for elementary and secondary education programs covered by NCLB has increased since the law's passage, states and school districts have argued that this amount does not even cover the extra costs of testing and administration. Congressional leaders have also claimed that this amount falls far short of what was promised by President Bush at the time the law went into effect. Fiscal equity and education adequacy litigations, which have been decided by dozens of state courts around the country in recent years, indicate that, if we take seriously the commitment to narrow significantly or eliminate achievement gaps, substantial additional funding for essential educational resources is required. Identification of schools for improvement must be coupled with the means for schools to improve. It is clear that the rapidly accelerating number of schools being designated as "needing improvement" far exceeds the capacity of states to provide technical assistance to them and undermines the credibility of NCLB.

Each of the next two chapters tackles critical resource gaps faced by our nation's schools and examines whether NCLB is successfully addressing them. Susannah Loeb and Luke Miller of Stanford University take on the gap in teaching quality between schools that serve poor and minority students and those that serve wealthier, white peers, which NCLB purports to remedy. Richard Elmore discusses the role of accountability systems in closing the capacity gap that keeps low-performing schools from being able to improve and explores what is needed to close that gap.

The only essential educational resource presently mandated by NCLB is teacher quality. Research shows that effective, experienced teachers are key to children's learning, and yet many have questioned the law's mechanisms for implementing this requirement. In Chapter 8, "A Federal Foray into Teacher Certification: Assessing the 'Highly Qualified Teacher' Provision of NCLB," Loeb and Miller investigate the effectiveness of NCLB's teacher quality provision and of the U.S. Department of Education's enforcement of its implementation. As they chronicle, initially lax USDOE enforcement and a serious lack of data and data-gathering capacity among the states led to delayed compliance with the provision. Nevertheless, at the midpoint of the law's timeline, Loeb and Miller conclude that NCLB has improved the supply of new, minimally qualified teachers to hard-to-staff schools. However, they question whether further improvement of teaching can be effected by a federal initiative, since the real work of fostering effective teachers happens locally.

Richard Elmore's chapter, "The Problem of Capacity in the (Re)Design of Educational Accountability Systems," makes the point that most schools get classified as failing under NCLB because *they don't know what to do to get better.* Regulatory enforcement cannot solve this problem, and can make it worse by focusing failing schools on compliance rather than addressing the lack of knowledge and skill that produced the problem in the first place. Elmore, of Harvard University, argues that an effective accountability system generates pressure for performance *and* provides support for the development of knowledge and skill required to meet those expectations. Not only does NCLB not qualify, Elmore argues, but it instead constitutes a federal preemption of educational accountability policy, setting unprecedented fixed parameters on state accountability systems. Driven by the law's faulty assumptions and rigid parameters, there has been a dramatic increase in schools classified as needing improvement, slow progress in schools leaving that classification, and a disproportionate number of schools in need of improvement in the most populous urban areas. To be truly effective, Elmore argues, NCLB must establish (1) reciprocity—an explicit statement of the amount of performance demanded and the amount of support to be supplied; (2) empirical validity—evidence to support the decisions upon which the standards are based; and (3) education policymaking at state and local levels of government—freeing states and localities to design and implement their own educational accountability policies and systems.

In the concluding essay, we (the editors of this volume, Michael Rebell and Jessica Wolff) argue that the role of NCLB in promoting educational equity in our nation's schools is even more important than when it was enacted, as a result of the U.S. Supreme Court ruling in *Parents Involved v. Seattle,* which largely gutted the equal educational opportunity decision in *Brown v. Board of Education.* To fulfill its important equity aims, we argue, NCLB needs more effectively to balance the current focus on accountability for results with a renewed focus on providing meaningful educational opportunities to allow students to attain those results. In defining "meaningful educational opportunity," we respond to the critique by Wells that begins this volume and argue that education policy must contend with the barriers to learning created by poverty in the United States today and create realistic means for dismantling them. We identify the five key revisions—establishing challenging but attainable achievement goals, recruiting and retaining effective teachers, providing comprehensive supports to minimize the impact of poverty, ensuring full and fair funding, and fostering capacity building in low-performing schools and districts—that are critical for ensuring that the law truly promotes meaningful educational opportunities for all students.

CHAPTER 1

"Our Children's Burden"

A History of Federal Education Policies
That Ask (Now Require) Our Public Schools
to Solve Societal Inequality

Amy Stuart Wells

Much has been written about No Child Left Behind (NCLB) as a notable de-
parture from prior federal education policies, its strict guidelines, and its in-
trusiveness into state and local decision making (Cross, 2004; DeBray, 2005;
McGuinn, 2006).[1] While there is much validity to these claims, it is also true
that, given the evolving federal role in education, NCLB was also the logical next step. In fact, since Congress passed the Elementary and Secondary
Education Act in 1965, the federal government has been a legal and political
force to reckon with in education policy. Thus, despite the popularity of "local control" in U.S. political history, we have seen the federal influence over
how public schools operate and what they teach steadily increase. Therefore,
NCLB is both the boldest and most constraining federal education policy
thus far and the product of a half-century trend toward a more intrusive federal presence in American education.

At the same time that the federal government's influence over education intensified, the education policy agenda in this country shifted sharply
from one designed to guarantee the rights of students who had not been well
served in public schools to one that mandates better educational outcomes
for all students. Indeed, this shift in focus–from "equity" to "excellence,"
from inputs to outputs, from carrots to sticks to force schools to comply with
mandates–has been well documented (see McGuinn, 2006; Petrovich, 2005)
and clearly reflects the evolving political context from the civil rights era of
the 1950s through the early 1970s to the age of accountability and privatization of education from the early 1980s through today. In this way, NCLB was
and still is reflective of these broader changes.

And yet, while NCLB is indisputably emblematic of the social and political times in which it was conceived, it also underscores an age-old and remarkably consistent theme throughout the history of U.S. social welfare policy: *Instead of building a more comprehensive social safety net, policymakers in this country continue to lay the bulk of the burden of solving inequality at the schoolhouse door.* In other words, over the last century, as governments of other industrialized countries built and enlarged comprehensive social welfare systems to offset inequality among their citizens, U.S. policymakers have invested in public schools and relatively few other supportive social services. Thus, while other industrialized nations began subsidizing income, health care, child care, pensions, and housing to take care of their citizens' most urgent needs, in the United States the public schools became the central means by which the government would help improve the lives of the poor and disadvantaged (see Quadagno, 1987; Shapiro & Young, 1989; Weir, Orloff, & Skocpol, 1988).

As a result of this emphasis on education as an antipoverty program, U.S. policymakers have remained relatively resistant to expanding social welfare policies other than those that prepare young people for the labor market, namely public education or job training. Only Social Security has enjoyed a similar level of consistent public support. The public schools, therefore, have shouldered the responsibility of addressing the disadvantages of children who lack supports in other realms of their lives. Such a burden was problematic enough in the War on Poverty era when the economy was growing and workers on the lower end of the income spectrum had more opportunities for mobility (Silver & Silver, 1991). But the onus placed on our schools to solve these societal problems is even more challenging in the current era of growing income inequality, rapidly rising childhood poverty rates, and an alarming increase in the number of working-poor families in which parents lack both child care and time at home (see Wells, forthcoming, for an overview). These recent trends suggest that the out-of-school experiences of poor children are becoming even more disparate from those of their more affluent peers, making the schools' NCLB-mandated job of "closing the achievement gap" more, and not less, difficult (Broader, Bolder Approach to Education Task Force, 2008).

There are many theories attempting to explain so-called "American exceptionalism" or resistance to developing a more comprehensive set of social welfare policies to support families, children, and schools (Sunstein, 2004). A popular argument, for instance, is that the U.S. political culture is embedded in a "bootstrap ideology" that sees education as a *hand up* as opposed to a *handout* (see Hartz, 1991; Heidenheimer, 1984; Lemann, 1989). Other explanations highlight the history of racial politics in the United States, which first denied African Americans access to social services and later legitimized the lack of support for families in concentrated in urban ghettos. Any efforts to redistribute resources toward those urban neighborhoods were unpopular with many white voters—in the north and in the south. Yet another theory points to the relatively weak labor movement in the United States and how this led to a privatization of benefits such as health care and pensions, removing the struggle for them from the public sphere (Kantor & Lowe, 1995).

All of these interconnected factors—and others as well (see Sunstein, 2004)—no doubt played an important role in the evolution of our relatively weak social welfare policies, our bold education policies, and thus the enormous burden we have placed on the public schools to solve almost all of our social problems. The question this chapter poses as policymakers debate the reauthorization of No Child Left Behind and the future federal role in education is just how long we can continue to expect the public schools to accomplish this feat, absent broader efforts to make children's overall lives more equal. After several years of cutting back on the relatively few programs for poor families amid growing poverty and inequality, federal policymakers must be held accountable for the larger, social context of public schools and the children they serve.

The point of this chapter is not to argue against the central goal of NCLB, which is ostensibly to close the academic achievement gaps across racial and social class lines. Nor is it to argue that schools do not matter. They matter a great deal, especially when so few other social policies are addressing inequality. Nor is it to say that the War on Poverty policies that focused mainly on educational "inputs" and student access to schools and programs placed enough emphasis on the quality of the education students were receiving (Hill, 2000). But the historical record strongly suggests that neither in the earlier era nor today has there been enough consideration of the broader inequality in which schools and their students were situated (Kantor & Lowe, 1995). These historical lessons are particularly important as we move forward in an era of increasing economic uncertainty and inequality.

Educational mandates, therefore, absent efforts to create more equal lives for children outside of school and to provide the extra resources, expertise, and support that schools serving disadvantaged students need to close the achievement gaps, are cruel and degrading to students and educators in "failing schools." In fact, punitive measures such as those embodied in NCLB, without broader social policies that attempt to equalize children's lives in terms of income, access to health care, and social services, will, in most cases, punish the youngest victims of our increasingly unequal society (Broader, Bolder Approach to Education Task Force, 2008).

Indeed, it is patently clear from the historical record and social science research that the federal government can best meet the educational needs of disadvantaged children by supporting not only public schools but also the families and communities they serve. Clearly, a more comprehensive set of policies is needed to solve the comprehensive inequalities that poor children in our public schools now face.

AN AMERICAN TRADITION:
PUBLIC EDUCATION AS THE CENTRAL SOCIAL WELFARE POLICY

Comparative analyses of social welfare policies in industrial nations have continually shown that the United States has lagged behind in providing the kind of social safety nets that became fairly commonplace in Western European countries during the 20th century (Quadagno, 1987; Shapiro & Young, 1989). According to Weir, Orloff, and Skocpol (1988), "Core welfare state policies such as old-age pensions and social insurance were much slower to emerge in the United States than in Europe: some—such as national health insurance—have never been instituted at all" (p. 9).

In contrast, the United States was chronologically ahead of many of these same countries when it came to building a public education system that was, for the most part, free and open to at least white children regardless of their social class background since its inception via the common school movement of the 19th century (Heidenheimer, 1984). Indeed, the American construction of a system of publicly funded and universal schools that were, by the mid-1800s, at least in theory, "common" in terms of drawing white children from a particular community regardless of their social standing and teaching them a somewhat common Protestant-centric curriculum was truly "exceptional" in a different sort of way; namely, it established one of the most comprehensive and universal educational systems in the world (see Kaestle, 1983). And even though the federal government was not directly involved in establishing or running this extensive system of common public schools, Hirschland and Steinmo (2003) argue that, contrary to popular belief, at an early point in the common school era, the U.S. federal government exercised "remarkable influence" over national education policy (p. 343). They note, for instance, that a core group of so-called "national progressive elites" influenced the central U.S. government powerfully to shape the development of American public schools by providing much-needed resources, especially land, to state and local governments (see Hirshland & Steinmo, 2003, p. 345).

In fact, Weir and colleagues (1988) note that early American "social policy" established prior to the 1930s mainly included support for mass public education and generous federal benefits for elderly Civil War veterans and their dependents. In contrast to the European welfare state developments, they write, "neither old-age pensions or nor social insurance made much headway in the United States before the Great Depression" (p. 6). Thus, while the national governments in other industrialized countries, particularly in Western Europe, developed policies and programs designed to protect citizens' minimum standards of income, nutrition, housing, health, and education, the federal, state, and local governments in the United States placed much greater emphasis on providing universal public education and developed far fewer programs to address inequality in other realms of people's lives (Flora & Heidenheimer, 1984).

Heidenheimer (1984), who has written extensively about U.S. "exceptionalism" as it related to the public safety net, argues that perhaps the most significant difference between the social welfare policies of the United States versus Great Britain was the American emphasis on education, especially when it came to helping low-income populations. He wrote:

> Massive support for the expansion of public education, including higher education, in the United States, must be seen as a central component of the American notion of welfare—the idea that through public education both personal betterment and national and social and economic development would take place. (p. 274)

In a lengthy historical comparison of welfare states in Britain, Germany, and the United States, Heidenheimer (1984) argues that the three countries clearly selected "alternative governmental responses to the needs and demands for equality and security that came to be more strongly articulated at this time" (pp. 274–275). For instance, he noted that the German government placed priority on meeting the security needs of the lower classes by introducing compulsory insurance programs. In the United States, policymakers responded to equity demands by enhancing "mobility opportunities for individuals," most notably through the unprecedented expansion of educational opportunities. The United States, Heidenheimer (1984) wrote, employed a strategy of what he called "substituting education for techniques of social action." Britain, on the other hand, did not "initiate radical departures in either education or social insurance, but rather enhanced the ability of various subnational collectivities to offer both kinds of benefits on a voluntary basis" (Heidenheimer, 1984, p. 274).

Not only were Heidenheimer and other comparative policy scholars (Shapiro & Young, 1989; Weir et al., 1988; Wilensky, 1975) struck by the distinct focus of U.S. policymakers on education over other social welfare policies but also on the uneven nature of the American system of provision, particularly when it came to education. Most social policies in other countries—be they health care, social insurance, or education—are managed centrally through uniform formulae. In the United States, however, with its more complex and multilayered form of federalism and strong anticentralization politics, there were great discrepancies across policies and place. Heidenheimer (1984) wrote that although programs that are administered by the federal government, such as Social Security pensions, usually had nationally uniform benefit rates, "benefit levels in education and social assistance [welfare] have varied by factors of 4:1 among American states and localities" (p. 286).

Notwithstanding Hirschland and Steinmo's (2003) argument about the influence of "national progressive elites" and the U.S. government on the development of American public education, even this provision of resources in the early stages of the common school movement was filtered through state and local governments, which were deciding where schools would be located and, ultimately, what would be taught. Thus, in the one area of social policy in which the United States excelled—education—the delivery of services has been and still is the most uneven and dependent on local context. Ironically, the children in the public schools with the fewest resources also tend to be the same children who could benefit the most from a more secure and robust social welfare system, which never has existed in this country.

In fact, even by the mid-1970s—after what many would consider the peak years of implementing social welfare policies in this country—the United States had not yet established more than a "relatively inexpensive and programmatically incomplete system of public social provision" (Flora & Heidenheimer, 1984). At that time, total social spending for education, income maintenance, and health in the United States accounted for about 16% of GDP with the largest share spent on education, while most European nations devoted more than 20% of GDP to social expenditures. Thus, overall, although the United States had become "above average in educational expenditures" by the end of the Great Society, it lacked (and still lacks) national health insurance and family allowances provided by most European welfare states as well as Canada. Meanwhile, both public assistance (welfare) and unemployment insurance in the United States versus countries with similar economies remained ungenerous and uneven, as states differed in their coverage of population groups at risk (Weir, Orloff, & Skopol, 1988, p. 4). In more recent years, following the implementation of the 1996 welfare reform and the lack of federal support for the State Children's Health Insurance Program (SCHIP) programs for children, support for poor families in the United States is even less robust (Goodnough, 2007; Greenhouse, 2008; Handler & Hasenfeld, 2007). U.S. exceptionalism continues, even as the demands on public schools to solve inequality have become more intense.

The Exception to American Exceptionality: The New Deal

If American resistance to social welfare policies stands out in contrast with other industrialized countries, then the New Deal policies of the Great Depression must stand out collectively as a very important exception to that exceptionalism. Researchers and historians who have studied this period of U.S. history refer to the New Deal and the Social Security Act of 1935 in particular as the "big bang" of national social welfare legislation. This one act alone established social insurance and public assistance programs, creating a basic framework of U.S. public social provision (Weir et al., 1988, p. 6). Indeed, the New Deal was the only period in our history when the federal government stepped in to provide immediate and direct economic assistance to people who were hungry and often homeless. Still, the direct relief programs enacted during that time were temporary and ceased to exist after the World War II.

From cash assistance to families for much-needed food to public work projects that created immediate and decent-paying government jobs, the federal policies of the New Deal era did what many European governments have tried to do: namely, lift families out of poverty as quickly as possible. According to Kantor and Lowe (1995), "Faced with skyrocketing levels of unemployment and confronted with millions of Americans going hungry, the New Deal mobilized resources on a hitherto unheard of scale to help people avoid destitution" (p. 5).

Kantor and Lowe (1995) note that after 1935, when the economy had stabilized to some degree, the emphasis of New Deal policy shifted slightly from emergency cash support to work relief–creating government-paid public work jobs. Yet throughout the decade, the need to "provide economic assistance to those out of work or chronically ill and homeless remained a chief concern" of policymakers (Kantor & Lowe, 1995, p. 5).

Thus, much more like the leaders of many European countries, the U.S. New Deal policymakers attempted to promote work and security through employment programs. The largest of the employment relief programs, the Civilian Conservation Corps (CCC) and the Works Progress Administration (WPA), combined employed nearly 7 million Americans, often providing room and board. Vouchers for food, rent, or fuel and cash grants were sometimes distributed to the poor as well (Sunstein, 2004, p. 46).

Even in this "heyday" of federal social policy, President Franklin Delano Roosevelt stressed repeatedly that he was far more enthusiastic about "employment relief," or public works programs, than he was about cash assistance, or "the dole," as he called it. According to Sunstein (2004), Roosevelt believed that government handouts were "demoralizing and contrary to national ideals." He sought, therefore, ways to "provide relief to the masses of the unemployed that did not compromise the recipients' pride and self-respect. . . . Employment relief, although often more costly than cash payments, was preferred by the administration and recipients alike" (p. 45).

Missing from the array of New Deal policies were reforms or supports for the educational system. As Heidenheimer (1984) notes, the New Deal policies did surprisingly little to improve public education. In fact, there was virtually no change in the distribution of educational opportunities or the manner in which education was financed and administered throughout the Depression. Kantor and Lowe (1995) write that "during the 1930s education typically was not a conscious tool of federal policy and was of secondary importance compared to other federal measures to revive the economy and alleviate immediate economic suffering" (p. 4).

This finding is especially surprising, writes Heidenheimer (1984), in view of the centrality of public education to American welfare notions. While a few New Deal programs, including the CCC and the National Youth Administration, did link education (or job training) and employment opportunities more directly, these were among the many programs that were terminated as soon as unemployment became less severe. Other New Deal policies—most notably Social Security; federally required, state-run unemployment insurance; and federally subsidized public assistance (welfare)—remain in place today, even as they have been cut or challenged.

In fact, perhaps the most notable legacy of the New Deal era is a Social Security system that virtually eliminated poverty among the elderly by the last quarter of the 20th century. Yet, given the success and popularity of many other New Deal policies, there was an opportunity, at the end of the Depression, to sustain a more robust social policy system and ensure greater safety and security for families and children. FDR himself, in the early 1940s, argued for a new set of domestic polity initiatives that would build on the momentum of the New Deal's legislative success. According to Kantor and Lowe (1995), FDR contended that the government should expand opportunities for adequate medical care and gainful employment.

In January 1944, in his State of the Union address, President Roosevelt boldly proposed a Second Bill of Rights to establish an American standard of living "higher than even before known" (Sunstein, 2004, p. 13). His proposal included a set of "relevant rights" that would apply to all—regardless of "station, race or creed," including the right to a "useful and remunerative job," to earn enough money to "provide adequate food and clothing and recreation," to a decent home for every family, to "adequate medical care and the opportunity to achieve and enjoy good health," and to a good education. FDR said that after the war is won, "we must be prepared to move forward, in the implementation of these rights. . . . For unless there is security here at home there cannot be lasting peace in the world" (Sunstein, 2004, p. 13).

Thus, by the late 1930s and early 1940s, the political momentum to develop a more comprehensive and meaningful welfare state seemed likely to succeed in the United States. In fact, many observers, including FDR himself, predicted that the United States would, in the postwar era, "embrace the kind of social agenda later adopted by social democratic regimes in northern Europe and Scandinavia. That never happened" (Kantor & Lowe, 1995, p. 6).

Understanding American Exceptionalism in Social Welfare Policy

Many scholars have struggled to understand the profound policy differences between the United States and other affluent, Western European countries when it comes to social provisions for the most disadvantaged or vulnerable members of society. In trying to explain the United States' stingy safety net and why even these few provisions have come under intense political attack in the 1980s and 1990s, these authors have questioned the "anti-American" rhetoric applied to policies that provide resources and services to those who are poor, even as Americans have been more generous in providing free—although far from equal—public education (see Katz, 1996). "At the level of practical politics there was (and still is) a fundamental hostility in congressional and public opinion to the idea of an American welfare state, especially one that gives money to poor people" (Weir, Orloff, & Skopol, 1988, p. 6). Below, I describe some of the most popular explanations of this contradiction.

The "National Values" Explanation of American Exceptionalism

One of the most popular explanations of American resistance to non-educational social welfare policies is the strength of laissez-faire liberal values in this country that shape a strong commitment to "individualism" and "self-help" as opposed to dependence on the government. Such values, some scholars have argued, have led to a "tenacious . . . resistance to social protection" (Weir et al., 1988).

Citing public opinion poll data, Sunstein (2004) writes that "compared to Europeans, Americans are less likely to believe that government should provide a minimum income guarantee, a job for everyone, or a decent standard of living for the unemployed" (p. 128). In fact, he notes that Americans are far less enthusiastic about a welfare system that provides extensive protection to the disadvantaged and far less willing to moderate the capitalist free enterprise system to ensure more equality in terms of income and support. For instance, one poll finds that only 23% of Americans accept the view that government has a duty to "take care of very poor people who can't take care of themselves." And when asked whether the "government should provide everyone with a guaranteed basic income," only 12% of wealthy and 33% of the nonwealthy Americans said yes. By contrast, the same proposition "commanded majority support among less wealthy citizens of Great Britain, West Germany, the Netherlands, and Italy, and near majority support among wealthier citizens" (p. 131).

Sunstein (2004) and others (see Katz, 1996) argue that the strong current of individualism—and, indeed, a large dose of Protestant ethic—that courses through the veins of American society reinforces an ideology that "poverty can be escaped through sheer effort." Thus, public policies to redistribute resources from the wealthy to the poor are seen as problematic because they reward people who do not work hard and punish those who do. This belief system is illustrated by another poll that found that 70% of Americans said "people are poor because of laziness, not because of society, whereas 70% of West Germans said that people are poor because of society rather than laziness." Furthermore, when asked whether poor people are able to work their way out of poverty, a full 71% of Americans agreed, whereas only 40% of Europeans did (Sunstein, 2004, p. 135).

Where National Values Meet Racial Ideologies

A more focused version of the "national values" argument suggests that race has played a central role in the construction of this meritocratic and individualistic framework for explaining the winners and losers in American society. According to Sunstein (2004) and Quadagno (1994), racial politics has strongly influenced the shape and nature of redistributive programs in the United States.

Sunstein (2004) notes, for example, that Southern Democrats hostile to African Americans played a critical role in defeating President Truman's proposed Full Employment Act. The failure of this legislation and other policies aimed at helping the poor occurred largely because Americans are likely to think of poor people as coming from a non-white racial/ethnic group: "This history of American redistribution makes it quite clear that hostility to welfare comes in part from the fact that welfare spending in the United States goes disproportionately to minorities" (Sunstein, 2004, p. 135).

Quadagno (1994) makes the more direct argument that the central reason that the United States was slow to legislate national welfare programs and lacked programs other countries enacted as a matter of course, such as national health insurance, family allowance, or paid paternal leave, was that by the time these policies became popular abroad in the 1950s and 1960s, race had moved to the center of the policymaking debate in the United States. During this postwar era, in particular, Quadagno (1994) argues, "efforts to use government intervention to extend positive liberties to African Americans clashed with the negative liberties of whites to dominate local politics, to control membership in their unions, and to choose their neighbors." These conflicts established a "racial fault line in public policy that subsequently provided the rationale for welfare state retrenchment" (Quadagno, 1994, p. 6).

Both Sunstein (2004) and Quadagno (1994) point to the distinctions between the New Deal social welfare policies and those that came a little later
as part of the Great Society. The New Deal, they noted, served a wide range
of citizens from many ethnic and religious backgrounds–people who had
been, prior to the Depression, affluent and those who had historically been
less well off. These New Deal programs served the needs of many people in
the midst of an economic crisis and were not directly targeted at any particular ethnic or racial group. In fact, several of the New Deal programs excluded
African Americans through tactics such as denying agricultural or domestic
workers access to Social Security (Quadagno, 1994).

Still, both Quadagno (1994) and Sunstein (2004) argue that, after the New
Deal, the politics of social welfare policies became inextricably intertwined
with racial issues, as poverty problems were increasingly seen as synonymous
with the problems in the urban ghettos that had by then become homes to
millions of African Americans who had migrated from the rural south. This
racialization of social policies led to a sharp decline in public support for
post–New Deal welfare policies.

Political Class Struggle Argument

The class struggle argument, which overlaps with the racial argument
above, states that in other industrialized countries, capitalists generally op-
pose the emergence or expansion of a welfare state while the labor-based
political parties support it (Sunstein, 2004). In the United States, however,
the lack of a labor-backed political party, and a working-class population
that is politically fractured, often along racial/ethnic lines, has impeded the
formation of a more generous welfare state. For instance, Quadagno (1994)
cites comparative research that shows that the most advanced welfare states
have originated in countries where a labor-backed party fought for new
social legislation.

Meanwhile, Kantor and Lowe (1995) note that the absence of an organized labor-backed political party that represented the working class across
the country, regardless of their race/ethnicity or geographic location, pre-
cipitated a situation in which labor unions began negotiating with private
corporate employers for social welfare benefits. When this effort began to
bear fruit, corporation by corporation, in the 1940s–as FDR was making
his plea for a Second Bill of Rights–the momentum to organize politically
and push the government to provide universal social services subsided. In
fact, by 1950, labor leaders had retreated from their efforts to reorganize
the political economy in part because they had reached an "accommodation with business and the state in which an emphasis on productivity-linked
wage increases and employer-funded pensions and health benefits replaced

its earlier commitment to full employment planning and an expanded public welfare system" (Kantor & Lowe, 1995, p. 6).

The system that emerged of employer-provided benefits allowed many unionized workers to secure health care, pensions, and other benefits through their jobs, at least temporarily. Yet, as we see more recently, private employers have begun to cut back drastically on such benefits (Greenhouse, 2008). Meanwhile, the emergence of this privately provided system of benefits back in the 1940s and 1950s removed important social welfare policy issues from the public arena and left them to private negotiations between workers and management. As a result, "those who did not benefit from unionization and collective bargaining—primarily minorities and women—were left dependent on less generous public programs" (Kantor & Lowe, 1995, p. 6).

In this way, the relationship between the political and class struggle is most obvious when we consider the racial politics of U.S. labor unions, many of which historically excluded African Americans. Once union leaders realized they could get benefits for their workers through private channels, their motivation to fight for publicly funded benefits for unionized and nonunionized workers alike, including blacks, was less appealing (Kantor & Lowe, 1995; Quadagno, 1994).

"State Structure" and Constitutional Arguments

Other scholars have stressed structural and constitutional reasons explaining why the United States lacks a more developed welfare state and why the more universal U.S. educational system is so decentralized. For instance, Heidenheimer (1984) noted that in the immediate post-World War II era, the United States lacked an experienced central government bureaucracy. He wrote that the "American welfare state development must be interpreted in light of a marked 'low stateness' profile that the political system exhibited well into the twentieth century. . . . Thus a welfare state infrastructure had to be developed even in the absence of effective national policymaking potential in many areas" (p. 276).

Similarly, Weir and colleagues (1988) link the political class struggle argument outlined above to an argument about the U.S. state structure, which, they claim, discourages unified, persistent class politics. Thus, each cluster of social welfare policymaking is heterogeneous, "a product of disparate plans previously pursued by networks or policy intellectuals . . . rather than by any political party or nationwide economic group." In this way, Weir et al. (1988) write, new social policies are often "temporary, fragile, incapable of any permanent institutionalization, and very soon undone by conservative backlashes" (pp. 22–23).

And, finally, Sunstein (2004) makes a related argument about the ways in which judges, particularly Supreme Court justices, have interpreted the U.S. Constitution in the last 30 years, which has moved the country away from embracing FDR's Second Bill of Rights. As noted, FDR's proposal would have guaranteed every American the right to a decent job; adequate food, clothing, and recreation; a decent home; adequate protection from the economic fears of old age, sickness, accident, and unemployment; and a good education.

Sunstein (2004) argues that in the 1960s, the nation was rapidly moving toward accepting this Second Bill of Rights, not through constitutional amendments but through the Supreme Court's interpretations of the Constitution and what rights and privileges it guaranteed. Subsequently, as the Supreme Court has become more conservative, this interpretation has shifted to a far less generous view of what the Constitution guarantees ordinary U.S. citizens and toward a far more generous view of the rights and privileges of corporations. Sunstein (2004) writes that if Richard Nixon had not appointed four Supreme Court justices in rapid succession, the "significant parts of the second bill [of rights] would probably be part of our constitutional understandings today" (pp. 4–5).

To a certain extent, each of these explanations for the lack of a strong U.S. welfare state is probably both accurate and incomplete. In other words, it is unlikely that any one of them explains the whole picture or the complexity of the multiple forces that first set the United States off down the path toward becoming a social welfare policy laggard and has helped us stay the course throughout most of the 20th century. In fact, I believe, the interconnectedness of these different arguments needs to be explored more fully. For instance, how did racial politics and the "southern strategy" lead to Nixon's election, which in turn led to the four Supreme Court justices who shifted the constitutional interpretation away from the Second Bill of Rights?

In this way, none of these arguments alone helps us fully understand the seemingly contradictory development of a robust and universal public education system side by side with a dearth of public programs. In many ways, the "national values" argument, particularly as it relates to and promotes the race and class politics arguments, is most helpful. After all, providing every child access to free government-funded public schools in many ways symbolizes and promotes a philosophy of "self-help" or a "hand up" over "charity" or a "handout." This distinction between policies designed to further "equality of opportunity," or the self-help model, versus those designed to further "equality of results," or what is perceived to be a handout, seems to matter a great deal in American politics. Wilensky (1975) writes that such distinctions between public policies—those with a central thrust of furthering "absolute equality" versus those that aim to further "equality of opportunity"—were important in understanding the ideological orientations to welfare states across different political contexts.

According to Flora and Heidenheimer (1984), who use Wilensky's framework to explain differences between the United States and European countries when it comes to social welfare versus education,

> [Wilensky] wrote that the core of the welfare state is a nation's health and welfare effort that constitutes "clearly and directly a contribution to absolute equality." By contrast, he perceives a "nation's educational effort . . . as chiefly a contribution to equality of opportunity—enhanced mobility for those judged to be potentially able and skilled." He concedes that the ideological underpinnings of the welfare state reflect everywhere a tension between meritocratic and egalitarian values. "But the mix varies from program to program, with the meritocratic component for education far more prominent than it is for the rest of the welfare state." (pp. 30–31)

Wilensky's distinction can inform our understanding of what it means for children, educators, and parents to live in a society that has placed so much emphasis on an abstract notion of "equal opportunity" via free, universal public education and at the same time has rather strongly rejected the concept of "absolute equality" or "equality of results." Indeed, he argues that how "equality of opportunity" is juxtaposed to "equality of results" crucially affects how the discussion of welfare state boundaries is cast, and how countries are compared with regard to attainment of its goals (cited in Flora & Heidenheimer, 1984, p. 31).

More specifically, Wilensky states

> Equality of opportunity is associated more with "becoming," the attainment of statuses over a life-cycle or intergenerational development. Equality of results tends to reflect "being" more in terms of measures of income and "levels of living." (Flora & Heidenheimer, 1984, p. 31)

The profound question we need to ask ourselves as we reflect on the role of the federal government in educational and other social policies, is whether or not we can ever accomplish anything resembling "equality of opportunity" in terms of "becoming" through our public school systems when the children who arrive at our schoolhouse doors have day-to-day "levels of living" and "being" that are so profoundly unequal. In other words, without a better balance between "being" and "becoming" from the perspective of a child, can we really claim that we have approached the goal of equality of opportunity?

In this way, Wilensky's analysis helps us understand the "national values" argument for American exceptionalism and how these dominant values foster a contradiction between our espoused societal goal of equal opportunity and the reality of a social welfare system that ensures opportunities are never equal. The irony, however, is the contrast between the New Deal era, when there was more support for policies designed to create greater equality of results, and the post–World War II era, when the policy focus shifted sharply toward equality of opportunities. In trying to explain this shift, it is clear that the "national values" argument only goes so far and that issues of race and racial politics are central to this change of heart.

In the following section of this chapter, I trace the post–World War II evolution and history of the federal role in public education, beginning with the broader social and political context that made racial politics more salient than it had been during the New Deal era. It is far easier to understand where we are today once we acknowledge that larger context and thus appreciate the incredible pressure we have placed on the public schools to deliver more equal opportunities in a society that expects each child to earn his or her equal results.

"THE EDUCATIONAL WAR ON POVERTY": THE NEW DEAL DIES BEFORE THE GREAT SOCIETY BEGINS

On the 15th anniversary of the signing of the Social Security Act, John F. Kennedy, in a speech in New York, argued that the "opening battle" against "suffering and deprivation had been won in the 1930s; but the war against poverty and degradation was not yet over" (Silver & Silver, 1991, p. 7). The civil rights era, from the 1950s to the mid- to late 1970s, encompassed and was intertwined with both the War on Poverty and the Great Society efforts of the federal government. What happened in terms of federal policymaking during this era illustrates an important and significant shift from the policies of the New Deal. What this shift most clearly symbolizes is our country's retreat from FDR's dream of a Second Bill of Rights and the development of a comprehensive social welfare system that would include a guaranteed income, universal health care system, and decent housing for all. Indeed, the federal policies passed as part of the War on Poverty agenda placed far more emphasis on "equality of opportunity" than on "equality of result." In other words, public education and other education-related programs, such as job training, replaced the New Deal's cash and employment relief programs as the most popular policies for combating poverty.

Understanding how and why this shift took place and its relationship to racial politics and the flow of blacks from the south to the north and from rural to urban communities is critical to understanding our current federal education policies and why they demand what they do of our schools. There was a time when such demands would have seemed unreasonable to more people. That time was before the federal government became so heavily involved in public education. Over the years, Americans have become used to social policies that relied heavily on the public schools—as divided and separate and unequal as they are—to overcome all the gaps between rich and poor, black and white, and English-speaking and non-English-speaking.

From the Great Depression to the War on Poverty: The Politics of Race and Place

Like the New Deal before it, the War on Poverty was a concerted effort by the federal government to better the lives of people suffering from a lack of basic necessities. But the similarities end there, and, in fact, ultimately, there were more differences between the federal responses in the two eras—differences in terms of *who* was poor and *where* they lived and *how* policymakers responded to their needs. In many ways, the main distinction between the 1930s and 1960s was race, especially as it interacted with space/place and the economy.

For instance, the 1960s, unlike the 1930s, were a time of great economic expansion and relative affluence for most white Americans. At the same time, in terms of race and space, the postwar period marked the peak of the so-called "Great Migration" of blacks to the north and into the cities and the parallel exodus of whites and jobs from the cities to the suburbs. While the great migration was a constant 100-year flow of blacks into urban areas, the largest movement occurred between the early 1940s and the late 1960s, when more than 5 million blacks left the south for northern cities (Lemann, 1991). Furthermore, when they arrived in these northern cities, they were greeted by an increasingly sophisticated system of housing segregation. According to Massey and Denton (1993), no other racial group in the history of our country has experienced the sustained level of residential segregation imposed on blacks.

These historical events left poor blacks highly concentrated in urban ghettos, which became the focal points in the fight against poverty (Kantor & Lowe, 1995; Lemann, 1988; Massey & Denton, 1993). This focus on segregated, black urban neighborhoods gave the War on Poverty a racial dimension that distinguished it from the New Deal era, when antipoverty policies served many more whites than blacks. Indeed, as noted above, certain New Deal programs, such as Social Security, intentionally excluded blacks by denying benefits to agricultural and domestic workers, which included the vast majority of blacks at that time (Quadagno, 1994).

Thus, by the early 1960s, the majority of white Americans were enjoying the fruits of their labors in a strong economy in which both wages and suburban housing values were on the rise. Meanwhile, the majority of African Americans found themselves segregated in extremely poor urban neighborhoods with very few decent-paying jobs and little or no opportunity to build home equity (Massey & Denton, 1993).

At this time, social scientists and policymakers were beginning to understand that the poverty in these urban communities was characterized by a depth and persistence that had never been seen before in the United States. For instance, amid the postwar optimism, Michael Harrington published *The Other America: Poverty in the United States* (1962), in which he argued that between 40 and 50 million Americans (about 25% of the total) were living in poverty and that roughly a quarter of the poor were black, even though blacks made up only about 12% of the total population at that time.

As a result of these shifts and the concentrated poverty in black urban communities, the federal government's antipoverty efforts in the War on Poverty, in contrast to the New Deal, became inextricably tied to black interests and concerns. "In fact, by the 1960s, expanding economic opportunity for low-income citizens and people of color had become a major focus of federal social policy, and education had emerged as the fundamental mechanism for combating poverty and racial inequality" (Kantor & Lowe, 1995, p. 4).

Education as *the* Means to Overcoming Poverty

At a planning meeting on the War on Poverty in 1964, President Johnson is reported to have described the proposed educational programs as follows: "We are going to eliminate poverty with education. . . . This is not going to be a handout; this is going to be something where people are going to *learn* their way out of poverty" (Silver & Silver, 1991, p. 70).

Shortly after this pronouncement, in a 1964 "Message on Poverty" to Congress, Johnson announced the goal regarding the "unfinished work" of fighting poverty: "To finish that work I have called for a national war on poverty. Our objective: total victory." In his "Message on Education" to Congress the following year, Johnson announced a forthcoming education bill—what was to become the Elementary and Secondary Education Act of 1965—as having "a national goal of full educational opportunity," targeted particularly at the children of low-income families. Johnson stated that "poverty has many roots but the taproot is ignorance" (Silver & Silver, 1991, p. 70). Similarly, Vice President Humphrey summarized the administration's central theme on fighting poverty in 1964 by stating that increased investment in education is "the key to the door through which the poor can escape from poverty" (Silver & Silver, 1991, p. 70).

Silver and Silver (1991) describe how education came to be the main weapon in the War on Poverty in their book, *The Educational War on Poverty.*

They argue that President Johnson was well aware of the significant ways in which poverty in the 1960s was different from what it had been during the Great Depression. Johnson himself stated that, during the Depression, the concern had been "mainly with educated and trained people who had been temporarily dislocated by the sickness of the economy." In the 1960s, Johnson saw the "paradoxical poverty in the midst of plenty" as another breed. At that time, the economy was booming and jobs were plentiful, but the unemployed were incapable of filling them.

> The most significant aspects of this new poverty, once the spotlight of attention was thrown on it, were the dismaying nature of its stubborn entrenchment and the total entrapment of its victims from one generation to the next. . . . A man was poor if he had too little money, but he also had inadequate education, medical care and nutrition, and had no real chance to train for a job–a cycle which he handed on to his children. . . . The focus on educational weaknesses and potentials in a period of apparently unending economic growth is therefore easy to detect and to understand. . . . (Silver & Silver, 1991, p. 72)

Basically, three central and somewhat overlapping explanations or theories emerge from the literature as to why this shift toward education as the solution to poverty took place during the 1960s. The first implies that giving cash assistance and jobs directly to African Americans in poor ghettos was not politically popular, given the overlap between the "national values" explanation of American exceptionalism and the politics of race in the United States. Thus, the idea of a "hand up" instead of a "handout" was particularly important in a society built upon an ideology of racial inferiority. The second overlapping explanation argues that the popularity of the "cultural deprivation" theory for explaining ongoing black poverty led to "solutions" that would reenculturate poor black children. And, finally, there is the argument that the black leaders of the civil rights movement contributed to this shift in poverty policy focus by focusing on access to education as a central goal. I briefly explore each of these overlapping explanations below.

No Handouts for Black Folks. In an analysis of the shift in policymaking from the New Deal to the 1960s, Kantor and Lowe (1995) argue that "handouts," in the form of cash assistance, were acceptable during the Depression when the devastation of poverty was far and wide and when most recipients were white. But by the 1960s, when the problem of poverty was perceived to be mostly related to blacks in urban ghettos, "a transformed federal policy would substitute schools for direct intervention in society and the labor market as the fundamental mechanism for solving social and economic problems" (p. 5).

In fact, the bulk of the 1960s War on Poverty programs was intended chiefly to expand opportunities in education and training, and "not to provide services to relieve immediate economic distress" as the New Deal programs were (Kantor & Lowe, 1995, p. 5; see also Brown, 1999). Kantor and Lowe (1995) argue that, by the late 1950s and early 1960s, policies for full employment or income redistribution garnered little support from white middle-class and blue-collar workers who, at that time, were enjoying wage increases and generous benefits mainly through their private-sector jobs. Consequently, when policymakers in the Kennedy and Johnson administrations created poverty policies, they ruled out active government intervention to create jobs and redistribute income because such policies lacked widespread popular support.

> They turned instead to more politically palatable proposals such as tax cuts to stimulate economic growth and job training and compensatory education programs that promised to do something for the poor without either antagonizing business by interfering in the labor market or alienating working- and middle-class voters by transferring income to the least advantaged. (Kantor & Lowe, 1995, p. 7)

Still, despite this War on Poverty bias toward education and job training programs, several new programs to relieve the economic distress of the poor were developed and strengthened during the 1960s. For instance, both the Neighborhood Youth Corps and Job Corps operated less as education and job training programs than as forms of work relief and income maintenance. Furthermore, the Food Stamp program, which had been initiated in 1961 on a small scale, was enlarged to cover more families by 1970, when it was providing benefits to more than 4 million people. And, in 1965, Medicaid, or medical insurance for the poor, was enacted, although the bulk of the burden of this program—about 80%—was transferred to the states. Meanwhile, the number of poor women and children receiving Aid to Families with Dependent Children (AFDC) or "welfare" rose from about 3 million in 1960 to almost 11 million by 1973 as the eligibility requirements were loosened by Supreme Court decisions and civil rights laws that curtailed abuses, diminished state authority over eligibility, and ordered states to provide due process of law to poor women who lost their benefits (Brown, 2003; DeParle, 2004).

Yet, even as the government expanded these social welfare policies during the War on Poverty era, the value of the benefits declined dramatically in real dollars, falling 25% in real terms. In fact, by 1984, the combined net AFDC/food stamp benefit was only 5% higher than the AFDC benefit alone had been in 1960 because many states were substituting food stamps for welfare benefits (Brown, 2003). In fact, Brown (1999) notes that the War on Poverty and Great Society programs, although framed as a part of a "redistributive welfare state," were, in fact, "intended to redistribute opportunity rather than money, through provision of educational, social and employment training services" (p. 206).

Not only did federal policymakers fail to expand social welfare provisions in real dollars during the War on Poverty era, but the main public assistance program at the time—AFDC—became the focus of increasing political controversy (Weir et al., 1988, pp. 8–9). In fact, a growing political resistance to programs that provided a so-called "handout"—as opposed to a "hand up"—began in earnest in the mid-1960s, as the welfare rolls were increasing. These arguments were articulated quite clearly in the Goldwater campaign of 1964, when the overlapping issues of "race and taxes" permeated the Republican Party and created the foundation for a new ideological coalition by pitting "taxpayers" against so-called "tax recipients" and "those in the labor force against those who were jobless." This coalition would grow throughout the 1960s and 1970s, resulting in the election of Ronald Reagan, a disciple of Goldwater, in 1980. But the political impact of that coalition was already being felt by the early 1960s (Edsall & Edsall, 1991).

Indeed, the anti-redistributive politics was so powerful that a 1964 report issued by the President's Council of Economic Advisers both identified the need for more equal income distribution and less racial discrimination and outlined a set of compensatory policies that would do nothing to address these inequalities directly. Indeed, the report rejected income redistribution, public employment, or other direct interventions in the economy in favor of a "program based on tax cuts and the provision of new educational services to stimulate growth and equip the poor with the tools they needed 'to *earn* the American standard of living by their own efforts and contributions'"(Kantor & Lowe, 1995, p. 7).

Of course, not everyone agreed with this focus on tax cuts and new educational services as the means to combat poverty. Many, including Daniel Patrick Moynihan, argued that the government should fight poverty by redistributing income, increasing spending to create jobs, and intervening in specific labor markets to provide public employment. Moynihan, in particular, argued for a guaranteed annual income in which the government would make up the difference between what poor people earned and what they needed to pay for food, shelter, and clothing. According to Lemann (1989), Moynihan had always wanted the United States to become more like a Western European social democracy, with full employment and family allowances. The idea that a guaranteed income was the best way to fight poverty had become Moynihan's leading public cause by the late 1960s when he worked in the Nixon administration and convinced a Republican president to support it as well (Lemann, 1989; Quadagno, 1994).

But in the end, due to a lack of congressional support for such redistributive programs and the escalating cost of the Vietnam War, federal antipoverty policy focused on relatively inexpensive public programs, mainly those of education and job training. Such programs, Kantor and Lowe (1995) argue, were designed not to alter the outcomes of the economic system but to help those at the bottom of society acquire the skills and attitudes they need to compete more successfully in it.

> Absent a genuine social democratic politics, education thus became a conscious tool of government social and economic policy in the 1950s and 1960s. Indeed, whereas the postwar social democratic governments in Northwestern Europe and Scandinavia sought to reduce unemployment and eliminate economic deprivation mainly by institutionalizing active labor market policies and building a floor under incomes, in the United States, education emerged as the chief means to extending benefits and promoting social welfare. (p. 7)

The Shift Toward Cultural Deprivation Theories. Another central factor that led to the emphasis on education as opposed to other forms of social provision was the growing body of research on "cultural deprivation" theory, which described poor children and children of color as being culturally deprived based on the lack of enrichment and the cultural orientation in their homes. Seen at the time as a more enlightened view than genetic inferiority theories of the past, cultural deprivation theory often portrayed schools and formal education as a cure for a cultural deficit based in children's homes.

During the early 1960s, a growing awareness of urban poverty was accompanied by a movement in the behavioral and social sciences to confront "questions of the relationship between disadvantage and education, and their complex connections with the processes of change taking place in the United States . . ." (Silver & Silver, 1991, p. 39). Thus, educators and psychologists emphasized the importance of optimal learning environments as early as possible in order to "reverse intellectual retardation in culturally deprived children, who needed teaching of above-average quality but normally receive the opposite" (Silver & Silver, 1991, p. 35).

The concept of "cultural deprivation" and the "culture of poverty" (see Lewis, 1969) had, by the 1960s, "penetrated the academic community" and become one of the central themes in discussions of poverty and how to overcome it. Psychologists, in particular, emphasized the cumulative effects of these cultural handicaps on children and the responsibility of schools to correct them. According to Silver and Silver (1991), "The schools, teachers and educators in general were being allocated blame for the failure of, particularly, Negro and slum children to benefit from schooling" (p. 37).

Even as some researchers were blaming schools for not doing enough to help poor children, especially poor black children, overcome their cultural deficits, cultural deprivation theory helped to legitimize the basis for greater federal involvement in educational reform since schools were simultaneously seen as the answer. In other words, children who had previously been labeled as problem children, retarded, slow learners, underprivileged, underachievers, and the like were suddenly described as "culturally deprived," which implied a new cause of school failure and a new approach to addressing it through educational programs (Silver & Silver, 1991, pp. 67–68).

Of course, there were skeptics of the cultural deprivation arguments, particularly as the primary way in which poverty, poor people, and their values were being defined (see Clark, 1965; Rainwater, 1970; Valentine, 1969). Clark (1965) argued that the culture of poverty argument needs to be viewed against a backdrop of the politics of race and that historically one of the earliest explanations for the poor performance of black students in school was racial inferiority. Clark (1965) also noted that while it became unfashionable by the 1960s for educators to talk about the academic performance of black children in terms of inherent racial differences, the switch to a discussion of cultural differences did not erase the old assumptions about inferiority in racialized terms (Clark, 1965; Silver & Silver, 1991).

In other words, in a social context in which white, middle-class culture in particular is seen as the "norm" and black students' cultural backgrounds are seen as deficient, the goal of schools would necessarily be to assimilate black children into the cultural mores of their white and more affluent counterparts (Delpit, 1995). Perhaps no single study helped to fuel this culture of poverty thinking more than the federally funded *Equality of Educational Opportunity* report, more commonly known as "the Coleman report." This study entailed what was, for its time, a sophisticated statistical analysis of educational opportunities across racial groups. Coleman and his colleagues' conclusion was essentially that the attributes of other students in the school account for far more variation in the achievement of minority-group children than do any attributes of their school's facilities and slightly more than attributes of the school staff (Coleman et al., 1966, p. 322).

The most broadly publicized message from the Coleman report was that the family backgrounds of the students and their classmates were more important than the schools themselves (Wells et al., 1995). For instance, *The New York Times* reported the central finding from the report to be: "differences in schools had very little effect on the achievement scores of children with a strong educational background in the home" (cited in Grant, 1973, p. 30).

But over time, the Coleman report came to support two somewhat paradoxical messages: The first was that schools do not matter—at least not as much as people had believed—and that family background, especially parents' education and income, mattered much more (Grant, 1973). The second message was that certain educational programs such as school desegregation and compensatory education were even more important than previously believed because they could help disadvantaged children overcome the cultural deficits of their families. While the first message seemed to carry more weight in academic circles, the second message had a profound impact on the ways in which educational policies were conceived and implemented (Grant, 1973; Moynihan, 1991; Wells et al., 1995).

Within the broader social and political context described in this article, it is no wonder that this became the dominant interpretation of a report with ambiguous conclusions. The other important historical factor related to cultural deprivation theory that contributed to the federal government's focus on education during the War on Poverty era was the growing interest in the implications of school failure, the relationship between schooling and employment, the incidence of juvenile crime, and the question of school dropout strategies to motivate adolescents. In both the United States and Britain after World War II, there was a growing public concern about the "youth problem." In particular, the focus was on poor and working-class youth who were seen as increasingly disenfranchised from the mainstream workforce. Education and other War on Poverty programs—for example, Job Corps—were promoted as ways to reduce such delinquency by preparing youth for productive employment (Lemann, 1988; Silver & Silver, 1991, pp. 52–53). All of these social and cultural factors led to an emphasis on the critical role of educational programs in solving the entire problem of poverty and inequality in the larger society.

Race and the Civil Rights Strategy. Another explanation of why educational programs became so central to the Great Society and its War on Poverty is the civil rights movement and the historic role that education had always played in black political protest against a system of racial subordination. Most important, the legal strategy employed by the NAACP in its assault on school segregation energized the civil rights movement and made education a major public issue in the 1960s. According to Kantor and Lowe (1995), "much of what has come to be seen as the modern civil rights movement was associated until the 1960s chiefly with the NAACP's legal campaign to end segregated schools" (p. 7).

Yet there is also ample historical evidence that the NAACP's leadership did not initially view its legal campaign for school desegregation as a substitute for other social and economic policies, but rather just one dimension of a broader effort to attack the legal basis of racial subordination. But the lack of political support for active state intervention in society and the labor market meant that the chief focus of both the NAACP and the federal government during the Great Society's War on Poverty was education (Kantor & Lowe, 1995, p. 8). In fact, in 1965, sociologist Nathan Glazer argued that poverty in America was an issue because the civil rights movement had made it a race issue.

Clearly, this belief in education as a key element in overcoming social, and especially racial, problems was central to the Supreme Court's unanimous opinion in *Brown v. Board of Education.* The strongly worded *Brown* ruling discussed at length the importance of public education in preparing students for their adult lives as workers and citizens: "Today, education is perhaps the most important function of state and local governments. Compulsory school attendance laws and the great expenditures for education both demonstrate our recognition of the importance of education in our democratic society" (*Brown v. Board of Education,* p. 7; see also Wells, Holme, Revilla, & Atanda, 2005).

Clearly, *Brown* had many long-term implications, but one of the most important such implications is that it laid the groundwork for "further federal involvement in educational legislation, support and intervention." Indeed, *Brown* established the important link between education and opportunity in a manner that would help catapult the educational system into the center of the War on Poverty and burden it with solving many of the inequalities inherent in a "separate and unequal" society (Silver & Silver, 1991, p. 22).

In fact, shortly after the *Brown* decision in 1954, Francis Keppel, then the dean of the Harvard Graduate School of Education and soon to become the U.S. Commissioner of Education, wrote that the Supreme Court decision would most likely be one of the most important historic events in the field of education. At the same time, he foresaw what lay ahead, noting that the American people cheerfully put tasks on the shoulders of the public schools with little realization of the difficulties involved. He also said that the national optimism about what education can accomplish is both a blessing and a danger. More specifically, in reference to *Brown,* he noted:

> The vast majority of the teachers and administrators in the public school have every intention of going forward to carry out the letter and spirit of the law; there are many among them, however, who hope that the schools will not be expected to accomplish a social miracle in the face of the latent or active opposition in homes and communities in both North and South. (cited in Silver & Silver, 1991, p. 22)

Paradoxically, while the civil rights movement generally and the NAACP's legal strategy in school desegregation more specifically contributed to the federal government's emphasis on educational reform as the central strategy in its War on Poverty, many of the policies that were eventually legislated within that reform movement, including the Elementary and Secondary Education Act and Head Start, may have been designed to dampen African American protest. Kantor and Lowe (1995) argue that there is sufficient evidence that the Great Society's War on Poverty education legislation was at least partly motivated by a desire to provide a "politically feasible alternative to school desegregation (particularly for northern Democrats fearful of White backlash but dependent on Black votes) while still doing something for low-income Blacks" (p. 9).

The Major Policies of Educational War on Poverty: The New Federal Role in Education

The story of the War on Poverty politics and the central role that educational and job training programs played in federal policymaking during that era stands in contrast to the pre-1960s history in which the federal government had played a relatively small role in American public education. Of course, the launch of the Soviet Union's satellite, Sputnik, in 1957 prompted a great deal of deliberation about what the federal government *should* be doing to improve the educational system, thereby ensuring that the United States would win the Cold War (Cross, 2004). But due to several political hurdles—most important, the issue of "race" and whether federal funds could flow to segregated schools and the issue of "religion" and whether federal funds could flow to private, religious schools—no major piece of federal education legislation had yet been passed when JFK was assassinated (Cross, 2004).

In fact, a series of major education bills had been introduced to both houses of Congress in the late 1950s and early 1960s, but nothing was passed and signed into law until 1965. Each proposed bill reflected a slightly different interpretation of what the federal role in education should be—from general aid to all schoolchildren to construction funds that would help alleviate overcrowding as the Baby Boomers flooded the schools to science and technology funding to help ensure that we were keeping up with the Soviets. Thus, while the National Defense and Education Act did pass in 1958 and provided some federal funding for math, science, and foreign language instruction, the federal role in education remained very small—less than $1 billion and less than 2% of the total education budget (McGuinn, 2006).

President Kennedy, in particular, was eager to see a major federal education law pass. He argued that the time for discussion about federal aid to education was past and that the United States could no longer afford the "luxury of endless debate over all the complicated and sensitive questions raised by each new proposal on federal participation in education" (Silver & Silver, 1991, p. 49). In fact, one of his speeches began, "Education is the keystone in the arch of freedom and progress . . . ignorance and illiteracy, unskilled workers and school dropouts—these and other failures of our educational system breed failures in our social and economic system" (cited in Silver & Silver, 1991, p. 49).

Despite Kennedy's support of a large federal role in education, the "big bang" of federal educational policy—the Elementary and Secondary Education Act of 1965—took several years to formulate and pass as policymakers struggled to figure out what the federal government's role should be in a country that had so strongly valued local control in public education and remained segregated by race and religion in many schools (Cross, 2004). The issue of race and whether federal money could flow to segregated schools was resolved in 1964 with the passage of the Civil Rights Act, which stated that racially segregated institutions could not receive federal funding. The issue of religion and the Catholic schools, in particular, that wanted access to any federal money that would flow to private schools was resolved in 1965 when a group of Catholic and public school officials derived the "child benefit theory," which allowed federal education funds to serve individual children and not public or private schools per se. In other words, federal funding for education would be, for the most part, "categorical," requiring children to be within a certain "category" that is eligible for the services to be funded by the federal money—be it compensatory education for poor children or special education for handicapped children or bilingual education for children whose home language is not English (Cross, 2004; Hill, 2000; McGuinn, 2006).

This categorical policy structure of targeting federal funds toward certain children with certain needs served two purposes that relate to the evolving federal role in public education at that time. First of all, it allowed federal policymakers to sidestep the issue of directly funding private schools—under the child benefit theory, the money follows the child. This led to many interesting arrangements as public school teachers were sent to private schools to provide Title I services to eligible children. But it also allowed the Elementary and Secondary Education Act (ESEA) to pass both houses of Congress rather quickly in 1965, more than doubling the federal education funding (Cross, 2004).

But the categorical nature of most of the federal funding also allowed the federal government to fulfill its critical historic role, which began with *Brown,* as the guarantor of students' 14th Amendment rights within the educational system. Many of these categorical programs became a combination of legislated and litigated histories of students who had been denied equal protection within the public schools fighting for equal access to educational opportunities (Cross, 2004; Hochschild & Scovronick, 2003). In fact, virtually all major federal education programs established between the *Brown* decision of 1954 and the passage of No Child Left Behind in 2001 were designed to identify inequalities and discrimination and attempt to remedy them.

Within a decade of the 1965 passage of ESEA, with its Title I program targeted at poor children, federal legislation had been passed to help assure that non-English-speakers, children with disabilities, migrant children, Native American children, and girls and women were not denied access to educational opportunities. As a result of this stream of federal equity-minded education policies and subsequent funding streams, between 1960 and 1970, federal aid to elementary and secondary schools increased from less than $1 billion to $3.5 billion. The number of federal education programs increased from 20 to 130 (Cross, 2004). The federal government had become a force to reckon with in the field of education, particularly in terms of issues of equity and antidiscrimination.

Though the federal government has also mounted small educational programs that were not focused on equity per se—for example, those intended to train teachers, support research, or develop new instructional methods—historically, these programs have received less funding and have had short, uncertain lives, compared with the programs designed to address discrimination (Hill, 2000). According to Hill (2000), "Equity is the historic basis for federal initiatives in K–12 education" (pp. 27–28).

As Silver and Silver (1991) note, in the 1960s, when the federal government became involved in education as it never had before, it shifted the focus away from the educational issues that had dominated local and state policymakers in the 1950s—for example, expanding and modernizing the system in response to demographic pressures, responding to shortages and inadequacies, and international events. By the 1960s, education had become increasingly central to political and social policy, and its role in overcoming poverty and disadvantage was a matter of increasing public interest and debate. What had been called "the American public's love affair with education," Silver and Silver (1991) write, "had become something quite different in its formulations from what had been a decade earlier" (p. 48).

This so-called love affair with education, born in part out of the disdain for other forms of public support, led to a bold new role for the federal government in directing what local public schools could and could not do, particularly as it related to serving students who had historically been denied equal educational opportunities. The tension between the enhanced federal role and the history of local control in the United States was somewhat lessened by the influx of federal funds to districts and schools. But it has never completely subsided and, in fact, has reemerged in full force in recent years.

Meanwhile, the public education system, bolstered by a newly engaged and involved federal government, took on the burden of attempting to close the gaps between the rich and the poor students minus a strong social safety net to hold up children whose families lack money for food, shelter, or health care. But the die had been cast in the 1960s; the public schools would be the primary safety net, and there has been no concerted effort to reconsider that decision in the years that followed.

As Kantor and Lowe (1995) remind us:

> From the outset of the Great Society, the idea that the education would eliminate poverty and expand economic opportunity for racial minorities and the poor dominated thinking about social and economic policy. Indeed, though policy planners in the Kennedy and Johnson administrations were certainly not the first to embrace this faith in education as a solution to social problems, seldom has education occupied so central a place in the minds of those responsible for planning social and economic policy. (p. 4)

FEDERAL EDUCATION POLICY SHIFT:
FROM EQUITY TO EXCELLENCE, FROM INPUTS TO OUTPUTS,
BUT STILL THE SAFETY NET

As the dream of a Great Society faded into the slow economy, rising inflation, high unemployment, an oil crisis, and the Iranian hostage debacle of the late 1970s, more American voters became disenchanted with the policies designed to provide greater equality of opportunity. Opportunities were becoming scarcer for most families; wages were stagnant while the cost of living was skyrocketing. To the extent that middle-class whites had supported War on Poverty policies such as compensatory education during the 1960s and early 1970s, they were less likely to do so now. For those who were hurting economically in their suburban towns, even the "hand up" policies that provided extra funds for urban schools seemed overly generous (see Edsall & Edsall, 1991).

A strong antigovernment, antitax mood set in, spurred and fostered by Ronald Reagan's 1980 campaign for president. Big government—especially when it was funding social programs—was bad and anti-American. Federal education policies and programs quickly became the target of this type of criticism, particularly as a result of the categorical and thus seemingly inconsistent and incoherent nature of the funding, services and regulations. A 1979 study conducted by researchers at the Rand Corporation found that 26 or 27 students in one "regular" classroom were in pullout programs to receive federally mandated services most of the day. Another study criticized the federal role in education as too small, too unfocused, too inconsistent, unclear, and ad hoc (Cross, 2004).

Paul Hill (2000), an outspoken critic of the federal government's role in education and one of the authors of the Rand study, argued that the categorical federal programs that emerged in the 1960s and 1970s created a "picket fence" approach to educational policy, introducing the idea that the government could act on some parts of schools and not others, create programs for some children and not others, and institute different rules to control the work of different teachers as well as administrative roles to supervise some teachers and not others.

This critique of the fragmented nature of federal involvement in education and its negative impact on local control was compounded with concerns about the "outcomes" or evidence that the federal investment in education was not leading to improved results, at least narrowly defined. On April 27, 1983, President Reagan's Secretary of Education Terrel H. Bell released a report from his appointed 18-member panel, the National Commission on Excellence in Education. Titled *A Nation at Risk: The Imperative for Educational Reform,* the commission's report laid most of the blame for the sagging economy, the loss of jobs, and the declining international competitiveness of the United States on the substandard public education system. Thus, just as the burden of solving poverty and inequality had been laid on the public educational system in the 2 prior decades, by the 1980s, blame for a weak economy was also heaped upon the schools. Perhaps the most-often quoted phrase from *A Nation at Risk* is, "If an unfriendly foreign power had attempted to impose on America the mediocre educational performance that exists today, we might well have viewed it as an act of war" (National Commission for Excellence in Education, 1983, p. 1).

Left out of the commission's report is a discussion of the rapidly closing black–white test score gap between the mid-1960s and the mid-1980s (see Grissmer, Flanagan, & Williamson, 1998). Furthermore, the commission's report has few citations and compares apples to oranges by discussing many of its statistics out of the context of the changing demographics of an educational system that serves more students for longer periods of time (see Berliner & Biddle, 1995). But the report had a tremendous impact on the American psyche and on how people made sense of what was wrong with our schools and society.

This broader political context no doubt strongly influenced a sea change in how policymakers were making sense of the federal role in education. The federal policy focus shifted over the next 20 years from the 14th Amendment requirement to ensure greater access for all to one that would demand better outcomes (as measured mostly by standardized test scores) and greater accountability. In very simplistic terms, this meant that the federal government's central purpose in education was changing from "equity" to "excellence," from ensuring proper inputs (or targeted resources) to a focus on the "outputs" derived from those inputs, and from policies that primarily used "carrots" in the form of funds to get the states and locals to comply with mandates to those that use "sticks" or sanctions to force the schools to do what is ordered.[2] The other shift was away from the so-called piecemeal manner in which individual students with different special needs would be targeted and supported to a more holistic or whole-school approach to education at the school level (Cross, 2004; McGuinn, 2006). While many of these changes were welcomed throughout the educational system, the concern, in light of a more recent growth in the black–white test score gap (Grissmer et al., 1998), is whether the shift away from equity has gone too far, especially as the country itself has become far more unequal (see Wells, in press).

Yet this shift in the federal role and emphasis occurred, it is worth noting, with much bipartisan support–from the "systemic reform" movement of the early 1990s to the passage of No Child Left Behind in 2001 (McGuinn, 2006; Riley, 1995). First there was President Bill Clinton and his Secretary of Education, Richard Riley, touting the systemic benefits of the Goals 2000 legislation, which established the voluntary national standards and provided funding to states to develop their own accountability systems. They then supported the 1994 reauthorization of ESEA, titled the "Improving America's Schools Act" (IASA), which required schools serving Title I students to help them achieve to high standards (Riley, 1995).

And after a short backlash within the Republican Party against federally supported standards and accountability systems in the mid-1990s, by 2001, the GOP and President George W. Bush were poised to steal the education platform and the standards reform movement from the Democrats by ratcheting up the accountability mechanisms and gaining strong bipartisan support for their legislation. The passage of that legislation, No Child Left Behind, the most recent authorization of ESEA, created an entirely new level of federal control over public education by attaching strict sanctions to the mandated outcome or "adequate yearly progress" measures of student achievement (McGuinn, 2006).

In many ways, NCLB completed the dramatic shift in the federal role toward "excellence," "outputs," and "sticks"–and even took it to a new level of sanctions that now apply to all schools, even those without Title I funding (DeBray, 2005). But there is a central theme of this more recent era of federal educational policy that is a continuation, a legacy of the War on Poverty era–namely, a reliance on the public schools alone to close the gaps between rich and poor students' academic achievement, and, by implication, their lives. And, thus, the burden placed on the public schools today to improve the test scores of students whose lives outside of schools are most disadvantaged is reminiscent in some ways of the 1960s argument that compensatory education and a few community action programs (that include job training programs) can solve the problems of the urban ghettos.

Yet, in other ways, NCLB and the philosophical shift that it represents are even worse, given the focus on "outputs" as measured by standardized tests, many of which are high-stakes for the students and their teachers (DeBray, 2005). The cornerstone of NCLB is more testing for students and a strict accountability system of sanctions associated with schools' failure to make progress in meeting student outcomes. Furthermore, test score data are broken down by student subgroups defined according to race/ethnicity, poverty, gender, disability, and English proficiency. This provision, in theory, will help schools and the government ensure that no children are being left behind (Cross, 2004; Wells et al., 2005). According to President George W. Bush, NCLB is designed to attack "the soft bigotry of low expectations" ("Bush Warns Against," 1999).

In January 2002, President Bush flew to the small town of Hamilton, Ohio, to sign the NCLB Act into law. At the signing ceremony in the local high school's gymnasium, Bush proclaimed that the legislative process was done, "And now it's up to you, the local citizens of our great land . . . to stand up and demand high standards, and to demand that no child—not one single child in America—is left behind" (Robelen, 2002, p. 20).

President Bush's choice of a small town as the venue for signing this influential federal law was symbolic of how far removed—physically and politically—many of our policymakers tend to be from the day-to-day experiences of poor children in troubled urban communities. This space between lawmakers and the people they target with their policies is especially pronounced in the case of NCLB, a "tough love" policy that is grounded in a belief that schools alone can overcome virtually all of the inequality in society and does nothing to offset the unevenness in the system (Karp, 2004). In other words, the high-stakes sanctions and punishments for both students (in some states) and schools failing to achieve "adequate yearly progress" are laid down upon a highly unequal educational system in which some students—particularly those in high-poverty schools—have access to far fewer resources and opportunities (Darling-Hammond, 2004; Sizer, 2004). To make matters worse, the law has been underfunded since the year it was passed, meaning that such inequalities in the educational system are not being offset by federal funding targeted toward poor students (Davis, 2006; Sanger, 2003).

Still, in recent years, many policymakers have often argued that the best way to achieve "equality" is not through liberal policies such as compensatory education or school desegregation but, rather, through policies that hold separate and unequal schools equally accountable for student outcomes. Note the following excerpt from a 2004 U.S. Department of Education newsletter:

> "Raise the bar!" "Close the gap!" These enthusiastic exclamations may sound like new-age workout instructions, but to teachers in the era of *No Child Left Behind,* they are familiar educational objectives. And they are achievable, thanks to over a decade of research that has delivered promising school improvement models. (Office of Innovation and Improvement, 2004, p. 1)

Indeed, the larger context of schools—rapidly rising childhood poverty, increasing income inequality, and ongoing racial segregation—has been completely missing from recent debates about educational policy (Karp, 2004; Wells, in press). And yet social science research has shown a strong, consistent, and statistically significant relationship between these social factors and student test scores, with poorer and more racially isolated students consistently performing poorly (Rothstein, 2004; Wells & Frankenberg, 2007). This relationship, as Rothstein (2004) and others have pointed out, is not simply about schools that serve poor students being substandard and underfunded—although most are—or about educators who teach poor children being underprepared, overwhelmed, or unmotivated, although this is often the case as well (Darling-Hammond, 1997; Wells & Frankenberg, 2007). It is also caused by the missing safety net for children and families, which results in too many poor children without much-needed health care, dental care, secure housing, adequate child care, nutritious food, or parents who have jobs that pay a living wage (Gordon, 1999; Rothstein, 2004; Wells, in press).

While more funding for poor school districts serving poor students of color is worth fighting for, there is no reason to believe that, if all else remains the same—especially inequality and the high concentration of rich and poor students in separate communities and schools—it will create equal educational opportunities (Orfield & Lee, 2005; Reardon & Yun, 2001; Wells et al., 2005). Below, I highlight some of the recent evidence on this changing social context of public schools, evidence that illustrates why placing the full burden of solving inequality on the educational system is shortsighted.

The Larger Context of Trying to Accomplish Equality of Results via Education

Examining the larger social context of public schools illuminates what it is that federal policymakers have seemingly ignored or underestimated since the New Deal. Furthermore, it is clear that in the last 2 decades, the lives of the most marginalized children within this context are becoming more—not less—difficult, even as the stakes for school failure have gotten higher. In fact, three recent trends or policy developments in particular strongly suggest that out-of-school inequalities will play a greater and not a smaller role in the years to come: growing income inequality; the influx of poor immigrants into the United States coupled with a highly segregated and unequal educational system; and the 1996 welfare reform act, which has left many poor children still poor, but now less likely to have health and child care.

Even absent these three recent trends, educational policies that are enacted minus broader social policies designed to improve children's daily lives in terms of food, shelter, clothing, and care are most likely doomed to fail, especially if their goal is to close the gap in school achievement between rich and poor children. These three trends, however, make this gap even harder to close without a broader safety net.

Growth in Income Inequality. Economists have demonstrated that in the last 3 decades income in this country has become far more unequal, as those with the highest salaries have enjoyed large pay increases while the family incomes of those at the bottom and middle of the distribution have remained relatively flat, even as more members of these families join the workforce and work longer hours (Hungerford, 2007; Kopczuk, Saez, & Song, 2007; Lemieux, 2007). Contrasted to the previous era (1950s–1970s), when there was a compression of incomes and the creation of a strong and better-off middle class, the last quarter century has led to deeper and wider divisions in terms of income and wealth (Krugman, 2005). According to one report, between 1950 and 1970, for every dollar earned by the bottom 90% of the population, those in the top 0.01% earned an additional $162. But from 1990 to 2002, for every dollar earned by the bottom 90%, members of the top 0.01% earned $18,000 (Herbert, 2005).

Meanwhile, between 1989 and 2000, when median hourly wages grew by just 5.9%, CEO compensation increased by 342% to an average of $1.7 million per year. "In 1978, the average CEO made 37 times what the average worker made; by 2000, the average CEO made 310 times what the average worker earned" (Drier, Mollenkopf, & Swanstrom, 2004). According to Greenhouse (2008), as more U.S. companies felt the intense pressure from Wall Street to produce impressive quarterly earnings, they embraced what he calls "the just-in-time workforce"—temporary workers, freelancers, and on-call "occasionals" who are paid less and have no job security. This trend then undercut the wages, benefits, and job security of traditional workers. Under this form of capitalism, workers' needs and well-being are minimized: "In short, it's a great economy if you're a high-level corporate executive or someone who owns a lot of stock. For most other Americans, economic growth is a spectator sport" (Krugman, 2006, p. 2).

In short, by 2004, the United States held the distinction of having the greatest income and wealth disparities of any advanced industrial society (Drier, Mollenkopf, & Swanstrom, 2004). Furthermore, this growing income inequality was laid down on top of several layers of racial segregation and inequality that so strongly defined our country by the middle of the 20th century, so that it should come as no surprise that the vast majority of the "fortunate fifth"—the top 20% of the population in terms of income—who have most benefited from these economic shifts are white. In other words, the new form of hyper-income inequality did not replace the pre-existing racial inequality; it just exacerbated it. Indeed, one analysis of 2000 census data reveals that the period from 1990 to 2000, the decade of widespread prosperity, "did not yield greater income or neighborhood equality for Blacks and Hispanics" (Logan, 2002).

Meanwhile, children are disproportionately affected by this growing inequality. According to Bernstein and Greenberg (2006), since 2000, the number of American children living in poverty has risen 12%—to 13 million. Furthermore, this increase in childhood poverty occurred at a time of ongoing economic recovery from the recession and expansion. The authors explain this seeming paradox: "despite on-going expansion, the poverty rate for children on this side of the pond [Atlantic Ocean] keeps rising, largely because the benefits of the recovery have flowed so disproportionately to families at the top of the income scale" (p. A19).

Increased Immigration and Ongoing Segregation. From so-called "global cities" such as New York, London, and Los Angeles to small agricultural towns in North Carolina, affluent countries are experiencing a large influx of low-wage immigrant workers from poor countries, which further undermines the domestic middle class while polarizing the highly paid professionals and the poorly paid service workers into separate social, economic, and political spheres (Drier et al., 2004; Krugman, 2002).

In New York City alone, between 1990 and 2000, the number of foreign-born residents increased from 2.1 million to nearly 3 million. And by 2000, more than a third of the New York City population was foreign-born, the highest percentage since the 1920s, during the peak of European immigration. Reflecting immigration trends across the country, 53% of foreign-born New Yorkers were Hispanic—mostly Dominicans, Mexicans, and Guatemalans—while Asians constituted 24%. These recent immigrants disproportionately live in poverty, have low levels of educational attainments, and do not speak English as their first language (NYC Department of City Planning, 2004). In fact, 62% of minimum-wage workers in New York City are immigrants (Fiscal Policy Institute, 2006; Wells, Holme, & Duran, 2006).

Furthermore, we know that racial and ethnic segregation—of immigrants and nonimmigrants as well—is most pronounced in large cities, with the size of the city and its percentage of African Americans positively correlated to the degree of segregation. According to Cutler, Glaeser, and Vigdor (1999), despite a slight decrease in overall racial segregation in the last 35 years, segregation across cities is persistent and strongly related to city size. This city size effect could be related to the increase in housing segregation in cities experiencing a large influx of immigrant groups (Belsie, 2001).

Layered on top of this ongoing racial segregation is a profound growth of socioeconomic segregation across neighborhoods that has produced and solidified pockets of highly concentrated poverty in urban and inner-ring suburban neighborhoods. Mirroring the growth in income inequality, economic segregation increased rapidly between 1970 and 1990 as affluent families continued to isolate themselves in exclusive enclaves (Drier et al., 2004, p. 39).

"Although two-thirds of all new jobs are located in the suburbs, three-quarters of welfare recipients live in central cities or rural areas . . . exclusionary zoning often prevents low-wage workers from moving closer to such jobs." Such a spatial mismatch means that parents of poor students are home less often as they commute long distances to poor-paying jobs. Meanwhile, in global cities, central business districts house lawyers, management consultants, high-wage professional jobs—high-wage workers, many of whom commute from the suburbs (Drier et al., 2004, p. 67).

Welfare Reform—From Poor Relief to Poor Jobs. Related to both the dual economy and the spatial mismatch is the 1996 federal welfare reform act and its unequal effect on recipients in low-income areas where there are few jobs. The Personal Responsibility and Work Opportunity Reconciliation Act of 1996, more frequently known as "welfare reform," is generally considered a success because the welfare rolls were cut from 12.3 million recipients in 1998 to 4.9 million in 2003. We know, however, that many families who left welfare are not better off than they were before, and most research confirms that the reform has not helped poor women climb out of poverty (Brown, 2003; Handler & Hasenfeld, 2007; Polit, Nelson, Richburg-Haytes, Seith, & Rich, 2005).

The 1996 act set aside money for job training and day care, but made no formal provision to bridge the gap between where welfare recipients live and where the jobs are, although, as we noted above, two-thirds of all new jobs are located in the suburbs, and three-quarters of welfare recipients live in central cities or rural areas. Hence, not surprisingly, welfare rolls have fallen more slowly in cities than elsewhere, and white welfare recipients have been far more likely to get themselves off the welfare rolls and into jobs than have blacks or Latinos (Brown, 2003; Drier et al., 2004; Handler & Hasenfeld, 2007). According to Brown (2003), the proportion of white families in TANF (Temporary Assistance to Needy Families) sharply dropped to 31% of all cases; racial minorities now account for over two-thirds.

Finally, the relationship between welfare (or lack thereof) and the low-paying service sector jobs is tight, intertwined, and dependent upon place. For instance, researchers have found that switching from welfare to a low-paying service job does not help women escape poverty—they just become part of the "working poor" as opposed to being poor welfare recipients (Polit et al., 2005). For instance, Shipler (2004) recounts that when the welfare reform law passed, the economy was strong enough to send welfare caseloads plummeting. But most available jobs had three unhappy traits: they paid low wages, offered no benefits, and led nowhere. As a result, the 8 million former welfare recipients who did find jobs lost many other supports that were designed to help them, such as food stamps and health insurance, "leaving them no better off—and sometimes worse off—than when they were not working" (Shipler, 2004, p. 40).

In fact, Blank and colleagues (2006) point out that there were two fundamental flaws in the effort to shift so many poor people to work so quickly. The first was that the type of jobs former welfare recipients could get generally did not pay enough to lift them out of poverty. The second was that the policies designed to help them in their working lives, including the health care and child-care programs, were not as well supported—especially after the 1990s—as they needed to be, resulting in large numbers of working poor people whose basic needs are no longer being met.

Of course, another way to think about the relationship between the lack of a social safety net and the labor market is that the former feeds the later. For instance, according to Hamnett (1996): "In the U.S., the growth of a low-income consumer-service sector is partly dependent on the limited welfare state protection which is available: many individuals, including single parents and others, are effectively forced into the flexible low-wage labour market, whereas in the Netherlands or Scandinavia, they are insulated by the welfare state" (p. 108).

Researchers in the field of education rarely discuss the connection between welfare reform and the public schools. But given the spatial separation between the rich and poor, welfare policy reforms have major implications for schools and students in poor neighborhoods with large percentages of welfare (or former welfare) recipients. They would have little direct impact on more affluent schools. One area where far more research is needed is the impact of welfare reform on the children of former welfare recipients, and their schooling in particular.

CONCLUSION:
A CALL FOR COMPREHENSIVE SOCIAL AND EDUCATIONAL POLICIES

This chapter has traced the history of the federal government's role in public education and the interaction between that role, other social welfare policies (or lack thereof), and the broader inequality in our society. The central argument here is not to diminish the role of schools in students' lives or to argue that we do not need to better fund and staff schools in low-income communities. We have a moral imperative to support schools serving poor children, especially.

Rather, the central argument of this chapter is that we must reconsider the burden we have placed on our public schools for the last 50 years, even as we, as a society, have failed to provide the policies and programs that can improve the lives of poor children outside of school. To close the gap in test scores between poor and affluent students, we must think more seriously about the types of complementary policies and supplementary resources that are required to make children's lives more equal outside of schools (see Gordon, 1999; Gordon, Bridglall, & Meroe, 2004).

In their historical analysis of why the United States continues to have one of the least generous systems of public social provision of any of the capitalist democracies, Weir, Orloff, and Skopol (1988) argue that the current "understanding of crisis and policy alternatives" depends on the ways each nation's existing policies influence political alliances and arouse debates over further policy choices. "A nation's politics creates social policies," they explain, which then in turn "remake its politics, transforming possibilities for the future" (p. 5).

Weir and colleagues (1998) remind us that it will not be easy to alter "American exceptionalism" because it is ingrained in how we make sense of social policy and the role of public schools in our society. But we have to consider, as we examine recent trends in income inequality, segregation, global labor markets, and welfare reform in our society, what would have happened if FDR had spent much time pondering our "exceptionalism" before launching the New Deal.

NOTES

1. The name of this chapter comes from *Our Children's Burden*, the title of a book edited by Raymond Mack and published in 1968 by Vintage Books. Intended as a complementary book of qualitative research to the statistical Coleman report of 1966, *Our Children's Burden* provided in-depth case studies of towns and communities that were struggling to implement school desegregation at that time. The central argument of the book is that, absent a broader effort in the United States to

desegregate housing and other dimensions of society, the public schools were left to address issues of racial inequality almost entirely on their own, making their job that much more difficult. As Mack (1968) noted in his conclusion to the book: "In America we have deemed desegregation too difficult a social process to be dealt with by realtors, bankers, clergymen, and community leaders. We have assigned the task to the children" (p. 459).

This chapter is not about school desegregation policy per se, but rather about the larger role of the federal government in education. Still, Mack's conclusion about the ways in which our society has placed so much of the burden for righting wrongs on children and schools is the perfect analogy for the broader discussion of federal policies that have placed this and many additional burdens on the schools and our children.

2. Clearly, the federal courts have used plenty of "sticks" to force school districts and educators to comply with desegregation orders and other federal laws. But the legislated federal policies were, up until recently, more reliant on carrots—extra funding (albeit not enough) to get states and districts to buy into their programs.

REFERENCES

Belsie, L. (2001, March 14). Ethnic diversity grows, but not integration: New census figures show greater diversity, but communities are no more integrated. *The Christian Science Monitor*, p. 1.

Berliner, D. C., & Biddle, B. J. (1995). *The manufactured crisis*. Reading, MA: Addison-Wesley.

Bernstein, J., & Greenberg, M. (2006, April 3). A plan to end childhood poverty. *Washington Post*, p. A19.

Blank, R., Danziger, S., & Schoeni, R. (2006). *Working and poor: How economic and policy changes are affecting low wage workers*. New York: Russell Sage Foundation.

Broader, Bolder Approach to Education Task Force. (2008). *A broader, bolder approach to education*. Retrieved June 10, 2008, from www.boldapproach.org

Brown v. Board of Education, 347 U.S. 483 (1954).

Brown, M. (1999). *Race, money, and the American welfare state*. Ithaca, NY: Cornell University Press.

Brown, M. K. (2003). Ghettos, fiscal federalism, and welfare reform. In S. F. Schram, J. Soss, & R. C. Fording (Eds.), *Race and the politics of welfare reform* (pp. 47–71). Ann Arbor: University of Michigan Press.

Bush warns against the "soft bigotry of low expectations." (1999). *Education Week*. Retrieved June 14, 2005, from http://www.edweek.org/ew/articles/1999/09/22/03bushs1.h19.html?querystring=soft%20bigotry

Coleman, J. S., Campbell, E. Q., Hobson, C. J., McPartland, J., Mood, A. M., Weinfeld, F., & York, R. L. (1966). *Equality of educational opportunity*. Washington, DC: U.S. Government Printing Office.

Clark, K. B. (1965). *Dark ghetto: Dilemmas of social power*. New York: Harper.

Cross, C. T. (2004). *Political education: National policy comes of age*. New York: Teachers College Press.

Cutler, D. M., Glaeser, E. L., & Vigdor, J. L. (1999, June). The rise and decline of the

American ghetto. *The Journal of Political Economy, 107*(3), 455–507.

Darling-Hammond, L. (1997). *The right to learn: A blueprint for creating schools that work.* San Francisco: Jossey-Bass.

Darling-Hammond, L. (2004). From "separate but equal" to "No Child Left Behind": The collision of new standards and old inequalities. In D. Meier & G. Wood (Eds.), *Many children left behind* (pp. 3–32). Boston: Beacon Press.

Davis, M. R. (2006, February 15). "President's budget would cut education spending." *Education Week, 25*(23), 1, 24–26.

DeBray, E. H. (2005). Partisanship and ideology in the ESEA reauthorization in the 106th and 107th congresses: Foundations for the new political landscape of federal education policy. *Review of research in education: Special issue on the Elementary and Secondary Education Act at 40*: Vol. 29 (pp. 29–50). Washington, DC: American Educational Research Association.

Delpit, L. (1995). *Other people's children: Cultural conflict in the classroom.* New York: New Press.

DeParle, J. (2004). *American dream: Three women, ten kids, and a nation's drive to end welfare.* New York: Viking Penguin.

Drier, P., Mollenkopf, J., & Swanstrom, T. (2004). *Place matters: Metropolitics for the twenty-first century.* Lawrence, KS: University Press of Kansas.

Edsall, T., & Edsall, M. D. (1991). *Chain reaction: The impact of race, rights, and taxes on American politics.* New York: W.W. Norton.

Fiscal Policy Institute. (2006). *Immigrant workers and the minimum wage in New York City.* Report prepared for the New York Immigration Coalition. New York City: Author.

Flora, P., & Heidenheimer, A. J. (1984). The historical core and changing boundaries of the welfare state. In P. Flora & A. J. Heidenheimer, (Eds.), *The development of welfare states in Europe and America* (pp. 17–34). New Brunswick, NJ: Transaction.

Goodnough, A. (2007, August 29). Census shows a modest rise in U.S. income. *The New York Times.* Retrieved on August 29, 2007, from http://www.nytimes.com/2007/08/29/us/29census.html

Gordon, E. (1999). *Education & justice: A view from the back of the bus.* New York: Teachers College Press.

Gordon, E. W., Bridglall, B. L., & Meroe, A. S. (Eds.). (2004). *Supplementary education: The hidden curriculum of high academic achievement.* Lanham, MD: Rowman & Littlefield.

Grant, G. (1973). Shaping social policy: The politics of the Coleman report. *Teachers College Record, 75*(1), 17–34.

Greenhouse, S. (2008). *The big squeeze: Tough times for the American worker.* New York: Alfred A. Knopf.

Grissmer, D., Flanagan, A., & Williamson, S. (1998). Why did the black–white score gap narrow in the 1970s and 1980s? In C. Jencks & M. Phillips (Eds.), *The black–white test score gap* (pp. 182–226). Washington, DC: Brookings Institution.

Hamnett, C. (1996). Why Sassen is wrong: A response to Burgers. *Urban Studies, 33*(1), 107–110.

Handler, J. F., & Hasenfeld, Y. (2007). *Blame welfare, ignore poverty and inequality.* Cambridge, UK: Cambridge University Press.

Harrington, M. (1962). *The other America: Poverty in the United States.* New York: Scribner.

Hartz, L. (1991). *The liberal tradition in America.* San Diego, CA: Harcourt Brace.

Heidenheimer, A. J. (1984). Education and Social Security entitlements in Europe and America. In P. Flora & A. J. Heidenheimer (Eds.), *The development of welfare states in Europe and America* (pp. 269–304). New Brunswick, NJ: Transaction.

Herbert, B. (2005, June 6). The mobility myth. *The New York Times.* Retrieved June 7, 2005, from www.nytimes.com

Hess, F. M., & Finn, C. E., Jr. (2007, September). Can this law be fixed? A hard look at the No Child Left Behind remedies. *Education Outlook, 3,*1-6.

Hill, P. (2000). The federal role in education. In *Brookings papers on education policy, 2000* (pp. 11–57). Washington, DC: Brookings Institution.

Hirschland, M. J., & Steinmo, S. (2003, July). Correcting the record: Understanding the history of federal intervention and failure in securing U.S. educational reform. *Educational Policy, 17*(3), 343–364.

Hochschild, J., & Scovronick, N. (2003). *The American dream and the public schools.* New York: Oxford University Press.

Hungerford, T. L. (September 4, 2007). *Income inequality and the U.S. tax system.* CRS Report for Congress. Washington, DC: Congressional Research Service. Order Code: RL34155.

Kaestle, C. F. (1983). *Pillars of the republic: Common schools and American society 1780–1860.* New York: Hill and Wang.

Kantor, H., & Lowe, R. (1995, April). Class, race and the emergence of federal education policy: From the New Deal to the Great Society. *Educational Researcher, 24*(3), 4–11, 21.

Karp, S. (2004). NCLB's selective vision of equality: Some gaps count more than others. In D. Meier & G. Wood (Eds.), *Many children left behind* (pp. 53–65). Boston: Beacon.

Katz, M. B. (1996). *In the shadow of the poorhouse: A social history of welfare in America.* New York: Basic Books.

Kopczuk, W., Saez, E., & Song, J. (2007). Uncovering the American dream: Inequality and mobility in Social Security earnings data since 1937. Working Paper 13345. Cambridge, MA: National Bureau of Economic Research. Retrieved March 21, 2008, from http://www.nber.org/papers

Krugman, P. (2002, October 20). For richer. *The New York Times Magazine,* p. 62.

Krugman, P. (2005, June 10). Losing our country. *The New York Times,* p. A2.

Krugman, P. (2006, July 14). Left behind economics [electronic version]. *The New York Times.* Retrieved November 20, 2008, from http://select.nytimes.com/2006/07/14/opinion/14krugman.html

Lemann, N. (1988, December). The unfinished war. Part I [electronic version]. *The Atlantic Monthly.* Retrieved November 20, 2008, from http://www.theatlantic.com/politics/poverty/lemunf1.htm

Lemann, N. (1989, January). The unfinished war. Part II. *The Atlantic Monthly,* pp. 53–68.

Lemann, N. (1991). *The promised land: The great black migration and how it changed America.* New York: Alfred A. Knopf.

Lemann, N. (2000). *The big test.* New York: Farrar, Strauss and Giroux.

Lemieux, T. (2007, October). *The changing nature of wage inequality.* Working Paper 13523. Cambridge, MA: National Bureau of Economic Research. Retrieved March 21, 2008, from http://www.nber.org/papers

Lewis, O. (1969). The culture of poverty. In D. P. Moynihan (Ed.), *On understanding poverty: Perspectives from the social science* (pp. 187–200). New York: Basic Books.

Logan, J. R. (2002). *Separate and unequal: The neighborhood gap for blacks and Hispanics in metropolitan America.* Albany, NY: Lewis Mumford Center for Comparative Urban and Regional Research.

Mack, R. W. (Ed.). (1968). *Our children's burden.* New York: Vintage Books.

Massey, D., & Denton, N. (1993). *American apartheid: Segregation and the making of the underclass.* Cambridge, MA: Harvard University Press.

McGuinn, P. J. (2006). *No Child Left Behind and the transformation of federal education policy, 1965–2005.* Lawrence: University of Kansas Press.

Moynihan, D. P. (1991). Educational goals and political plans. *Public Interest, 102,* 32–84.

National Commission on Excellence in Education. (1983). *A nation at risk: The imperative for educational reform.* Washington, DC: U.S. Government Printing Office.

NYC Department of City Planning. (2004, October). *The newest New Yorkers 2000.* New York: Author.

Office of Innovation and Improvement. (2004). *Americans' choice lifts students to reach the achievement bar.* Washington, DC: U.S. Department of Education.

Orfield, G, & Lee, C. (2005). *Why segregation matters: Poverty and educational inequality.* Cambridge, MA: The Civil Rights Project, Harvard University.

Petrovich, J. (2005). The shifting terrain of educational policy: Why we must bring equity back. In J. Petrovich & A. S. Wells (Eds.), *Bringing equity back: Research for a new era in American educational policy* (pp. 3–15). New York: Teachers College Press.

Polit, D. F., Nelson, L., Richburg-Haytes, L., & Seith, D., with Rich, S. (2005, August). *Welfare reform in Los Angeles: Implementation, effects and experiences of poor families and neighborhoods.* Washington, DC: MDRC.

Quadagno, J. (1987). Theories of the welfare state. *Annual Review of Sociology, 13,* 109–128.

Quadagno, J. (1994). *The color of welfare: How racism undermined the war on poverty* (pp. 3–15). New York: Oxford University Press.

Rainwater, L. (1970). *Behind ghetto walls: black families in a federal slum.* London: Allen Lane.

Reardon, S. F., & Yun, J. T. (2001). Suburban racial change and suburban school segregation, 1987–95. *Sociology of Education, 74* (April), 79–101.

Riley, R. W. (1995). Reflections on Goals 2000. *Teachers College Record, 96*(3), 380–388.

Robelen, E. W. (2002, January 16). Amid heartland hoopla, Bush signs the ESEA. *Education Week, 21*(18), 20, 23.

Rothstein, R. (2004). *Class and schools: Using social, economic, and educational reform to close the black–white achievement gap.* New York: Teachers College Press.

Sanger, D. E. (2003). Bush defends financing for schools. *The New York Times.* Retrieved September 6, 2004, from http://www.nytimes.com/2003/09/09/politics/09BUSH.html?ex=1064133497&ei=1&en=40edb153596f5cda

Shapiro, R. Y., & Young, J. T. (1989). Public opinion and the welfare state: The United States in comparative perspective. *Political Science Quarterly, 104*(1), 59–89.

Shipler, D. (2004). *The working poor: Invisible in America.* New York: Vintage.

Silver, H., & Silver, P. (1991). *An educational war on poverty: American and British policy-making 1960–1980.* Cambridge, MA: Cambridge University Press.

Sizer, T. R. (2004). Preamble: A reminder for Americans. In D. Meier & G. Wood (Eds.), *Many children left behind* (pp. xvii–xxii). Boston: Beacon.

Sunstein, C. R. (2004). *The Second Bill of Rights.* New York: Basic Books.

Thomas, J. Y., & Brady, K. P. (2005). The Elementary and Secondary Education Act at 40: Equity, accountability and the evolving federal role in public education. In L. Parker (Ed.), *Review of research policy implementation, critical perspectives and reflections* (pp. 51–67). Washington, DC: American Educational Research Association.

Valentine, C. A. (1969). Culture and poverty: Critique and counter-proposals. *Current Anthropology, 10*(2/3), 181–201.

Weir, M., Orloff, A. S., & Skocpol, T. (1988). Introduction: Understanding American social politics. In M. Weir, A. S. Orloff, & T. Skocpol (Eds.), *The politics of social policy in the United States* (pp. 3–27). Princeton, NJ: Princeton University Press.

Wells, A. S. (in press). The social context of charter schools: The changing nature of poverty and what it means for American education. In M. G. Springer, H. J. Walberg, M. Berends, & D. Ballou (Eds.), *Handbook of research on school choice.* Philadelphia: Lawrence Erlbaum.

Wells, A. S., & Crain, R. L. (1997). *Stepping over the color line: African American students in white suburban schools.* New Haven, CT: Yale University Press.

Wells, A. S., & Frankenberg, E. (2007, November). The public schools and the challenge of the Supreme Court's integration decision. *Phi Delta Kappan, 89*(3), 178–188.

Wells, A. S., Hirshberg, D., Lipton, M., & Oakes, J. (1995). Bounding the case within its context: A constructivist approach to studying detracking reform. *Educational Researcher, 24*(5), 18–24.

Wells, A. S., Holme, J. J., & Duran, J. (2006, April). *A spatial understanding of the schools left behind: Scapegoating poor urban schools in an era of accountability and school choice.* Paper presented at the annual meeting of the American Educational Research Association, San Francisco.

Wells, A. S., Holme, J. J., Revilla, A. T., & Atanda, A. K (2005). How society failed school desegregation policy: Looking past the schools to understand them. *Review of Research in Education, 28,* 47–100.

Wilensky, H. L. (1975). *The welfare state and equality: Structural and ideological roots of public expenditures.* Berkeley: University of California Press.

CHAPTER 2

The Challenge and Opportunity of African American Educational Achievement

----

Michael T. Nettles,
Catherine M. Millett, and Hyeyoung Oh

Academic achievement gaps between African American and white students in this country continue to be wide and growing. These gaps begin at a very young age. By grade 4, they are evident in math, science, and reading; by grade 8, the gaps, especially in math, are even larger. The performance gaps between student groups remain present through high school and beyond. African American students' SAT scores, for example, have been well below the scores of their white peers and the national average as reported annually by the College Board. In 2007, African American students on average scored 433 on the critical reading section, 429 on the math, and 425 on the writing, compared with whites who, on average, scored 527 on the critical reading, 534 on the math, and 518 on the writing sections of the SAT (College Board, 2007). Black students' scores were also below the national average: 69 points below the national critical reading average score (502), 86 points below the national math average score (515), and 69 points below the national writing average score (494).

On the Graduate Record Examinations (GRE), in 2005–2006, African Americans scored a 394 on the verbal section, 418 on the quantitative, and 3.6 on the analytical writing section, in comparison with whites, who scored a 495 on the verbal, 563 on the quantitative, and 4.4 on the analytical writing sections. Black students are also scoring below the national GRE averages as well: 88 points below the verbal average (482), 129 points below the quantitative average (547), and 0.7 average points below the analytical writing section (4.3) (Graduate Record Examinations Board, 2007).

African American educational achievement in the United States is a veridical paradox. On the one hand, as a population group, African Americans place the greatest stress on the nation's education system, requiring the most attention while delivering the weakest results. On the other hand, African Americans provide the best target of opportunity for the nation to realize the greatest overall gains in achievement and return on investment. The challenge for the nation and especially for policymakers is twofold: first, to acknowledge that African American student achievement is vitally important to the nation's future and merits being the highest priority and receiving substantial sustained investment of resources; and, second, to produce a compelling new strategy that adequately addresses the specific challenges of meeting African Americans' educational needs.

The Elementary and Secondary Education Act of 2001 (No Child Left Behind) can be an initial step. The central focus of the act is making a national imperative of academic gains for everyone and closing gaps among people of various race/ethnic groups and social classes. The emphasis on gains signals the sensitivity of policymakers to the genuine need to improve the nation's overall system of education. The focus on gaps reflects policymakers' sense of the national crisis of achievement among minority and disadvantaged populations and responsibility for the nation's economy and general well-being, especially at this time of growing diversity. The largest and seemingly most intractable of the gaps is between African American and white students. It may be politically unfeasible and even unconstitutional for national policies explicitly to single out any race, ethnic group, or class for special treatment. Consequently, national policies give attention to addressing gaps generally, leaving the tailoring that is required to fit each segment of the population to those who implement the policies. The result has been slow and modest progress overall, and very modest and nearly unnoticeable progress for African American students, the population group with the greatest barriers and challenges. For African American students, as for other groups, closing gaps may require actions to address their specific challenges.

This chapter explores the human, institutional, and societal elements of African American underachievement and the gaps that African American students must overcome to be on par with their white peers in reaching the laudable educational targets that policymakers are setting for America's youth. This exploration is intended as a step toward solving the puzzle of black–white achievement gaps, as this nation debates the reauthorization of No Child Left Behind and weighs options for revising the law to better accomplish its goal of closing these gaps. It is our hope that this examination of the elements of African American underachievement and gaps will provide directions for shaping strategies and identifying further research required to eliminate the gaps.

EXPLANATIONS FOR
AFRICAN AMERICAN STUDENT UNDERACHIEVEMENT

While the relatively low performance of African American students has been observed for many years, the enactment of the No Child Left Behind Act has brought a more intense focus on both measuring and understanding black–white achievement gaps. Though research on these gaps has proliferated, it has covered much of the same territory that has been traversed over the past 3 decades. Scientists and theoreticians have examined most elements of human character, behavior, and endeavor to try to identify meaningful correlates and cures for the vast difference between African American and white student achievement. Included among the most notable recurring explanations are oppositional culture, racism, socioeconomic factors, family- and community-based factors, and school-based factors. In the section that follows, we examine the literature on each of these topic variables for their plausibility as explanations of African American achievement and the gaps between their performance and that of their white peers.

Oppositional Culture

Over the past 2 decades, numerous theories have emerged to explain the black–white achievement gap.[1] Among the most popular, albeit not the most persuasive, has been the oppositional culture theory. This theory, when ascribed to African American students, has often been focused on peer pressure and especially the charge by peers that people who are serious students are "acting white." This phenomenon was initially reported by Signithia Fordham and John Ogbu (1986) as a plausible explanation for the achievement gap. Their research led them to conclude that when high-achieving African American students are faced with the burden of peer pressure resulting from being characterized as "acting white," they respond by developing oppositional orientations and approaches to schooling that are counterproductive. The evidence for this view is at best inconclusive, although the view has been a darling of broadcast media. In fact, substantial recent evidence has been produced that suggests that such behaviors and attitudes are not pervasive among African American students, nor are they more prevalent among African Americans than among students of other racial/ethnic backgrounds (Ainsworth-Darnell & Downey, 1998; Carter, 2005; Tyson, Darity, & Castellino, 2005) Some have argued that it is not necessarily a burden of acting white, but rather, a burden of high achievement that students of all races and ethnic groups confront (Tyson, Darity, & Castellino, 2005).

For many students, school is an environment with conflicting expectations and norms. One expectation is for high achievement, as emphasized by teachers, administrators, parents, and often by students themselves.

On the other hand, among peers, academic disengagement, rather than achievement, is encouraged and understood to be "cool" (Ogbu, 2003). Accordingly, Tyson, Darity, and Castellino (2005) highlight a distinction they feel must be made between associating a universal attitude pushing mediocrity versus an attitude toward academic achievement that is understood to be typical within a specific racial group (e.g., among black students). Thus, they separate the notion of oppositional culture into three types of oppositionality: general, racialized, and class-based. General oppositionality is the push for academic underachievement, in response to taunts such as "dork" and "nerd," a phenomenon that is found across all youth groups, regardless of race, ethnicity, or social class. Racialized oppositionality would be what Fordham and Ogbu have defined as the "burden of acting white," where black students respond with academic underachievement as a result of taunts such as "Oreo"—implying that these students are actively trying to mimic, or become, their white counterparts. Lastly, class-based oppositionality focuses more on social class, making it a universal culture across all racial groups; students are taunted with labels such as "snooty" and other words indicating that they feel that they are better than their peers. The taunts—whether they are socially, racially, or class motivated—are constant reminders of the attitudes and behaviors that are deemed acceptable by one's peers. Consequently, many children respond to the comments and strive for academic disengagement and underachievement.

Racism

After thoroughly examining the research literature, John Diamond (2006) argues that the key to understanding achievement gaps is the academic achievement constraints faced by African Americans as a result of the racial stratification of society:

> What is abundantly clear from prior research on race and education is that there is a material and symbolic cost to being black in the contemporary United States. These disadvantages are embedded in our social fabric and reflected in our social structures, schools, and perceptions of race and intellectual ability. Black students face a racialized educational terrain that creates material and symbolic disadvantages for them. (p. 10)

Diamond elucidates some of the distinctive experiences of African American students based on their race:

- The schools that black students attend are often less conducive to their educational success (Bryk & Schneider, 2003; Diamond & Spillane, 2004).

- While the mechanisms are complicated to sort out, school segregation—in particular the concentration of low-income African American students in certain schools—leads to lower outcomes for students attending these schools even after controlling for students' prior achievement (Bankston & Caldas, 1996), and schools in the United States have become increasingly (re)segregated in recent years (Orfield & Eaton, 1996).
- African Americans pay higher prices for lower-quality housing that is more likely to be located in segregated neighborhoods; they have lower levels of employment and occupational mobility, lower home loan approvals, and more negative interactions with the legal system (Bonilla-Silva, 2001).

Some scholars argue that the African American experience is unlike any other experience of a minority group in the United States and that this difference plays a crucial role in African American pathways to success. Unlike Latin or Asian immigrants, who are often labeled as voluntary immigrants—individuals who made an active decision to come to the United States, whether it be for better job opportunities or to pursue an education—African Americans are seen as involuntary immigrants, forced to enter the United States by someone else's hand (Ogbu, 2003). Thus, their perceptions of the American dream and American success may differ from those shared by other minority groups in the United States. Black Americans are thus seen to have formed a collective identity that is defined by oppression, resulting in many perceiving and fearing the adoption of "white ways" as a mechanism for fracturing African American solidarity and identity.

Others argue that the exclusion and collective mistreatment of African Americans by whites purely on the basis of skin color has affected some black individuals by molding the perceptions they hold of themselves and those around them. As the efforts of African Americans to gain legitimate places in academia and the workforce are rebuffed, a greater number internalizes these beliefs (Ogbu, 2003). They may experience feelings of self-doubt and resignation as they begin to question their intelligence in comparison to whites (Ogbu, 2003). With the many obstacles blacks experience as a result of a racially stratified society, combined with the obstacles they may create for themselves through internalization of racist beliefs, the black–white achievement gap is unsurprising.

Socioeconomic Status

Socioeconomic status is a critical issue for the achievement gap debate because it dictates the environments, resources, and opportunities that children encounter as they grow up.

- black children are more likely to live in poor households than white children.
- Because of a history of social policy that limited African Americans' access to the major avenues toward wealth accumulation (e.g., purchasing suburban homes), black families have far fewer assets than their white counterparts who earn the same incomes (Oliver & Shapiro, 1995).

Studies have repeatedly shown that lower socioeconomic status and lower academic performance are linked (Nettles, Millett, & Ready, 2003). High-poverty, high-minority schools have a greater likelihood of having unqualified teachers (Olson, 2003) and have a more difficult time attracting and retaining highly qualified teachers (Sunderman & Kim, 2005).

Socioeconomic status–social class–not only affects the resources to which students have access in school, but it also affects the resources to which students have access at home. Social class has been shown to affect the ability to provide the necessary family support for children to succeed academically. There are several theories about the interplay of social class and academic achievement, all of which may shed additional light on black–white achievement gaps. One theory argues that parents from low socioeconomic backgrounds may place too little importance on education and may be ineffective or too little involved in their children's education. Children may assimilate these attitudes, so that they, too, place little value on education (Lareau, 1989; Sewell & Hauser, 1980; Sewell & Shah, 1968a, 1968b). Another perspective emphasizes the importance of parents' social networks and affiliations to provide parents with the tools necessary to support their children's education (Carbonaro, 1998; Coleman, 1988; Coleman & Hoffer, 1987; Hao & Bonstead-Bruns, 1998; Hofferth, Boisjoly, & Duncan, 1998; McNeal, 1999). This social capital perspective emphasizes social class as key to gaining access to many educational, occupational, and personal opportunities (Carbonaro, 1998; Coleman, 1988; Coleman & Hoffer, 1987; Hao & Bonstead-Bruns, 1998; Hofferth, Boisjoly, & Duncan, 1998; McNeal, 1999; Wong, 1998).

The third perspective holds schools accountable for treating parents of low socioeconomic status differently from those of high socioeconomic status (for example, by making them feel less welcome at school), resulting in the disengagement of low-income families from their children's education (Comer, 1980; Connell, Ashenden, Kesslerr, & Dowsett, 1982; Epstein & Dauber, 1991; Lareau, 1987). The fourth perspective, based on Bourdieu's cultural capital theory, stresses that a parent's social class limits the cultural resources to which he or she has access (Bourdieu, 1986; Bourdieu & Passeron, 1990). Furthermore, the resources that low-income parents are able to offer tend to be disregarded or dismissed, in comparison to the resources that wealthier families are able to provide (Bourdieu, 1986; Bourdieu & Passeron, 1990).

Parenting and Parent Involvement

Other researchers focus their attention on the family and parenting as key factors in preventing children from falling through the cracks (Furstenberg, Cook, Eccles, Elder, & Sameroff, 1999). The process of learning begins at the home, even before children start to attend school. Some researchers have argued that the family is the primary determining force behind student performance, not schools (Coleman et al., 1966). Parenting involves a variety of behaviors and roles, including teaching, disciplining, nurturing, setting an example for, and supporting children (Brooks-Gunn & Markman, 2005; Ogbu, 2003). Recent literature has shown that parental involvement in children's academic and social lives plays a crucial role in children's academic learning and achievement (Epstein, 2001; Steinberg, 1997).

In his study of Shaker Heights families, Ogbu (2003) found that even though black parents had high academic expectations for their children, they often were limited in their involvement in their children's education and extracurricular activities and had low participation in various school organizations and activities organized for parents (Ogbu, 2003). Although, in theory, African American parents wished to push their children to succeed academically, they failed to engage in practices (e.g., supervision of homework, teaching time management, monitoring television time, encouraging their children to work hard in school, teaching children to avoid negative pressures) that facilitate such success (Furstenberg, Cook, Eccles, Elder, & Sameroff, 1999; Ogbu, 2003). Furthermore, black parents were often unaware of the existence of honors and advanced placement (AP) courses and the significance of enrolling in such courses during high school (Ogbu, 2003).

School-Based Factors

Schools play a significant role in the widening of the black–white achievement gap. Diamond (2006) presents the following characteristics of the racialized terrain of their schools and classrooms:

- Black students are typically taught by less qualified teachers (e.g., noncertified teachers and teachers with limited experience) than their white counterparts (Uhlenberg & Brown, 2002).
- Black students face a number of educational disadvantages in their schools and classrooms when compared with white students. For

example, they are concentrated in lower educational tracks, which provide students with less challenging course work and result in less learning (Hallinan, 1994; Oakes, Ormseth, Bell, & Camp, 1990).
• The teachers of black students also hold lower expectations for them than for other students.

Tracking. Through academic leveling and tracking of students, many schools create pathways of achievement for some and not for others. This practice can exacerbate achievement gaps because students are frequently divided on perceived ability, which, in practice, often translates into divisions across racial lines. Whites are frequently enrolled in upper-level courses while blacks are enrolled in lower-level ones (Ogbu, 2003). Furthermore, African American students are disproportionately placed in special education courses (Blanchett, 2006), which contributes to reducing their access to critical educational resources.

Tracking often occurs as early as elementary school, which poses a problem and can explain the widening of the achievement gap as students continue through their secondary education. Tracking designates a specific pathway for students from which it is often hard to break out. Ogbu found that these mechanisms can also have a negative impact on how students perceive their academic abilities: Some black students avoided taking honors and AP courses because they felt the work would be too difficult for them; consequently, they never gave themselves a chance to try and succeed.

Teacher Expectations. Teachers' perceptions of race play a critical role in the academic expectations teachers hold for their students (Carter, 2005; Rosenthal & Jacobson, 1968; Sleeter & McLaren, 1995). Teachers' sensitivity to race can also affect instruction and mold the experiences of students within their classroom (Delpit, 1995; Kinchloe, Steinberg, Chennault, & Rodriguez, 1998; King, Hollins, & Hayman, 1997; Ladson-Billings, 1994; Paley, 1979). Teachers' reduced academic expectations of students from a particular race or socioeconomic status can become a self-fulfilling prophecy and result in the diminished academic performance of those students (Rosenthal & Jacobson, 1968). Race also plays a factor in which students are labeled as in need of disciplinary action and in the ways in which teachers try to intervene and help their students (Gregory & Mosely, 2004).

The lack of availability of sufficient guidance counseling may also play a critical role in the achievement gap. Counselors typically help students decide which courses to take and guide them to focus on their academic futures, especially college. In underfunded, understaffed schools, however, counselors often have little time to help students or encourage them to take higher-level classes (Ogbu, 2003).

The disproportionate academic underachievement of African American students and their inadequate resources leads to an observable gap in achievement between them and their white contemporaries. The evidence of the gaps is abundant. The next section presents some of the most prominent indicators of academic achievement gaps between African American and white students.

THE EVIDENCE ON BLACK–WHITE ACHIEVEMENT GAPS

For a number of the theories to explain achievement gaps, sufficient data for serious secondary analyses are not available. We concentrate in the following section on the factors for which adequate data do exist. The principal source of data is the National Center for Education Statistics, and our analysis includes data from the National Assessment of Educational Progress (NAEP), the Educational Longitudinal Survey (ELS), and the Schools and Staffing Survey (SASS).

Effects of Racial Composition of Schools:
School Performance on NAEP by the Percentage of Black Students

In the United States, schools have become increasingly resegregated over the past 2 decades. Compared with low-minority schools, high-minority schools are much more likely to be high-poverty and underperforming. According to Orfield and Lee (2007), "On average, segregated minority schools are inferior in terms of the quality of their teachers, the character of the curriculum, the level of competition, average test scores, and graduation rates" (p. 5). Given these facts, we examined the effects of the racial composition of schools on black–white achievement gaps, using NAEP 2007 math, 2005 science, and 2007 reading assessments of 4th and 8th graders. A series of scatter plots is presented below that reveals the extent of achievement gaps and compares how the gaps among 4th graders with the gaps among 8th graders are distributed based on the percentage of black students in school. The two horizontal lines through the scatter plots represent the overall average scale scores for blacks and whites, revealing the overall gap between blacks and whites (see Figures 2.1–2.6; all figures and tables for this chapter are presented in an appendix at the end of the chapter).

In general, by grade 4, the achievement gap between black and white students has already formed, with national performance averages 26 points apart in math (at 222 and 248, respectively), 33 average points apart in science (at 128 and 161, respectively), and 27 average points apart in reading (at 203 and 230, respectively) (see Figures 2.1–2.3). In grade 4, the achievement gap between blacks and whites persists regardless of the racial composition of the school. It is noteworthy that there are black school averages below the black mean throughout the school race composition distribution. But there is also clustering of black and white students' scores above their respective means in each subject at schools with black student populations of less than 40%. There are also a few black student averages above the white mean in the distribution of schools up to 60% black. Of the black students performing below the national black average, those who attended schools with over 70% black student population perform better than a large share of those attending schools with black student populations of less than 70%.

In grade 8 math, science, and reading, trends similar to those for grade 4 can be found, with an observable achievement gap between black and white students regardless of the size of the black student population in their schools. As expected across the various schools, white and black students are consistently performing both above and below their national means. As in grade 4, in grade 8 subject assessments, students with the lowest scores in schools with black student populations of more than 70% are outperforming many of the students who perform poorly at schools with black student populations of less than 70%.

Given that the NAEP samples of 4th and 8th graders represent different cohorts and that neither sample is longitudinal, one must interpret with caution comparisons of the gaps between the two grades. They should not be interpreted as one cohort widening or narrowing in achievement over time between the two grades, but rather as gaps of two different cohorts. At the same time, however, since they are both nationally representative samples and are on the same score scale, it is interesting to compare the two grades. For grade 8, the gap is wider in math and science and slightly narrower in reading than for 4th graders (see Figures 2.4–2.6). White students averaged 290 in comparison with black students averaging 259 points on NAEP grade 8 math assessments, 159 compared with 123 in 8th-grade science and 270 compared with 244 in 8th-grade reading. The comparison of black–white gaps between the two grades shows that, in math, the 8th-grade gap was 31 points and the 4th-grade gap was 26 points; in science, the gap was 33 points in 4th grade compared with 36 points in 8th grade; and in reading, the gap was 27 points in 4th grade compared with 26 points in 8th grade.

NAEP Performance Trends in Urban Districts

Among the starkest racial distinctions in the student population distribution is the overrepresentation of African American youngsters in urban schools, where they are most often in the majority. These students also represent the lowest achievers, and their schools yield the poorest results and the largest gaps in performance. The Trial Urban District Assessment (TUDA), a special project within NAEP, began assessing reading and writing performance in five large urban districts in 2002. By 2003, it had expanded its assessments to include both reading and mathematics across nine urban districts, and, by 2005, across 11 urban districts. Analyses of TUDA not only allow comparisons of the performance of different districts, but of student performance levels in large central cities with the national student performance levels. In math, TUDA analyses show that students across the nation in large central cities and within the selected urban districts all improved their average scale scores from grade 4 to grade 8. However, the percentage of students performing below the basic skill level increased within each district and across the nation as well (see Figures 2.7 and 2.8). By grade 8, the majority of students in Atlanta, the District of Columbia, Cleveland, Los Angeles, and Chicago were performing below the basic level in grade 8 math. In contrast, assessments of grade 4 and grade 8 reading showed not only an increase in average scale scores among students, but also lower percentages of students below the basic reading level by grade 8 (see Figures 2.9 and 2.10). In grade 4, the majority of students in the District of Columbia, Los Angeles, Cleveland, Chicago, and Atlanta were performing below the basic level. By grade 8, only students in the District of Columbia, Atlanta, Los Angeles, and Cleveland were more likely to be performing below than above the basic level in reading.

The Effects of Academic Tracking

As discussed earlier, academic tracking is sometimes viewed as an instrument of race and class segregation in schools and may be an important contributor to achievement gaps. In light of current research emphasizing the importance of a rigorous high school curriculum in preparing students for college, analyses of students' high school curriculum tracks can be meaningful for understanding gaps. The Educational Longitudinal Survey (ELS): 2002, a nationally representative survey of 10th graders in 2002, provides a valuable source of such data. ELS data reveal some interesting curricular patterns among high school students across racial and socioeconomic lines.

We examined the data on the relationship of race and high school tracking. More than 50% of the surveyed students who responded to the question (6,898 of 12,478, unweighted) indicated that they were enrolled in a college preparatory program; the majority of these students were white (4,427 of 6,898, or 64%) (see Table 2.1). Significance tests determining whether racial classification is associated with a student's likelihood to take a college preparatory program were inconclusive. However, analyses did show that black students were less likely to enroll in general high school programs than whites but more likely than white students to enroll in vocational high school programs.

Using ELS data, we also examined the relationship between socioeconomic class and tracking. We found that students from the highest socioeconomic status quartile were more likely to be enrolled in a college preparatory program than students from the lowest quartile. These students were less likely to be enrolled in a general or vocational high school program than their counterparts from the lowest socioeconomic status quartile (see Table 2.2).

Analyses of the relationship between students' racial background and their likelihood of enrolling in a special education program revealed that, of the students who indicated that they were enrolled in such a program, whites were slightly less likely than blacks to be enrolled in special education (8% versus 9%) (see Table 2.1). Eleven percent of students in the lowest SES quartile, however, were enrolled in special education programs compared with 6% of their counterparts from the highest SES quartile (see Table 2.2).

Analyses of whether students were ever enrolled in a remedial English class were similar. Blacks were more likely to have been enrolled in a remedial English class than whites (see Table 2.1), and students from the lowest socioeconomic quartile were more likely to have been enrolled in remedial English than students from the highest socioeconomic quartile (see Table 2.2). These patterns partially persist regarding the likelihood for students to have ever taken a remedial math class. While black students were no more likely than white students to have ever taken a remedial math class (see Table 2.1), students from the lowest socioeconomic quartile were more likely than students from the highest quartile to have been enrolled in remedial math (see Table 2.2).

Academic tracking not only involves separating students for specialized teaching that concentrates on establishing stronger foundations in academic subjects, but it also consists of placing some students on a path to an accelerated or honors track. An example of such tracking is enrollment in advanced placement (AP) courses in high school. Although a statistically significant connection could not be made between race and the likelihood of a student to have ever participated in an AP class (see Table 2.2), a connection could be drawn with socioeconomic status (see Table 2.1). Similar to the pattern found for enrolling in a college preparatory program, students from the highest socioeconomic quartile are typically more likely to enroll in an AP class than students from the lowest quartile.

The Relationship of Home and Family to Performance on NAEP

As was mentioned in earlier, students' family background and home environment have been scrutinized for their possible contribution to the growing achievement gap between white and black students. Parents' educational attainment is commonly considered to be a contributor to students' academic success. Parents' education is a component of socioeconomic status and often thought of as a proxy for the value that families place on education in their household. The relatively low average achievement of black students may in part be the result of a higher proportion of their parents being of lower educational attainment than the parents of white students.

However, the 2007 NAEP math scores of white and black students with parents with the same educational attainment appear to contradict conventional findings (see Figure 2.11). Black students whose parents have the highest educational attainment are performing below the level of white students whose parents have the lowest educational attainment. In addition, on average, while the scores of white students increase with each successive increase of their parents' educational attainment, the scores of black students do not. The scores of black students increase when their parents complete some postsecondary education compared with just completing high school, but their scores do not appear to benefit further by their parents going on to complete college over just attending college.

Researchers have found that the availability of various types of educational resources (e.g., books, computers, and so forth) within students' households correlates with academic achievement. Analyses of NAEP 2007 data bear this out. An examination of the number of books in students' households shows that in grade 4, 40% of white students reported more than 100 books in their households, compared with 22% of black students (see Figure 2.12). In contrast, approximately 21% of white students stated they had 25 or fewer books in their homes, in comparison with 50% of black students, resulting in the majority of black students reporting having 25 or fewer books at home. Analyses in grade 8 presented similar trends. Nearly 40% of white students reported having more than 100 books at home, compared with 18% of black students (see Figure 2.13). Approximately 25% of white students have 25 or fewer books in their homes, compared with approximately 47% of black students.

As students progressed from grade 4 to grade 8, both black and white students reported having fewer books at home. This was unexpected, for it would seem that as students continue to advance in school they would acquire more books. However, this trend could be a result of Internet access, and the availability of free online resources.

Another predictor of children's academic success is parents' availability to spend time with their children. Data from the Early Childhood Program Participation Survey (ECPP) of the 2005 National Household Education Survey Program (NHES, 2005) show that black and white parents reported that they spent time doing similar activities with their children (3 to 5 years of age) (see Figure 2.14). The exception was that white parents were somewhat more likely than black parents to report that they spent time working with their children on arts and crafts. It was promising to find that there were no stark race differences in parents spending time on activities with their children. However, these data are self-reported by parents, which can result in some parents feeling pressure to answer in what they consider to be a socially acceptable way. In addition, this survey question does not measure the quality or frequency of these activities or the amount of time parents spent on them. Without this information, it is difficult to know the true effectiveness of such activities. Nonetheless, from these data, it is observed that white and black parents alike make efforts to spend time with their children and to engage in various activities, ranging from telling them a story to working on arts and crafts projects together.

The Relationship of School Poverty Level to Performance on NAEP

As we have described, existing research literature and ELS:2002 data indicate that there is a correlation between school socioeconomic status and academic performance. For this reason, a closer examination of the likelihood of students of different races attending low- versus high-poverty schools is useful for understanding achievement gaps. Some 43% of white students attended schools where approximately 0–25% of the student population was eligible for free or reduced lunch, compared with 11% of African American students (see Figure 2.15). In contrast, 37% of African American students were enrolled in schools where 76–100% of the student population was eligible for free or reduced lunch, while only 4% of white students were enrolled in such schools.

Though the differences in scores by both race and socioeconomic status could not be found, the NAEP 2007 data show the average scores of students in math, science, and reading in grades 4 and 8, by eligibility to enter the National School Lunch Program. On average, in grade 4, students who were not eligible for the lunch program scored at least 22 points higher on average than their peers who were eligible to participate in the program (see Figure 2.16). Grade 8 scores were similar to the pattern at grade 4, with students who were ineligible to enroll in the lunch program scoring at least 24 points above their counterparts as well.

Teacher Quality and Teacher Demographics

Of the many factors examined by the current literature, teacher quality is one of the frontrunners for affecting achievement gaps. Common indicators of teacher quality are the extent to which teachers are certified, experienced, and teaching in their major field and "in license." The NCES 1999–2000 Schools and Staffing Survey (SASS) generated data on the public school students who were being taught by teachers both outside of their major and without certification. Students of relatively low SES and black students have high rates of both. It is not uncommon to see a positive relationship between the percentage of free or reduced-price lunch students and the percentage of teachers who are uncertified or teaching out of license (see Figure 2.17).

Moreover, data show that middle school students are more likely than high school students to have uncertified or out-of-license teachers. Nearly one-third of students in schools with 25–49% and 50–74% of the student population eligible for free or reduced-priced lunch are in classrooms with teachers without certification or a major in math. This is interesting because of the growing achievement gap in math from grade 4 to grade 8, as shown by Figures 2.1 and 2.4. Middle school math is the subject and grade level that has the highest percentage of students being taught by less qualified teachers regardless of the percentage of students eligible for free or reduced-priced lunch (see Figure 2.17). The highest percentages of students being taught by such teachers are within schools with the majority of the population qualifying for free or reduced-price lunch (see Figure 2.17).

Another proxy for teacher quality is experience. The NAEP 2007 assessment produced data on the likelihood of students having teachers with various numbers of years of teaching experience. In grade 8 math, white students were more likely to have a teacher with over 20 years of teaching experience (25%) than black students were (19%) (see Figure 2.18). In grade 8 math, white students were also less likely to have a teacher with 9 or fewer years of experience (44%) in comparison with black students (55%). Generally speaking, white students were more likely than black students to have teachers with 10 or more years of teaching experience, and were less likely to have teachers with less than 4 years of experience.

Typically, schools in which minority students comprise the majority population of the school have the highest percentages of students being taught by unqualified teachers. Aside from middle school science, schools with a 25–49% minority population had the largest percentage of students with teachers teaching both outside of their major and without certification (see Figure 2.19). Perhaps most problematic was middle school math, with nearly 40% of the students attending schools with a 75% or greater minority population in classrooms with unqualified teachers. Similarly, in middle school English nearly one-third of students in schools with 50–74% minority populations were being taught by unqualified teachers.

The data presented on middle school math (see Figure 2.19) are especially interesting in combination with the NAEP 2007 grade 4 and grade 8 math assessment scores. The NAEP data indicate a widening of the white–black achievement gap in math from grade 4 to grade 8. One factor may be the larger percentage of teachers without a major in the field or teacher certification. Even in schools with less than 10% minority populations, nearly one-quarter of the student population is being taught by unqualified teachers (see Figure 2.19). Regardless of the type of public school the students attend, middle school math has the highest percentage of students being taught by teachers teaching outside of their major and or without certification.

Teaching is a complex process that involves not only disseminating academic information but also forming relationships with students. Current literature acknowledges the important and multifaceted roles of teachers in students' lives, and researchers have begun to examine the relationships of awareness and understanding that form between teacher and student. Concerns have been raised about the ability of white teachers to relate to black students, and for these same students to be able relate to white teachers. Differences in race and socioeconomic status may result in communication barriers that prevent teachers and students from forging a closer, supportive bond, which, in turn, would be expected to help students persevere and succeed in their academic pursuits. If having teachers of similar ethnicity and/ or race is the only way to bridge gaps between a teacher and student, then there may be some cause to worry based on NAEP 2007 data. Across the nation, the majority of black students (60%) have white teachers (see Figure 2.20). In the South, 52% of the black student population is being taught by white teachers (see Figure 2.21). This is especially telling because of the high concentration of African Americans in the South.

The sparseness of diversity among teachers within schools is troublesome at all tiers of education and needs to be examined. Such homogeneity within the teaching corps may result in decreased cultural awareness or diversity in schools, feelings of isolation among some minority students within schools, and fewer role models for minority students to look up to and try to emulate in their own academic endeavors. However, regardless of region or teachers' ethnicity, African American students scored at least 25 points lower than their white counterparts on NAEP 2007 grade 8 math assessments (see Figures 2.22 and 2.23).

The Students

Looking to the family, schools, and teachers to explain the persistence of achievement gaps is crucial, but these are not the only variables that should be investigated as causes of the gaps; consideration must also be given to the students themselves. Researchers have tried to link student involvement both inside and outside of school as indicators of academic success in schools. The types of activities in which students choose to engage can reinforce behaviors that are conducive to learning and academic success, and place students among peers who are pursuing similar goals. In contrast, other extracurricular activities may be seen as contributing to perpetuating behaviors that are less conducive to behaviors that are necessary for high academic achievement. The *Digest of Education Statistics 2005* provides data that differentiated between some of the popular activities in which high school sophomores participated inside and outside of school, distinguishing the students by race (see Figures 2.24 and 2.25).

Among both blacks and whites, the majority of students reported that they used a personal computer at home. Excluding this activity, in general the data showed that white students tend to be less involved in the listed extracurricular activities, aside from those activities related to sports. Black students, on the other hand, are more likely to engage in a variety of activities, from community service to taking a music, art, or language class. However, black students also are more likely to spend 3 or more hours per weekday playing video or computer games and watching 6 or more hours of television on a weekday.

CONCLUSION AND RECOMMENDATIONS

The foregoing data and analyses present evidence of enormous black–white achievement gaps at the precollegiate level that show few signs of narrowing. Closing these gaps will require many years of targeted and sustained investment. Despite 2 decades of national government efforts to reform the U.S. education system, only since 2001 has the policy been explicit about closing gaps across race and social class lines. No Child Left Behind is a start, but for African American students, much more action is required to close gaps. The unique characteristics and challenges of these students need to be taken into account in shaping policies directed toward their measurable progress. At the same time, it is important to recognize the challenge of the politics of persuading the public that it is in the national interest to invest in raising the achievement of each race/ethnic group and social class. For African Americans, the climb to the highest levels of achievement is the steepest. The review of research and the analyses presented in this chapter suggest that the keys to addressing African American achievement gaps involve a combination of actions involving research, measurement, policies, and program interventions. Much more needs to be learned through research and measurement about the specific educational conditions and needs of African American students. To the extent possible, policies and actions that relate to the foregoing analyses include the following: (1) strengthening schools, (2) compensating for socioeconomic disadvantage, (3) enhancing family support and involvement, and (4) improving the measurement and communications about achievement gaps. The following are aspects of each of them that our analyses suggest are in need of attention:

Strengthening Schools

- Eliminate the undersupply of African American teachers by attracting more African Americans to the teaching profession. African American teachers comprise only 7.8% of the nation's teacher workforce (only 3% of white students have African American teachers, and 60% of African American students have white teachers).
- Increase access, participation, and achievement of African American students in more rigorous curricula in schools where they are in the minority.
- In the short term, strengthen the segregated schools that more than half of African American students presently attend.
- Ensure that the teaching staff in schools where African American students are in the majority are qualified by requiring that the teachers have bachelor's degrees in the subjects that they teach.
- Given the relatively low performance of African American urban schools and students compared with their counterparts in the rest of the nation, and the limitation of finances, enact instructional and assessment policies that are aimed at addressing the particular problems of urban schools.

Compensating for Socioeconomic Disadvantage

- Given that 65% of African American 8th-grade students attend schools where the majority of students are eligible for free and reduced-priced lunch compared with just 19% of white students, polices aimed at African American students and their families need to address problems of poverty that impede learning and development. Access to books and computers and to other human and material resources to compensate for having parents with relatively low levels of educational attainment needs to be developed.

Enhancing Family Support and Involvement

- While there is ample evidence that family involvement is vitally important in student achievement, too little is known about the involvement of the families of African American students and the constraints and capacity for them to contribute substantially to improving their children's educational achievement and for closing gaps.

Improve Measurement and Communications about the Gap

- Produce student assessments that may be conducted more frequently, with narrower foci, and that generate more information about the mastery of the content and the process of teaching and learning. Use such information to help students and teachers to improve student performance.
- Current national policy makes a large investment in assessing student performance and progress through testing. More information needs to be generated about how schools and school districts use the assessment results to improve student learning.

APPENDIX

Table 2.1. Educational Longitudinal Survey (ELS): 2002. Data on High School and Class Enrollments by Race (in percentages)

	Asian	Black or African American	Hispanic	white
High School Program				
General	30.36	34.053*	44.095	38.561*
College	58.57	49.58	43.24	52.531
Vocation	11.07	16.367*	12.664	8.907*
Ever in Special Education				
No	92.71	91.142	90.229	92.475
Yes	7.288	8.858*	9.771	7.525*
Ever in Remedial English				
No	92.02	91.19	89.816	91.955
Yes	7.983	8.81*	10.184	8.045*
Ever in Remedial Math				
No	90.16	88.662	88.798	90.839
Yes	9.841	11.338	11.202	9.161
Ever in an AP Program				
No	78.9	84.426	82.389	81.94
Yes	21.1	15.574	17.611	18.06

Source: U.S. Department of Education, National Center for Education Statistics, 2002. Produced by ETS, September 2006.

Note: Tests were only run for African American and white students.

*p < .05

Table 2.2. Educational Longitudinal Survey (ELS): 2002. Data on High School and Class Enrollments by Socioeconomic Status (in percentages)

	Lowest quartile	Second quartile	Third quartile	Highest quartile
High School Program				
General	42.768*	42.122	39.43	29.932*
College	41.58*	44.763	51.82	64.533*
Vocational	15.651*	13.116	8.75	5.535*
Ever in Special Education				
No	88.554	91.626	92.837	94.12
Yes	11.446*	8.374	7.163	5.88*
Ever in Remedial English				
No	89.879	91.523	91.746	92.805
Yes	10.121*	8.477	8.254	7.195*
Ever in Remedial Math				
No	88.019	89.921	90.716	91.579
Yes	11.981*	10.079	9.284	8.421*
Ever in an AP Program				
No	86.751	85.636	82.103	74.916
Yes	13.249*	14.364	17.897	25.084*

Source: U.S. Department of Education, National Center for Education Statistics, 2002. Produced by ETS, September 2006.

Note: Tests were only run for lowest and highest quartile.

*p < .05

Figure 2.1. NAEP 2007 Grade 4 Math Assessment: Average Within-School Scale Scores for Black and White Students in Public Schools, by Percentage of Black Students in School

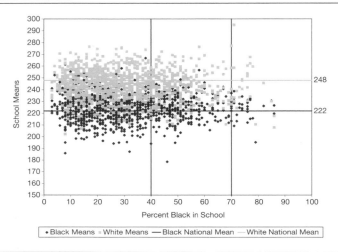

Source: U.S. Department of Education, Institute of Education Sciences, National Center for Education Statistics, and National Assessment of Educational Progress (NAEP), 2007a. Produced by ETS, March 2008.

Figure 2.2. NAEP 2005 Grade 4 Science Assessment: Average Within-School Scale Scores for Black and White Students in Public Schools, by Percentage of Black Students in School

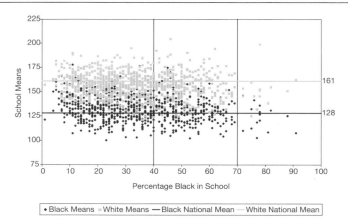

Source: U.S. Department of Education, Institute of Education Sciences, National Center for Education Statistics, and National Assessment of Educational Progress (NAEP), 2005a. Produced by ETS, September 2006.

Figure 2.3. NAEP 2007 Grade 4 Reading Assessment: Average Within-School Scale Scores for Black and White Students in Public Schools, by Percentage of Black Students in School

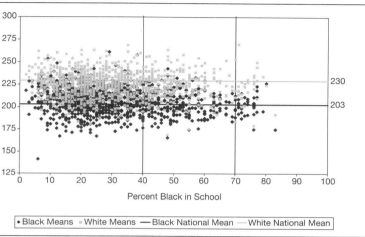

Source: U.S. Department of Education, Institute of Education Sciences, National Center for Education Statistics, and National Assessment of Educational Progress (NAEP), 2007b. Produced by ETS, March 2008.

Figure 2.4. NAEP 2007 Grade 8 Math Assessment: Average Within-School Scale Scores for Black and White Students in Public Schools, by Percentage of Black Students in School

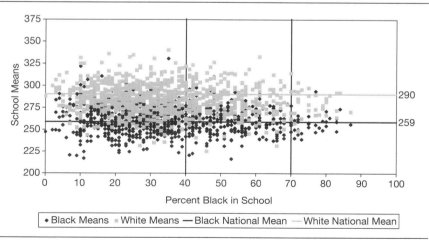

Source: U.S. Department of Education, Institute of Education Sciences, National Center for Education Statistics, and National Assessment of Educational Progress (NAEP), 2007a. Produced by ETS, March 2008.

Figure 2.5. NAEP 2005 Grade 8 Science Assessment: Average Within-School Scale Scores for Black and White Students in Public Schools, by Percentage of Black Students in School

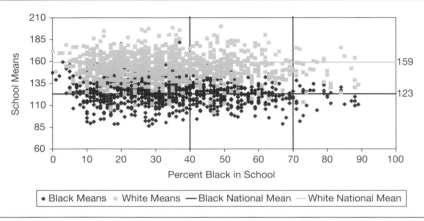

Source: U.S. Department of Education, Institute of Education Sciences, National Center for Education Statistics, and National Assessment of Educational Progress (NAEP), 2005a. Produced by ETS, September 2006.

Figure 2.6. NAEP 2007 Grade 8 Reading Assessment: Average Within-School Scale Scores for Black and White Students in Public Schools, by Percentage of Black Students in School

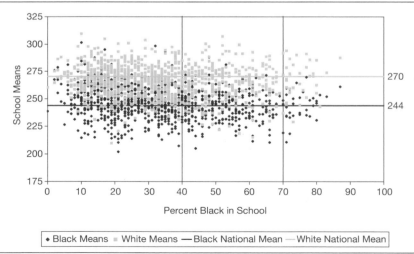

Source: U.S. Department of Education, Institute of Education Sciences, National Center for Education Statistics, and National Assessment of Educational Progress (NAEP), 2007b. Produced by ETS, March 2008.

Figure 2.7. Average NAEP Mathematics Scale Scores and Percentage of Students Within Each Achievement Level, Grade 4 Public Schools, by Urban District, 2005

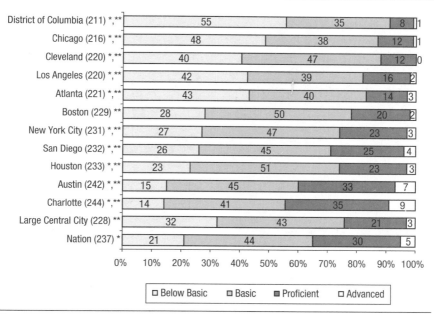

Source: U.S. Department of Education, Institute of Educational Sciences, National Center for Education Statistics, NAEP-Trial Urban District Assessment (TUDA), 2005b.

Notes: * = Average scores are significantly different from large central city public schools.
** = Average scores are significantly different from nation (public schools).
Significance testing was conducted at the .05 level only.
Detail may not sum to totals because of rounding.

Figure 2.8. Average NAEP Mathematics Scale Scores and Percentage of Students Within Each Achievement Level, Grade 8 Public Schools, by Urban District, 2005

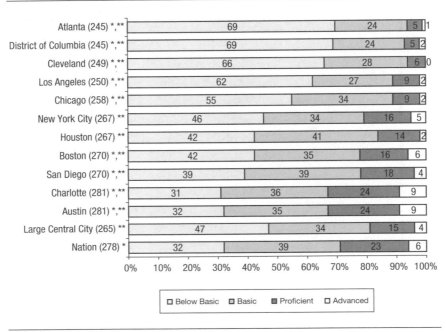

Source: U.S. Department of Education, Institute of Educational Sciences, National Center for Education Statistics, NAEP-Trial Urban District Assessment (TUDA), 2005b.

Notes: * = Average scores are significantly different from large central city public schools.
** = Average scores are significantly different from nation (public schools).
Significance testing was conducted at the .05 level only.
Detail may not sum to totals because of rounding.

Figure 2.9. Average NAEP Reading Scale Scores and Percentage of Students Within Each Achievement Level, Grade 4 Public Schools, by Urban District, 2005

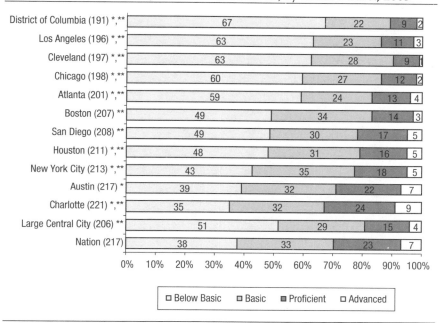

Source: U.S. Department of Education, Institute of Educational Sciences, National Center for Education Statistics, NAEP-Trial Urban District Assessment (TUDA), 2005b.

Notes: * = Average scores are significantly different from large central city public schools.
** = Average scores are significantly different from nation (public schools).
Significance testing was conducted at the .05 level only.

Detail may not sum to totals because of rounding.

Figure 2.10. Average NAEP Reading Scale Scores and Percentage of Students Within Each Achievement Level, Grade 8 Public Schools, by Urban District, 2005

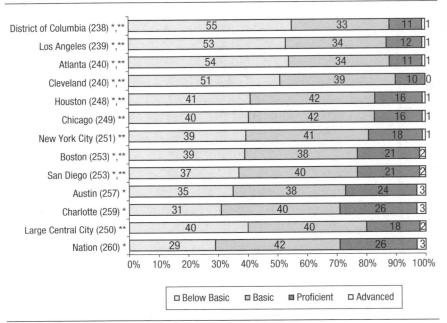

Source: U.S. Department of Education, Institute of Educational Sciences, National Center for Education Statistics, NAEP-Trial Urban District Assessment (TUDA), 2005b.

Notes: * = Average scores are significantly different from large central city public schools.
** = Average scores are significantly different from nation (public schools).
Significance testing was conducted at the .05 level only.

Detail may not sum to totals because of rounding.

Figure 2.11. Students' Average Scale Scores on the 2007 National Assessment of Educational Progress on Grade 8 Math and Parents' Highest Level of Education, by Race

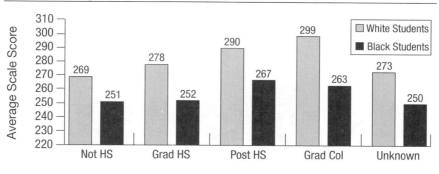

Source: U.S. Department of Education, Institute of Education Sciences, National Center for Education Statistics, NAEP, 2007a. Produced by ETS, March 2008.

Figure 2.12. In Grade 4, Students' Reports of Number of Books Present in the Household, by Race

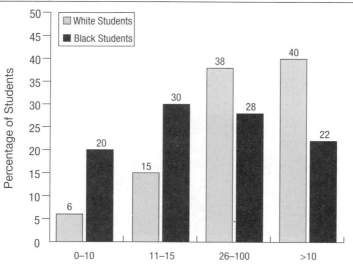

Note: Students took the 2007 Grade 4 NAEP math assessment.

Source: U.S. Department of Education, Institute of Education Sciences, National Center for Education Statistics, NAEP, 2007a. Produced by ETS, March 2008.

Figure 2.13. In Grade 8, Students' Reports of Number of Books Present in the Household, by Race

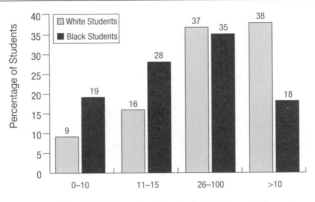

Students' Reports of Books in the Home, 8th grade

Note: Students took the 2007 Grade 8 NAEP math assessment.

Source: U.S. Department of Education, Institute of Education Sciences, National Center for Education Statistics, NAEP, 2007a. Produced by ETS, March 2008.

Figure 2.14. Percentage of Children from Age 3 Through Age 5 and Not Yet in Kindergarten Whose Parents Reported Participating in Home Activities with Child in the Past Week, by Type of Involvement and Child's Race/Ethnicity: 2005

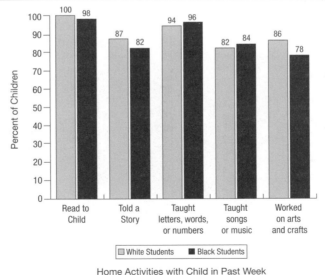

Home Activities with Child in Past Week

Source: U.S. Department of Education, National Center for Education Statistics, 2005.

Figure 2.15. Student Populations Found in Schools of Varying Socioeconomic Levels, by Race

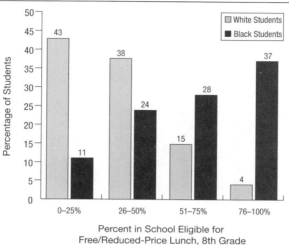

Note: Students took the 2007 Grade 8 NAEP math assessment.

Source: U.S. Department of Education, Institute of Education Sciences, National Center for Education Statistics, NAEP, 2007a. Produced by ETS, March 2008.

Figure 2.16. Average Scale Scores in Math and Reading in Grades 4 and 8, by Eligibility for National School Lunch Program

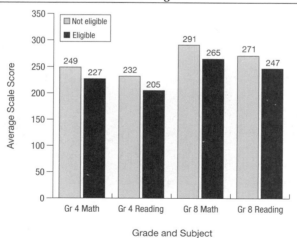

Source: U.S. Department of Education, Institute of Education Sciences, National Center for Education Statistics, National Assessment of Educational Progress (NAEP), 2007a, 2007b. Produced by ETS, March 2008.

Figure 2.17. Percentage of Public School Students in Classes Taught by Teachers Without a Teaching Certificate or a Major in the Field They Teach, by Subject Area, School Level, and Poverty Characteristics: 1999–2000

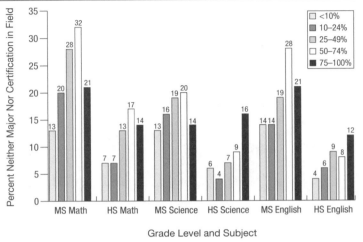

Note: Middle school includes grade 5–9 and high school includes grades 10–12.

Source: U.S. Department of Education, National Center for Education Statistics, 2004, Tables 24-1, 24-2, and 24-3.

Figure 2.18. In Grade 8 Math, Teachers' Years of Experience for White and Black Students

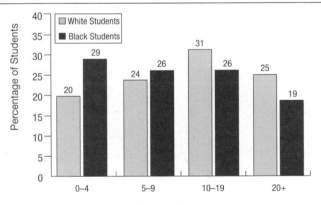

Note: Students took the 2007 Grade 8 NAEP math assessment.

Source: U.S. Department of Education, Institute of Education Sciences, National Center for Education Statistics, National Assessment of Educational Progress (NAEP), 2007a. Produced by ETS, March 2008.

Figure 2.19. Percentage of Public School Students in Classes Taught by Teachers Without a Teaching Certificate or a Major in the Field They Teach, by Subject Area, School Level, and Percentage of Minority Students: 1999–2000

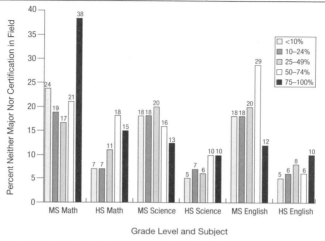

Note: Middle school includes grade 5–9 and high school includes grades 10–12.

Source: U.S. Department of Education, National Center for Education Statistics, 2004, Tables 24-1, 24-2, and 24-3.

Figure 2.20. Ethnicity and Race of Teachers for White and Black Students in Grade 8 Math

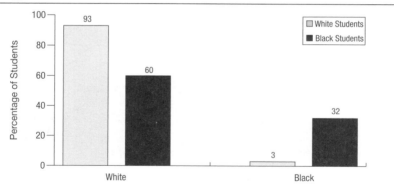

Note: Students took the 2007 Grade 8 NAEP math assessment.

Source: U.S. Department of Education, Institute of Education Sciences, National Center for Education Statistics, National Assessment of Educational Progress (NAEP), 2007a. Produced by ETS, March 2008.

Figure 2.21. Race/Ethnicity of Teachers for White and Black Students in Grade 8 Math in the South

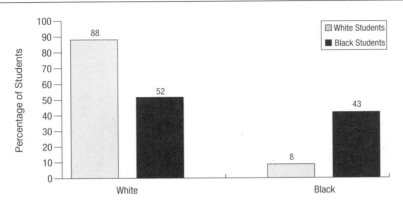

Note: Students took the 2007 Grade 8 NAEP math assessment.

Source: U.S. Department of Education, Institute of Education Sciences, National Center for Education Statistics, National Assessment of Educational Progress (NAEP), 2007a. Produced by ETS, March 2008.

Figure 2.22. Race of Teachers by Grade 8 NAEP 2007 Math Performance for White and Black Students

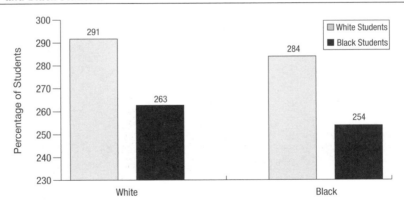

Source: U.S. Department of Education, Institute of Education Sciences, National Center for Education Statistics, National Assessment of Educational Progress (NAEP), 2007a. Produced by ETS, March 2008.

Figure 2.23. Race of Teachers by Grade 8 NAEP 2007 Math Performance for White and Black Students in the South

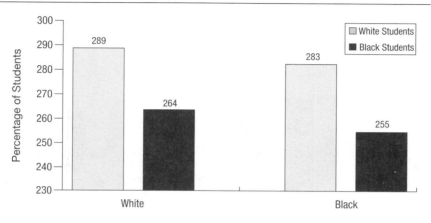

Teachers' Race/Ethnicity

Source: U.S. Department of Education, Institute of Education Sciences, National Center for Education Statistics, National Assessment of Educational Progress (NAEP), 2007. Produced by ETS, March 2008.

Figure 2.24. 10th Grade Students' Participation in Extracurricular Activities, by Race

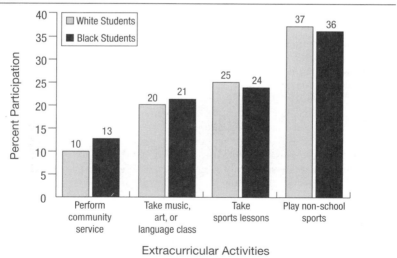

Extracurricular Activities

Source: U.S. Department of Education, Institute of Education Sciences, National Center for Education Statistics, 2006, Table 137.

Figure 2.25. 10th-Grade Students' Participation in Extracurricular Activities, by Race (continued)

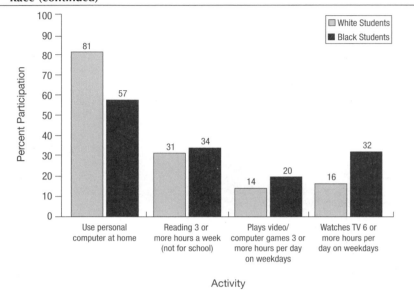

Activity

Source: U.S. Department of Education, Institute of Education Sciences, National Center for Education Statistics, 2006, Table 137.

NOTE

1. At one extreme of the attempts to explain African American underachievement are a few psychologists and biologically oriented pseudo-scientists proffering genetic theories about human intelligence. Despite being an idea that is unpopular, even distasteful, in public discourse, the hereditability theory of intelligence often lurks not far from the surface of debates about achievement gaps, especially pertaining to race. Proponents believe that performance gaps between American blacks and whites are due to inherent and unalterable differences in intelligence between the races, rather than to the effects of poverty, discrimination, inequities, or other remediable factors (Deutsch, Katz, & Jensen, 1968; Herrnstein & Murray, 1994; Jensen, 1969, 1972). They contend that the majority of performance differences is accounted for by nature or heredity, leaving only a minor share to nurture or environmental circumstances (Chipuer, Plomin, Pedersen, McClearn, & Nesselroade, 1993; Jensen, 1992). Scholars on the opposing side of this controversial position argue—on grounds ranging from the frailty of the instruments used to measure intelligence to the inadequacy of research data and methodologies—that the evidence of genetic differences is much too feeble to support social policies that would lead to denying programs and assistance to blacks and other minorities (Kamin, 1974; Lewontin, Rose, & Kamin, 1984). Very early in this nature versus nurture debate, Light and Smith (1971) produced

a model that showed that even if intelligence were 80% determined by genes, the vast share of the black–white difference in measured performance could still be accounted for by environmental factors. More recently, scientists have begun to look at the interplay between biology and culture. Li (2003) conducted a study showing that nature and nurture influence each other such that the anatomy of the brain can be altered by environment (e.g., taxi drivers' brains were enlarged in the region where cognition of maps would normally take place). This research provides an interesting compromise for the nature-nurture argument, proposing the existence of a reciprocal relationship between what has been understood to be two dichotomous entities.

REFERENCES

Ainsworth-Darnell, J. W., & Downey, D. B. (1998). Assessing the oppositional culture explanation for racial/ethnic differences in school performance. *American Sociological Review, 63*(4), 536–553.

Bankston, C. L. I., & Caldas, S. J. (1996). Majority African American schools and social injustice: The influence of desegregation on academic achievement. *Social Forces, 75*(2), 535–555.

Blanchett, W. J. (2006). Disproportionate representation of African American students in special education: Acknowledging the role of white privilege and racism. *Educational Researcher, 35*(6), 24–28.

Bonilla-Silva, E. (2001). *White supremacy and racism in the post-civil rights era.* Boulder, CO: Lynne Rienner.

Bourdieu, P. (1986). The forms of capital. In J. G. Richardson (Ed.), *Handbook of theory and research for the sociology of education* (pp. 241–258). New York: Greenwood Press.

Bourdieu, P., & Passeron, J. C. C. (1990). *Reproduction in education, society, and culture* (2nd ed.). Beverly Hills, CA: Sage.

Brooks-Gunn, J., & Markman, L. B. (2005). The contribution of parenting to ethnic and racial gaps in school readiness. *The Future of Children, 15*(1), 139–168.

Bryk, A. S., & Schneider, B. L. (2003). Trust in schools: A core resource for school reform. *Educational Leadership, 60*(6), 40–44.

Carbonaro, W. J. (1998). A little help from my friends' parents: Intergenerational closure and educational outcomes. *Sociology of Education, 71*(4), 295–313.

Carter, P. L. (2005). *Keepin' it real: School success beyond black and white.* New York: Oxford University Press.

Chipuer, H. M., Plomin, R., Pedersen, N. L., McClearn, G. E., & Nesselroade, J. R. (1993). Genetic influence on family environment: The role of personality. *Developmental Psychology, 29*(1), 110–118.

Coleman, J. S. (1988). Social capital in the creation of human capital. *American Journal of Sociology, 94 Supplement,* S95–S120.

Coleman, J. S., Campbell, E. Q., Hobson, C. J., McPartland, J., Mood, A. M., Weinfeld, F. D., et al. (1966). *Equality of educational opportunity.* Washington, DC: U.S. Government Printing Office.

Coleman, J. S., & Hoffer, T. B. (1987). *Public and private high schools: The impact of communities.* New York: Basic Books.

College Board. (2007). *2007 college-bound seniors: Total group profile report*. New York: Author.

Comer, J. P. (1980). *School power: Implications of an intervention project*. New York: The Free Press.

Connell, R. W., Ashenden, D. J., Kessler, S., & Dowsett, G. W. (1982). *Making the difference: Schools, families, and social division*. Sydney, Australia: George Allen and Unwyn.

Delpit, L. D. (1995). *Other people's children: Cultural conflicts in the classroom*. New York: New Press.

Deutsch, M. R., Katz, I., & Jensen, A. R. (1968). *Social class, race, and psychological development*. New York: Holt, Rinehart, and Winston.

Diamond, J. B. (2006, June). *Are we barking up the wrong tree? Rethinking oppositional culture explanations for the black/white achievement gap*. Paper presented at the Achievement Gap Initiative, Harvard University.

Diamond, J. B., & Spillane, J. P. (2004). High-stakes accountability in urban elementary schools: Challenging or reproducing inequality? *Teachers College Record, 106*(6), 1145–1176.

Epstein, J. L. (2001). *School, family, and community partnerships: Preparing educators and improving schools*. Boulder, CO: Westview Press.

Epstein, J. L., & Dauber, S. L. (1991). School programs and teacher practices of parent involvement in inner-city elementary and middle schools. *Elementary School Journal, 91*(3), 289–305.

Fordham, S., & Ogbu, J. U. (1986). Black students' school success: Coping with the "burden of 'acting white.'" *The Urban Review, 18*(3), 176–206.

Furstenberg Jr., F. F., Cook, T. D., Eccles, J., Elder Jr., G. H., & Sameroff, A. (1999). *Managing to make it: Urban families and adolescent success*. Chicago: The University of Chicago Press.

Graduate Record Examinations Board. (2007). *Factors that can influence performance on the GRE general test: 2005–2006*. Princeton, NJ: Educational Testing Service.

Gregory, A., & Mosely, P. M. (2004). The discipline gap: Teachers' views on the over-representation of African American students in the discipline system. *Equity and Excellence in Education, 37*(1), 18–30.

Hallinan, M. T. (1994). Tracking: From theory to practice. *Sociology of Education, 67*(2), 79–84.

Hao, L., & Bonstead-Bruns, M. (1998). Parent-child differences in educational expectations and the academic achievement of immigrant and native students. *Sociology of Education, 71*(3), 175–198.

Herrnstein, R. J., & Murray, C. (1994). *The bell curve: Intelligence and class structure in American life*. New York: The Free Press.

Hofferth, S. L., Boisjoly, J., & Duncan, G. J. (1998). Parents' extra-familial resources and children's school attainment. *Sociology of Education, 71*(3), 246–268.

Jensen, A. R. (1969). How much can we boost IQ and scholastic achievement? *Educational Review, 39*, 1–123.

Jensen, A. R. (1972). *Genetics and education*. New York: Harper and Row.

Jensen, A. R. (1992). Mental ability: Critical thresholds and social policy. *Journal of Social, Political and Economic Studies, 17*(2), 171–182.

Kamin, L. J. (1974). *The science and politics of I.Q.* Potomac, MD: Lawrence Erlbaum.

Kinchloe, J. L., Steinberg, S. R., Chennault, R. E., & Rodriguez, N. M. (Eds.). (1998). *White reign: Deploying whiteness in America.* New York: St. Martin's Press.

King, J. E., Hollins, E. R., & Hayman, W. C. (Eds.). (1997). *Preparing teachers for cultural diversity.* New York: Teachers College Press.

Ladson-Billings, G. (1994). *The dreamkeepers: Successful teachers of African American children.* San Francisco: Jossey-Bass.

Lareau, A. (1987). Social class differences in family-school relationships: The importance of cultural capital. *Sociology of Education, 60*(2), 73–85.

Lareau, A. (1989). *Home advantage.* New York: Falmer Press.

Lewontin, R. C., Rose, S., & Kamin, L. J. (1984). *Not in our genes: Biology, ideology, and human nature* (Vol. 322). New York: Pantheon Books.

Li, S.-C. (2003). Biocultural orchestration of developmental plasticity across levels: The interplay of biology and culture in shaping the mind and behavior across the life span. *Psychological Bulletin, 129*(2), 171–194.

Light, R. J., & Smith, P. V. (1971). Statistical issues in social allocation models of intelligence: A review and a response. *Review of Educational Research, 41*(4), 351–367.

McNeal, R. B., Jr. (1999). Parental involvement as social capital: Differential effectiveness on science achievement, truancy, and dropping out. *Social Forces, 78*(1), 117–144.

Nettles, M. T., Millett, C. M., & Ready, D. D. (2003). Attacking the African American–white achievement gap on college admissions tests. In D. Ravitch (Ed.), *Brookings papers on education policy 2003* (pp. 215–252). Washington, DC: Brookings Institution.

Oakes, J., Ormseth, T., Bell, R. M., & Camp, P. (1990). *Multiplying inequalities: The effects of race, social class, and tracking on opportunities to learn mathematics and science* (No. NSF-R-3928). Santa Monica, CA: Rand.

Ogbu, J. U. (2003). *Black American students in an affluent suburb: A study of academic disengagement.* Mahwah, NJ: Lawrence Erlbaum.

Oliver, M. L., & Shapiro, T. M. (1995). *Black wealth/white wealth: A new perspective on racial inequality.* New York: Routledge.

Olson, L. (2003). The great divide. *Education Week, 22*(17), 9–16.

Orfield, G., & Eaton, S. E. (1996). The growth of segregation. In G. Orfield & S. Eaton (Eds.), *Dismantling desegregation. The quiet reversal of Brown v. Board of Education* (p. 424). New York: The New Press.

Orfield, G., & Lee, C. (2007). *Historic reversals, accelerating resegregation, and the need for new integration strategies.* Los Angeles: The Civil Rights Project.

Paley, V. (1979). *White teacher.* Cambridge, MA: Harvard University Press.

Rosenthal, R., & Jacobson, L. (1968). Self-fulfilling prophecies in the classroom: Teachers' expectations as unintended determinants of pupils' intellectual competence. In M. Deutsch, I. Katz, & A. R. Jensen (Eds.), *Social class, race, and psychological development* (pp. 219–253). New York: Holt, Rinehart, and Winston.

Sewell, W. H., & Hauser, R. M. (1980). The Wisconsin longitudinal study of social and psychological factors in aspirations and achievement. In A. Kerckhoff (Ed.), *Research in sociology of education and socialization* (pp. 59–100). Greenwich, CT: JAI Press.

Sewell, W. H., & Shah, V. P. (1968a). Parents' education and children's educational aspirations and achievements. *American Sociological Review, 33*(2), 191–209.

Sewell, W. H., & Shah, V. P. (1968b). Social class, parental encouragement, and educational aspirations. *American Journal of Sociology, 73*(5), 559–572.

Sleeter, C., & McLaren, P. (Eds.). (1995). *Multicultural education, critical pedagogy, and the politics of difference.* Albany: State University of New York Press.

Steinberg, L. (1997). *Beyond the classroom.* New York: Simon & Schuster.

Sunderman, G. L., & Kim, J. (2005). *Teacher quality: Equalizing educational opportunities and outcomes.* Cambridge, MA: The Civil Rights Project at Harvard University.

Tyson, K., Darity, W., & Castellino, D. R. (2005). It's not "a black thing": Understanding the burden of acting white and other dilemmas of high achievement. *American Sociological Review, 70*(4), 582–605.

Uhlenberg, J., & Brown, K. M. (2002). Racial gap in teachers' perceptions of the achievement gap. *Education and Urban Society, 34*(4), 493–530.

U.S. Department of Education, Institute of Education Sciences, National Center for Education Statistics. (2005a). *National Assessment of Educational Progress (NAEP). 2005 science assessment.* Washington, DC: U.S. Government Printing Office.

U.S. Department of Education, Institute of Education Sciences, National Center for Education Statistics. (2005b). *National Assessment of Educational Progress (NAEP) trial urban district assessment, 2005.* Washington, DC: U.S. Government Printing Office.

U.S. Department of Education, Institute of Education Sciences, National Center for Education Statistics. (2006). *Digest of education statistics 2005.* Retrieved September 1, 2006 from http://snipurl.com/255pg

U.S. Department of Education, Institute of Education Sciences, National Center for Education Statistics. (2007a). *National Assessment of Educational Progress (NAEP) 2007 mathematics assessment.* Washington, DC: U.S. Government Printing Office.

U.S. Department of Education, Institute of Education Sciences, National Center for Education Statistics. (2007b). *National Assessment of Educational Progress (NAEP) 2007 reading assessment.* Washington, DC: U.S. Government Printing Office.

U.S. Department of Education, National Center for Education Statistics. (2002). *Educational longitudinal study of 2002 (ELS: 2002).* Washington, DC. CD-ROM.

U.S. Department of Education, National Center for Education Statistics. (2005). *Initial results from the 2005 NHES early childhood program participation survey* (No. NCES 2006–075). Retrieved September 1, 2006, from http://nces.ed.gov/pubs2006/earlychild/02.asp

U.S. Department of Education, National Center for Education Statistics. (2004). *The condition of education 2004 (NCES-077).* Washington, DC: U.S. Government Printing Office.

Wong, R. S. (1998). Multidimensional influences of family environment in education: The case of socialist Czechoslovakia. *Sociology of Education, 71*(1), 1–22.

CHAPTER 3

Educational Policy for Linguistically and Culturally Diverse Students

Foundation or Barrier?

Eugene E. García

Educating children from non-English-speaking immigrant and nonimmigrant families is a major challenge for school systems throughout the United States. Historically, education has not been a successful experience for many of these students (August & Shanahan, 2006), and there are currently wide achievement gaps between these language-minority students and their English-speaking peers (García, Kleifgen, & Falchi, 2008; National Task Force on Early Education for Hispanics, 2007). Moreover, this challenge is growing: The population of students who come to school not speaking English has increased over 60% in the last decade (García, 2005; Hernandez, 2006) and is expected to continue to grow. Confronted with this reality, policymakers and the public have urged changing teaching methods, adopting new curricula, allocating more funding, and holding educational institutions accountable in order to improve the educational opportunities and outcomes of these students. Unfortunately, present federal and state (and, to some degree, local district) policies remain largely out of sync with the practices that can assist in the reduction of the achievement gap for language-minority students in this country.

Since the historic 1954 ruling in *Brown v. Board of Education,* our national goal has been to provide equal educational opportunity to disadvantaged students. Today, under the No Child Left Behind Act (NCLB), we have the additional challenge of producing excellence in academic outcomes for *all* children. For students from non-English-speaking families, however, educational "reform" as we have practiced it, particularly since the NCLB legislation, has had almost no impact; 6 years into the NCLB reforms, wide achievement gaps persist between these students and their English-only peers. According to the 2005 National Assessment for Educational Progress (NAEP), only 28% of ELL 4th graders scored at or above the basic achievement level for reading, compared with 75% of white students. In math, 55% of ELL 4th graders scored at or above proficient, compared with 89% of white students (Fry, 2007). In 8th grade, only 29% of ELLs scored at or above the basic achievement level for reading, compared with 75% of non-ELL students. Only 29% of ELL 8th-grade students scored at or above the basic achievement level for mathematics, compared with 71% of non-ELL 8th graders (Kohler & Lazarin, 2007).

Recent analyses of the Early Childhood Longitudinal Study–Kindergarten (ECLS-K) indicate that achievement gaps between various Hispanic ethnic groups and whites differ across a number of dimensions from kindergarten through 5th grade (García & Miller, 2008). Mexican-origin students, from first-generation immigrant families with limited opportunities to access English in the home and Spanish in school, are the most at risk for academic underachievement. Moreover, access to resources prior to schooling, especially preschool and support outside of school, can significantly affect early school performance in both reading and math. In addition, academic underachievement is primarily related to the absence of "complex" language structures that most standardized tests associated with NCLB do not assess adequately. This evidence would suggest that a simple "reform" accountability policy whose primary focus is to demonstrate adequate yearly progress (AYP) on standardized tests does not do justice to the challenges of raising academic achievement for linguistically and culturally diverse students.

In this chapter, I describe our nation's linguistically and culturally diverse students and discuss recent federal, state, and local policy changes, resulting from either litigation or legislation, that affect these students. My goal is to further an understanding of how such policies either disadvantage or enhance the education of these students. Finally, I argue that federal education policy, and the state policy it drives, must be more responsive to the needs of English language learners, both in designing the assessments that drive accountability for the achievement of these students and in fostering capacity building among schools and districts to ensure that necessary educational "innovations" take into consideration the language and cultural characteristics of students.

THE DIVERSITY OF OUR NATION'S "ENGLISH LANGUAGE LEARNERS"

Today, there are some 7,000 living languages throughout the globe, with many individuals speaking more than one of them. Moreover, many countries around the world have a great diversity of languages within their own borders. Papua New Guinea records 820 distinct languages, ranking first in diversity of languages within its borders. The United States ranks fifth, with more than 300 languages serving as primary or first language for its residents.

So, clearly, the U.S. students referred to in the literature as English language learners (ELLs) are not a homogenous group. While most students coming to U.S. schools with a primary language other than English are children of Hispanic (or Latino) heritage, some 25% of the non-English-speaking students speak languages other than Spanish (National Task Force on Early Education for Hispanics, 2007). Moreover, "English language learners" come to school with various levels of proficiency both in English and in their native language, and some may speak several languages prior to being introduced to English in U.S. schools. For instance, Southeast Asian immigrants may have learned their native language as well as French in refugee camps while they awaited immigration clearance to the United States (García, 2005). Recent Mexican immigrant children may speak Spanish and an indigenous Mexican language upon entry into U.S. schools (Hernandez, 2006).

The ELL population has been growing rapidly over the past few decades. Between 1979 and 2006, the number of school-age children (ages 5–17) who spoke a language other than English at home increased from 3.8 to 10.8 million, or from 9% to 20% of the school-age population (Planty, Hussar, Snyder, Provasnik, Kena, Dinkes, Kewal Ramani, & Kemp, 2008). Some 72% of them spoke Spanish as their native language (Planty et al., 2008).

WHAT ARE THE LEGAL RIGHTS OF ENGLISH LANGUAGE LEARNERS?

The *Lau* Decision

The 1974 U. S. Supreme Court decision of *Lau v. Nichols* is the landmark case that made clear that schools are under a legal obligation to afford additional supports or services to ensure meaningful educational opportunities to English language learners. The Court stated in unequivocal language,

> [T]here is no equality of treatment merely by providing students with English instruction. Students without the ability to understand English are effectively foreclosed from any meaningful discourse. Basic English skills are at the very core of what these public schools teach. Imposition of a requirement that, before a child can effectively participate in the education program he must already have acquired those basic skills is to make a mockery of public education. We know that those who do not understand English are certain to find their classroom experiences wholly incomprehensible and in no way meaningful. (*Lau v. Nichols*, 1974, p. 18)

The class action lawsuit was filed against the San Francisco Unified School District on March 25, 1970, and involved 12 American-born and foreign-born Chinese students. Prior to the suit, the district had initiated a pullout program in 1966, at the request of parents of limited English proficient (LEP) students–the legal term used for these students at that time. In a 1967 school census, the district identified 2,456 LEP Chinese students. By 1970, the district had identified 2,856 such students. Of this number, more than half (1,790) received no special instruction. In addition, more than 2,600 of these students were taught by teachers who could not speak Chinese. Still, the district argued that it had made initial attempts to serve this population of students. The Supreme Court's majority opinion overruled an appeals court that had ruled in favor of the district. The Supreme Court ruled in favor of the students and parents, holding that they were entitled to "a meaningful educational opportunity." The Court did not, however, prescribe a specific remedy. It left to the school district's discretion the design and implementation of specific programs to meet the children's needs.

The *Lau* opinion relied on statutory and regulatory grounds and did not reach the constitutional issues, although plaintiffs had argued that the equal protection clause of the 14th Amendment to the U.S. Constitution was relevant to the case. A student's right to special educational services flowed from the district's obligations under the Title VI of the 1964 Civil Rights Act, which prohibits discrimination on the grounds of race, color, or national origin in programs or activities receiving federal financial assistance. A May 25, 1970, memorandum issued by the Department of Health, Education, and Welfare (HEW) required special educational services for LEP students.

Court Action after *Lau*

After *Lau,* the litigation regarding language minority students almost exclusively involved Hispanic litigants. Although some cases were litigated to ensure compliance with the *Lau* requirements of "affirmative steps," most subsequent cases involved issues left unanswered by *Lau:* Which students are eligible for services under the ruling? What form of additional educational services must be provided? In *Aspira of New York, Inc. v. Board of Education* (1975), a suit was brought by an advocacy group on behalf of all Hispanic children in the New York City school district. The plaintiffs argued that these students could not successfully participate in regular education classes because of their lack of English proficiency, but that they could successfully participate in a Spanish-language curriculum (Roos, 1984). The U.S. district court hearing this case developed a specific instrument and procedure to identify those students eligible for Spanish-language instructional programs.

The procedure called for children to be tested in parallel Spanish and English standardized achievement tests to obtain estimates of their linguistic abilities. All students scoring below the 20th percentile on an English-language test were given the same (or a parallel) achievement test in Spanish. Students who scored higher on the Spanish achievement test and a Spanish-language proficiency test were to be placed in a Spanish-language bilingual program. These procedures assumed adequate reliability and validity for all of the language and achievement tests—a highly questionable assumption then, and now.

In the key Fifth Circuit decision of *Castaneda v. Pickard* (1981), the court interpreted Section 1703(f) of the Equal Educational Opportunities Act of 1974 (EEOA) as substantiating *Lau*'s holding that schools cannot ignore the special language needs of students. The EEOA extended Title VI of the Civil Rights Act to all educational institutions, not just those receiving federal funding. Section 1703 (f) provides:

> No state shall deny equal educational opportunities to an individual on account of his or her race, color, sex, or national origin, by . . . the failure of an educational agency to take appropriate action to overcome language barriers that impede equal participation by its students in its instructional programs. (EEOA, 1974, sec. 1703 (f))

Furthermore, the court then pondered whether the statutory requirement of the EEOA that districts take "appropriate action to overcome language barriers" should be further delineated. The plaintiffs urged on the court a construction of "appropriate action" that would necessitate bilingual programs that incorporated bilingual students' primary language. The court concluded, however, that Section 1703(f) did not embody a congressional mandate that any particular form of remedy be uniformly adopted. However, the court did conclude that Congress required districts to adopt an appropriate program and that, by creating a cause of action in federal court to enforce Section 1703(f), it left to federal judges the task of determining whether a given program was appropriate. It then articulated a tripartite mode of analysis for determining whether a school district has complied with its obligations under Section 1703(f):

1. The court will determine whether a district's program is "informed by an educational theory recognized as sound by some experts in the field or, at least, deemed a legitimate experimental strategy." The court explicitly declined to be an arbiter among competing theorists.
2. The court will determine whether the district is implementing its program in a reasonably effective manner (e.g., adequate funding, qualified staffing).

3. The court will determine whether the program, after operating long enough to be a legitimate trial, produces results that indicate the language barriers are being overcome. (*Castañeda v. Pickard*, 1981, p. 73)

In the *Castañeda* decision, therefore, the court spoke firmly to the issue of program implementation. In particular, the court indicated that the district must provide adequate resources, including trained instructional personnel, materials, and other relevant support, that would ensure effective program implementation. Implicit in these requirements is the notion that districts staff their programs with language-minority education specialists, typically defined by state-approved credentials or professional course work (similar to devices used to judge professional expertise in other areas of professional education).

Looking Forward:
The Tentative Legacy of *Lau*

In recent years, the courts' role in promoting the rights of English language learners has eroded as the power of *Lau v. Nichols* has been undermined. Through the cumulative impact of three cases—*Guardians Association v. Civil Service Commission, Alexander v. Choate,* and *Alexander v. Sandoval*—the court has now established that plaintiffs can sue under Title VI only for intentional discrimination, which has left enforcement of the large area of nonintentional discriminatory "impact" almost entirely in the hands of the executive branch. While enforcement of the core elements of *Lau v. Nichols* is on increasingly shaky ground, the central holding remains uncontested: An English-only curriculum that provides no meaningful instruction to non-English-speaking students is discriminatory, whether or not that was the intent of school officials (Gándara, Moran, & García, 2004).

U.S. federal courts have played a significant role in shaping educational policy for English language learners. They have spoken to issues of student identification, program implementation, resource allocation, professional staffing, and program effectiveness. Moreover, they have obligated both state and local educational agencies to language-minority education responsibilities. Most significantly, they have offered to language-minority students and their families a forum in which minority status is not disadvantageous. It has been a highly ritualized forum, extremely time- and resource-consuming. Still, the federal courts have been a responsive institution and will likely continue to be used as a mechanism to air and resolve the challenges of educating language-minority students.

NO CHILD LEFT BEHIND
AND THE DEMISE OF THE BILINGUAL EDUCATION ACT

Federal legislation has also historically played an important role in establishing rights and ensuring educational opportunities for English language learners. In enacting the No Child Left Behind Act, the 2001 reauthorization of the Elementary and Secondary Education Act of 1965, Congress eliminated the Bilingual Education Act (BEA), the central source of federal support for English language learners. Title III of the new law, Language Instruction for Limited English Proficient and Immigrant Students, has now become the source of federal funds to support the education of bilingual students, who are referred to in the new law as LEP students. However, Title III differs markedly from the initial enactment of the Bilingual Education Act and all of its five subsequent reauthorizations.

The Bilingual Education Act

From its inception in 1968 until its final reauthorization in 1994, Title VII of ESEA, the Bilingual Education Act, stood as the United States' primary federal legislative effort to provide equal educational opportunity to language-minority students. The legislation was reauthorized on five occasions (1974, 1978, 1984, 1988, and 1994). While the aim of the legislation was never one of establishing language policy, the role of language became a prominent marker as the legislation articulated the goals and nature of education for language-minority students.

The initial Title VII legislation originated as part of the War on Poverty legislation and, like *Lau v. Nichols,* built on the Civil Rights Act of 1964. The legislation was primarily a "crisis intervention" (García & Gonzalez, 1995), a political strategy to funnel poverty funds to the second largest minority group in the Southwest, Mexican Americans (Casanova, 1991). The Bilingual Education Act was designed as a demonstration program to meet the educational needs of low-income, limited-English-speaking children. It was intended to be a remedial effort, aimed at overcoming students' "language deficiencies," and these "compensatory efforts were considered to be a sound educational response to the call for equality of educational opportunity" (Navarro, 1990, p. 291). No particular program of instruction was recommended; in fact, financial assistance was to be provided to local educational agencies "to develop and carry out new and imaginative . . . programs" (Bilingual Education Act, 1968, sec. 702). Among the approved activities were programs in bilingual education, history and culture, early childhood education, and adult education for parents.

While the role of native language instruction was not specifically addressed until the 1974 reauthorization, as a practical matter, all of the programs funded under the BEA in its early years featured native language instruction. The 1974 reauthorization even defined bilingual education as "instruction given in, and study of, English, and, to the extent necessary to allow a child to progress effectively through the educational system, the native language" (sec. 703(a)(4)(A)(i)).[1] Other significant changes in terms of eligibility included the elimination of poverty as a requirement, the inclusion of Native American children as an eligible population, and a provision for English-speaking children to enroll in bilingual education programs to "acquire an understanding of the cultural heritage of the children of limited English-speaking ability" (sec. 703 (a)(4)(B)).

Over the next 15 years, national sentiment shifted to focus on English acquisition as the primary goal of education for language minority students. The 1978 reauthorization added language to the 1974 definition of bilingual education emphasizing the goal of English language proficiency. Bilingual education programs that encouraged native language maintenance would only foster children's allegiance to minority languages and cultures, and this was not considered an acceptable responsibility for schools. Native language maintenance was the responsibility of families, churches, and other institutions outside the school (Casanova, 1991; Crawford, 1999). So, while bilingualism was viewed as a laudable goal, the ultimate benefit of programs would be judged in terms of English-language acquisition and subject-matter learning (Birman & Ginsburg, 1983).

The 1984 reauthorization of the BEA targeted funds to transitional bilingual education: 60% of Title VII funds were allocated to the various grant categories, and 75% of these funds were reserved for transitional bilingual education programs. Transitional bilingual education programs were specified as providing "structured English-language instruction, and, to the extent necessary to allow a child to achieve competence in the English language, instruction in the child's native language" (sec. 703 (a)(4)(A)). So, the purpose of native language instruction was to support transition to English instruction. In contrast, developmental bilingual education programs were defined as providing "structured English-language instruction and instruction in a second language. Such programs shall be designed to help children achieve competence in English and a second language, while mastering subject matter skills" (sec. 703 (a)(5)(A)). So, the goal of this program included native language and English language competence, yet no funding allocations were specified.

In addition to delineating these two bilingual education programs, the grant categories included special alternative instructional programs (SAIPS) that did not require the use of native language, and 4% of Title VII funds were allocated to SAIPS. These programs were created in recognition "that in some school districts establishment of bilingual education programs may be administratively impractical" (sec. 702 (a)(7)). While the 1984 grant categories remained the same for the 1988 reauthorization, funds allocated to SAIPS were increased to 25%. Furthermore, the 1998 legislation included a 3-year limit on an individual's participation in transitional bilingual education programs or SAIPS: "No student may be enrolled in a bilingual program . . . for a period of more than 3 years" (sec.7021 (d)(3)(A)).

From Bilingual to English-Only Education

The 2001 reauthorization of the ESEA marks a complete reversal from the reauthorization in 1994 with regard to limited English proficient students. Whereas the 1994 version of the Bilingual Education Act included among its goals "developing the English skills and to the extent possible, the native-language skills" of LEP students, the new law focuses only on attaining "English proficiency." In fact, the word *bilingual* has been completely eliminated from the law and any government office affiliated with the law. A new federal office, the Office of English Language Acquisition, Language Enhancement, and Academic Achievement for Limited-English-Proficient Students (commonly referred to as OELA), replaces the Office of Bilingual Education and Minority Languages Affairs (OBEMLA) and oversees the provisions of the new law. What was formerly known as the National Clearinghouse for Bilingual Education is now known as the National Clearinghouse for English Language Acquisition and Language Instruction Educational Programs.

Through Title III of NCLB, federal funds to serve ELL students are no longer federally administered via competitive grants designed to ensure equity and promote quality programs, programs that served as guiding lights to the larger nation. Instead, resources are allocated primarily through a state formula grant for language instruction educational programs (LIEPs) based on "scientifically-based research" (U.S. Department of Education, 2002). LIEPs are defined as "an instruction course in which LEP students are placed for the purpose of developing and attaining English proficiency, while meeting challenging State and academic content and student academic achievement standards. A LIEP may make use of both English and a child's native language to enable the child to develop and attain English proficiency" (U.S. Department of Education, 2003, p. 20).

The formula grants are distributed to each state based on the state's enrollments of LEP and immigrant students.[2] Each state must then allocate 95% of the funds to individual local education agencies (LEAs). The argument for the formula grants claims that the previous system of competitive grants "benefited a small percentage of LEP students in relatively few schools"

(U.S. Department of Education, n.d.). In fact, resources are now spread more thinly than before–among more states, more programs, and more students. Through competitive grants, Title VII support for instructional programs previously served about 500,000 "eligible" bilingual students out of an estimated 3.5 million nationwide. Under the new law, districts automatically receive funding based on the enrollments of LEP and immigrant students. However, the impact of federal dollars is reduced. Pre-NCLB, for example, about $360 was spent per student in Title VII–supported instructional programs. Post-NCLB, despite the overall increase in appropriations, Title III provides less than $135 per student. Funding for all other purposes–including teacher training, research, and support services–has been restricted to 6.5% of the total budget. That amounts to about $43 million. In 2001, pre-NCLB, by contrast, $100 million was spent on professional development alone in order to address the critical shortage of teachers qualified to meet the needs of bilingual students.

Accountability provisions mandate annual assessment in English for any student who has attended school in the United States (excluding Puerto Rico) for 3 or more consecutive years and attainment of "annual measurable achievement objectives" (U.S. Department of Education, 2002). States are required to hold school districts accountable for making adequate yearly progress (AYP).[3] Districts must report every second fiscal year and include a description of the program as well as the progress made by children in learning English, meeting state standards, and attaining English proficiency. Districts failing to meet AYP must develop an improvement plan with sanctions if they continue to fail for 4 years (U.S. Department of Education, 2002). In fact, failure to meet AYP can eventually result in the loss of Title III funds.

In summary, federal policies have begun to emphasize the teaching and learning of English with little regard for the development of academic bilingual competency for students coming to school speaking a language other than English. State policies have begun to mirror this shift, and in particularly dramatic ways in two states with significant populations of bilingual children.

THE CONVERGENCE/NONCONGRUENCE
OF POLICIES AND ACHIEVEMENT

The contemporary educational *Zeitgeist* that embraces excellence and equity for all students–as reflected in *A Nation at Risk* (National Commission on Excellence in Education, 1983), *Goals 2000* (1994), and the more recent initiatives by President Bush in the No Child Left Behind Act of 2001–has brought attention to ELL and immigrant children and their families. The major thrust of efforts aimed at these populations has been to identify why such populations are not thriving and how institutions serving them can be "reformed" or "restructured" to meet this educational challenge.

California and Texas are the states with largest populations of ELL students. To understand the impact of recent policy changes on these students, I will briefly discuss state-level changes in these two places.

California

With the passage of Proposition 227 in 1998 (García & Curry, 2000), and soon thereafter an English-only state school accountability program (García, 2001b), California has targeted ELL students with "language of instruction" policies. These two state policies, supported by district-level policies, dictated a move toward English-only reading programs (Stritikus, 2002). From the perspective of teachers and principals at the local level, these policies have significantly altered the educational landscape for California's student population, especially for ELL students (Stritikus, 2002). Teachers experience these policies as top-down reforms that reduce teacher autonomy in classroom instruction. They argue that current educational trends posit higher test scores and a school's API ranking as the educational goals of students and teachers—a misplaced focus that leads to the impoverishment of student learning in the classroom (Stritikus, 2002). For bilingual educators, this further means the erosion of their primary language instruction and curriculum.

Most disheartening is the recent analysis of the achievement gap between bilingual and nonbilingual students in California. According to Stanford 9 data published in 2004 (California State Department of Education, 2004), the gap between English-fluent and non-English-fluent students has increased. According to these same data, since California's Proposition 227 passed in 1998, 88% of California's non-English-fluent students have been placed into English immersion classes that are normally designed not to exceed 1 year. Since 1998, Stanford 9 achievement test scores in reading have shown a widening gap between non-English-fluent and English-fluent students.

Texas

The impact on bilingual students of California's English-only reform policies finds strong parallels in Texas. Emerging research on high-stakes testing identifies a set of alarming educational trends regarding the impact of the Texas Assessment of Academic Skills (TAAS): TAAS-based teaching and test preparation are usurping a substantive curriculum; TAAS is divorced from children's experience and culture and is widening the educational gap between rich and poor, and between mainstream and language-minority students (McNeil, 1988, 2000; Valenzuela, 1997, 1999). According to McNeil and Valenzuela (2001), the TAAS system in Texas is "playing out its inherent logic at the expense of our poorest minority children" (p. 63).

In both California and Texas, one test is used to assess student academic outcomes. Both states have placed a tremendous emphasis on school ranking and are witness to a drastic increase in the implementation of mandated scripted reading programs at the expense of other effective instructional practices for second language learners (Stritikus, 2002). California's educational system is growing more and more prescriptive, just as Texas has, discrediting the cultural and linguistic assets that students bring to the classroom (García, 2005). In sum, in California, and to some degree in other states such as Texas, English-only policy initiatives continue to have negative effects on ELL students. They are subtractive in nature, ignoring the linguistic resources that bilingual students bring to the classroom, and disregard responsive attributes of programs that work well for these students.

THE IMPACT OF NCLB ON ASSESSMENT AND ACCOUNTABILITY FOR ENGLISH LANGUAGE LEARNERS

NCLB requires that schools and districts be accountable for the academic progress of ELL students, referred to under the law as LEPs. Under NCLB, these students must take an English-language proficiency test and, in addition, meet the same content proficiency requirements as other students. The scores of this subgroup of students are disaggregated and schools, districts, and states can be penalized if these students miss test score targets. (Only the scores of students who have attended school in the United States for less than a year are not counted for accountability purposes.) Unfortunately, assessing these students appropriately for accountability purposes is a significant challenge. Test development and assessment practices for culturally and linguistically diverse students raise numerous validity concerns (and have been the basis of several lawsuits).

Almost none of the tests that states use to measure the subject-matter knowledge of LEP students has been validated for use with these students; thus, it is not possible to have an accurate understanding of their achievement (Rebell & Thurston, 2008). And while NCLB allows LEP students to take assessments in their native language for 3 years, plus 2 additional years, if necessary, only 11 states provide such assessments (Zehr, 2005). Not only are these assessments costly to develop, especially in areas of great linguistic diversity, but their development is difficult.

To be effective, NCLB must rely on assessments that accurately measure the progress of all students. At the present time, we fundamentally lack such assessments. To ensure that language-minority students are assessed fairly, assessments should take into account children's cultural and linguistic backgrounds, so as to not penalize those who fall outside the cultural mainstream. Such tests create culturally and linguistically relevant means and scores that accurately portray the abilities and concurrent performance levels for a diverse body of children. Though important strides have been made in the development of appropriate tests and testing procedures for culturally and linguistically diverse students (Rhodes, Ochoa, & Ortiz, 2005), much research and development are still needed. Current tests are limited in terms of their overall number as well as the domains and skills they cover (Espinosa & López, 2006). Moreover, tests developed for specific language-minority groups that are merely translations of original English versions tend to be based on Euro-American cultural values and not be applicable to other groups with different backgrounds. Furthermore, tests with appropriate content and construct validity should be standardized with representative samples of Hispanic children from diverse national origins, language backgrounds, and socioeconomic conditions.

The National Association for the Education of Young Children recently adopted a series of recommendations on the screening and assessment of young ELL students (2005). These are particularly useful for those serving young Hispanic children. First, they recommend that assessments be guided by specific purposes with appropriate applications to meet the needs of the child. Assessments and screenings should be used to offer better services and to develop more informed interventions. Moreover, this approach encourages ELL students to be included into accountability systems and to provide meaningful measures that improve learning outcomes.

Second, instruments used to assess young ELL students should align with the specific cultural and linguistic characteristics of the child being assessed. This means the cultural and linguistic content and context of the tests are congruent with the child's background.

Third, the main purpose of assessment should be to improve the learning and development of the child. In order for this to occur, multiple methods, measures, and people should be incorporated in an assessment of the child's ongoing performance, given the curricular content and instructional approaches used in class.

Fourth, formal standardized assessments should be used wisely. Such assessments are appropriate to identify disabilities, evaluate programs (for accountability purposes), and/or to monitor and improve individual learning. However, test developers, evaluators, and decision makers should be aware of the limitations and biases many of these tests introduce—e.g., sampling and norming, test equivalence, test administration, and test content.

Fifth, those conducting assessments should have cultural and linguistic competence, knowledge of the child being assessed, and specific assessment-related knowledge and skills. It is important to remember that assessments are more likely to be reliable when carried out by teams of professionals who are bicultural, bilingual, and knowledgeable about first and second language acquisition.

Lastly, the families of young ELL students should play a critical role in the assessment process. Parents (or legal guardians) should be queried as sources of data and should be involved in the interpretation process of comprehensive assessments. In addition, parents (or legal guardians) should always be aware of reasons for assessment, the procedures involved, and the significance of the outcomes. Their voices should be sought out and should influence program placement and other intervention strategies (Lazarin, 2005).

RECOMMENDATIONS FOR ADDRESSING CULTURAL AND LINGUISTIC DIVERSITY

With NCLB up for reauthorization, scholars, policymakers, researchers, and practitioners alike are weighing in with recommendations for revisions to the legislation. The law should be revised to address more effectively the needs of culturally and linguistically diverse students. Revisions are required in two areas primarily. First, the law must be revised to improve the current means for assessing the performance of these students—the basis for accountability for the achievement of this vulnerable population. Second, and perhaps more importantly, the law must be revised to include the means to improve the capacity of schools and districts to educate these students and effectively respond to their needs.

Improving the Assessment and Accountability of English Language Learners

The Commission on No Child Left Behind, a bipartisan, independent effort dedicated to improving NCLB (Commission on No Child Left Behind, 2006) made particular recommendations regarding ELL students that I will briefly summarize here. First, the commission recommends withholding a portion of the state's administrative funding if that state has not fully developed and implemented English-language proficiency standards, assessments, and annual measurable objectives. Second, the commission recommends extending the time period, from 2 years to 3 years, that ELLs can remain the LEP subgroup for AYP purposes, after attaining proficiency in English. This would help schools more accurately measure the achievement of ELLs. Third, the commission recommends that states use their allocation of funding to create and implement alternate assessments for

English learners, to develop plans for establishing universally designed assessment systems, and to further develop and implement high-quality science assessments now required under law. Fourth, the commission recommends that the U.S. Department of Education develop a common scale across states to determine English-language proficiency. Finally, the commission recommends ensuring that teachers of English language learners receive the training and support they need by requiring states to create an endorsement for teacher certification for those who spend more than 25% of their teaching time with English learners. These recommendations touch on key elements of the present policy that, if NCLB is reauthorized, could be very useful in achieving the overall goals of NCLB, particularly for ELL students. To its credit, NCLB places ELL students directly in the realm of the accountability goals. These recommendations would much improve achieving the overall goals for these students, nationally.

Building Capacity to Meet the Needs of English Language Learners

NCLB has brought important attention to the needs of language-minority students by disaggregating data on their achievement and requiring schools, districts, and states to be accountable for their progress. However, even if Congress could solve the law's problems with fairly identifying, testing, and measuring progress with these students, NCLB has nothing to say about how to improve schooling to meet the real needs of this population. The law does nothing to promote the kinds of educational policies that would actually build the capacity of our nation's schools to educate language-minority students in a way that is responsive to their particular needs.

Developing Responsive Pedagogy and Learning Communities. Providing meaningful educational opportunities for language-minority students requires important changes in classroom practices. From a policy perspective, NCLB's efforts to provide highly qualified teachers, clear definitions of ELL students, resources directed to these students, and accountability inclusive of these students can do much to create education environments in and out of school that maximize the achievement gap reductions that are necessary for this student population. Research that supports this policy effort suggests that the educational failure of "diverse" student populations is related to the culture clash between home and school. If the contribution of culture is not fully considered, educational endeavors for these culturally distinct students are likely to fail (García, 2001b). The challenge for educators is to identify critical differences between and within ethnic minority groups and individuals within those groups and to incorporate this information into classroom practice.

Equally important, instructional programs must also ensure the implementation of appropriate general principles of teaching and learning. The academic failure of any student rests on the failure of instructional personnel to implement what we know "works." A meta-analysis by Walberg (1986) suggests that educational research has identified robust indicators of instructional conditions that have academically significant effects across various conditions and student groups. In this vein, a number of specific instructional strategies—including direct instruction, tutoring, frequent evaluation of academic progress, and cooperative learning—have been particular candidates for the "what works" category.

Expectations also play an important role. Noguera (2004) has suggested that students, teachers, and school professionals in general have low academic expectations of culturally and linguistically diverse students. Raising student motivation in conjunction with enhancing academic expectations with challenging curriculum is a prescribed solution. Implied in this "general principle" position is that the educational failure of "diverse" populations can be eradicated by the systemic and effective implementation of these understood general principles of instruction that work with "all" students.

Other significant conceptual contributions attempt to explain the academic underachievement of culturally and linguistically diverse students. Paulo Freire (1970) has argued that educational initiatives cannot expect academic or intellectual success under social circumstances that are oppressive. He and others suggest that such oppression taints any curriculum or pedagogy and that only a pedagogy of empowerment can fulfill the lofty goals of educational equity and achievement (Cummins, 1986; Pearl, 1991). Similarly, Bernstein (1971), Laosa (1982), and Wilson (1978) point to socioeconomic factors that influence the organization of schools and instruction. Extensive exposure, over generations, to poverty and related disparaging socioeconomic conditions significantly influence the teaching/learning process at home, in the community, and in schools. The result is disastrous, long-term educational failure and social disruption of family and community. Ogbu (1999) offers an alternative, macrosociological perspective with regard to the academic failure of culturally and linguistically diverse students. He explains underachievement by arguing that immigrant and minority populations form a layer of our society that is not expected to excel academically or economically and is therefore treated as a "caste-like" population. These expectations are transformed into parallel self-perceptions by these populations, with academic underachievement and social withdrawal as the result.

No quick fix is likely under social and schooling conditions that mark the student for special treatment of his or her cultural difference without consideration for the psychological and social circumstances in which that student resides. This approach warns us against the isolation of any single attribute (poverty, language difference, learning potential, and so on) as the only variable of importance. This more comprehensive view of the schooling process includes an understanding of the relationship between home and school, the psycho-socio-cultural incongruities between the two and the resulting effects on learning and achievement (Brown & Campione, 1998).

Such thinking has profound implications for the teaching/learning enterprise with culturally diverse students (García, 2001a). It requires a new pedagogy that views the classroom as a community of learners in which speakers, readers, and writers come together to define and redefine the meaning of the academic experience. It has been described as a pedagogy of empowerment (Cummins, 1986), as cultural learning (Heath, 1986; Trueba, 1987), and as a cultural view of providing instructional assistance/guidance (Tharp & Gallimore, 1989). In any case, it argues for the respect and integration of the students' values, beliefs, histories, and experiences, and recognizes the active role that students must play in the learning process. It is therefore a *responsive pedagogy,* one that encompasses practical, contextual, and empirical knowledge and a "worldview" of education that evolves through meaningful interactions among teachers, students, and other school community members. This responsive set of strategies expands students' knowledge beyond their own immediate experiences while using those experiences as a sound foundation for appropriating new knowledge.

Of course, a teaching and learning community that is responsive to the dynamics of social, cultural, and linguistic diversity within the broader concerns for high academic achievement both requires and emerges from a particular schooling environment. While considerable work has been devoted to restructure schools and change the fundamental relationships that exist among school personnel, students, families, and community members, seldom have these efforts included attention to the unique influences of the linguistic and sociocultural dimensions of these same relationships and structures. The environments that potentially support and nurture the development of responsive learning communities are not unlike those promoted by leading school reform and restructuring advocates; however, we further suggest that the incorporation of social, cultural, and linguistic diversity concerns creates a set of educational principles and dimensions that are more likely to address the challenges faced by schools that must attend to the needs of growing populations of diverse students.

The learning environments that we consider essential to the development of a responsive pedagogy are referred to as "effective schooling" (García, 2001a, 2005) and "high performance learning communities" (Berman, 1996). The focus on the social, cultural, and linguistic diversity represented by students in today's public schools further challenges us to consider the theoretical and practical concerns relative to ensuring educational success for diverse students. That is, responsive learning communities must necessarily address issues of diversity in order to maximize their potential and to sustain educational improvement over time.

Capacity-Building Recommendations for English Language Learners

The following policies and practices would help to foster responsive learning communities for ELL students.

Federal, State, and Local Policy

- Federal efforts to produce or underwrite solid longitudinal experimental and qualitative studies linking nonschool variables with school-related variables associated with student academic outcomes with the goal of sparking innovation
- Federal investments in the development of "language and literacy specialists" who work in Title I and Title III schools and classrooms with ELL students
- Federal and state accountability that considers longitudinal academic development outcomes for ELL students over a minimum period of 3 years
- Federal and state elimination of prohibitions on the use of the students' nonschool languages(s) for instruction
- Local district and school development of language and global education architectures that generate multilanguage and multicultural learning for all students

Schoolwide Practices

- School-level promotion of a vision defined by the acceptance and valuing of diversity
- Schoolwide treatment of classroom practitioners as professionals and colleagues in school development decisions
- School-level collaboration, flexibility, and provision of enhanced professional development
- School-level elimination of policies that categorize diverse students and render their educational experiences inferior or limiting for further academic learning
- School-level reflection of and connection to surrounding community, particularly with the families of the students attending the schools

Instructional Practices

- Bilingual/bicultural skills and awareness among teachers
- High expectations of diverse students

- Treatment of diversity as an asset to the classroom
- Participation by teachers in ongoing professional development on issues of cultural and linguistic diversity and effective practices
- Curriculum development to address cultural and linguistic diversity, including

> Attention to and integration of home culture/practices
> Focus on maximizing student interactions across categories of English proficiency, academic performance, time since immigration, and so on
> Regular and consistent attempts to illicit ideas from students for planning units, themes, activities
> Thematic approach to learning activities—with the integration of various skills, events, and learning opportunities
> Focus on language development through meaningful interactions and communications combined with direct grammatical skill-building in content-appropriate contexts

CONCLUSION

In summary, present federal and state (and, to some degree, local district) policies are out of sync with the practices that can assist in the reduction of the achievement gap for ELL students in this country. The architects of these policies have not drawn on the designs of the practitioners as they both move, through NCLB and related policies, to address the academic shortfalls of a growing population of U.S. students. In practice, a responsive learning community recognizes that academic learning has its roots in both out-of-school and in-school processes. Such a conceptual lens extends beyond the policy and practice frameworks of "equal educational opportunity" and concludes that a focus on broader issues of culture, like those represented in the multicultural education movement, is useful but not enough for effectively serving culturally and linguistically diverse students in today's schools. Instead, diversity must be perceived and acted on as a resource for teaching and learning instead of a problem. A focus on what students bring to the schooling process generates a more asset/resource-oriented approach versus a deficit/needs-assessment approach. Within this knowledge-driven, responsive and engaging learning environment, skills are tools for acquiring knowledge, not a fundamental target of teaching events.

In addition, the search for general principles of learning that work for all students must be redirected. This mission requires an understanding of how individuals with diverse sets of experiences, packaged individually into cultures, "make meaning," communicate that meaning, and extend that meaning, particularly in the social contexts of schools. Such a mission requires in-depth treatment of the processes associated with producing diversity, issues of socialization in and out of schools, coupled with a clear examination of how such understanding is actually transformed into pedagogy and curriculum that results in high academic performance for all students. Policy must align itself with this mission.

NOTES

1. The inclusion of native language instruction in the definition of bilingual education was influenced by bilingual programs in Dade County, Florida, which were founded to address the needs of the first wave of professional-class Cuban immigrants. The Cuban immigrants saw themselves as temporary residents of the United States who would soon return to their country, and, therefore, wanted to preserve their culture and language. Thus, the bilingual programs encouraged Spanish-language maintenance and English-language acquisition (Casanova, 1991). At the same time, the success of the programs gave encouragement to the idea of bilingual education as a method of instruction for students from disadvantaged backgrounds (Hakuta, 1986). Native language instruction could serve as a bridge to English-language acquisition, by providing equal access to the curriculum until students were English proficient. While the BEA acknowledged the role native language could play in supporting a transition to English, it did not promote bilingual education as an enrichment program where the native language was maintained.

2. Those programs awarded funds under the 1994 reauthorization will continue to be eligible.

3. As of February 2004, for AYP calculations, states can include for 2 years in the LEP subgroup students who have achieved English-language proficiency to ensure that they receive credit for improving English-language proficiency from year to year.

REFERENCES

Aspira of New York v. *Board of Education of the City of New York*, 394 F. Supp. 1161 (1975).

August, D., & Shanahan, T. (Eds.). (2006). *Developing literacy in second language learners: Report of the National Literacy Panel on Language Minority Youth and Children.* Mahwah, NJ: Lawrence Erlbaum.

Berman, P. (1996). *High performing learning communities.* Berkeley: University of California Press.

Bernstein, B. (1971). A sociolinguistic approach to socialization with some reference to educability. In B. Bernstein (Ed.), *Class, codes and control: Theoretical studies towards a sociology of language* (pp. 146–171). London: Routledge and Kegan Paul.

Bilingual Education Act, Pub. L. No. (90–247), 81 Stat. 816 (1968).

Bilingual Education Act, Pub. L. No. (93–380), 88 Stat. 503 (1974).

Bilingual Education Act, Pub. L. No. (95–561), 92 Stat. 2268 (1978).

Bilingual Education Act, Pub. L. No. (98–511), 98 Stat. 2370 (1984).

Bilingual Education Act, Pub. L. No. (100–297), 102 Stat. 279 (1988).

Bilingual Education Act, Pub. L. No. (103–382), 106 Stat. 1422 (1994).

Birman, B. F., & Ginsburg, A. L. (1983). Introduction: Addressing the needs of language minority children. In K. A. Baker & A. A. D. Kanter (Eds.), *Bilingual education: A reappraisal of federal policy* (pp. ix–xxi). Lexington, MA: D.C. Heath and Company.

Brown, A., & Campione, J. (1998). Design experiments: Theoretical and methodological challenge in creating complex intervention in classroom settings. *The Journal of the Learning Sciences, 2,* 141–178.

California, Proposition 227: English Language in Public Schools (1998).

California State Department of Education. (2004). *Public school accountability act.* Retrieved June 8, 2004, from http://www.cde.ca.gov/psaa/

Casanova, U. (1991). Bilingual education: Politics or pedagogy. In O. Garcia (Ed.), *Bilingual education* (Vol. 1, pp. 167–182). Amsterdam: John Benjamins.

Castañeda v. *Pickard,* 64b F.2d 989 (1981).

Commission on No Child Left Behind. (2006). *Beyond NCLB: Fulfilling the promise to our nation's children.* Washington, DC: The Aspen Institute.

Crawford, J. (1999). *Bilingual education: History, politics, theory, and practice* (4th ed.). Los Angeles: Bilingual Education Services.

Cummins, J. (1986). Empowering minority students: A framework for intervention. *Harvard Educational Review, 56,* 18–36.

Department of Health, Education, and Welfare, 35 Fed. Reg. II, 595 (1970).

Equal Educational Opportunities Act of 1974, Pub. L. No. (93–380), 88 Stat. 514 (1974).

Espinosa, L., & López, M. (2006). *Assessment considerations for young English language learners across different levels of accountability.* Paper prepared for the National Early Childhood Accountability Task Force.

Freire, P. (1970). *The pedagogy of the oppressed.* New York: Continuum.

Fry, R. (2007). *How far behind in math and reading are English Language Learners?* Washington, DC: Pew Hispanic Center.

Gándara, P., Moran, R., & García, E. (2004). Legacy of *Brown: Lau* and language policy in the United States. *Review of Research in Education, 28,* 27–46.

García, E. (2001a). *Hispanic education in the United States: Raices y alas.* Lanham, MD: Rowman and Littlefield.

García, E. (2001b). *Understanding and meeting the challenge of student diversity* (3rd ed.). Boston: Houghton Mifflin.

García, E. E. (2005). *Teaching and learning in two languages: Bilingualism and schooling in the United States.* New York: Teachers College Press.

García, E., & Curry, J. E. (2000). The education of limited English proficient students in California schools: An assessment of the influence of Proposition 227 in selected districts and schools. *Bilingual Research Journal, 24*(1–2), 15–36.

García, E. E., & Gonzalez, R. (1995). Issues in systemic reform for culturally and linguistically diverse students. *Teachers College Record, 96*(3), 418–431.

García, E. E., & Miller, L. S. (2008). Findings and recommendations of the National Task Force on Early Childhood Education for Hispanics. *Child Development Perspectives, 2*(2), 53–58.

Garcia, O., Kleifgen, J. A., & Falchi, L. (2008, January). *From English language learners to emergent bilinguals. Equity matters: Research review No. 1.* New York: Campaign for Educational Equity, Teachers College, Columbia University.

Goals 2000: Educate America Act, H.R. 1804 (1994).

Hakuta, K. (1986). *Mirror of language: The debate on bilingualism.* New York: Basic Books.

Heath, S. B. (1986). Sociocultural contexts of language development. In California State Department of Education (Ed.), *Beyond language: Social factors in schooling language minority students* (pp. 143–186). Los Angeles: Evaluation, Dissemination, and Assessment Center, California State University.

Hernandez, D. (2006). *Young Hispanic children in the US: A demographic portrait based on Census 2000.* State University of New York at Albany: A Report to the National Task Force on Early Childhood Education for Hispanics.

Kohler, A. D., & Lazarin, M. (2007). Hispanic education in the United States. *NCLR Statistical Brief, 8,* 9.

Laosa, L. M. (1982). Psychometric characteristics of Chicano and non-Hispanic white children. *Journal of Applied Developmental Psychology, 3*(3), 217–245.

Lau v. Nichols, 414 U.S. 563, 566 (1974).

Lazarin, M. (2005). *To the extent practicable: Inclusion of English language learners in assessment and accountability systems under the No Child Left Behind Act.* Washington, DC: National Council of La Raza.

McNeil, L. M. (1988). *Contradictions of control: School structure and school knowledge.* New York: Routledge.

McNeil, L. M. (2000). *Contradictions of reform: The educational costs of standardization.* New York: Routledge.

McNeil, L. M., & Valenzuela, A. (2001). The harmful impact of the TAAS system of testing in Texas: Beneath the accountability rhetoric. In M. Kornhaber & G. Orfield (Eds.), *Raising standards or raising barriers? Inequity and high-stakes testing in public education.* New York: Century Foundation.

National Association for the Education of Young Children. (2005). *Screening and assessment of young English-language learners.* Washington, DC: Author.

National Commission on Excellence in Education. (1983). *A nation at risk: The imperative for educational reform.* Washington, DC: Author.

National Task Force on Early Education for Hispanics. (2007). *National Task Force on the Early Education for Hispanics: Final Report.* Tempe: Arizona State University.

Navarro, R. A. (1990). The problems of language, education, and society: Who decides? In E. E. García & R. V. Padilla (Eds.), *Advances in bilingual education research* (pp. 289–313). Tucson: University of Arizona Press.

Noguera, P. A. (2004). Social capital and the education of immigrant students: Categories and generalizations. *Sociology of Education, 77*(2), 180–183.

Ogbu, J. (1999). *Collective identity and schooling.* Paper presented at the annual meeting of the Japan Society of Education and Sociology, Tokyo.

Pearl, A. (1991). Democratic education: Myth or reality. In R. Valencia (Ed.), *Chicano school failure and success* (pp. 101–118). New York: Falmer Press.

Planty, M., Hussar, W., Snyder, T., Provasnik, S., Kena, G., Dinkes, R., Kewal Ramani, A., & Kemp, J. (2008). *The condition of education 2008.* NCES 2008–031. Washington, DC: National Center for Education Statistics, Institute of Education Sciences, U.S. Department of Education.

Rebell, M. A., & Thurston, E. K. (2008). Ensuring quality standards, assessments, and progress requirements. In M. A. Rebell & J. R. Wolff, *Moving every child ahead: From NCLB hype to meaningful educational opportunity* (pp. 109–131). New York: Teachers College Press.

Rhodes, R., Ochoa, S. H., & Ortiz, S. (2005). *Assessing culturally and linguistically diverse students: A practical guide.* New York: Guilford.

Roos, P. (1984, July). *Legal guidelines for bilingual administrators.* Austin, TX: Society of Research in Child Development.

Stritikus, T. (2002). *Immigrant children and the politics of English-only: Views from the classroom.* New York: LFB Scholarly Publishing.

Tharp, R. G., & Gallimore, R. (1989). Rousing schools to life. *American Educator, 13*(2), 20–25, 46–52.

Trueba, H. T. (1987). *Success or failure? Learning and the language minority student.* New York: Harper & Row.

U.S. Department of Education. (n.d.) *Executive summary of the No Child Left Behind Act of 2001.* Retrieved June 8, 2004, from http://www.ed.gov/nclb/overview/intro/execsumm.html

U.S. Department of Education, Office of Elementary and Secondary Education. (2002). *Outline of programs and selected changes in the No Child Left Behind Act of 2001.* Washington, DC: Author.

U.S. Department of Education, Office of English Language Acquisition, Language Enhancement, and Academic Achievement for Limited English Proficient Students. (2003). *Non-regulatory guidance on the Title III state formula grant program.* Washington, DC: Author.

Valenzuela, A. (1997). Mexican American youth and the politics of caring. In E. Long (Ed.), *From sociology to cultural studies* (pp. 322–350). London: Blackwell.

Valenzuela, A. (1999). *Subtractive schooling: U.S.–Mexican youth and the politics of caring.* Albany: State University of New York Press.

Walberg, H. J. (1986). Synthesis of research on teaching. In M. C. Wittrock (Ed.), *Third handbook of research on teaching* (pp. 214–229). Washington, DC: American Educational Research Association.

Wilson, W. J. (1978). *The declining significance of race.* Chicago: University of Chicago Press.

Zehr, M. A. (2005, June 15). State testing of English language learners scrutinized. *Education Week,* pp. 3, 12.

CHAPTER 4

Standards, Assessments, and Accountability for Students with Disabilities

An Evolving Meaning of a "Free and Appropriate Public Education"

Margaret J. McLaughlin,
Meredith Miceli,
and Amanda Hoffman

The education of students with disabilities in today's schools is shaped by two very powerful laws: the 2004 Individuals with Disabilities Education Improvement Act (IDEA) and the No Child Left Behind Act (NCLB), enacted in 2002. These two laws signal a new vision for special education and require a major reconsideration of the role of special education in schools and the students who should receive it. However, this reshaping of special education occurs within a context of great ambiguity and contention resulting from the inherent tension between the fundamental entitlement of students with disabilities to an individual education, as laid out in IDEA, and the concept of universal standards and accountability that forms the foundation of NCLB.

This chapter explores the sources of that tension, including the core policy goals and assumptions that underlie both disability and standards-based policies, and examines the preliminary results, that is, how students with disabilities are faring under the new accountability systems mandated by NCLB. It concludes with speculation about where the evolving policies may lead educators as they grapple with the meaning of special education.

THE TENSION BETWEEN NCLB AND IDEA

There is a fundamental tension between NCLB's concept of universal or common standards for all students and the core policies of IDEA. To understand the source of the tension better, it is important to recognize the policy goals underlying disability legislation. As conceptualized by Silverstein (2000), four major goals guide all federal laws and other policies pertaining to children and adults with disabilities. These are *individualization, integration or inclusion, economic self-sufficiency*, and *self-determination or self-advocacy*.

The goal of individualization is central to all disability policies and arises from the very heterogeneous nature of disabilities and of their impact on functioning. It requires that each person with a disability be considered in terms of his or her strengths and needs and that accommodations, supports, and services be provided on an individual basis in relation to those particular needs. No program or policy should be designed solely on the basis of general categories, labels, or other classification schema. In IDEA, the concept of individualization is centered on the core entitlement to a "free and appropriate public education" (FAPE), which is developed through an individualized educational program, or IEP.

A second important policy goal is the full integration or inclusion of persons with disabilities into all aspects of the school, community, and workplace as well as in the policies that govern these entities. Within IDEA, the focus on inclusion comes from the "least restrictive environment" (LRE) provision, requiring that an appropriate education be provided in or as close to the regular classroom as feasible in the school that the child would have attended if he or she did not have a disability. It is also found in IEP requirements that students with disabilities access and progress in the general education curriculum. This goal was also a driving force behind the inclusion of students with disabilities in standards reforms, beginning with Goals 2000: Educating America's Children Act of 1994.

The third goal is preparing individuals with disabilities for meaningful and self-sustaining employment. Enhancing employability is a major focus of Section 504 of the Vocational Rehabilitation Act (Sec. 504), IDEA, and the Americans with Disabilities Act (ADA), as well as several programs under the Social Security Act (SSA). Within IDEA, transition planning and articulation with post-school institutions and agencies that support or promote employment dominates secondary school special education.

Finally, self-determination and self-advocacy are emerging as a fourth major goal in policy for individuals with disabilities; this is a reaction to a historic paternalism, protectiveness, and lack of regard for the preferences and choices of persons with disabilities. New policies, including the transition provisions in IDEA, require that students with disabilities be involved in making decisions about their lives, such as their course of study, post-school goals, and the services and supports they need to achieve their goals.

The four policy goals respond to the significant variation in functioning among persons with disabilities as well as their history of exclusion, segregation, and discrimination. They focus on support and habilitation of the individual and on the rights and entitlements of the individual with a disability. Disability policy assumes that the individual is the bearer of rights and, thus, equality of opportunity must be interpreted on an individual basis.

These individually oriented policy goals for students with disabilities contrast and are in tension with the central policy goal driving current models of standards-based reforms, which is to close the achievement gap between privileged students and those who are members of historically disadvantaged groups. The standards-based theory of action behind NCLB assumes that individuals in all groups can and should attain the same outcomes and that outcome differences among groups result from lack of opportunity. The standards-based theories were developed in relation to the problems of racial and ethnic minority groups and do not fit as easily into the special education context.

While both IDEA and NCLB intend to increase opportunities and improve outcomes, there is a tension between the two policy frameworks. To help to elucidate the complexity of the policies governing their education, we need first to review the characteristics of students with disabilities.

STUDENTS WITH DISABILITIES

Students who are identified as having disabilities in U.S. schools are covered primarily by one or both of two federal laws: IDEA and Section 504 of the Rehabilitation Act. Eligibility under IDEA requires first that a student be determined to have one or more of the 13 disabilities specified in the law and, second, that the disability have an adverse educational impact on the student. As mentioned above, under IDEA, eligible students are entitled to an individually designed education that includes tailored instruction and related services as determined through the development of an IEP. The IEP requirements within IDEA are quite extensive and prescriptive, and can encompass any level of specialized or unique service or support that an individual student may require to obtain a "free and appropriate public education." We will discuss what constitutes "appropriate" later in this chapter.

Section 504 of the Rehabilitation Act typically includes students who meet the broad definition of having a physical or mental impairment that substantially limits one or more major life activities. (The Americans with Disabilities Act [ADA] reinforces Section 504 and the Office of Civil Rights interprets

ADA as incorporating all Section 504 protections.) Most, but not all, students covered under Section 504 meet the eligibility requirements of IDEA. Under Section 504, students are entitled to reasonable accommodations that enable them to access the same education provided to their nondisabled peers, including alterations to the physical environment as well as instructional and assessment accommodations as specified in an individual accommodation plan (Council of Administrators of Special Educators, 2006).

Data on Students with Disabilities

The U.S. Department of Education requires that states report annually on the number, type of disability, and race/ethnicity of students served under IDEA. As of fall 2006, the most recent date for which data are available, a total of 6,081,890 students with disabilities, ages 6–21, were served under IDEA. This number represented about 9% of the general 6- to 21-year-old population living in the United States at the time (U.S. Department of Education, 2007a).

Students with learning disabilities accounted for 46% of the students with disabilities (U.S. Department of Education, 2007a), down from 51% in 1997, but representing an increase of over 300% since the passage of the original federal special education legislation in 1975 (U.S. Department of Education, 2003). Following this group are the students with speech and language impairments (19%); mental retardation (9%); emotional disturbance (8%); and "other health impaired" (10%), which includes students identified as having attention-deficit/hyperactivity disorder (ADHD). All other categories account for about 9% of all students with IEPs (U.S. Department of Education, 2007a). According to a national report on the implementation of IDEA (O'Reilly et al., 2006), in 2003, males accounted for almost two-thirds of the students ages 6–17 served under IDEA. In students ages 6–12, males represent 80% of students with emotional disturbance and 83% of the students with autism, and in ages 13–17, males represent 77% of students with emotional disturbance and 85% of students with autism.

Cross-sectional data such as those presented above provide a snapshot of which students have IEPs, but they mask the variation across and within states. Also, the numbers and disability classifications change across grades as students move in and out of special education. The number of students entering special education peaks in upper elementary grades and in middle school and then begins to drop off through high school (U.S. Department of Education, 2007d). There are several possible reasons for this peak, including the fact that many students are referred for evaluation only after experiencing several years of failure and/or behavioral problems. In part, the peak may reflect the fact that elementary schools are better able to deal with or tolerate some of the problems presented by low achievers, but it is also possible that the severity of problems, particularly behavioral and emotional disorders, increases over time. At the secondary level, dropping out is a major problem and likely accounts for the decrease in numbers (U.S. Department of Education, 2008b).

Some students are declassified. Data obtained from several nationally representative studies found that, overall, 17% of elementary- and middle-school-age students with disabilities were declassified over a 2-year period that extended from 2000 to 2002 (O'Reilly et al., 2006). Most of these were students with speech and language impairments. The likelihood of leaving special education services was not associated with students' grade level, gender, or race/ethnicity. However, students living in households with annual incomes greater than $50,000 were more likely to be declassified (21%) than those in the lowest income bracket of below $25,000 (13%) (O'Reilly et al., 2006).

Classification of Learning Disabilities

A growing number of students have been identified as having a learning disability. As noted earlier, this group has increased some 300% since the disability was included among those covered under IDEA. Its inclusion did not occur until 2 years after the passage of the 1975 Education of All Handicapped Children Act, and only after a great deal of contentious debate. At the time, governors and state education officials were concerned that, without a clear and reliable definition, the number of children identified as having a learning disability would explode and overwhelm school budgets (Levine & Wexler, 1981).

The 2004 IDEA included amendments changing how schools may identify learning disabilities. Local school districts may now use a new evaluation procedure that determines whether the child responds to scientific, research-based interventions (IDEA, 2004, sec. 1414). The model, commonly referred to as "response to intervention" (RTI), requires that a set of increasingly intensive academic interventions, including small-group and one-on-one instruction, be provided in the general education classroom by the general education teacher with careful monitoring of progress. Only students who fail to progress after receiving the controlled interventions are referred for special education evaluation (Fuchs & Deshler, 2007).

Racial and Ethnic Disproportionality

Table 4.1 presents the racial and ethnic composition by disability categories for students with IEPs.

Table 4.1. Students Age 6 Through 21 Served under IDEA, Part B, by Race/ Ethnicity and Disability Category (in Percentages): Fall 2006

Type of Disability	American Indian/ Alaskan Native	Asian/ Pacific Islander	Black (Not Hispanic)	Hispanic	White
Specific learning disabilities	1.74	1.70	20.52	21.22	54.82
Speech or language impairments	1.35	3.15	15.44	17.53	62.52
Mental retardation	1.28	2.11	32.75	14.08	49.79
Emotional disturbance	1.56	1.12	28.79	11.09	57.44
Multiple disabilities	1.36	2.70	20.91	13.23	61.79
Hearing impairments	1.26	4.98	16.25	22.71	54.81
Orthopedic impairments	0.97	3.52	14.82	20.94	59.75
Other health impairments	1.25	1.49	17.39	9.85	70.02
Visual impairments	1.36	4.23	17.18	18.04	59.18
Autism	0.74	5.35	14.36	11.56	67.98
Deaf-blindness	1.91	4.10	13.87	18.61	61.50
Traumatic brain injury	1.62	2.53	16.49	13.19	66.17
Developmental delay[a]	3.69	2.66	22.43	9.83	61.40

[a]Developmental delay is applicable only to children ages 3 through 9.
Source: IDEAData.org, https://www.ideadata.org/tables30th/ar_1-19.xls

National data such as these indicate that black students are 2.99 times more likely to be classified as having mental retardation and 2.21 times more likely to be classified as having emotional disturbance than all other racial/ ethnic groups combined. Meanwhile, Asian/Pacific Islander students are less than half as likely to be identified as having specific learning disabilities, mental retardation, emotional disturbance, or other health impairments than all other groups combined.

The issues surrounding disproportionate representation are not new to special education; they have been examined by two National Research Council committees (Donovan & Cross, 2002; Heller, Holtzman, & Messick, 1982). A major conclusion of these committees was that the disproportionate representation of black and Hispanic students in special education results from the failure of general education to support individual students who have learning and/or behavioral difficulties. In this view, the "disability" is constructed or created as a result of barriers imposed by curriculum policies and inadequate human and other resources rather than a deficit within the child (Donovan & Cross, 2002). Other factors noted by the committees that contribute to disproportionate representation are ambiguous or broad definitional criteria and longstanding issues with the biased psychometric assessment tools used in diagnosis, specifically IQ tests (Donovan & Cross, 2002; Heller et al., 1982).

While race issues have been studied extensively, relatively less is known about the relationship between poverty and special education classification. One national study reported that 36% of elementary and secondary students who are identified as having a disability and who are receiving special education services live in households with an income less than $25,000. This compares with about 24% of general education students (O'Reilly et al., 2006).

Early Intervention Services

In recognition of the critical role of early intervention in reducing inappropriate referrals and special education identification, the 2004 IDEA amendments included a new provision, Early Intervening Services (EIS). This provision requires local school districts with a "significant disproportionality" based on race or ethnicity in classification, LRE, and/or suspensions and expulsions of students with disabilities to spend 15% of their federal special education funds on students who have not been identified as needing special education or related services but who need additional academic and behavioral support to succeed in a general education environment.

The new IDEA provisions, Early Intervention Services and response to intervention, signal that the construct of "disability" as it pertains to the entitlement to special education is changing. These changes affirm that special education is not a remedial or compensatory program for hard-to-teach students or a safety net for poor general education curriculum and instruction. Rather, specially designed education as defined by the IDEA is intended for students "with a disability." In today's policy environment, however, it is less clear which students fall into that group; given the focus on educating students with disabilities in the least restrictive environment and the specific policy demands of NCLB, the line between what is special education and what is general education is blurring.

WHERE STUDENTS WITH DISABILITIES ARE EDUCATED

Moving students with disabilities from separate schools and self-contained special education classrooms into the educational mainstream has been one of the centerpieces of IDEA policy. Current federal regulations define *least restrictive environment* in terms of a continuum of placements, ranging from the regular classroom to separate residential schools, hospitals, and even the home. Least restrictive environment is measured in terms of the proportion of a school day that a student is educated outside of a general education classroom. In 2006, nearly 54% of students were educated in a general education classroom 80% or more of their school day, 24% were outside the general education classroom 21–60% of the time, and 17% were educated in separate classrooms more than 60% of their day. An additional 5% received their education in a separate public or private school, residential facility, or other setting (e.g., correctional facility, home, or hospital environment) (U.S. Department of Education, 2007b). The movement of children into general education classrooms has accelerated over recent years. For example, in 2001, around 48% of students with disabilities were educated in general education classrooms 80% or more of the time (U.S. Department of Education, 2006b).

The least restrictive environment data vary by disability and by race/ethnicity as well as across states. For example, in 2006, on average 55% of students identified as having a learning disability were educated 80% or more each day in general education classrooms, compared with 35% of the students with emotional disturbance and 16% of students with mental retardation (U.S. Department of Education, 2007b). As a group, black students are more likely to receive their education in segregated settings. In 2005, nearly one-fourth of black students with disabilities were educated outside of the regular classroom more than 60% of the time, compared with 20% of Hispanic students and 13% of white students (U.S. Department of Education, 2006a).

Students with Disabilities and NCLB

Under NCLB, states must establish challenging standards, implement assessments that measure students' performance against those standards, and hold schools and school systems accountable for the achievement of all students. Indeed, under the law, *all* students must reach proficiency levels on challenging tests in reading and mathematics by 2014. Each year between 2002 and 2014 schools must achieve a designated rate of adequate yearly progress (AYP) toward that goal. NCLB also requires schools to be accountable for the proficiency and achievement of AYP targets by each specific student subgroup of sufficient size in each school, including the subgroup of students who receive special education services.

- The focus on subgroups of students in NCLB is important, as it permits an unprecedented level of scrutiny of the performance of diverse groups of students. It marks a victory of sorts for disability advocates who lobbied unsuccessfully to include students with disabilities in the original ESEA.
- Students with disabilities are expected to participate in all aspects of Title I of NCLB. The regulations define how students with disabilities will be assessed and how schools will be held accountable for their performance. The U.S. Department of Education expects that the majority of students with disabilities will take the regular assessment with or without accommodations, but some exceptions and variations to the general rules have been put into effect for students with disabilities.

Prior to the passage of NCLB, students with disabilities were required to participate in state and local assessments; however, IDEA did not specifically mandate inclusion of assessment results in state or district accountability systems (Thurlow, 2004). In fact, as states implemented their assessment and accountability systems throughout the latter part of the 1990s, students with disabilities were erratically and inconsistently included. Few states reported the assessment results of all of their students with disabilities, and even fewer states had implemented and reported student performance on alternate assessments (Thurlow, 2004).

Alternate Achievement Standards. Two specific NCLB regulations attempt to consider the heterogeneity of the subgroup of students with disabilities. In December 2003, the USDOE issued regulations for the inclusion of students with "the most significant cognitive disabilities" in Title I assessments (p. 68702). These regulations grant states the flexibility to measure the achievement of students with disabilities, not to exceed 1% of the tested population, against alternate achievement standards (NCLB, 2002, sec. 200.1(d)) and to count at the local and state levels the scores of these students deemed proficient or advanced under the alternate standards as proficient in the calculation of AYP (NCLB, 2002, sec. 200.13(c)(1)(i)). An alternate achievement standard was defined as "an expectation of performance that differs in complexity from a grade-level achievement standard" (U.S. Department of Education, 2005, p. 20). It is important to note that only the achievement standards are permitted to be altered. All students with disabilities must be instructed in grade-level content regardless of the student's cognitive functioning (Kohl, McLaughlin, & Nagle, 2006).

Modified Achievement Standards. In April 2007, the USDOE issued another set of regulations permitting states to adopt "modified" achievement standards. These modified standards are intended for a small group of children, in addition to the "1% students," whose disabilities preclude them from achieving grade-level proficiency and whose progress is such that they will not reach grade-level achievement standards in the same time frame as other students. Proficient scores of students who are held to modified standards may be included in AYP calculations at any level, up to 2% of the tested population. The regulations require that states provide guidance to IEP teams regarding how to determine which students should be held to modified achievement standards. But modified academic achievement standards must be based on a state's grade-level academic content standard and the student's IEP must include goals that are based on the academic content standards for the grade in which the student is enrolled. The state must ensure that students are not assessed based on modified academic achievement standards merely because of their disability category or their racial or economic background (U.S. Department of Education, 2007c).

Requiring that students with disabilities have access to the same grade-level subject-matter content standards as well as achieve at specific levels is a significant shift from the notion of an "appropriate" education as one that is individually determined through the IEP team. As a result of the movement toward standards-based education, there has been a shift in thinking about the role of the IEP, the central document in the IDEA procedural system.

The IEP and Standards-Based Education

In 1997, some major changes were made to the IEP provisions in IDEA. Language was added to require students with disabilities to participate in state and local assessments and to require IEP teams to consider how these students would access and progress in the general education curriculum. The 2004 IDEA amendments went further in aligning the IEP to NCLB and in ensuring that students with IEPs have the full opportunity to learn the same content specified in state standards.

To reconcile the IEP policies with the NCLB requirements, there is a move by states to create "standards-based IEPs" whose goals are based on state-defined content standards (Ahearn, 2006). These IEPs are distinguished by goals that align with or restate state standards but that "individualize" the specific supports and services that will be provided to students to enable them to progress toward attainment of the standards. In addition, the IEPs may include additional individualized nonacademic goals or access skills (e.g., vocational, social/behavioral, or therapeutic) required to meet the standards.

This represents a significant shift as, historically, the IEP has been both individually determined and divorced from general education curriculum and instruction. At the time of passage of the 1975 Education for All Handicapped Children Act (P.L. 94–142) Congress clearly indicated that the requirement for written IEPs was essential to achieving the ambitious goals of the special education legislation (Levine & Wexler, 1981; Zettel & Ballard, 1977). Individualized educational goals and services were considered necessary given the heterogeneity among the population and the lack of appropriate programs in many schools. Advocates also lobbied strenuously for the IEP provisions believing that a formal written document was necessary to hold states and local districts accountable for providing what was appropriate for an individual child. The IEP mandate prevailed in part because its development was to be a team process involving parents and local school representatives, who presumably would not agree to something that schools could not provide. Also, while the district was legally responsible for providing the services specified on the IEP, it was not legally responsible for failure in performance of a child with a disability (Levine & Wexler, 1981). However, the IEP soon began to be used as a contract that documented that a child was not denied his or her due process under the law (National Council on Disability, 1993; U.S. Department of Education, 1982; Wright, Cooperstein, Renneker, & Padilla, 1982).

Over the years, as the courts became involved in defining the meaning of a student's entitlement to a free and appropriate public education, they reinforced the use of the IEP as the manifestation of what constituted an "appropriate" education. *Board of Education of Hendrick Hudson Central School District* v. *Rowley* (1982) is the first and only Supreme Court case to have ruled on the "appropriate" standard. The Court held that, in order to be "appropriate," the special education and related services provided to a child with a disability must be designed in conformity with mandated procedures and timelines and must be reasonably calculated to confer some educational benefit. Lower courts, in applying the *Rowley* standard, have had no difficulty in judging procedural integrity, but tend to defer to educators' opinions about what constitutes educational benefit for any given child (McDonnell, McLaughlin, & Morison, 1997; Pullin, 2008). Over the years, there have been various attempts to raise the substantive requirements for what constitutes a free and appropriate public education (see, for example, Johnson, 2003), but without great success.

As yet, it is unclear exactly what a "standards-based IEP" will look like, but undoubtedly its legal and accountability functions would remain. It seems likely that IEP teams would have less discretion in determining what content an individual student is taught, but rather their role would be to determine what constitutes "appropriate" instruction and necessary supports and services to enable the student to learn the content. In this way, the policy goal, as opposed to the legal standard, for interpreting a free and appropriate public education is shifting from individual determinations of "reasonable educational benefit" to attainment of universal standards.

CLOSING THE ACHIEVEMENT GAP

In the previous sections we have described some of the more pertinent changes that have been made to IDEA and NCLB in an attempt to align standards-driven reforms with traditional special education policy goals, specifically individualization and inclusion. However, these changes are not sufficient unless they also lead to better post-school outcomes. Thus, it is important to examine the degree to which the goal to close the achievement gap is being realized for students with disabilities.

Educational Outcomes and Academic Performance

Until recently, very little was known about the aggregate academic performance or other educational outcomes of students with disabilities. These students were routinely exempted from the National Assessment of Educational Progress (NAEP) as well as from state and local assessments unless they were able to participate without accommodations. Moreover, when these students did participate, their scores were often excluded from assessment reports or not disaggregated (McLaughlin & Thurlow, 2003).

Since the 1997 reauthorization of IDEA, students with disabilities have had to be included in state and local assessments with appropriate accommodations, and their results have been reported both as part of overall student performance and disaggregated, as is now also required by NCLB. In addition, beginning in 1998, students with disabilities were permitted to have accommodations on the NAEP test and their scores were disaggregated.

NAEP Data. In 1996, the U.S. Department of Education began efforts to study the effect of assessment accommodations for students with disabilities on NAEP results. It initiated a transition in which official NAEP reporting samples would come to include students assessed with accommodations. The national samples for the NAEP science and mathematics assessments were split between settings in which testing accommodations were allowed and settings in which they were not. This enabled the program to link data trends to the past, to study the effects of providing assessment accommodations, and to begin new trend baselines in which accommodations were allowed. NAEP's guidelines to schools for determining which students should participate in the assessment were also revised.

Beginning with the 2002 assessments, NAEP has offered accommodations to all students who need them. The provision of accommodations increased the numbers of students with disabilities included in NAEP testing. As an example, in the 2006 civics test, between 10% and 13% of the 4th-, 8th-, and 12th-grade samples were identified as students with disabilities, and between 2% and 3% of these students were excluded from testing because the IEP team had determined that the student could not participate in assessments such as NAEP or the student required accommodations that NAEP did not permit (U.S. Department of Education, 2008a).

Figures 4.1–4.6 display the assessment data from the NAEP data viewer (U.S. Department of Education, n.d.). For each of the years the NAEP data were reported, mean outcomes in reading for students with disabilities were significantly lower than mean outcomes for students without disabilities at 4th, 8th, and 12th grades. The reading data indicate that 4th-grade students with disabilities had a higher average score and a higher percentage scoring at or above proficient in 2007 than in any of the previous year's data. Eighth-grade students with disabilities had a higher average score in 2007 than in 2003, but the apparent increase between 1998 and 2007 was not statistically significant. In addition, the percentage of 8th graders with disabilities who performed at or above proficient in 2007 was not significantly different from any of the previous years, and was lower in 2005 than in 2002. The NAEP reading data for 12th-grade students were reported in 1998, 2002, and 2005 only. Average reading scores in 2005 for students with disabilities were not significantly different from average reading scores in 2002 or 1998.

Figure 4.1. Percentages of 4th-Grade Students with and without Disabilities at or Above Proficiency and Below Proficiency for Reading: 1998, 2000, 2002, 2003, 2005, and 2007

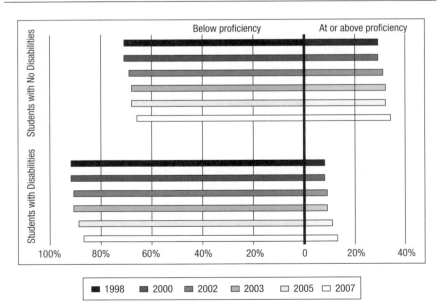

Figure 4.2. Percentages of 8th-Grade Students with and without Disabilities at or Above Proficiency and Below Proficiency for Reading: 1998, 2002, 2003, 2005, and 2007

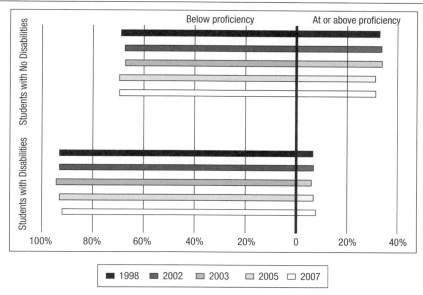

Figure 4.3. Percentages of 12th-Grade Students with and without Disabilities at or Above Proficiency and Below Proficiency for Reading: 1998, 2002, and 2005

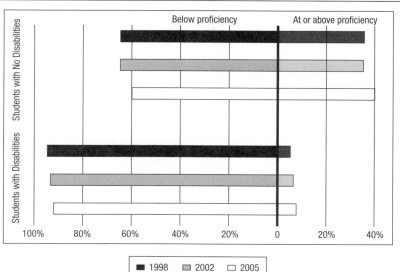

It is notable that the percentage of students at or above proficient for 12th-grade students with disabilities was lower than for 8th-grade students and 4th-grade students, and that the percentage at or above proficient was lower for 8th-grade students than for 4th-grade students in 2005, the only consistent year across all grades. In addition, the disparity between students with disabilities and students without disabilities was greater in the 12th and 8th grades than in the 4th grade.

The trends for the students with disabilities in mathematics were similar to the trends in reading, although there appeared to be greater increases in the percentage of students at or above basic for 4th-grade and 8th-grade students in math than in reading (Figures 4.4, 4.5, and 4.6). It is important to note that the NAEP math assessment for 12th-grade students was updated in 2005, and the difference in the assessment should be considered in making comparisons. As in reading, for each of the years the NAEP data were reported, mean outcomes in mathematics for students with disabilities were significantly lower than mean outcomes for students with no disabilities at 4th, 8th, and 12th grades. In mathematics, students with disabilities had a higher average score and a higher percentage performing at or above proficient in 2005 than in any previous assessment year at grades 4, 8, and 12. However, less than 10% of 8th-grade and 12th-grade students with disabilities were at or above proficient in 2005.

Figure 4.4. Percentages of 4th-Grade Students with and without Disabilities at or Above Proficiency and Below Proficiency for Math: 1998, 2000, 2003, 2005, and 2007

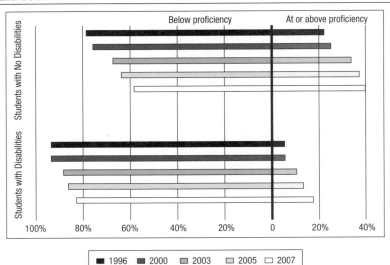

Figure 4.5. Percentages of 8th-Grade Students with and without Disabilities at or Above Proficiency and Below Proficiency for Math: 1996, 2000, 2003, 2005, and 2007

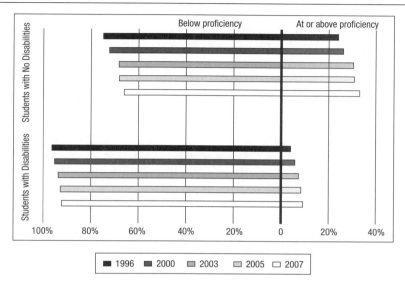

Figure 4.6. Percentages of 12th-Grade Students with and without Disabilities at or Above Proficiency and Below Proficiency for Math: 1996, 2002, and 2005

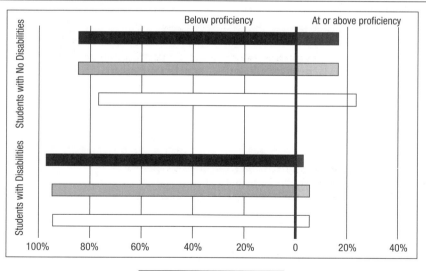

State Assessments for NCLB. It is difficult to draw any definitive conclusions about the overall performance of students with disabilities on state assessments due to the variation among state assessment instruments and accommodation policies. However, states' annual performance reports (APR) contain information on a variety of indicators, including assessment participation and performance results for state assessments. The state assessment data submitted by states are summarized by the National Center on Educational Outcomes (NCEO) using a common approach to construct numerators and denominators for determining percentages. Under NCLB, each state is required to establish, at minimum, three performance levels–basic, proficient, and advanced–for the state assessments. However, some states report five levels (e.g., below basic, basic, proficient, advanced, very advanced). Each state has established a level of performance regarded as proficient.

The data, as reported to the NCEO, include the numbers of students with disabilities tested and the percentage scoring at each of the state's performance levels. We collapsed the data from each state into two categories: proficient and nonproficient, and then aggregated them at the national level. Figures 4.7 and 4.8 display the percentages of students with disabilities at the proficient and nonproficient levels, as reported by the states. This includes all students taking regular assessments with and without accommodations. In general, approximately 61–65% of students with IEPs used accommodations on the regular assessment.

Figure 4.7 displays the percentages of special education students at proficient and nonproficient levels on state reading assessments as reported by the NCEO. In 3rd grade, less than 40% of the students scored in the proficient range, with some variability across the years. There is a decreasing trend in the percentage of students at the proficient level as grade level increases, although the percentage of 12th-grade students at the proficient level is slightly higher than the percentage of 8th-grade students at or above the proficient level for each of the 3 years reported.

Figure 4.8 displays the percentages of special education students at proficient and nonproficient levels on state mathematics assessments as reported by the NCEO. At the 3rd-grade level, a greater percentage of the special education students scored at the proficient level than on the reading assessment, with more than 40% achieving proficiency in 2003–2004 and in 2005–2006. However, the decreasing trend as grade level increases is greater for the math assessment than for the reading assessment; on the 8th-grade assessment, less than 20% of the students scored at the proficient level for 2 of the 3 years, including the 2005–2006 year.

A number of researchers have noted that both the characteristics of students with disabilities and assessment policies (i.e., accommodation policies) can significantly influence interpretations of performance (Almond, Lehr,

Figure 4.7. Percentages of Special Education Students at Proficient and Nonproficient Levels on State Reading Assessments as Reported by the NCEO: 2002–2003, 2003–2004, 2005–2006

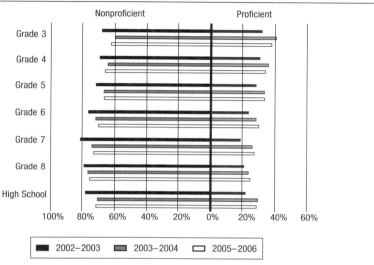

Figure 4.8. Percentages of Special Education Students at Proficient and Nonproficient Levels on State Math Assessments as Reported by the NCEO: 2002–2003, 2003–2004, 2005–2006

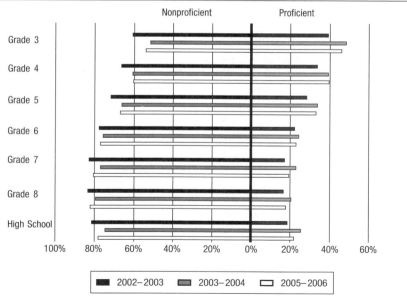

Thurlow, & Quenemoen, 2002; Embler, 2006; McLaughlin & Thurlow, 2003). Ysseldyke and Nelson (2002) identified 20 factors that are critical to an accurate understanding of assessment data for students with disabilities. Among these are the heterogeneity and size of the subgroup, the movement of students in and out of special education, and assessment accommodation policies. For example, in examining the relationship between mobility and academic achievement within one state, Ysseldyke and Bielinski (2003) found that the achievement scores of students who exited special education were a much higher-achieving group (roughly 0.50 standard deviations higher) than those who remained in special education. In contrast, the achievement scores of students who entered special education were much lower than those who exited special education (an average of 0.75 standard deviations below). This movement of students in and out of special education results in unstable groups from year to year. Moreover, the relationship of this movement to academic achievement leads to a subgroup of increasingly lower-achieving students. This was addressed in the April 2007 NCLB regulations that permit schools to include in the subgroup of students with disabilities, for up to 2 years, those students who have exited special education (NCLB Regulation, 2007). Other factors that confound interpretation are the number of changes that state assessment and accountability programs have undergone in recent years, specifically those affecting students with disabilities, such as changing test accommodation policies and alternate assessments.

In terms of alternate assessments, the 1997 IDEA amendments required states to have alternate assessments for students with disabilities in place by July 2000. States responded to these policies in different ways (Browder, Spooner, Ahlgrim-Delzell, Flowers, & Karvonen, 2003; Kohl, McLaughlin, & Nagle, 2006). For instance, states used more than one type of alternate assessment and a number of these assessments were based on an alternate curriculum or set of standards that were essentially nonacademic (e.g., functional and vocational skills). The guidelines for who should participate in alternate assessments also differed substantially across the states. In 2003, the NCLB regulations clarified which students should participate in alternate assessments but also stated that they were to be aligned with grade-level content standards. The assessments had to be technically adequate, "off-level" assessments were not permitted and states were required to have clear participation guidelines. As a result, almost every state was forced to change its alternate assessments (Kohl et al., 2006).

Test accommodation policies have also been subject to changes as new assessments have been developed and the number and types of allowable accommodations have increased. Nevertheless, there is a great deal of variation across states in terms of which accommodations are permitted for which types of assessments (Lazarus, Thurlow, Eisenbraun, Lail, Matchett,

& Quenemoen, 2006). In addition, teachers and IEP team members are not always well informed about accommodation policies or how to administer them (Lazarus, Thompson, & Thurlow, 2006). All of these factors make it difficult to compare their performance with other students. However, other indicators, beyond test scores, test participation rates, and the achievement gap, may help gauge the benefits of current accountability policy for students with disabilities. One such indicator is changing special education practices in schools.

Changing the Role of Special Education

From the beginning of the standards movement, advocates and many special educators have pushed for students with disabilities to be included in all aspects of the new educational policies so that they, too, could benefit from increased accountability and achievement expectations (McLaughlin & Thurlow, 2003). Advocates and policymakers also hoped that including students with disabilities in the curriculum and assessments would push schools toward educating more students with disabilities in general education classrooms. There is evidence that the standards movement is changing the historic separation of special education from mainstream education and providing students with disabilities opportunities to have greater access to high-quality curriculum. Results from a longitudinal four-state study conducted by researchers at the University of Maryland and National Center on Educational Outcomes documented that many teachers and administrators perceive that students with disabilities are benefiting from NCLB policies despite the fact that the achievement data from the four states indicated a widening gap (Educational Policy Reform Research Institute, 2007). Among the findings from the case studies of the four states are those emphasizing how the expectations for students with disabilities have been altered and how schools have had to confront the reality that the poor performance of these students can be attributed to their lack of opportunity to receive grade-level instruction. Further, more of these students are receiving instruction in challenging grade-level subject matter, and many administrators who were interviewed reported surprise at the gains some students were making. The case studies also pointed to other areas that are changing, including a greater focus on increasing the skills of general education teachers so that they can work more effectively with students with disabilities and encouraging co-teaching and other collaboration between general and special education. The research clearly pointed to special education becoming less isolated within schools, but administrators also reported facing some major challenges as they attempted to raise achievement levels of students with disabilities. The two greatest challenges are the lack of both general and special education teachers who can instruct students with disabilities and the entrenched attitudes and beliefs about what students with disabilities can achieve.

The finding about the lack of teacher capacity to respond to the new demands is substantiated by national data showing that fewer than three-quarters of all beginning special education teachers report being certified for their main teaching assignment (O'Reilly et al., 2006). In an effort to provide students with disabilities access to general education curriculum, schools are including more of the students with disabilities in general education academic classrooms taught by general education teachers (O'Reilly et al., 2006). General and special education teachers also report using a variety of strategies, including co-teaching and differentiating instruction, to support the inclusion of students with disabilities in these classrooms (Educational Policy Reform Research Institute, 2007). As a result, the case studies revealed that in many schools, special and general education teachers share roles, teaching models, and professional development, not to mention a shared language grounded in a common curriculum.

An interesting example of "shared language" that emerged from the case study research is the emergence of a new way of classifying students with disabilities that is based on the "type" of assessment (i.e., alternate or grade level) a student will be using (Nagle & Thurlow, 2006). In the case study schools, it was common for special and general education teachers and administrators to refer to a student with a disability as "an alternate assessment" or "a regular assessment" student. Moreover, typically, those students who were taking an alternate assessment based on alternate achievement standards were seen as belonging to special education while other students were more likely to be considered a shared responsibility with general education.

In spite of the greater collaboration and merging of teachers' roles, special educators still perceive that they are primarily responsible for the achievement of students with disabilities. As part of the research noted above, a "collective responsibility" survey, adapted from the work of Lee and Smith (1996), was developed and administered to all special and general education teachers in a total of 10 elementary schools in three of the states. The survey that was administered as part of the interviews and site visits to schools that were considered high performing asked teachers to rate on a 1–5 scale the degree to which "all teachers in this school share responsibility" for improving the achievement and the behavior of students with and without disabilities. Results of surveys obtained from 140 teachers (108 general education versus 32 special education/specialists) indicated that most teachers (89% of general educators versus 85% of special educators) believe that their colleagues feel responsible for improving the performance of general educations students, but a lower percentage (75% of general educators versus 46%

of special educators) perceive that all teachers feel responsible when students with disabilities perform poorly. Further, 95% of general educators and 93% of special educators believe that most or nearly all general education teachers set high standards and expectations for students in their classrooms; 95% of general educators also believed that teachers set high standards and expectations for students with disabilities, compared with about 52% of the special educators (Nagle, Hernandez, Embler, McLaughlin, & Doh, 2006; Nagle & Malmgren, 2006).

One additional study supporting the finding of the interdependence of general and special education was conducted by Malmgren, McLaughlin, and Nolet (2005) based on data obtained from one of the local districts involved in the four-state study described earlier. It examined school-level variables that predict aggregate performance of students with disabilities. Assessment results in reading and math in 3rd, 5th, and 8th grades across two grade levels were analyzed using a series of hierarchical linear regressions. Of the variables considered, only the school-level performance of general education students added any predictive value to the model, after accounting for race and poverty.

THE FUTURE OF NCLB POLICIES AND STUDENTS WITH DISABILITIES

It is evident from the information presented earlier in this chapter that students with disabilities have posed a number of unique challenges to the implementation of standards-driven reforms and to NCLB. Thus far, we are not able to determine how many students and/or which students we might expect to reach current standards . . . even if the time were extended beyond 2014. Yet, closing the gap in achievement is not the only measure of success, and we cannot deny that students with disabilities are being provided the chance to learn what other students are learning. As we approach the reauthorization of NCLB, a number of proposals have been put forth for "fixing" the law for students as it pertains to students with disabilities. However, tinkering with the current law is unlikely to solve the fundamental tension between the policy goals of individualization and closing the achievement gap.

The goal of closing the achievement gap is grounded in the assumption that factors extrinsic to students, such as poor instruction and lack of resources, are holding back certain students and that these factors are alterable. Thus, better teachers, more resources, a more rigorous curriculum, and greater accountability will result in all student groups reaching the same level of achievement. This assumption, however, cannot be applied to all or even most students with disabilities. The standards for determining eligibility for special education require that potential causes of low achievement such as child's primary language and lack of prior exposure to evidence-based instruction must be ruled out. Thus, to consider that improving instruction will somehow be sufficient to permit a student to reach the same standard suggests that the student should not be eligible to receive special education in the first place.

No doubt the same factors that are assumed to close the achievement gap for low-income or minority students will also raise the achievement of students with disabilities. We also do not want to deny any individual student the opportunity to benefit from inclusion in the curriculum, assessments, and most of all, the accountability. However, we must be alert to the possibility that inclusion may also mean loss of opportunities for some students with disabilities to receive an education that may, in fact, better help them achieve the goals of economic self-sufficiency. The conundrum is how to find the middle ground between individualization and the fully inclusive educational policies and inclusion, and education that leads to meaningful employment. The resolution to the tension will lie in a reconsideration of both the construct of "disability" as it pertains to eligibility under IDEA and a reconsideration of the role and function of special education.

Redefining Special Education

The NCLB regulations governing the participation of students with disabilities in NCLB policies are attempts to accommodate the very heterogeneous group of students served under IDEA. At the same time, we are witnessing changes in the integration of special education personnel and practices in some schools and the assimilation of the majority of students with IEPs into general education. These developments, coupled with the recent changes to IDEA eligibility discussed earlier, point to a future scenario that may considerably alter special education policies and redefine the population that will be served.

In reality, there has always been a substantial overlap between the group of students who receive special education and other subgroups of low-achieving students, including low-income and African American and Hispanic students. In fact, there are basically three groups of students served under IDEA at any one time: a large group of mostly young students with speech and language delays; a larger group consisting of middle elementary through high school students with "socially constructed" (Donovan & Cross, 2002) disabilities, such as learning disabilities, emotional disturbance, "mild" mental retardation, and attention deficit disorders; and a much smaller group of students composed of those with clear and marked medically defined disabilities such as autism, significant mental retardation, sensory deficits, and the like. Many of the students in the first group are declassified, while those in the second group are often identified only after repeated failure in general education. Despite the meaningless labels, the majority of these students may in fact be products of inadequate general education instead of learners with unique or idiosyncratic needs that require vastly different or highly specialized curriculum and instruction. The students differ, for the most part, only in the degree of underachievement and/or behavior problems they exhibit compared with other students in the school and should be able to achieve at levels that correspond to their peers without IEPs if they are provided high-quality instruction in general education. Both the Early Intervention Services and response to intervention provisions represent initial efforts to deal with these problems.

It is the third group, comprised of students who are most likely held to alternate achievement standards as well as perhaps new modified achievement standards, that will require the highly individualized educational planning that has characterized the IEP. This group is estimated to represent a third or less of all students who currently have IEPs. It is also a group of students whom the federal special education law was designed to address . . . those for whom even the best regular education would not be enough or would be irrelevant. These students will certainly require instruction in some academic areas, but they will also need far more personalized planning and instruction and supports to realize post-school outcomes such as employment.

This "educational triage" would alter the current construct of "disability" as currently defined in IDEA and take special education policy back to its roots as an educational law constructed for students with clear and evident disabilities. It would also focus the resources on those students most in need of long-term specialized education and related services that support both access to general education curriculum as well as vocational and career education, as opposed to providing compensatory services to students whose only "disability" is poor or insufficient general education. While IDEA and NCLB policies support this direction, it will require that the expectations and standards for what constitutes general education be raised.

This new "vision" for special education might have arisen independent of NCLB. Certainly, the move to educate students with disabilities in general education classrooms was reducing the separation of general and special education. However, the mandatory public accountability required by NCLB clearly accelerated the changes in how special education operates in schools and school districts. In this respect, the theory of action underlying NCLB, that the standards, assessments, and accountability will motivate schools and teachers to change instruction, appears to be borne out when considering special education.

NOTE

Funding for this work was provided in part through the U.S. Department of Education, Office of Special Education Programs (Grant #H324P000004). Opinions expressed in this chapter are those of the authors, and do not necessarily reflect the views of the U.S. Department of Education or the Office of Special Education Programs.

REFERENCES

Ahearn, E. (2006). *Standards-based IEPs: Implementation in selected states.* Alexandria, VA: National Association of State Directors of Special Education.

Almond, P. J., Lehr, C., Thurlow, M. L., & Quenemoen, R. (2002). Participation in large-scale state assessment and accountability systems. In T. M. Haladyna (Ed.), *Large-scale assessment programs for all students: Validity, technical adequacy, and implementation* (pp. 341–370). Mahwah, NJ: Lawrence Erlbaum.

Board of Education of the Hendrick Hudson Central School District v. *Rowley*, 458 U.S. 176 (1982).

Browder, D., Spooner, F., Ahlgrim-Delzell, L., Flowers, C., & Karvonen, M. (2003). What we know and need to know about alternate assessment. *Exceptional Children, 70*(1), 45–61.

Council of Administrators of Special Educators. (2006). *Section 504 and ADA: Promoting student access. A resource guide for educators* (3rd ed.). Fort Valley, GA: Author.

Donovan, M. S., & Cross, C. T. (Eds.). (2002). *Minority students in special education and gifted education.* Washington, DC: National Academy of Sciences.

Educational Policy Reform Research Institute. (2007). *Profiles of reform: Four states' journeys to implement standards-based reform with students with disabilities.* College Park: University of Maryland.

Embler, S. D. (2006). *Evaluating schools based on the performance of students with disabilities: A comparison of status and value-added approaches.* Unpublished doctoral dissertation, University of Maryland, College Park.

Fuchs, D., & Deshler, D. D. (2007). What we need to know about responsiveness to intervention (and shouldn't be afraid to ask). *Learning Disabilities Research & Practice, 22,* 129–136.

Goals 2000: Educating America's Children Act, 20 U.S.C. § 5801 (1994).

Heller, K. A., Holtzman, W. H., & Messick, S. (Eds.). (1982). *Placing children in special education: A strategy for equity.* Washington, DC: National Academy Press.

Individuals with Disabilities Education Act of 1997, 20 U.S.C. § 1401 et seq.

Individuals with Disabilities Education Improvement Act of 2004, 20 U.S.C. § 1415 et seq.

Johnson, S. F. (2003). Reexamining *Rowley*: A new focus in special education law. *The Beacon: Journal of Special Education Law and Practice, 2*(2). Retrieved March 27, 2008, from http://www.harborhouselaw.com/articles/rowley.reexamine.johnson. htm

Kohl, F. L., McLaughlin, M. J., & Nagle, K. M. (2006). Alternate achievement standards and assessments: A descriptive investigation of 16 states. *Exceptional Children, 73*(1), 107–122.

Lazarus, S. S., Thompson, S. J., & Thurlow, M. L. (2006). *How students access accommodations in assessment and instruction: Results of a survey of special education teachers.* College Park: University of Maryland, Educational Policy Reform Research Institute.

Lazarus, S. S., Thurlow, M. L., Eisenbraun, K. D., Lail, K. E., Matchett, D. L., & Quenemoen, M. (2006). *State accommodations policies: Implications for the assessment of reading.* Minneapolis: University of Minnesota, Partnership for Accessible Reading Assessment.

Lee, V. E., & Smith, J. B. (1996). Collective responsibility for learning and its effects on gains in achievement for early secondary school students. *American Journal of Education, 104*(2), 103–147.

Levine, E. L., & Wexler, E. M. (1981). *PL 94–142: An act of Congress.* New York: Macmillan.

Malmgren, K., McLaughlin, M. J., & Nolet, V. (2005). Accounting for the performance of students with disabilities on statewide assessments. *Journal of Special Education, 39*(2), 86–96.

McDonnell, L. M., McLaughlin, M. J., & Morison, P. (Eds.). (1997). *Educating one and all: Students with disabilities and standards-based reform.* Washington, DC: National Academy Press.

McLaughlin, M. J., & Thurlow, M. (2003). Educational accountability and students with disabilities: Issues and challenges. *Journal of Educational Policy, 17*(4), 431–451.

Nagle, K., Hernandez, G., Embler, S., McLaughlin, M. J., & Doh, F. (2006). Characteristics of effective rural elementary schools for students with disabilities. *Rural Special Education Quarterly, 25*(3), 3–12.

Nagle, K., & Malmgren, K. W. (2006, April). *Increasing teacher collective responsibility for academic achievement and development of students with disabilities.* Paper presented at the annual meeting of the American Educational Research Association, San Francisco.

Nagle, K., & Thurlow, M. L. (2006, June). *Issues in the classification of students with disabilities revisited: Perspectives and purposes of disability classification systems.* Paper presented at the 4th Anglo-American Conference, Cambridge University, UK.

National Council on Disability. (1993). *Serving the nation's students with disabilities: Progress and prospects.* Washington, DC: Author.

No Child Left Behind Act of 2001, P.L. 107–110, § 1001 et seq. (2002).

No Child Left Behind Act Regulation, 34 C.F.R § 200.20 (2007).

O'Reilly, F., Fafard, M., Wagner, M., Brown, S. C., Fritts, J., Luallen, J., Carlson, E., blackorby, J., Hebbeler, K., & Chambers, J. (2006). *Improving results for students with disabilities: Key findings from the 1997 national assessment studies.* Bethesda, MD: Abt Associates.

Pullin, D. (2008). Individualizing assessment and opportunity to learn: Lessons from the education of students with disabilities. In P. Moss, D. Pullin, J. Gee, E. Haertel, & L. Young (Eds.), *Assessment, equity, and opportunity to learn* (pp. 109–135). New York: Cambridge University Press.

Silverstein, R. (2000). Emerging disability policy framework: A guidepost for analyzing public policy. *Iowa Law Review, 85*(5), 1691–1797.

Thurlow, M. L. (2004). Biting the bullet: Including special-needs students in accountability systems. In S. Fuhrman & R. Elmore (Eds.), *Redesigning accountability systems for education* (pp. 115–140). New York: Teachers College Press.

U.S. Department of Education. (n.d.). *NAEP data explorer.* Retrieved October 5, 2007, from http://nces.ed.gov/nationsreportcard/nde/

U.S. Department of Education. (2008a). *NAEP inclusion policy: Inclusion of special-needs students.* Retrieved May 23, 2007, from http://nces.ed.gov/nationsreportcard/about/inclusion.asp#history

U.S. Department of Education. (2008b). *Table 4–3. Students with disabilities served under IDEA, Part B, in the U.S. and outlying areas who exited school, by exit reason, reporting year, and student's age: 1995–96 through 2004–05* [Data file]. Retrieved April, 30, 2008, from https://www.ideadata.org/tables30th/ar_4–3.xls

U.S. Department of Education. (2007a). *Table 1–3. Students ages 6 through 21 served under IDEA, Part B, by disability category and state: Fall 2006* [Data file]. Retrieved from https://www.ideadata.org/tables30th/ar_1–3.xls

U.S. Department of Education. (2007b). *Table 2–2. Students ages 6 through 21 served under IDEA, Part B, by educational environment and state: Fall 2006* [Data file]. Retrieved from https://www.ideadata.org/tables30th/ar_2–2.xls

U.S. Department of Education. (2007c). Title I–Improving the Academic Achievement of the Disadvantaged; Individuals with Disabilities Education Act (IDEA); Final Rule. *Federal Register.* (34 CFR Parts 200 and 300). Retrieved from http://www.ed.gov/legislation/FedRegister/finrule/2007-2/040907a.html

U.S Department of Education. (2007d). *Table 1-1. Children and students served under IDEA, Part B, by age group and state: Fall 2006* [Data file]. Retrieved December 15, 2007, from https://www.ideadata.org/tables30th/ar_1–19.xls

U.S. Department of Education. (2006a). *Table 5-6: Number, percentage of racial/ethnic group, and difference from national baseline of children ages 6–21 served in different educational environments percentage based on total number of children ages 6–21 in racial/ethnic group: December 1, 2005* [Data file]. Retrieved from http://www.monitoringcenter.lsuhsc.edu/04–05%20B%20RANKED%20DATA%20OSEP%20POST%20030107/artbl5_6s.xls

U.S. Department of Education. (2006b). *Table 5-8: Number, percentage, difference from national baseline, and percent change in the percentage of students of children ages 6–21 served in different educational environments: Under IDEA, Part B: 2001 through 2005* [Data file]. Retrieved from http://www.monitoringcenter.lsuhsc.edu/04–05%20B%20RANKED%20DATA%20OSEP%20POST%20030107/artbl5_8s.xls

U.S. Department of Education. (2005). *U.S. Department of Education's fiscal year 2005 performance and accountability report.* Washington, DC: Author.

U.S. Department of Education. (2003). *Twenty-fifth annual report to Congress on the implementation of the Individuals with Disabilities Education Act.* Washington, DC: Office of Special Education and Rehabilitative Services.

U.S. Department of Education. (1982). *Fourth annual report to Congress on the implementation of Public Law 94–142: The Education for All Handicapped Children Act.* Washington, DC: Author

Wright, A. R., Cooperstein, R. A., Renneker, E. G., & Padilla, C. (1982). *Local implementation of P.L. 94–142: Final report of a longitudinal study.* Menlo Park, CA: SRI International.

Ysseldyke, J., & Bielinski, J. (2002). Effect of different methods of reporting and reclassification on trends in test scores for students with disabilities. *Exceptional Children, 68*(2), 189–200.

Ysseldyke, J. E., & Nelson, J. R. (2002). Reporting results of student performance on large-scale assessments. In G. Tindal & T. Haladyna (Eds.), *Large-scale assessment programs for all students: Development, implementation, and analysis.* New York: Lawrence Erlbaum.

Zettel, J., & Ballard, J. (1977). The Education for All Handicapped Children Act of 1975 (P.L. 94–142): Its history, origins, and concepts. In J. Ballard, B. A. Ramirez, & F. J. Weintraug (Eds.), *Special education in America: Its legal and governmental foundations* (pp. 11–22). Reston, VA: Council for Exceptional Children.

CHAPTER 5

"Proficiency for All"

- -

An Oxymoron

Richard Rothstein,
Rebecca Jacobsen, and Tamara Wilder

The No Child Left Behind Act (NCLB) states that all children shall "reach, at a minimum, proficiency on challenging State academic achievement standards and state academic assessments" (sec. 1001) by 2014 and that these standards must "contain coherent and rigorous content" and "encourage the teaching of advanced skills" (sec. 1111 (b)(1)(D)). The law does not further define "challenging" standards, but it is reasonable to infer such standards would challenge typical children to achieve at a higher level than their past performance. This inference is supported by the law's requirement that the National Assessment of Educational Progress (NAEP) be administered biennially in math and reading to a sample of 4th- and 8th-grade students in each state, providing a standard by which state judgments about proficiency can be compared. Furthermore, NCLB uses language to describe proficiency that parallels that of NAEP, whose definition of proficiency is "demonstrated competency over challenging subject matter" (Perie, Grigg, & Dion, 2005, p. 2). As Christopher T. Cross, appointed by the Department of Education in 2002 to coordinate rulemaking for NCLB, noted, NAEP "is supposed to be the benchmark for states, and that is why its use was expanded" in the act ("Chat Wrap Up," 2006).

The NCLB requirement that proficiency be "challenging" can also be traced to a series of articles on "systemic school reform" in the late 1980s and early 1990s that had an important influence on the development of federal accountability. In these, Marshall Smith and Jennifer O'Day proposed a program to create schools with "coherent and challenging instructional programs that genuinely engage all, or at least most of their students" (Smith & O'Day, 1991, p. 236).[1] They called for new standardized tests for accountability purposes that would "stand as a serious intellectual challenge for the student" (p. 244). The reform goal of "challenging content for all children," O'Day and Smith (1993) wrote, should take on "an aura of official policy," and although NAEP is not explicitly aligned with any state's curriculum, "we expect that it will be moderately sensitive to effects of curricula that emphasize challenging content" (pp. 262–263, 301).

Yet NCLB's requirement that *all* students be proficient in math and reading at the same "challenging" standards ignores the reality that, even under the best of circumstances and in the best schools, children's abilities vary widely. Indeed, human variation characterizes any trait we want to measure, whether it is academic achievement, height, weight, athletic ability, artistic inspiration, resistance to disease, or courage. Even if the law were to succeed in giving schools and teachers the incentive to pay inordinate attention to math and reading, it is practically and conceptually ludicrous to expect all students to reach identical levels of challenging proficiency. The law hopes to eliminate disparities based on children's race and socioeconomic status, but overlooks the reality that disparities within any race or social group are greater than the disparities between these groups.

Thus, while NAEP tests are excellent, their cut-off scores, defining a single point of proficiency that all students should achieve, have no credibility. The proficiency passing points are arbitrary, fancifully defined by panels of teachers, politicians, and lay people.

There is a considerable difference between feasible goals, which must be grounded in reality, and appropriate goals, which can mean anything the goal setters choose. In the 1988 congressional reauthorization of NAEP, the Senate bill instructed the National Assessment Governing Board (NAGB), NAEP's overseer, to "identify feasible achievement goals for each age and grade in each subject area under the National Assessment" (Vinovskis, 1998, p. 42). The final bill that emerged from the conference committee somehow substituted the word *appropriate* for *feasible*, so NAGB was now instructed to identify *appropriate*, not *feasible*, achievement goals (Vinovskis, 1998).

When NAGB attempted to carry out Congress's intent, it asked Terry Hartle, as Senator Edward Kennedy's chief education staff member and a drafter of the bill, to explain what it meant. Hartle stated that Congress's choice of language was "deliberately ambiguous" because neither congressional staff nor education experts were able to formulate it more precisely. "There was not an enormous amount of introspection" on the language, Hartle reported (Vinovskis, 1998, p. 42).

A few experts protested at the time. One was Harold Howe II, former U.S. Commissioner of Education, who had played an important role in developing the NAEP some 20 years before. Howe wrote to the Commissioner of Education Statistics,

> . . . [M]ost educators are aware that any group of children of a particular age or
> grade will vary widely in their learning for a whole host of reasons. To suggest
> that there are particular learnings or skill levels that should be developed to
> certain defined points by a particular age or grade . . . defies reality. (Vinovskis,
> 1998, p. 43)

Nor was Howe the first to sound such a warning. Six years before, when
momentum was first building for NAEP reports that went beyond scale
scores, the federal governing body for NAEP, then called the Assessment
Policy Committee, asked three foundations (Carnegie, Ford, and Spencer)
to finance a year-long study of NAEP and how it should be improved. The
foundations commissioned former U.S. Labor Secretary Willard Wirtz and
his colleague Archie Lapointe to conduct the study and they, in turn, convened an advisory council including the president of the Educational Testing
Service, prominent scholars, a corporate (IBM) official, and the deputy director of Great Britain's comparable educational assessment program (Lapointe
& Koffler, 1982; Wirtz & Lapointe, 1982).

The Wirtz-Lapointe report, presented to the Assessment Policy Committee in 1982, recommended that NAEP develop descriptions of what students
know and can do if they achieve scale scores at various levels. But the report
warned that NAEP should not define passing points or cut scores, which, the
report said, "would be easy, attractive, and fatal. . . . Setting levels of failure,
mediocrity, or excellence in terms of NAEP percentages would be a serious
mistake . . ." (pp. 32–33).

Most policymakers, however, endorsed the idea of a defined achievement level that would indicate whether U.S. students passed or failed the
NAEP exam. So, in 1990, while retaining the NAEP scale scores, NAGB
adopted performance level reporting as well (Vinovskis, 1998, p. 44).
Although initially NAGB intended to define only one achievement level,
proficiency, it eventually decided to establish three points on each NAEP
scale to describe achievement levels—basic, proficient, and advanced.

Proficiency was defined as the level of performance that *all* students
should achieve or, as NAGB policy further explained it, "the knowledge
and skills all students need to participate in our competitive economy . . .
and the levels of proficiency needed to handle college-level work" (Vinovskis, 1998, p. 44).

At the time NAGB made this pronouncement, approximately 29% of all
17-year-olds eventually went on to graduate from college. NAGB's unex-
amined assumption that the NAEP proficiency standard could be defined
at a level that would more than triple this rate to something like 100%
is another illustration of the fanciful thinking underlying the achievement
level process.

SUBJECTIVITY IN DETERMINING CUT SCORES

Today, many state standardized tests, used for measurement purposes under NCLB, employ similar terminology about the competitive economy and college readiness to describe their cut scores. In fact, there is nothing scientific about establishing these cut scores. All available methods require subjective decisions of panels of judges who decide what constitutes proficiency for a particular subject and grade. One common method is to ask each judge to imagine what a barely proficient student can generally do, and then estimate, for each question on a test, the probability that such a student will answer the question correctly. When each judge's estimates for such a probability for each question on the test are averaged together, and all the judges' average estimates are averaged together, the result is the minimum test score (in percentage correct) that a student must achieve to be deemed proficient. This is the method used to set the proficiency cut score for NAEP. Similar exercises were used to define basic and advanced performance (Livingston & Zieky, 1982).

The National Assessment Governing Board, consisting of 26 governors and other state education officials, classroom teachers, teachers' union officers, school administrators, and academic experts, hired contractors who, in turn, appointed panels of teachers, professors, business leaders, and other citizens to decide which NAEP questions a student should be expected to answer correctly if that student were deemed to be at the basic, proficient, or advanced level.[2] The panelists were given no standard by which to make these judgments except their own opinions.

In the case of mathematics, for example, NAGB established three panels of 20 judges, one for each of the grade levels tested—4th, 8th, and 12th. Of the 60 judges, 33 were schoolteachers, 9 were other educators, and 18 were members of the general public (Loomis & Bourque, 2001a). After each panelist decided what percentage of NAEP questions a basic, proficient, or advanced student should be able to answer correctly on each test, the percentages established by all panelists were then averaged together (General Accounting Office, 1993, p. 12). There was wide variation in the panelists' opinions, confirming that an average might incorporate great subjectivity.

It might be hoped that those making these judgments have in mind students they have known who get adequate grades, but if so, the judgments will likely be flawed. Few teachers have had deep experience with a fully representative group of students. Most teachers spend their careers in similar communities where students' demographic characteristics and average ability levels are different from those of students who live in other types of communities.

Yet even if it were reasonable to expect that the judgment of teachers and other educators who have had experience with a representative group of pupils in the targeted grades would be valid regarding whether students would be likely to answer particular questions correctly, there is no reason to defer to their judgment (or taste) regarding whether answering those questions correctly should be deemed proficiency. Defining proficiency is a subjective process that does not rely mainly on experience.[3]

It is apparent that determination of the cut point is a function of the identity and qualifications of the judges upon whose subjective opinions the decision rests. NAGB was more interested in getting judges who were representative of various constituencies (teachers, business leaders, and so on) than it was in worrying too much about how judges could be qualified to make valid judgments about what students ought to be able to do, as distinct from what most students are *actually* able to do.

These subjective judgments, although well intentioned, would lead to overestimates of proficient performance even if judges had personal experience with a fully representative group of students. This overestimation occurs because when teachers and educators, as well as members of the general public, think about proficiency, they don't only have in mind students they have known who get adequate grades. Rather, they tend to think of a performance level that is higher than what students actually achieve, but one that they hope students will achieve or think students should achieve. It is a rare teacher who considers that her students' average performance should not have been higher than it was, if only the students had tried a little harder, parents could have been persuaded to be a little more supportive, the teacher had organized the curriculum a little differently, or some distracting event had not occurred during the school year. So it is not surprising that the NAGB judges established definitions of NAEP achievement levels that were unreasonably high, despite the judges having gone through several days of training designed to avoid that very result.

In 1978, long before NAGB began to define cut scores for NAEP, a measurement expert warned that judges will almost invariably set unrealistically high criteria. He described the mental process that judges typically apply as one of "counting backwards from 100%":

> An objective is stated and a test item is written to correspond to it. Since the objective is felt to be important—or else it wouldn't have been stated—its author readily endorses the proposition that everyone should be able to answer the test question based on it. . . . But reason and experience prevail and it is quickly recognized that perfection is impossible and concessions must be made for mental infirmity, clerical errors, misinformation, inattention, and the like. Just how great a concession should be made becomes distressingly arbitrary. . . . (Glass, 1978, p. 244)

If this is an accurate description of how NAGB judges approached their task, it is not surprising that NAEP proficiency is defined unreasonably stringently. The mental burden of proof, as it were, falls on deviations from perfection.

Following the work of the first panels in 1991, NAGB determined that the math cut scores that had been established were in fact too high, so it simply reduced the judges' decisions (Loomis & Bourque, 2001a, p. 3). NAGB's action was arbitrary, as were the judges' decisions themselves. After the first achievement levels for math were established, NAGB conducted a forum to hear public comments about the new standards. Mary Harley Kruter, one of the judges who participated in the process to establish cut scores, was the mathematics education project director for the National Academy of Sciences. At the NAGB forum, Kruter testified that her panel had too little time to make reasonable judgments about the cut scores: "We were uncomfortable that we did not do the best job we could do," she said. "It was a rushed process" (Rothman, 1991). Greg Anrig, president of the Educational Testing Service, which was administering NAEP, urged NAGB to delay employing achievement levels until it could be certain that they had been established properly (Rothman, 1991).

In response, Chester E. Finn Jr., a former NAGB chairman and still a board member, explained why the board was unwilling to delay the use of cut scores to report on the percentage of students who are proficient: If we delay, Finn stated, "we may be sacrificing something else–the sense of urgency for national improvement" (Rothman, 1991).

NAGB itself has issued contradictory statements regarding how seriously its achievement levels should be taken. In 1990, it stated that the proficiency level represented merely "acceptable" achievement (Popham, 2000, p. 164). More recent NAGB publications acknowledge that the definitions are indefensible, although NAGB continues to use them. As a NAGB report put it in 2001:

> Nor is performance at the Proficient level synonymous with "proficiency" in the subject. That is, students who may be considered proficient in a subject, given the common usage of the term, might not satisfy the requirements for performance at the NAEP achievement level. Further, Basic achievement is more than minimal competency. Basic achievement is less than mastery but more than the lowest level of performance on NAEP. Finally, even the best students you know may not meet the requirements for Advanced performance on NAEP. (Loomis & Bourque, 2001a, p. 2)

In the early 1990s, NAGB, Congress, and the Department of Education all commissioned studies to evaluate the achievement level setting process and the validity of the results. Each study concluded that the achievement levels were flawed and urged NAGB to discontinue their use, or to use them only with the most explicit warnings about their unscientific nature. The government's response to each of these studies was to commission yet another study, hoping that a different group of scholars would emerge with a more favorable conclusion.

The first of these studies, by three well-known and highly respected statisticians (Daniel L. Stufflebeam, Michael Scriven, and Richard M. Jaeger), was conducted in 1991, following the initial efforts of judges to establish math cut scores. According to the statisticians' preliminary report, "the technical difficulties [with NAGB's achievement level definitions in math] are extremely serious" and to repeat the process in new standards-setting exercises for other subjects would be "ridiculous" (Vinovskis, 1998, pp. 46–47). The statisticians charged that NAGB was technically incompetent and that Congress should reconstitute it with members who had more psychometric sophistication. NAGB's response was to cancel the statisticians' contract before their final report was issued (Vinovskis, 1998).

But the statisticians' views had been publicized, so the House Education and Labor Committee asked the General Accounting Office (GAO) to decide whether the statisticians were right in their indictment of NAGB's standards-setting process. In 1993, the GAO released its report entitled, *Educational Achievement Standards: NAGB's Approach Yields Misleading Interpretations,* and concluded that defining cut scores is not a task that lay people can reasonably perform. For example, the GAO found that NAGB panel members, whose judgments were averaged regarding the probability of students at different achievement levels answering each test item correctly, could not properly distinguish between easier and more difficult test items. For example, judges had a tendency to classify open-ended items as difficult, when they were not necessarily so, and multiple-choice items as easy, even when they were not. Therefore, the GAO concluded, the cut scores for basic and proficient students could have been set considerably lower than they were, based on the NAGB panel's own stated criteria. This would result in much larger numbers of students being deemed proficient (General Accounting Office, 1993, pp. 31–32). The GAO reached these conclusions:

> We conclude that NAGB's . . . approach was inherently flawed, both conceptually and procedurally, and that . . . the approach not be used further until a thorough review could be completed. . . .
>
> These weaknesses are not trivial; reliance on NAGB's results could have serious consequences. For example, policymakers might conclude that since nearly 40 percent of 8th grade students did not reach the basic level . . . , resources should be allocated so as to emphasize fundamental skills for most classes. Since many students who scored below 255 [the cut score for basic performance] were in fact able to answer basic-level items (according to our analysis), this strategy could retard their progress toward mastering more challenging material. . . .

> In light of the many problems we found with NAGB's approach, we recommend that NAGB withdraw its direction to NCES that the . . . NAEP results be published primarily in terms of levels. The conventional approach to score interpretation [i.e., reports of scale scores] should be retained until an alternative has been shown to be sound. (General Accounting Office, 1993, p. 38)

Indeed, the GAO's warning of the "serious consequences" to follow from use of NAEP achievement levels predicted almost precisely how a decade later, NCLB, based on use of such levels, has caused a distortion in the curriculum for lower-scoring students, leading to an undue emphasis on basic skills that "retard[s] their progress toward mastering more challenging material" (U.S. General Accounting Office, 1993, p. 38). In response to the GAO's criticism, the Department of Education acknowledged that "one reason the judges may have set such high standards is that they did not have the disciplining experience of comparing their personal estimates of what students at a given level *will* do with what students like those at that level actually *did*" (Elliott, 1992, p. 71).

Then the Department of Education commissioned its own study of the NAGB achievement levels, to be performed by a National Academy of Education (NAE) panel. Confirming the GAO's findings, the NAE panel concluded that the procedure by which the achievement levels had been established were "fundamentally flawed," were "subject to large biases," and that the achievement levels by which American students had been judged deficient were set "unreasonably high" (National Academy of Education, 1993, pp. xxii, 148). The NAE recommended that the method used for establishing NAEP achievement levels should be abandoned and that the achievement levels themselves should not be used. In fact, the NAE panel stated, continued use of these standards could set back the cause of education reform because it would harm the credibility of NAEP itself (p. xxiv).

Still not satisfied, the Department of Education next contracted with the National Academy of Sciences to conduct yet another evaluation of NAEP. The Academy's panel held a conference in 1996 on the achievement-level-setting process and published its conclusions 3 years later. The "process for setting NAEP achievement levels is fundamentally flawed," the Academy report repeated. "[P]rocesses are too cognitively complex for the raters, and there are notable inconsistencies in the judgment data. . . . Furthermore, NAEP achievement-level results do not appear to be reasonable compared with other external information about students' achievement" (Pelligrino, Jones, & Mitchell, 1999, p. 7).

None of this advice has been followed. In the 1994 reauthorization of the Elementary and Secondary Education Act (ESEA), of which NCLB is the subsequent reauthorization, Congress acknowledged these scientific judgments by instructing that the achievement levels should be used only on a "developmental basis" until the Commissioner of Education Statistics reevaluates them and determines that the levels are "reasonable, valid, and informative to the public" (Vinovskis, 1998, p. 56). As noted above, similar language remains in NCLB. However, the only reevaluation that has been performed was that of the National Academy of Sciences, noted above, which reiterated the prior studies' condemnations of NAEP achievement levels. A result of that reevaluation has been that NAEP reports now include disclaimers about the validity of the proficiency levels being used. Yet the same NAEP reports continue to use them, while officials continue to issue pronouncements about the percentages of students who are not proficient, without mentioning the disclaimers. For example, recent NAEP reports include a caution, buried in the text, defending the use of achievement levels only for observing trends, that is, changes in the percentage of students who achieve proficiency over time, but not for validating the percentages at any given point in time. The caution concludes by offering no defense of achievement-level definitions other than the fact that the government continues to use them:

> As provided by law, NCES, upon review of congressionally mandated evaluations of NAEP, has determined that achievement levels are to be used on a trial basis and should be interpreted with caution. However, NCES and NAGB have affirmed the usefulness of these performance standards for understanding *trends* in achievement. NAEP achievement levels have been widely used by national and state officials [emphasis added]. (Grigg, Lauko, & Brockway, 2006, p. 5)

NCLB imposes sanctions on schools and school districts for failing to meet levels of proficiency on state tests that, although lower in many cases than NAEP levels, were established using similar processes. Irrespective of the actual level of state cut scores, NCES asserts that achievement levels established in this way should only be used "on a trial basis and . . . interpreted with caution," and then only for purposes of understanding trends over time, not for purposes of judging how many students are truly proficient at any given time.

Because the establishment of proficiency levels is necessarily subjective, no matter how well informed the opinions of judges may be, an almost inevitable consequence of a decision by both the federal and state governments to use such levels has been the politicization of standardized testing. When proficiency criteria were established for NAEP in the early 1990s, the criteria were made unreasonably high because policymakers wanted to spur school reform by demonstrating (or exaggerating) how poorly American students perform. In none-too-subtle language, the General Accounting Office concluded that NAGB established these standards, despite their lack of scientific credibility, because the benefits of sending an important message about U.S. students' school achievement appeared considerable, and NAGB saw little risk in publishing scores and interpretations that had yet to be fully examined. . . . NAGB viewed the selection of achievement goals as a question of social judgment that NAGB, by virtue of its broad membership base, was well suited to decide. (U.S. General Accounting Office, 1993, p. 57)

Political, not scientific, considerations continue to explain NAGB's stubborn refusal to abandon achievement level cut scores that have no scientific or scholarly credibility. In 2000, NAGB commissioned yet another review of the controversy by James Popham, a nationally respected psychometrician. Acknowledging that the cut scores are widely regarded as being too high, Popham (2000) noted that resistance to lowering them was based on a belief that doing so "would present a clear admission to the world that the nation's much touted pursuit of *demanding* levels of student performance was little more than public-relations rhetoric. [Lowering the cut scores] would forever damage NAEP's credibility because it would be seen as little more than a self-serving education profession's adjust-as-needed yardstick" (p. 176). Nonetheless, Popham concluded, "if not modified, [the achievement levels policy] may make NAEP an educational anachronism within a decade or two" (p. 176).

NCLB AND THE NAEP STANDARDS

In the NAEP administrations immediately prior to the adoption of NCLB, only 22% of 4th graders in public schools nationwide were deemed proficient in math and 27% in reading. For 8th graders, only 25% were deemed proficient in math and 29% in reading (Institute of Education Sciences, 2006).[4]

This gives us a rough way to estimate how much improvement would be required for all students in all subgroups to be proficient. At present (the most recent data are from 2005), 71% of all 8th graders in public schools are below proficiency in reading on the NAEP. For the typical student, becoming proficient would require a gain of 0.6 standard deviations (Institute of Education Sciences, 2006).[5] In other words, by 2014 the median student would perform similarly to a student who is at about the 72nd percentile of performance today.[6] For a student whose performance is below the median, but still similar to that of most same-age students (i.e., those who are below the median but still performing better than the lowest-performing 16% of all students), becoming proficient would require a gain of up to 1.6 standard deviations.[7] In other words, a student who is at the 16th percentile in today's achievement distribution would also perform similarly to a student who is now at the 72nd percentile. Approximately one-sixth of all students would require a gain even greater than 1.6 standard deviations.

NAEP'S PROFICIENCY DEFINITION
IS INCONSISTENT WITH OTHER ACHIEVEMENT DATA

Other data we have on student achievement provide evidence that NAEP cut scores for achievement levels are unreasonably high.[8] For example, the NAEP definitions tell us that in 2000, the number of 12th-grade students who performed at the advanced level in mathematics was equal to only 1.5% of all U.S. 17 year olds.[9] Yet, as Figure 5.1 shows, in the same year, nearly double that number (2.7%) of all 17 year olds were awarded college credit in calculus because they passed highly demanding advanced placement exams—designed to measure not merely mastery of the high school curriculum, but mastery of beginning college mathematics itself. Advanced placement exams are given in only some U.S. high schools and, if available to all students, more than 2.7% of all 17 year olds would likely have achieved passing scores.

Similarly, in 2000, 8% of all 17 year olds, five times the number deemed to be at the advanced level by NAEP, scored over 600 on the SAT math test, a score that most college admissions officials consider reflects advanced math achievement; the actual number of students who achieve at this level could be half again as high as 8%, because this number does not account for the fact that the SAT is not taken by many high-scoring college-bound students in states where the ACT is more common.

Figure 5.1. Comparison of NAEP Advanced Achievement Level with Other Achievement Data, 2000 (for 17 Year Olds)

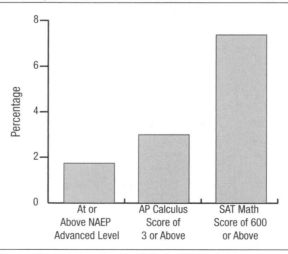

Source: Census Bureau, 2006; College Board, 2000a, b; NCES, 2000

WORLD-CLASS STANDARDS

Let's examine another approach to estimating proficiency. In the 1994 legislation, Goals 2000, a congressionally mandated objective was that U.S. students should be "first in the world in math and science" by the year 2000. Many education reformers, even those who boasted of having the highest expectations, later acknowledged that this goal was absurd. As the federal government's National Education Goals Panel, established to monitor progress toward these goals, acknowledged, the first-in-the-world aim "led to a certain amount of derision and sarcasm" (Wurtz, 1999, p. 19). So, in 2001, reformers trimmed their expectations, saying in effect, "We don't need to be first in the world; all we require is to be minimally proficient." NCLB's expectation that all students should be proficient seemed to be a more modest and achievable goal than first-in-the-world standing.

Yet this expectation had matters backwards. Reaching proficiency for all is an even higher and more unreachable aspiration than being first in the world, because even first-in-the-world educational systems have a wide range of performance. No matter how much more time were permitted to achieve NCLB's goal, all American students would not be proficient, even if the United States became demonstrably the world's highest-performing nation.

We can compare these slogans: "proficiency-for-all" versus "first-in-the-world." In 1993, the National Center for Education Statistics (NCES) computed an approximate equation of performance between American students on the 8th-grade NAEP test, given in 1992, and an international exam, the Second International Assessment of Educational Progress (IAEP), given the previous year.[10] This comparison requires assuming that NAEP and IAEP tests are similar in content and in scaling, and so is not usable for any precise purposes. We describe it here only to provide a very rough idea of how foolish is the goal of proficiency for all.

According to these experimental data, Taiwan was first in the world in math in 1991. If Taiwanese 13 year olds had taken the American NAEP exam the following year, their estimated average NAEP score would have been 285, compared with American 8th graders' average score of 262 (Salganik, Phelps, Bianchi, Nohera, & Smith, 1993, p. 56, Table 9a). But NAEP defines 8th graders as proficient if they achieve a score of 299, not only far higher than the U.S. average score, but considerably higher than the average Taiwanese score as well (Reese, Miller, Masseor, & Dussey, 1997, p. 44, figure 3.2). Although Taiwanese students were first in the world in math, *approximately 60% of them scored below what NAEP defines as proficient* (Pashley & Phillips, 1993, p. 25, Table 4).Thus, even if the United States were first in the world in math, we would still be far from meeting the NCLB goal of all students being proficient.

According to more recent (2003) data from the Third International Mathematics and Science Survey (TIMSS), American 8th graders had an average scale score of 504 in math and 527 in science, compared with scores in the highest-scoring country (Singapore) of 605 and 578, respectively (Gonzales et al., 2004, p. 5, Table 3; p. 15, Table 9).[11]

Yet still, approximately 25% of students in Singapore are below what NAEP defines as proficient in math, and 49% are less than proficient in science. We display these comparisons in Figures 5.2 and 5.3. In Korea, the second-highest-scoring country in math and third-highest-scoring country in science, one-third are less than proficient in math and 60% are less than proficient in science. In Chinese Taipei, the second-highest scorer in science, 53% of 8th-grade students are less than proficient. And in Hong Kong, the third-highest scorer in mathematics and the fourth-highest scorer in science, one-third are less than proficient in math and 62% are less than proficient in science.[12]

On the Progress in International Reading Literacy Study (PIRLS), a 2001 reading test administered by the International Association for the Evaluation of Educational Achievement (IEA), America's 10 year olds scored ninth highest in the world—the highest-scoring countries were Sweden, the Netherlands, England, Bulgaria, Latvia, Canada, Lithuania, and Hungary, all of which, including the United States, were closely bunched together—the average U.S. performance was only 0.2 standard deviations below that of Sweden

Figure 5.2. Percentage of Students Predicted to Score Below NAEP 8th-Grade Math Proficiency Cut Score

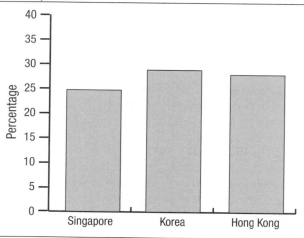

Sources: TIMSS, 2003; Gonzales et al., 2004; NAEP cut scores: Reese et al., 1997

Note: Percentages estimated using Linn's (2000) linking method.

Figure 5.3. Percentage of Students Predicted to Score Below NAEP 8th-Grade Science Proficiency Cut Score

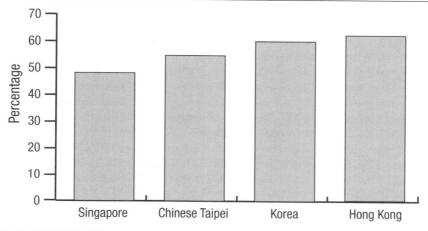

Sources: TIMSS, 2003; Gonzales et al., 2004; NAEP cut scores: Grigg et al., 2006

Note: Percentages estimated using Linn's (2000) linking method.

(Mullis, Martin, Gonzalez, & Kennedy, 2003, p. 24 and p. 26, Exhibit 1.1).[13] But on NAEP's achievement level report, only 30% of U.S. 10 year olds were deemed proficient in reading the next year.

We repeat here the caution that applications of NAEP proficiency levels to international tests are only rough approximations to suggest orders of magnitude and are not technically defensible for precise uses. Having said that, *by comparing the NAEP scale with scores on this international reading test, we estimate that about two-thirds of all Swedish students, the highest-scoring students in the world, were not proficient in reading as NAEP defines it.*

In short, being first in the world is a very modest aspiration compared with NCLB's expectation that all students will be proficient. Proficiency for all is a standard that no country in the world comes close to meeting, nor is it one that any country can reasonably expect to meet.

THE SUBJECTIVITY OF STATE PROFICIENCY STANDARDS

When proficiency criteria have been established by state officials for purposes of accountability under NCLB, political considerations have also prevailed. Several states have established proficiency cut scores that are in NAEP's below-basic range.[14] These relatively low criteria ensure that more schools can escape NCLB sanctions. Colorado has two cut scores for proficiency:

One is termed "proficient" for purposes of compliance with NCLB, but the same cut score is termed only "partially proficient" for purposes of compliance with state educational accountability policies (Kingsbury, Olson, Cronin, Hauser, & Houser, 2003). Other states, such as South Carolina, have set criteria that are relatively high, presumably for reasons similar to those of federal officials who set NAEP standards (Kingsbury et al., 2003). Eighth-grade mathematics students in Montana who achieve far above their state's proficiency standard can walk across the border to Wyoming and, with the same math ability, fall far below proficiency in that state (Kingsbury et al., 2003). In Missouri, 10% fewer students are deemed proficient on the state 8th-grade math test than on NAEP, while in Tennessee, 66% more students are deemed proficient on the state test than on NAEP (Linn, 2006).

South Carolina's case is particularly interesting. In the mid-1990s, the state's students were four times as likely to be deemed proficient by South Carolina's own accountability system as were proficient on the NAEP (Linn, 2000, p. 10, Figure 6). Today, however, the state's students are no more likely to be proficient by state than by NAEP criteria (Lee, 2006, p. 68, Table B-1). This does not reflect a change in student learning, only a change in arbitrary definition.

Capricious state standards in other states produce anomalies of their own. In the 1990s, for example, Massachusetts established cut scores on its state test that resulted in only 28% of its 8th graders being deemed proficient in science. But at approximately the same time, Massachusetts' 8th graders scored higher, on average, than students in every country in the world (except Singapore) on the TIMSS (Horn, Ramus, Blumerr, & Madaus, 2000, pp. 24–25).

One state, Louisiana, found that its proficiency definition was so high that adequate yearly progress under NCLB could not be fulfilled, so it simply decreed that, for NCLB purposes, its basic cut score would be considered a challenging standard of proficiency (Hoff, 2002). As Linn (2006) has observed, "the variability in the stringency of state standards defining proficient performance is so great that the concept of proficient achievement lacks meaning" (p. 6).

AIMING LOWER—FOR BASIC, NOT PROFICIENT, PERFORMANCE

Can the problems we have described be fixed by reducing NCLB's expectations—for example, by abandoning the demand that all students achieve "challenging" standards of performance and instead accepting that all students should only be required to achieve at something more like the "basic" level on NAEP? In other words, should NCLB concede to states that have sabotaged NCLB's intent by setting very low standards of proficiency?

Unfortunately, such an attempt to rescue NCLB's intent is inadvisable from a policy perspective, and also unworkable. Requiring all students to achieve above a basic, as opposed to proficient, cut score has been tried before. In the 1970s, in response to federal requirements that states assess student performance to show that federal aid was being properly utilized, states adopted standardized testing regimes in which mostly basic skills were tested (Linn, 2000).

Educators and policymakers soon developed contempt for such exams, and they were abandoned after about a decade of use. The National Commission on Excellence in Education, in its influential 1983 indictment of American schools, *A Nation at Risk,* had this to say: "'Minimum competency' examinations (now required in 37 states) fall short of what is needed, as the 'minimum' tends to become the 'maximum,' thus lowering education standards for all" (p. 20). Accountability for only basic skills, the commission found, had created incentives to deliver curriculum that did not challenge typical students. The commission recommended that minimum competency exams be abandoned, to permit creation of curriculum emphasizing more advanced skills.

A few years later, O'Day and Smith's (1993) proposal for accountability and testing aligned with challenging curriculum (systemic school reform) was an explicit rejection of the minimum competency movement in American education. Minimum competency tests, they wrote, "emphasized recognition of facts, word analysis, mathematical computation skills, routine algorithmic problem solving, and little else" (p. 258). Such tests, Smith and O'Day noted, were aligned with the curriculum for disadvantaged children because, with the incentives provided by such tests, teachers only taught such basic skills. Test scores of the most disadvantaged children did increase in such a system, but the academic needs of students higher in the achievement distribution were ignored: "because the scores of more well-to-do and majority students did not change during this time, the achievement gap narrowed" (p. 258).[15] Smith and O'Day's call for systemic school reform was for "the coherence and clarity of the back-to-basics movement [to be] replaced with a similar coherence and clarity in support of the new, challenging content" (p. 262).

If we were to forget these lessons from a generation ago and modify NCLB to require only a basic level of achievement, not a challenging standard of proficiency, the logical flaws would still apply that are inherent in attempts to apply a single standard to students across the full range of the ability distribution. Standards that are a challenge for students at the bottom of the distribution cannot be a challenge for students higher up.

NAEP's basic level of performance would also be unworkable as NCLB's minimum standard because even NAEP's basic cut scores are too high for too many students. We noted that many students in the highest-scoring countries in the world achieve at less than proficiency as NAEP defines it. Fewer, though still a significant proportion of students in the highest-scoring countries, achieve at less than basic as NAEP defines it.

INEVITABLE INDIVIDUAL VARIABILITY: WHY "PROFICIENCY FOR ALL" IS AN OXYMORON

As these illustrations show, achieving proficiency for all is not simply a matter of adjusting the 2014 goal date by a few years. The slogan of "proficiency for all" is an oxymoron, confusing a minimum standard, one that all (or almost all) students should meet, with a challenging standard, one that requires typical students to reach beyond their present level of performance. Even if schools were to improve so that typical students achieved a challenging level of performance, below-average students, even if challenged, would not reach the same level. If a challenging standard were achievable by below-average students, it would no longer be a standard that was challenging for typical students.

Think of it this way. Imagine you are teaching a class with a typical range of students. There are many C students, but there are also quite a few Bs, a few As, a few Ds, and maybe even an A+ student in the mix. Imagine that your principal tells you to ignore the As and A+s—you won't be held accountable for whether they learn much new this year. But for the rest of the students, you are told you must teach effectively enough so that you can conclude the year with a test that has two characteristics: First, all students will pass. Second, the test will be hard enough so that both your B students and your D students will find it a challenge to get a passing grade. We defy you to design such a test, no matter how effective your teaching may be. It is a logically impossible task.

In its administration of NCLB, the U.S. Department of Education barely acknowledges this human variability. It permits the lowest-performing 1% of all students to be held to a vague "alternate" standard of proficiency, and the next-lowest-performing 2% to be held to a "modified" standard of proficiency, which still must lead to "grade level" achievement and to a regular high school diploma (U.S. Department of Education, 2005b). Let's be clear about what this means: Under NCLB, children with IQs as low as 65 must achieve a standard of proficiency in math that is higher than that achieved by 60% of students in Taiwan, the highest-scoring country in the world (in math), and a standard of proficiency in reading that is higher than that achieved by 65% of students in Sweden, the highest-scoring country in the world (in reading).[16]

Nonetheless, Secretary of Education Margaret Spellings rejects calls for substantial modifications to NCLB, claiming that the law is "99.9% pure" (Klein, 2006). And although this may have been a flippant comment, she later clarified her remark, saying that she "meant to convey only that no changes were needed to its 'core principles'" (Dillon, 2006).

NCLB'S GOAL CONFUSION

What NCLB has done is the equivalent of demanding not only that, nationwide, all C students become A students, but that D and F students also become A students. As noted above, this confuses two distinct goals—that of raising the performance of typical students and that of raising the minimum level of performance we expect of all or almost all students. Both are reasonable instructional goals. But given the nature of human variability, no single standard can possibly describe both of these accomplishments. If we define proficiency for all as the minimum standard, it cannot possibly be challenging for most students. If we define proficiency for all as a challenging standard (as does NCLB), the inevitable patterns of individual variability dictate that significant numbers of students will still fail, even if they all improve. This will be true no matter what date is substituted for NCLB's 2014.

In response to this argument, some note that commonplace tests do exist in which all test takers are expected to be proficient. A state written driver's license exam is, it is said, an example, and if we can expect all drivers to be proficient at understanding the rules of the road, we can also expect all 4th graders to be proficient in math. This analogy fails for two reasons. First, not *all* test takers pass the written exam to get a driver's license, although almost all do, eventually, having taken the test multiple times, something not permitted in contemporary school accountability systems. Second, anyone who has taken a driver's license test knows that the level of difficulty is extraordinarily low. Passing can be ensured by devoting only a few minutes to review of the state manual published for this purpose. Nobody would call a state driver's test "challenging." If it were indeed challenging, the goal of having everyone pass would be no more in reach than the goal of having all 4th graders be proficient in math. If we define proficiency low enough (perhaps something less than the basic level on NAEP), it is certainly possible to achieve the NCLB goal of having almost all students be proficient by some future date. But such a standard would not be challenging to most students and would do little to spur typical students to perform at higher levels than they do today.

DETERMINING REALISTIC GOALS FOR IMPROVEMENT

More reasonable supporters of contemporary school accountability policies acknowledge that not all children are alike and that there is an inevitable distribution of achievement, but say that, at least, the distribution can be narrowed by targeted policies that raise the performance of students at the bottom at a faster rate than performance improves for students overall. Then the gap between a proficient and a minimum standard need not be as great as it is today.

In addition to raising all parts of the distribution (i.e., shifting the distribution "to the right"), it is also possible to narrow the distribution somewhat, but probably not by very much. As Daniel Koretz (2006) points out in an important paper, the typical variation in children's achievement, the gap between children at lower and higher levels of academic competence, is not primarily a racial or ethnic gap; it is a gap within race and ethnic groups, including whites. The range of student performance in Japan and Korea, more homogeneous societies than ours whose average math and science scores surpass those of the United States, is similar to the range here. Koretz estimates that if the black–white gap were entirely eliminated, the standard deviation of U.S. 8th-grade math and reading scores would shrink by less than 10%. Perhaps some additional shrinkage would result if we were able to reduce the race-neutral achievement gap by family income, but even so, most of the existing variability in student performance would remain (Koretz, 2006). It would still be just as impossible to craft a standard that was a simultaneous challenge to students at the top, the middle, and the bottom of the distribution.

One way to establish boundaries on what might be reasonable expectations for improvement would be to examine historical precedent. It is generally agreed that, since about 1963, U.S. student achievement has gone through three distinct phases. At first, and until the late 1970s, achievement declined. Then, until the late 1980s, achievement rose. And from about 1990 to the present, math scores have continued to climb while reading scores have been mostly stagnant or have declined slightly (Campbell, Hombo, & Mazzeo, 2000; Grissmer, Kirby, Berends, & Williamson, 1994; Koretz, 1986).

The test-score decline of the 1960s and 1970s was considered very significant, a national crisis. The necessity of arresting this decline, a "rising tide of mediocrity," was an important motivation behind the *Nation at Risk* report of 1983. How large was the decline? As the report stated, on the College Board's SAT, average verbal scores fell by about 50 points and math scores by about 40 (National Commission on Excellence in Education, 1983, pp. 8–9). Overall, average test scores dropped by a similar amount, about 0.4 standard deviations (Koretz, 1986, 2006). Social, cultural, and economic factors were responsible for some of this decline—for example, children from larger families typically achieve at lower average levels than children from smaller families, perhaps because children from large families get less adult attention, and the score decline corresponds to the period when Baby Boomers moved through schools (Koretz, 1987; Rothstein, 1998; Zajonc, 1986). So perhaps (this is just a guess) the decline in average achievement attributable to deterioration in school quality was about 0.2 standard deviations. In other words, at the end of this period, typical students (i.e., those at the 50th percentile in a ranking of all students by their performance) scored similarly to students who were at about the 34th percentile at the beginning of the period, and if we controlled for nonschool factors, we might say that deteriorating school quality caused a typical student to fall to about the 42nd percentile.

So if we thought a school-improvement program could cause a student achievement gain equal in size to the decline caused by the deterioration of school quality some 4 decades ago, we might aim for a situation where, 15 years hence, typical students achieve at about the level that students at the 58th percentile achieve today.

The second phase, from about the mid-1970s to the late 1980s, saw student achievement (on NAEP math tests) rise by 0.2 standard deviations in the 12th grade, and by more than 0.3 standard deviations in the 4th and 8th grades (Koretz, 2005; Linn, 2000). David Grissmer and colleagues have estimated that the black–white gap was cut in half during this period, and that about half of that cut was attributable to family factors (smaller black families and higher levels of black parental education). This would leave about half of the decline in the black–white gap otherwise unexplained, possibly attributable to school improvements (Grissmer et al., 1994). Using this period of improvement as a yardstick, we might try to improve schools again at a similar rate, to get typical students, 15 years from now, up to achievement levels of today's students who are in the mid-50s in percentile ranks. Keep in mind, as always, that this aspiration describes the movement of typical students, those at about the middle of a national distribution. Some will improve to higher levels, and some will regress to lower ones.

In behavioral science, an intervention designed to improve human performance is generally considered effective but small if it improves average performance by 0.2 standard deviations; medium if it improves average performance by 0.5 standard deviations; and large if it improves average performance by 0.8 standard deviations (Cohen, 1988). In other words, at the conclusion of a moderately successful intervention, average individuals will perform at the level that individuals who were previously at the 69th percentile were performing. Other individuals, those above and below average, would also perform at a correspondingly higher level. But such interventions are rare, especially if measured over reasonably proximate time spans.[17]

However, in education, where good experimental controls are absent, large effect sizes are less probable than in fields such as experimental psychology or medicine (Cohen, 1988, p. 13; Valentine & Cooper, 2003, p. 5). In the field of education, it seems reasonable to classify an effect size of 0.5 as quite large; a more practical standard for successful educational reform would be one that shifted average performance by something like a quarter to a third of a standard deviation within the foreseeable future, or one that enabled typical students to perform at the level that students who were previously at the 60th to 63rd percentile were performing.

If the United States were to revamp its schools and child welfare practices to be first in the world in math, this would require that typical American 8th graders (those who were at the 50th percentile rank in a national distribution of student achievement) would perform at the level that 8th graders who were at the 90th percentile of math achievement performed before the intervention began (Gonzales et al., 2004, p. 5, Table 3; p. 88, Table C12). This would be an upward shift in average performance of about 1.3 standard deviations, a magnitude of accomplishment that would be extraordinary in any field. And, as noted above, even if all students' achievement improved under such a regime, about half would still perform below the new, higher average level.

We can again translate this to classroom reality. Any teacher understands how it works. She can set high expectations for student performance and may successfully elicit high average performance for her class. A teacher, for example, might expect C students to raise their sights so that they produce B work. But this teacher would never make B-level work the minimum passing grade. She would understand that some students would earn only a C and would still be eligible to advance to the next grade, even under the strictest of no-social-promotion policies.

CONCLUSION

The goal of all students, in all subgroups, achieving proficiency by 2014, or by any subsequent date, is not achievable because

- Inevitable variation in student performance makes it logically necessary that all students cannot be at or above a level that typical students find "challenging." Achievement that is challenging for students at the middle of the distribution of ability cannot also be challenging for students at the top, and would be impossibly difficult for students at the bottom.

- The concept of proficiency in multiple academic subjects and grade levels is impossibly subjective, so subjective that basing an accountability system upon it, involving sanctions and rewards, will almost inevitably impose these sanctions and rewards either on too many or too few schools, depending on the political objectives of the standards-setting process.
- Evidence of the flaws in using subjective proficiency standards for purposes of accountability comes from comparing the share of "proficient" students on the NAEP with the share of students with similar achievement levels in the highest-scoring countries in the world. Even in these countries, many students would not meet the NAEP standard.
- Schools should be accountable for performance in math and reading, and it is not unreasonable to set targets for improvement. Reasonable targets would expect the full distribution of student achievement to show relative improvement, but would not expect all students to end up at the same place. Establishing goals for such improvement should take account of changes in educational performance known to have been achieved in the past.

NOTES

The full version of this chapter is available at http://devweb.tc.columbia. edu/manager/symposium/Files/101_Rothstein%20-%20Prof%20for%20All%20 -%20TC%20Symposium%2011–14–06.pdf or at http://www.epi.org/content.cfm/ webfeatures_viewpoints_nclb20061114

1. Marshall Smith was education advisor to Governor Bill Clinton when the latter co-chaired the National Governors Association education task force at the 1989 Charlottesville Education Summit where federal education goals were adopted; Dr. Smith then chaired the task force on education standards established by federal law in 1991 to develop a national accountability system, and went on to serve as President Clinton's deputy secretary and undersecretary of education.

2. NAGB required that 55% of these judges be classroom teachers, and another 15% be other educators (curriculum specialists, principals, and so on). The remainder could be noneducators such as parents of schoolchildren or business executives who employ recent high school graduates. The contractor, American College Testing (ACT), selected all the teacher judges from nominees of school district superintendents, teacher union officers, and private school executives. The nonteacher educator judges were selected from nominees of faculty of schools of education. The noneducator judges were selected from nominees of local chambers of commerce, mayors, and chairs of school boards (ACT, 1992).

3. We do successfully define proficiency for professional certifications. Physicians, accountants, hairdressers, and others obtain licenses to practice only after satisfying

boards of examiners that they possess proficiency in their fields, and passing examinations is part of these processes. But the professional boards that establish cut scores
on such examinations usually attempt to maintain existing professional standards in
the licensing of new practitioners. These boards do not use cut scores as a way of radically raising the existing level of professional practice. As a result, the boards can rely
on experience to determine what competent physicians, accountants, or hairdressers
can actually do; they do not use cut scores to require newly licensed practitioners
to perform at radically higher levels than most existing practitioners. In practice,
cut scores on such licensing examinations are often changed based on supply and
demand factors: If there is a shortage of job seekers in a profession, licensing boards
lower the cut scores for passing the test, confirming that even for licensing exams,
the concept of proficiency has no objective meaning (Glass, 1978). Further, there is
considerable selectivity in the pool of candidates. NCLB achievement levels must apply to all students. But not all young people are qualified to enter training to become
candidates in medicine, accounting, or hairdressing, so the variability in performance
among candidates is much narrower than among all students. And then, professional
schools are expected to weed out students who were admitted, but are not likely to
pass the licensing exam at the end of their training.

4. Data for 4th graders in reading, and for 4th and 8th graders in mathematics, are
from NAEP administrations in 2000. Data for 8th graders in reading are from NAEP
1998. NAEP was not given for 8th grade reading in 2000. Data are for all public
school students, including those who took the test with accommodations. These data
include the percentage of all students whose scores were above the proficient cut
score, including those whose scores were above the advanced cut score.

5. These and similar estimates in this chapter are approximations because the
distributions of test scores are not perfectly normal and therefore the median (or
typical) student may not be identical to the mean (or average) student. Our estimates,
however, are calculated from the mean, assuming perfect normality. In 2005, the
proficiency cut score was 281 in reading, the mean score was 260, and the standard
deviation was 35.

6. Throughout this chapter, we adopt a convention of describing percentile ranks
as ascending with improved performance. In other words, the best-performing 1%
of students is described as being at or above the 99th percentile, and the poorest-
performing 1% of students is described as being at or below the 1st percentile.

7. Students who perform "similarly" to most same-age students are defined here,
consistent with conventional terminology, as those who are between one standard deviation below and one standard deviation above the mean, or students who perform
better than approximately the poorest-performing 16% of students, but not as well as
approximately the best-performing 16% of students.

8. One of us has previously published criticisms of the NAEP proficiency standards that are substantially similar to those expressed here (see Rothstein, 1998, pp.
71–74, and Rothstein, 2004, pp. 86–90).

9. This estimate takes the number of 12th graders who performed at the advanced
level, divided by the Census Bureau (2006) report of the size of the 17-year-old cohort in the year 2000. Other estimates in this paragraph are calculated with a similar
methodology.

10. The International Assessment of Educational Progress was funded by the National Science Foundation and administered by the Educational Testing Service for the U.S. Department of Education, National Center for Education Statistics. NCES referred to its equating of the two tests as "experimental"; we use the term "approximate" instead, to avoid suggesting that NCES conducted an actual experiment using the two tests.

11. Singapore is not really comparable to other countries; it is a city-state, much of whose working class commutes on a daily basis from Malaysia, the country where its children attend school. If the achievement of other countries were also based on testing only (or predominantly) their middle classes, scores more appropriately comparable to Singapore's might be obtained.

12. These approximate comparisons of TIMSS 2003 in mathematics and science with NAEP 2003 in mathematics and NAEP 2005 in science were calculated using a method demonstrated by Linn (2000) when he compared TIMSS 1994–1995 with NAEP 1996. Linn estimated where NAEP cut scores would fall on the TIMSS scale, assuming that the percentage proficient or above would be the same for U.S. students on the 8th-grade TIMSS mathematics assessment as it was on the 8th-grade NAEP mathematics assessment. In 2003, 27% of U.S. 8th graders were at or above the NAEP proficiency cut score. Using Linn's linking method, the approximate equivalent of the NAEP proficiency cut score on the TIMSS 2003 is the score that only 27% of U.S. students reached, or the score that corresponds to the 73rd percentile in the U.S. distribution. We estimated the percentage below this proficiency standard for each country from the predicted percentile score of a student in that country scoring one point below the estimated NAEP cut score on the TIMSS scale.

13. On the IEA scale, the U.S. mean was 542 and the Swedish mean was 561. The scale was constructed so that the standard deviation of test scores was 100.

14. Of eight states whose 4th-grade reading standards were examined by the Northwest Evaluation Association, four (California, Colorado, Iowa, and Montana) have proficiency cut scores that are below NAEP's basic cut score (see Table 4 in Kingsbury et al., 2003, versus Table 1 in Perie, Grigg, & Donahue, 2005; the data are not from the same year, however).

15. At about the time that Smith and O'Day were challenging the value of curriculum that emphasized only basic skills, others were beginning to notice that a significant portion of the increase in test scores during the "minimum competency" period was not real, and reflected teaching to tests, excessively narrowed curricula, and some cheating. See, for example, Cannell (1988, 1989) and Koretz (1988). In the present chapter, we do not discuss score inflation in high-stakes testing systems, which is as inevitable in NCLB-mandated tests as it was in the standardized tests of the 1970s (Koretz, 2006). It is, however, yet another flaw in accountability systems, such as NCLB, that rely exclusively on high-stakes tests.

16. Initially, department regulations permitted schools to exempt only students with the most severe cognitive disabilities, not to exceed 1% of all students, from regular accountability testing. Such students were still required to show adequate yearly progress toward a "modified" grade level proficiency standard, established by a similar process to that used for defining proficiency for all students (Lee, 2003). In other words, the department assumed that students who were approximately 2.3

standard deviations and more below average should have been expected to perform reasonably similarly to average and above-average students. This group includes students who are classified as mildly mentally retarded, expected under NCLB to meet a somewhat modified "grade-level" proficiency standard. (Students are classified as mildly mentally retarded if they have IQ scores between 50 and 70. A little less than half of such students, those with IQs below 65, are in the bottom 1% of all students in cognitive ability. A little more than half of mildly mentally retarded students have IQ scores between 65 and 70. These students typically can be expected to finish high school with academic achievement up to a 6th-grade level [Gurian, 2002].) The expectation that grade-level proficiency could be modified only for the bottom 1% was so egregious that in 2005 the Department responded to complaints by proposing that an additional 2% of students (including, most probably, students with IQs between 65 and 72) could be assessed based on "modified achievement standards" (Saulny, 2005; U.S. Department of Education, 2005a, b), and it now characterized the standard required of the bottom 1% as an "alternate," not modified, achievement standard. However, the proposed rule specifies that the modified standards should still be "aligned with grade-level content standards, but are modified in such a way that they reflect reduced breadth or depth of grade-level content," yet would not preclude such "a student from earning a regular high school diploma" (U.S. Department of Education, 2005b). Such language leaves it entirely unclear how the achievement standards can actually be modified, and suggests that ineffective and unaccountable school practices are the cause of even the most able of these students typically achieving only 6th-grade academic levels and failing to earn regular high school diplomas. The department's proposed rule states that requiring such students to achieve adequate yearly progress toward grade-level standards "would provide a safeguard against leaving children behind due to lack of proper instruction" (U.S. Department of Education, 2005b). The department's rule also asserts that students between the bottom 1% and bottom 3% can achieve proficiency, but these students may need more time to do so, which is the only reason for using temporary modified standards: "[W]e acknowledge that, while all students can learn challenging content, certain students, because of their disability, may not be able to achieve grade-level proficiency within the same time-frame as other students . . ." (U.S. Department of Education, 2005b). As Koretz (personal communication, Sept. 26, 2006) has observed, "The proposed regulations are impractical, I think. They call for standards and assessments that are 'modified in such a manner that they reflect reduced breadth or depth of grade-level content.' But if, each year, you cover grade-level material in less breadth or depth, over time, students will fall behind grade level." Three states (Kansas, Louisiana, and North Carolina) have now begun to use modified assessments for these students (Samuels, 2006), with panels of teachers and other "educational stakeholders" establishing proficiency cut scores for students with IQs as low as 50 (North Carolina Board of Education, 2006, p. 19). The proposed U.S. Department of Education rule, permitting a total of 3% of students to be held accountable for alternate, or modified, but standardized, proficiency standards, was published in the *Federal Register* on December 15, 2005, but has not yet been formally adopted, although the comment period closed on February 28, 2006. Even this new 3% exemption will doubtlessly be modified in any NCLB reauthorization that passes Congress. But the fact that we are even debating whether children with below-normal mental capacity should achieve a standardized definition of proficiency is breathtaking. Even if the intent of the proposed regulation were clear, it would still hold schools accountable for getting students with IQ scores as low as 72 to proficiency according to the regular, unmodified, grade-level standards.

17. Certainly, the effectiveness of medical doctors is more than one standard deviation higher than it was 100 years ago, survival rates for most diseases are more than one standard deviation above what they were 100 years ago, and life expectancy is more than one standard deviation longer than it was 100 years ago. Occasionally, a technological breakthrough has a short-term result of such magnitude. Survival rates of HIV patients jumped by more than a standard deviation with the development of antiretroviral drugs, as did survival rates from heart disease with the development of surgeries such as pacemakers and bypasses. "If the statistics of 1940 had persisted, fifteen thousand mothers would have died [in childbirth] last year (instead of fewer than five hundred)—and a hundred and twenty thousand newborns (instead of one-sixth that number)" (Gawande, 2006). But breakthroughs are rare and cannot be the model for ongoing educational reform efforts, which, absent unforeseeable breakthroughs, must be incremental.

REFERENCES

American College Testing. (1992, October 21). *Description of writing achievement-levels setting process and proposed achievement level definitions. 1992 National Assessment of Educational Progress.* Presented to the National Assessment Governing Board. ERIC # ED 351 697.

Campbell, J. R., Hombo, C. M., & Mazzeo, J. (2000, August). *NAEP 1999 trends in academic progress. Three decades of student performance.* NCES 2000–469. Washington, DC: U.S. Department of Education, Office of Educational Research and Improvement.

Cannell, J. J. (1988). Nationally normed elementary achievement testing in America's public schools: How all 50 states are above the national average. *Educational Measurement: Issues and Practice, 7*(2).

Cannell, J. J. (1989). *How public educators cheat on standardized achievement tests: The "Lake Wobegon" report.* Albuquerque, NM: Friends for Education.

Chat wrap up: The changing federal role in education. (2006, November 1). *Education Week, 26*(10).

Cohen, J. (1988). *Statistical power analysis for the behavioral sciences* (2nd ed.). Hillsdale, NJ: Lawrence Erlbaum.

Dillon, S. (2006, September 28). As 2 Bushes try to fix schools, tools differ. *The New York Times.* Retrieved April 9, 2008, from http://www.nytimes.com/2006/09/28/education/28child.html?_r=1&scp=1&sq=As%202%20Bushes%20Try%20to%20Fix%20Schools,%20Tools%20Differ&st=cse&oref=slogin

Elliott, E. J. (1992, March 25). Letter from Emerson J. Elliott, Acting Assistant Secretary, U.S. Department of Education, to Eleanor Chelimsky, Assistant Comptroller General. Washington, DC: General Accounting Office.

Gawande, A. (2006, October 9). The score. How childbirth went industrial. *The New Yorker.* Retrieved April 9, 2008, from http://www.newyorker.com/archive/2006/10/09/061009fa_fact

Glass, G. (1978). Standards and criteria. *Journal of Educational Measurement, 15*(4), 237–261.

Gonzales, P., Guzmán, J. C., Partelow, L., Pahlke, E., Jocelyn, L., Kastberg, D., & Williams, T. (2004, December). *Highlights from the trends in international mathematics and science study (TIMSS) 2003.* NCES 2005–005. Washington, DC: U.S. Department of Education, Institute of Education Sciences.

Grigg, W., Lauko, M., & Brockway, D. (2006, May). *The nation's report card: Science 2005.* NCES 2006–466.Washington, DC: U.S. Department of Education, National Center for Education Statistics.

Grissmer, D. W., Kirby, S. N., Berends, M., & Williamson, S. (1994). *Student achievement and the changing American family.* Santa Monica, CA: Rand.

Gurian, A. (2002, March 19). *About mental retardation.* Retrieved September 25, 2006, from http://www.aboutourkids.org/aboutour/articles/about_mr.html# introduction

Hoff, D. J. (2002, October 9). States revise the meaning of proficient. *Education Week, 22*(6), 1, 24–25.

Horn, C., Ramos, M., Blumer, I., & Madaus, G. (2000, November 1). Cut scores: Results may vary. *National Board on Educational Testing and Public Policy Monograph, 1*(1).

Institute of Education Sciences, National Center for Education Statistics. (2006). *NAEP data explorer.* Retrieved September 16, 2006, from http://www.nces.ed.gov/ nationsreportcard/nde/criteria.asp

Kingsbury, G. G., Olson, A., Cronin, J., Hauser, C., & Houser, R. (2003). *The state of state standards. Research investigating proficiency levels in fourteen states.* Lake Oswego, OR: Northwest Evaluation Association.

Klein, A. (2006, September 6). Spellings: Education law needs only a soft scrub. *Education Week, 26*(2).

Koretz, D. (1986). *Trends in educational achievement.* Washington, DC: Congress of the United States, Congressional Budget Office.

Koretz, D. (1987). *Educational achievement: Explanations and implications of recent trends.* Washington, DC: Congress of the United States, Congressional Budget Office.

Koretz, D. (1988). Arriving in Lake Wobegon: Are standardized tests exaggerating achievement and distorting instruction? *American Educator, 12*(2), 8–15, 46–52.

Koretz, D. (2005, October 17). Understanding today's educational testing. Course lecture, Harvard Graduate School of Education, Cambridge, MA.

Koretz, D. (2006, November 16). *The pending reauthorization of NCLB: An opportunity to rethink the basic strategy.* Paper presented at the Civil Rights Project/Earl Warren Institute Roundtable Discussion on the Reauthorization of NCLB, Washington, DC.

Lapointe, A. E., & Koffler, S. L. (1982, December). Your standards or mine? The case for the National Assessment of Educational Progress. *Educational Researcher, 11*(10), 4–11.

Lee, J. (2006). *Tracking achievement gaps and assessing the impact of NCLB on the gaps: An in-depth look into national and state reading and math outcome trends.* Cambridge, MA: The Civil Rights Project at Harvard University. Retrieved April 9, 2008, from http://www.civilrightsproject.harvard.edu/research/esea/nclb_naep_lee.pdf

Lee, S. (2003, March 20). *No Child Left Behind and students with disabilities.* Presentation to the Office of Special Education Programs Staff.

Linn, R. L. (2000). Assessments and accountability. *Educational Researcher, 29*(2), 4–16.

Linn, R. L. (2006, June). *Educational accountability systems.* CSE Technical Report 687. Los Angeles: National Center for Research on Evaluation, Standards, and Student Testing.

Livingston, S. A., & Zieky, M. J. (1982). *Passing scores. A manual for setting standards of performance on educational and occupational tests.* Princeton, NJ: Educational Testing Service.

Loomis, S. C., & Bourque, M. L. (Eds.). (2001a, July). *National Assessment of Educational Progress achievement levels, 1992–1998 for mathematics.* Washington, DC: National Assessment Governing Board.

Mullis, I. V. S., Martin, M. O., Gonzalez, E. J., & Kennedy, A. M. (2003). *PIRLS 2001 international report: IEA's study of reading literacy achievement in primary schools.* Chestnut Hill, MA: Boston College.

National Academy of Education Panel on the Evaluation of the NAEP Trial State Assessments. (1993). *Setting performance standards for student achievement. A report of the National Academy of Education panel on the evaluation of the NAEP trial state assessments: An evaluation of the 1992 achievement levels.* Stanford, CA: National Academy of Education.

National Commission on Excellence in Education. (1983, April). *A nation at risk: The imperative for educational reform. A report to the nation and the Secretary of Education.* Washington, DC: U.S. Government Printing Office.

North Carolina Board of Education. (2006, August). *Recommended interim academic achievement standards (cut scores) and descriptors for the NCEXTEND2 EOG writing assessments grades 4 and 7.* Retrieved from http://www.ncpublicschools.org/sbe_meetings/0608/0608_hsp/hsp0608.pdf

No Child Left Behind Act of 2001, 20 U.S.C. sec. 6301 et seq. (2002).

O'Day, J. A., & Smith, M. S. (1993). Systemic reform and educational opportunity. In S. H. Fuhrman (Ed.), *Designing coherent education policy. Improving the system* (pp. 250–312). San Francisco: Jossey-Bass.

Pashley, P. J., & Phillips, G. W. (1993). *Toward world class standards: A research study linking international and national assessments.* ETS-24-CAEP-01. Princeton, NJ: Educational Testing Service.

Pelligrino, J. W., Jones, L. R., & Mitchell, K. J. (Eds.). (1999). *Grading the nation's report card.* Washington, DC: National Academies Press.

Perie, M. W., Grigg, W., & Dion, G. (2005, October). *The nation's report card: Mathematics 2005.* NCES 2006–453. Washington, DC: U.S. Department of Education, National Center for Education Statistics.

Perie, M. W., Grigg, W., & Donahue, P. (2005, October). *The nation's report card: Reading 2005.* NCES 2006–451. Washington, DC: U.S. Department of Education, National Center for Education Statistics.

Popham, J. (2000). Looking at achievement levels. In M. L. Bourque & S. Byrd (Eds.), *Student performance standards on the National Assessment of Educational Progress: Affirmation and improvements.* Washington, DC: National Assessment Governing Board.

Reese, C. M., Miller, K. E., Masseo, J., & Dossey, J. (1997, February). *NAEP 1996 mathematics report card for the nation and the states: Findings from the National Assessment of Educational Progress.* NCES 97–488. Washington, DC: U.S. Department of Education, Office of Educational Research and Improvement.

Rothman, R. (1991, January 16). NAEP board urged to delay standards-setting plan. *Education Week.*

Rothstein, R. (1998). *The way we were? The myths and realities of America's student achievement.* New York: Century Foundation Press.

Rothstein, R. (2004). *Class and schools: Using social, economic, and educational reform to close the black–white achievement gap.* New York: Teachers College Press.

Salganik, L. H., Phelps, R. P., Bianchi, L., Nohara, D., & Smith, T. M. (1993, October). *Education in states and nations: Indicators comparing U.S. states with the OECD countries in 1988.* NCES 93–237. Washington, DC: U.S. Department of Education, Office of Educational Research and Improvement.

Samuels, C. A. (2006, September 13). Regulations on "2 percent" testing awaited. *Education Week, 26*(3), 31–32.

Saulny, S. (2005, May 11). U.S. provides rules to states for testing special pupils. *The New York Times.* Retrieved from http://www.nytimes.com/2005/05/11/politics/11child.html?ei=5090&en=ce8fc28635802fc8&ex=1273464000&adxnnl=1&partner=rssuserland&emc=rss&pagewanted=print&adxnnlx=1215108562-LeHCAiuU3s+nVnqPDtsbRA

Smith, M. S., & O'Day, J. A. (1991). Systemic school reform. In S. H. Fuhrman & B. Malen (Eds.), *The politics of curriculum and testing* (pp. 233–267). Bristol, PA: Falmer Press.

U.S. Census Bureau. (2006). *Population estimates.* Retrieved September 16, 2006, from http://www.census.gov/popest/estimates.php

U.S. Department of Education. (2005a, December). *Raising achievement of students with disabilities.* Retrieved April 9, 2008, from http://www.ed.gov/admins/lead/speced/achievement/factsheet.pdf

U.S. Department of Education. (2005b, December 15). 34 CFR Parts 200 and 300. Title I–Improving the academic achievement of the disadvantaged; Individuals with Disabilities Education Act (IDEA)–Assistance to states for the education of children with disabilities. Proposed Rule. *Federal Register, 70*(240), 74624–74638.

U.S. General Accounting Office. (1993). *Educational achievement standards. NAGB's approach yields misleading interpretations.* GAO/PEMD 93–12. Washington, DC: Author.

Valentine, J. C., & Cooper, H. (2003). *Effect size substantive interpretation guidelines: Issues in the interpretation of effect sizes.* Washington, DC: What Works Clearinghouse.

Vinovskis, M. (1998). *Overseeing the nation's report card: The creation and evolution of the National Assessment Governing Board (NAGB).* Washington, DC: National Assessment Governing Board, U.S. Department of Education.

Wirtz, W., & Lapointe, A. (1982). *Measuring the quality of education: A report on assessing educational progress.* Washington, DC: Authors.

Wurtz, E. (1999). *National education goals: Lessons learned, challenges ahead.* Washington, DC: National Education Goals Panel.

Zajonc, R. B. (1986). The decline and rise of scholastic aptitude scores: A prediction derived from the confluence model. *American Psychologist, 41*(8), 862–863.

CHAPTER 6

Improving the Accountability Provisions of NCLB

Robert L. Linn

The No Child Left Behind Act of 2001 (NCLB, 2002), which reauthorized the Elementary and Secondary Education (ESEA) Act of 1965, was the centerpiece of the Bush administration's educational agenda. For the 2006 fiscal year, NCLB provided $14 billion in financial assistance to states, districts, and schools with high percentages of poor children to help improve student achievement. NCLB has much that is praiseworthy, particularly for its emphasis on the achievement of all children, the special attention it gives to improving learning for children who have lagged behind in the past, and the attention given to closing persistent gaps in achievement.

A critical, albeit less praiseworthy, feature of NCLB is its heavy reliance on test-based accountability. Although there is widespread support for the general idea that schools and educators should be held accountable for improving student achievement, some of the specific NCLB accountability requirements are unrealistic or counterproductive and threaten to undermine the praiseworthy aspects of the law.

The NCLB accountability system has several fundamental problems that need to be addressed. Five of the most serious problems will be discussed in this chapter, and proposals for improvement will be provided. A brief summary of them is presented below before turning to more detailed consideration of each problem.

1. *Expectations.* The expectations for student performance, which include the adequate yearly progress (AYP) targets that lead to all students performing at the proficient level or above by the 2013–2014 school year, are unrealistic and unobtainable (Lee, 2006; Linn, 2003a; Rothstein, Jacobsen, & Wilder, this volume). More realistic expectations need to be established that are ambitious but obtainable given sufficient effort on the part of educators and students.

2. *Proficiency.* Proficient student achievement, although fundamental to the determination of AYP, is so poorly defined and varies so much from state to state that it has become meaningless. A better definition of acceptable or desirable levels of student achievement is needed.

3. *Fixed Targets versus Improvement.* Although the "P" in AYP stands for "progress," the definition of AYP focuses on current student achievement each year in comparison to a fixed target. With the exception of the safe harbor provision, improvement in student achievement is not considered in determining the AYP status of a school. A revised NCLB accountability system should consider both improvement and status.

4. *Narrow Measures.* NCLB focuses narrowly on state assessments of mathematics and reading or English language arts. Although achievement in these subjects is obviously important and state assessments can provide relevant measures of achievement, there are other important subjects and other indicators of student achievement. An improved NCLB accountability system should allow for the use of multiple sources of information about student achievement.

5. *Multiple Hurdles.* There are many ways that a school can fail to meet the AYP requirements in a given year, but only one way that it can meet them. It must meet or exceed the participation rate requirements (95% of eligible students) for mathematics and reading/English language arts for the student body as a whole and for each subgroup of students where disaggregated reporting is required, and must meet or exceed the percentage proficient or above targets for all students and for all subgroups. An improved NCLB accountability system would allow for high performance in one area to compensate to some degree for lower performance in another area.

UNREALISTIC EXPECTATIONS

The NCLB goal for student achievement is that all students perform at the "proficient" level or above by the 2013–2014 school year. As discussed in detail in the following section, proficient achievement is, in reality, a poorly defined concept that has come to have wildly different meanings in different states. The stated intention of NCLB, however, is that the proficient achievement standard should correspond to a high level of student achievement. Specifically, NCLB requires states to set challenging academic achievement standards that (I) are aligned with the academic content standards; (II) describe two levels of high achievement (proficient and advanced) that determine how well children are mastering the material in the State academic content standards; and (III) describe a third level of achievement (basic) to provide complete information about the progress of lower-achieving children toward mastering the proficient and advanced levels of achievement. (NCLB, 2002, Part A, Subpart 1, Sec. 1111 (b) (D) (ii))

Although the actual definition of academic achievement standards defining the basic, proficient, and advanced performance levels is left to the states, it is clear that the intent of the law is to set ambitious proficient and advanced levels. Ambitious achievement standards are in keeping with the sprit of the standards movement that has dominated educational assessment and accountability for more than a decade. Certainly, when achievement levels were set on the National Assessment of Educational Progress (NAEP) for the first time in 1990, they were set at quite high levels. When NAEP mathematics results were first reported in terms of achievement levels in 1990, a 4th-grade student had to be at the 87th percentile to be counted as proficient. The minimum to be counted as proficient corresponded to the 85th percentile at the 8th-grade level and the 88th percentile at the 12th-grade level (Braswell, Lutkus, Grigg, Santapau, Tay-Lim, & Johnson, 2001). Thus, 15% or fewer of all students performed well enough to be considered to be proficient or above on the 1990 NAEP mathematics assessments at any of the three grade levels assessed.

Although the NAEP standard for proficient achievement was clearly set at an ambitious level in mathematics at all three grade levels, there were no consequences for students or schools that failed to meet the standard. Under NCLB, however, there are real consequences for falling short of the proficient level on state assessments. Targets for making AYP are established in terms of the percentage of student scoring at the proficient level or above on state assessments and those targets must increase in a pattern that leads to 100% of the students being proficient in both reading or English language arts and mathematics by 2013–2014.

The expectation that a high level of achievement is required to reach the proficient level is in keeping with the achievement levels set on NAEP and on the assessments in a number of states prior to the enactment of NCLB. But is it realistic to require that all students perform at such a high level in 2013–2014? When the year for achieving the goal was selected, it was 12 years away from the initial year of NCLB, 2002, and thus corresponded to the 12 years of elementary and secondary education, or to the idea that a 1st-grade student in 2002 should reach the proficient level by the 12th grade. Even if that trajectory were reasonable for all students, which is highly debatable, it doesn't allow many years for the student who is in the 3rd grade in 2013–2014 and may have started with an extremely low level of achievement as a 1st-grade student in 2011–2012. That student is nonetheless expected to be proficient in 2013–2014.

Each state must have its own assessment and set its own proficiency level. Starting in 2003, states must also participate every other year in state administrations of NAEP in reading and mathematics at grades 4 and 8. The requirement to participate in NAEP does not specify how the state NAEP results will be used, but it is clear that NAEP is expected to provide a benchmark against which performance on individual state assessments could be compared. NAEP provides the only common measure of student achievement at grades 4 and 8 and the only uniform definition of proficient achievement across states.

One of the potential uses of the NAEP results is to evaluate the reasonableness of the expectation that all students will achieve at proficient level or above by 2013–2014 where the high level of achievement demanded by NCLB is needed to be proficient. Some would like to have NAEP become an official benchmark for judging state standards. For example, Florida governor Jeb Bush and New York City mayor Michael Bloomberg suggested that NAEP "should become the official benchmark for evaluating state standards." They went on to suggest that "states should be required to bring their standards into line" with NAEP (Bush & Bloomberg, 2006, p. 3).

In the years since NAEP achievement levels were first established in mathematics in 1990, there have been fairly substantial increases in the percentage of students performing at the proficient level or above on the NAEP mathematics assessments. The gains have been most noticeable at the 4th grade, but there have also been substantial increases at the 8th grade. On the 2007 NAEP mathematics assessment, 39% of students at grade 4 were at the proficient level or above, compared with only 13% in 1990. At grade 8, the percentage of students proficient or above on the mathematics assessments increased from 15% in 1990 to 32% in 2007 (Lee, Grigg, & Dion, 2007). Although these increases in performance are encouraging, the rate of improvement is not nearly rapid enough to reach the goal of 100% of students at the proficient level or above by 2013–2014. From 1990 to 2007, the percentage of students at the proficient level or above increased by an average of 1.53% per year at grade 4 and 1.0% per year at grade 8. If those trends continued for the 7 years from 2007 to 2014, the percentage of students who would be at the proficient level or above in 2014 would be 50% at grade 4 and 39% at grade 8. Half the students is a long way from all students.

The achievement levels for the reading assessments were set in 1992. In that year, the proficient cut score corresponded to the 71st percentile at both grades 4 and 8, that is, 29% of the students were at the proficient level or above. Since that time, there has been very little increase in the percentage of students performing at the proficient level or higher in reading. Thirty-three percent of public school students were at the proficient level or above in 2007 at grade 4 and 37% were at the proficient level or above at 8 (Lee, Grigg, & Donahue, 2007). If that same trend of a 4% increase at grade 4 over 15 years were to continue for the next 15 years, there would still be only 37% of the 4th-grade students at the proficient level or above in reading in 2022. The corresponding number for 8th-grade students would be only 33% proficient or above in 2022. Thus, 8 years after the 2014 NCLB deadline for having all students reach at least the proficient level, two-thirds of the grade 8 students would fail to achieve that level of performance. Radical changes clearly would be needed in the trends even to come close to the NCLB 100% goal, and there is no reasonable basis for thinking that such changes are feasible.

The national trends on NAEP do not auger well for reaching the 100% proficiency goal by 2014. It is simply unrealistic to expect that there would be a sudden and sustained acceleration in the percentage of students reaching the proficient level to achieve the NCLB goal (Lee, 2006; Linn, 2003a). But what about results for individual states? Are there states that have shown better achievement in general and in rate of improvement as measured by NAEP? As was required by NCLB, all 50 states participated administered NAEP in reading and mathematics at grades 4 and 8 in 2003, 2005, and 2007. Certainly, there are states that have better achievement than the nation as a whole and there are states that had greater increases in student performance than was observed for the nation. Of course, it is also true that students in some states performed more poorly than the nation.

In 2007, the percentage of students at the proficient level or above in reading at grade 4 ranged from a low of 19% in Mississippi to a high of 49% in Massachusetts. At grade 8, the range was from 17% in Mississippi to 43% in Massachusetts. For mathematics, the ranges were slightly larger than the ones for reading—from 21% proficient or above in Mississippi to 58% in Massachusetts at grade 4 and from 14% in Mississippi to 51% in Massachusetts at grade 8. Clearly, the states differ in both subjects and both grade levels in the percentage of students who are at the proficient level or above on NAEP, but no state has even half its students at that level in reading and a substantial majority of states had less than half their students at that level in mathematics at either grade in 2007.

Trends in the percentage proficient for 2003, 2005, and 2007 were reviewed to see whether there were states where the trajectories might lead to an expectation that all or nearly all students might reasonably be expected to perform at or above the proficient level by 2014. Figures 6.1 through 6.4 display the 2003, 2005, and 2007 trend lines in the percentage of students at the proficient level or above for reading at grades 4 and 8 and mathematics at grades 4 and 8, respectively, for six selected states. The selected states are the three with the largest gains in percentage proficient or above and the three with the smallest gains (which, in some cases, were actually losses) for that grade and subject.

Figures 6.1 and 6.2 show not only how far states are from the 100% goal but also that trend lines are generally flat for reading at both grade levels, even for the three states with the largest gains. Only Massachusetts at grade 4 shows a clear positive trend where the percentage proficient or above moved from 40 in 2003 to 44 in 2005 to 49 in 2007. The increases in percentage proficient or above shown in Figures 6.3 and 6.4 were usually larger for mathematics than for reading, but only two states—Montana and Pennsylvania—had increases that averaged three or more percentage points per year at grade 4, and only one state—Massachusetts—had an increase at grade 8 that averaged as much three percentage points per year.

If the proficient achievement standard is set at a high level as prescribed by NCLB and reflected on NAEP, then the goal of having *all* students perform at that level by 2014 is out of reach, despite intensive efforts of educators and students. Unobtainable goals might not be a bad thing if there were no consequences for failing to reach them. Failure to meet NCLB goals, however, has serious consequences for schools, educators, and students. Schools that fail to meet AYP targets 2 years in a row are placed in the "needs improvement" category. Those schools must develop an improvement plan, offer supplemental educational services such as tutoring, and offer school choice. Failure to make AYP for a third year in a row can result in corrective action, such as extending the school year or replacing school staff. Schools that fail to make AYP 5 years in a row are subject to restructuring. Setting unrealistically ambitious goals and sanctioning schools that fail to meet them does more to demoralize than motivate educators. This is not an argument against sanctions or ambitious goals. Rather, it is an argument that goals should be realistically obtainable given sufficient effort.

At the very least, there should be an "existence proof," that is, evidence that goals are obtainable. In the case of NCLB, it should be possible to identify some schools that have either already achieved or are on a clear trajectory for achieving the goals that are set for all schools. One way of ensuring that goals are ambitious but still within reach is to use empirical results to set the goals. Schools might be rank-ordered in terms of the rate of improvement in student achievement on the state's assessments in reading or English language arts and in mathematics over the past 4 or 5 years. The highest-ranking schools in terms of gains made on each assessment—say, the top 20%—could then be used to set the goal for all schools. If the top 20% increased the percentage of students performing at the proficient level or above by an

Figure 6.1. Trends in Percentage Proficient or Above on NAEP Grade 4 Reading for 2003, 2005, & 2007 for the 3 States with the Largest and the 3 with the Smallest Gains

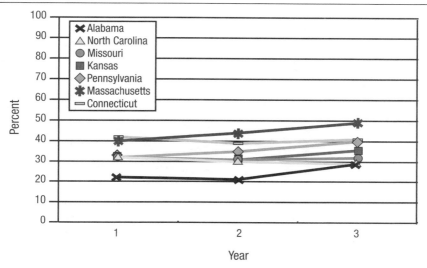

Figure 6.2. Trends in Percentage Proficient or Above on NAEP Grade 8 Reading for 2003, 2005, & 2007 for the 3 States with the Largest Gains and the 3 with the Smallest Gains

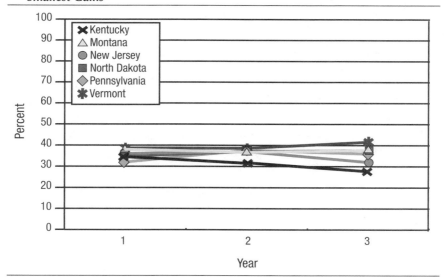

Figure 6.3. Trends in Percentage Proficient or Above on NAEP Grade 4 Mathematics for 2003, 2005, & 2007 for the 3 States with the Largest and the 3 with the Smallest Gains

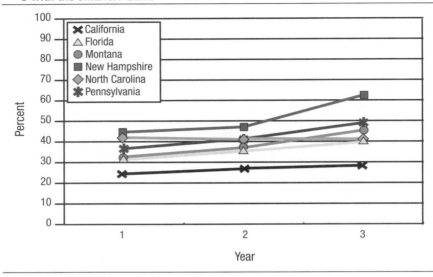

Figure 6.4. Trends in Percentage Proficient or Above on NAEP Grade 8 Mathematics for 2003, 2005, & 2007 for the 3 states with the Largest and the 3 with the Smallest Gains

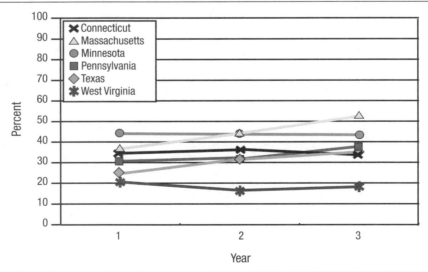

average of 2% per year in reading/English language arts and 3% per year in mathematics, then increases of 2% and 3% per year could be set as the goals for all schools. Those would certainly be ambitious goals for schools that had shown little or no improvement or possibly even declined during the past 4 or 5 years, but they would also be based on the knowledge that continued improvement at the identified rate is possible.

It is recognized that the target percentage improvement for assessments in the content areas might vary in how challenging they are to achieve for schools starting out with low student achievement compared with schools starting out with high achievement. The comparability of the challenge would certainly be more similar for schools starting at different levels of student achievement, however, than the current system, which sets the same target each year for all schools and sets the goal to be achieved by 2013–2014 at 100% of students at the proficient level or above. The improvement targets could also be combined with an overall status target so that schools that reached some relatively high level of achievement would not be expected to continue to show substantial improvements in student achievement each year.

PROFICIENCY

The standards movement has its roots in the 1980s, starting with the publication of *A Nation at Risk* (National Commission on Excellence in Education, 1983) and the efforts of the National Governors Association (NGA) that led to the 1989 Charlottesville Education Summit. President George H. W. Bush and the governors concluded that national goals were needed to stimulate reform of the educational system. President Bush announced the goals in his 1990 State of the Union address and the National Educational Goals Panel (NEGP) was established later that year (see, for example, Vinovskis, 1999). The NEGP played a leadership role in establishing and defining the standards-based reform movement. Standards-based educational reform involves the identification of two types of standards: content standards that specify the subject-matter material to be taught, and performance standards that specify expected levels of knowledge and understanding of that material for students.

The 1989 Charlottesville Education Summit and the NEGP encouraged the establishment of ambitious performance standards and provided the context in which the performance standards, referred to as achievement levels, were set for NAEP. As described above, the NAEP achievement levels defined quite high expectations. Standards-based education and accountability were prominent features of two pieces of legislation enacted during Bill Clinton's presidency—Goals 2000: Educate America Act of 1994 and the reauthorization of ESEA by the Improving America's Schools Act of 1994 (IASA) (see, for example, Hess & Petrilli, 2006, Chapter 1).

Using performance standards, or student academic achievement standards, as they are called by NCLB, to report results of student assessments is seen as preferable to the older ways of reporting test results in terms of averages and national norms. The achievement standards are meant to provide a way of reporting the degree to which student achievement is meeting expectations rather than merely indicating how students are performing in comparison with other students. The achievement standards are supposed to provide a means to identify the level of performance that is considered good enough and thereby to establish a goal for student achievement.

Reporting assessment results in terms of academic achievement standards would be sensible if there was a good way of deciding the level of achievement that corresponds to proficient performance. Unfortunately, setting achievement standards is fraught with difficulties. Many measurement professionals, even those who are most in favor of setting achievement standards, agree that "there is *no* true standard that the application of the right method, in the right way, with enough people, will find" (Zieky, 1995, p. 29). Furthermore, there is no scientific basis for defining proficient performance or translating that definition into a cut score on an assessment. Rather, the achievement standards are set by judges using one of several different methods. Where the cut scores get set depends on the method used, the context in which judgments are made, and the judges who participate in the process (Glass, 1978; Jaeger, 1989; Linn, 2003b, 2007).

Given the uncertainties in standard setting, it is not surprising that there is wide variability in the stringency of cut scores that states have set to define proficient achievement on their assessments. Olson (2005) published the percentage of students who were reported to be proficient or above on reading or English language arts and mathematics assessments at grades 4 and 8 in 2005 for each of 47 states that had assessments in place at that point (for the few states that did not have assessments in place at either grade 4 or 8 in 2005, the closest grade with assessments was used). The percentage of students who were proficient or above on the state reading/English language arts assessments ranged from a low of 35% in Missouri to a high of 89% in Mississippi at grade 4. The corresponding range at grade 8 was from 30% in South Carolina to 88% in North Carolina. The ranges of percentages proficient or above according to state mathematics assessments ranged from 39% in Maine and Wyoming to 92% in North Carolina at grade 4 and from 16% in Missouri to 87% in Tennessee at grade 8.

Although, as was illustrated in Figures 6.1 through 6.4, there certainly are real differences in achievement among states, the differences are not nearly as great is suggested by the variation in reported percentage of students who are at proficient level or above in either subject at both grade levels. Maine, Missouri, South Carolina, and Wyoming have clearly defined proficient achievement in a much more demanding way than Mississippi, North Carolina, and Tennessee. It is nonsensical to think that achievement in mathematics at grade 8 in Tennessee is so much better than it is in Missouri that the percentage of students who reach the proficient level or above is more than five times as large in Tennessee as it is in Missouri.

State-by-state NAEP mathematics results in 2005 at grade 8 stand in sharp contrast with the state assessment results reported for Tennessee and Missouri. The NAEP percentages of students who were proficient or above for those two states differed little, but the percentage was slightly lower for Tennessee (21%) than Missouri (26%). The NAEP results are dramatically different from the 87% and 16% reported for the state assessments. The definitions of proficient achievement vary so wildly from state to state that the concept lacks a common meaning. Certainly, reporting results in terms of the percentage proficient on state assessments lacks comparability from state to state.

Tracking the percentage of students above a cut score, whether it is called proficient level or something else, is not necessarily the best way to monitor progress. If the percentage of students who are above a cut score on a state assessment is to be used, however, the cut score should be more meaningful than the state-established proficient levels. There are several approaches that would be preferable to reporting results. One simple approach would be to define the standard or cut score on a state assessment to be equal to the median score in a base year, presumably 2002. The percentage of students scoring above that constant cut score would then be used to monitor improvement in achievement with target increases set at reasonable levels—for example, 3% per year. With a target increase of 3% a year, the proportion of students scoring above the 2002 median would need to increase from 50% in 2002 to 86% in 2014. That would represent a dramatic improvement in the achievement of the nation's students, but might not be totally unrealistic, and surely is not as poorly defined as 100% proficient or above given the huge state-to-state variability in the meaning of proficiency.

Another alternative would be to compare change over time with the current variability of student performance. This is usually done by dividing the change in mean scores by the standard deviation of scores, a measure often called an "effect size." The use of effect size does not suggest any acceptance of the current distribution of performance as adequate. Rather, effect-size statistics are used routinely because they make available a variety of evidence that can used to gauge the rate of change—for example, historical data on trends, international comparisons, and evaluations of the effects of past educational interventions.

An effect size for 2003 would be equal to the difference in the mean achievement score in 2003 and the mean in 2002 divided by the standard deviation in 2002. Using effect-size statistics for the top-performing, say, 20% of schools, an annual target increase in effect size could be set. This might result in an annual target increase in effect size of, say, 0.03. Thus, a school would need to have a cumulative effect size of 0.36 when 2014 was compared with the 2002 base year. An effect size of 0.36 would mean that an average student in 2014 would be performing at a level equivalent to roughly the 64th percentile in the 2002 distribution. That would represent a larger increase in student achievement of the nation's students than has been achieved in any similar period of time during the last 50 years. Although effect-size statistics are seemingly less transparent to the public than the percentage of students scoring above a cut score, effect-size statistics are widely used and are certainly less complicated to explain than the confidence intervals now used by most states to determine AYP.

FIXED TARGETS VERSUS IMPROVEMENT

Although the NCLB accountability system might appear to focus on improvement, as suggested by the word *progress* in "AYP," it actually focuses on current status. Schools where students are already achieving at relatively high levels, for example, can actually have a decline in achievement from one year to the next, and still make AYP. Schools with very low achievement initially, on the other hand, will routinely fail to meet AYP, even if they show rather sizeable year-to-year gains in student achievement. This is because, with the exception of the safe harbor provision, AYP focuses on current achievement in a given year in comparison to an annual measurable objective (AMO) for that year, rather than on changes in achievement from one year to the next.

Basing evaluations of schools almost exclusively on the current performance of students in relationship to fixed targets ignores the fact that schools differ substantially in the achievement levels of their students when they enter school. It privileges schools that serve students who are already high-achieving and puts schools serving initially low-achieving students at a substantial disadvantage. The inference that School A is of low quality or that the teachers in School A are less effective than those in School B, based solely on the fact that the percentage of students who are at the proficient level or above in a given year is smaller in School A than School B, is simply not justified. There are too many other possible explanations for the difference, most notably that the students in the two schools differed in their levels of achievement at the start of the year or when they entered 1st grade.

Many state-devised school accountability systems base their evaluations of schools on a combination of current status measures and improvement in student achievement from one year to the next. Therefore, it is not surprising that a number of states have expressed interest in the possibility of changing the way in which AYP is determined for NCLB to allow greater emphasis on improvement.

A change in the NCLB accountability system that would allow schools to meet AYP either because their current achievement met a target or because the improvement in achievement met a target seems desirable. This might be accomplished with a less stringent safe harbor criterion. Consistent with the proposals above, both the current year achievement target and the improvement target should be set in light of what has been shown to be possible by schools that have shown substantial gains over a period of 4 or 5 years.

An alternative way of evaluating change in achievement that is attractive to several states is the use of longitudinal student records to track growth in achievement for individual students. Analytical procedures, commonly referred to as value-added models, are used to estimate the school effects on student growth. Consideration should be given to the possibility of allowing states to use results of value-added analyses to provide evidence of improved achievement. The value-added results could be used, possibly in combination with status measures, to satisfy AYP requirements.

In response to widespread interest in approaches that focus on growth for purposes of determining AYP, the U.S. Department of Education authorized a pilot program that allowed states to submit proposals to use a growth model to make AYP determinations. The pilot program was announced by Spellings on November 21, 2005. Several "core principles" that must be met for a proposal to be approved were identified in a letter from Secretary Spellings to the chief state school officers regarding the pilot program. The first and perhaps most constraining principle specifies that the growth model "must ensure that all students are proficient by 2013–2014 and set annual goals to ensure that the achievement gap is closing for all subgroups of students" (Spellings, 2005). Thus, despite the argument that the expectation is unrealistic, the fixed achievement target of 100% proficient or above in 2013–2014 is maintained.

Eight states submitted proposals to participate in the growth model pilot program. Two of those proposals (from North Carolina and Tennessee) were approved for implementation of growth model pilots in 2005–2006 (Spellings, 2006). Since the approval of the first two states an additional eight states were approved for implementation of growth models for the determination of AYP.

The pilot program takes one step toward a system that would use information about growth in student performance to determine whether schools are performing adequately. This is an important step, but so far, it will be applicable for only 20% of the states. It is also limited by the continuing requirement that the amount of growth will lead to all students reaching at least the proficient level by 2014. The option of using improvement as well as current status to determine AYP needs to be available to more states and, as was argued above, more realistic achievement goals need to be set.

Many states lack a longitudinal data system that would allow them to implement a value-added model. Improvement in performance of students in those states could still be used in the determination of AYP by comparing the performance of student cohorts from one year to the next. Comparisons of successive cohorts of students (e.g., 4th-grade students in 2006 compared with 4th-grade students in 2005) lacks some of the advantages of longitudinal tracking of student achievement, but can still provide information on changes in student achievement that would complement the comparisons of current performance to fixed targets each year.

NARROW MEASURES

The NCLB school accountability system uses student achievement results on state assessments in just two subjects, mathematics and reading or English language arts, to determine AYP. Reading and mathematics are obviously of critical importance. But these are not the only subjects that are vital for students to learn. Other subjects (e.g., science, history, civics) are also important for students to understand in order to function in modern society.

State assessments are not the only means of measuring student achievement. Student achievement in reading, mathematics, and other subjects is routinely measured in a variety of ways, including district benchmark assessments, formative classroom assessments, and teacher grades. These other indicators can provide relevant information about student achievement not only in the two subject areas that are privileged by NCLB, but in other content areas as well.

In a summary report of public hearings on NCLB, the Public Education Network (2006) reported that the public believes that the focus of the NCLB accountability system is too narrow. Concern was expressed that the results often conflict with the results of a state's own accountability system and with the personal evaluations of schools by members of the public. The public thinks there is too much emphasis on a single assessment as the determining factor for AYP and would like to see the emphasis reduced by making greater use of formative evaluation information.

The public has good reason to be concerned about the narrow focus on state assessment results in mathematics and reading/English language arts for the determination of AYP. A survey of school districts conducted by the Center on Education Policy (CEP) (2006) found that 71% of the districts said that they had reduced the time devoted to at least one other subject to allow more time to be devoted to reading and mathematics (p. 89). Although some of the districts indicated that the additional time spent on reading and mathematics had helped low-achieving students make gains in those subjects, "others reported that students were shortchanged in important subjects like social studies and science" (CEP, 2006, p. 89).

The CEP finding that less time was devoted to nontested subjects is consistent with results reported in other studies. A substantial majority of teachers in two districts surveyed by Sunderman, Tracey, Kim, and Orfield (2004), for example, reported that AYP requirements caused some teachers to increase the amount of time spent on activities specifically aimed at preparing students for state-mandated assessments while deemphasizing or neglecting the content of untested topics.

The nearly exclusive emphasis on reading and mathematics can not only narrow the curriculum by overemphasizing those subjects at the expense of other subjects, but it can also narrow the teaching of the two target subjects by limiting instruction to the material that appears on the assessments. Narrow teaching to the test, emphasizing formats and predictable patterns of questions, can lead to inflated test scores. Koretz (2005) has defined score inflation "as a gain in scores that substantially overstates the improvement in learning it implies" (p. 99). Score inflation is not unusual in high-stakes accountability uses of assessment results. Several studies have found that gains in scores on high-stakes tests do not generalize well to other indicators of student achievement, such as results on the National Assessment of Educational Progress (NAEP) or the ACT (Klein, Hamilton, McCaffrey, & Stecher, 2000; Koretz & Barron, 1998; Koretz, Linn, Dunbar, & Shepard, 1991; Linn, Graue, & Sanders, 1990).

Koretz (2005) has noted that the measurement community has frequently spoken out against the use of a single test score for making important decisions largely because errors of measurement, which are an unavoidable part of any test, may lead to incorrect decisions. The use of multiple measures can mitigate problems associated with measurement error. Koretz (2003, 2005) also noted that there is an additional reason for favoring the use of multiple measures in high-stakes, test-based accountability—namely, that a single assessment can intensify score inflation by exacerbating undesirable incentives to teach narrowly to the test, to say nothing of the occasional educator who will succumb to the temptation to cheat.

The state accountability system that has been in place in Kentucky for more than a decade provides a good illustration of a school-building accountability system that encourages the teaching of a broad array of academic subjects. Student assessments in seven content areas (reading, writing, mathematics, science, social studies, arts and humanities, and practical living/vocational studies) are used by the Kentucky accountability system in judging the academic progress of a school (http//www.kde.state.ky.us/). Although the heaviest weight is given to reading and mathematics at the elementary school level, science, social studies, and writing also are given substantial weight. For middle school and high school, reading, mathematics, science, social studies, and writing are given equal weight, while somewhat lower weight is assigned to arts and humanities and practical living/vocational studies. The Kentucky approach to school accountability clearly encourages educators to attend to more than just reading and mathematics.

Although college admissions decisions differ in many ways from school accountability decisions, there are lessons to be learned from experience with college admissions that may have relevance for school accountability. There is a vast literature on the use of standardized tests to predict performance in college (see, for example, Zwick, 2002). The research is quite consistent in showing that college admissions tests such as the SAT and ACT provide reasonably good prediction of student performance in college as measured by grade point average. In most instances, however, high school grades or rank in class provide better prediction of college grades than standardized tests do. This is so, despite the fact that there are obvious between-school differences and between-course differences in the stringency of high school grades. Moreover, the combination of high school grades or rank in class and the standardized test scores do a better job of prediction than either alone.

The results of studies that have investigated the prediction of performance in college suggest that teacher-assigned grades contain useful information about student achievement despite the fact that the grades are not standardized. The use of teacher-assigned grades or systematic ratings of student achievement provided by teachers, together with a common set of district-selected benchmark assessments and formative classroom assessments selected by teachers, would likely improve the quality of information about student achievement, and could increase the validity of school evaluations when combined with the results of state assessments.

Teacher ratings of student achievement in selected subjects or teacher-selected classroom assessments could broaden the sources of information about student achievement. Combining teacher-produced scores with state assessments would require that teacher scores be reported in a common metric, such as a 1 to 5 scale, but the potential gain in information would be worth the added effort needed to obtain and use teacher-produced scores.

A concern that would have to be addressed if teacher-assigned grades were to become a part of the accountability is that teachers might give inflated ratings or grades to make their school look better. One way of addressing this would be to audit a subset of student work from classrooms where teachers have assigned grades and have that work independently rated. This has been done with teacher scoring of Regents examinations in New York State for many years. It is also the approach used in Kentucky with writing portfolios that are scored locally. Another approach would be to introduce a form of moderation, as is done in some other countries. Teacher grades are compared with performance on a common test, and when differences become too large, the test scores are used to moderate or adjust the teacher-assigned grades.

MULTIPLE HURDLES

A school can fail to make AYP for many different reasons. At a minimum, a school must clear five distinct hurdles to make AYP in a given year. It must have at least 95% of its eligible students participate in the mathematics and reading or English language arts assessments. The percentage of students who perform at the proficient level or above must meet or exceed the annual measurable objective for mathematics and the AMO for reading/English language arts. It must also meet the criterion set for the additional academic indicator selected by the state (e.g., attendance rate for elementary and middle schools and graduation rate for high schools). Because of disaggregated reporting requirements for subgroups, schools with diverse student bodies are frequently confronted with many more than the five hurdles based on all students in the school. As the number of subgroups for which disaggregated reporting is required increases, the number of hurdles that a school must clear rapidly increases (Marion, white, Carlson, Erpenbach, Rabinowitz, & Sheinker, 2002).

Thus, a school with more than the minimum number of students in each of several subgroups identified for disaggregated reporting has substantially more than five hurdles to clear. For example, a school with six subgroups (African American students, Hispanic students, white students, students with limited English proficiency, economically disadvantaged students, and students with disabilities) meeting the minimum size requirement would have not five, but 29, hurdles to clear—the five when all students in the school are considered as a whole, plus 24 for the four hurdles (participation rates in reading and mathematics, and achievement in reading and mathematics), for each of the six subgroups. Thus, the latter school could fail to make AYP in 29 different ways but could make AYP in only one way—by clearing all 29 hurdles.

Requiring schools to meet AYP requirements for separate subgroups of students is consistent with the NCLB goal of closing gaps in achievement for the identified subgroups. Nevertheless, it is clear that NCLB's multiple-hurdle approach makes it considerably more difficult for large schools with diverse student bodies to meet AYP requirements than it is for small schools or schools with homogeneous student bodies (Kim & Sunderman, 2005; Linn, 2005).

There are alternatives to the conjunctive system of multiple hurdles used in the NCLB school accountability system. The most obvious alternative is some form of a compensatory system. With a compensatory approach, achievement that is above the goal in one content area can be used to compensate for achievement that falls below the goal in another area. If the AMO for a given year was 50% proficient or above in reading and 40% proficient or above in mathematics, for example, then a school where, say, 55% of its students were proficient or above in reading but only 38% of its students were proficient or above in mathematics could make AYP under a compensatory system, while it would fail to do so under the current multiple-hurdle system. A number of state accountability systems that were in place prior to the enactment of NCLB used a compensatory approach. The California and Kentucky state accountability systems provide illustrations of compensatory approaches.

California's accountability is based on a compensatory approach. The California Academic Performance Index (API) is a weighted combination of scores on tests of English language arts, mathematics, history–social science, and science as well results of the California Alternate Performance Assessment. Schools are evaluated based on their overall API results rather than separately by comparing results with fixed targets subject by subject. The Kentucky state accountability system also uses a compensatory approach. An academic index is calculated for the Kentucky accountability system as a weighted composite of assessment results at selected grades in the seven content areas assessed by the state. An overall accountability index is then computed by combining the academic index with nonacademic indicators, such as attendance and retention, that are assigned modest weights. Relatively low achievement in one or two content areas can be compensated by achievement that exceeds expectations in other content areas.

A conjunctive, multiple-hurdle approach such as that used to determine AYP has at least two disadvantages. First, as was already noted, it places large schools with diverse student bodies at a disadvantage in comparison with schools that may serve students who are equally at risk but are more homogeneous demographically. Second, overall reliability of a school's classification can be no greater than the reliability of the least reliable indicator. A compensatory system can ameliorate both of these disadvantages. The first disadvantage is alleviated by reducing the number of indicators and associated targets. The second disadvantage is mitigated because the composite measure is more reliable than the individual measures that make up the composite.

Hybrid systems are also possible and, in the case of NCLB, might be preferable to either a pure compensatory system or a pure conjunctive system with many hurdles. A composite index could replace the five separate hurdles of participation rates and performance in the two subjects and on the other indicator. Composite indices for subgroups could also be created for the subgroups for which disaggregated reporting is needed based on a combination of participation rates and performance in reading/English language arts and mathematics. The multiple-hurdle feature of the hybrid system would then be the requirement that targets be met for subgroups as well as for all students in a school. Such a system would retain the focus on subgroup performance and closing of achievement gaps while allowing compensation across subject areas. It would also be a way to add the science assessments that will be required in 2007–2008 into the mix for determining AYP without adding to the number of hurdles that a school must clear. Moreover, it would make it relatively easy to add other measures of achievement obtained from district benchmark assessments and formative assessments selected by teachers. An overall achievement index could be formed as a weighted combination of all the measures included in the system.

CONCLUSION

NCLB has the potential to make substantial positive contributions to education. It can contribute to the improvement of student achievement and, through its focus on students who have lagged behind and too often have been ignored in the past, to the closing of achievement gaps among racial/ethnic groups, between economically disadvantaged students and their more affluent counterparts, between limited English proficient students and native English speakers, and between students with and without disabilities. Some features of the NCLB accountability system, however, need to be modified if the praiseworthy goals of NCLB are going to be achieved.

The most important modification is to set performance targets for judging adequate yearly progress that are more reasonable and that have a realistic hope of being achieved given sufficient effort. The need for more realistic goals applies to both the safe harbor provision of the law and to the annual performance targets. The current definitions of proficient achievement established by states lack any common meaning. Alternatives to defining proficiency should be considered that would provide more meaningful and comparable achievement targets. Past data on schools showing exemplary gains in achievement should be used to set goals that are ambitious, but obtainable with hard work. These goals should be expressed more clearly than current proficiency standards, which are poorly defined and vary wildly from state to state.

Changes to AYP requirements should be made that would allow schools to get credit for gains in achievement as well as absolute performance in a given year. The 2005 pilot program that allows the use of longitudinal growth models by a small number of states is a step in that direction, but the fact that the unrealistic 100% proficiency requirement in 2013–2014 is maintained undercuts the value of the program. It is limited to just 10 states. Furthermore, gains made by schools in states without longitudinal tracking systems do not count toward making AYP if the school fails to meet the AMO for either reading/English language arts or mathematics.

The narrow measures used to determine AYP should be expanded to encourage attention to subjects in addition to reading and mathematics and thereby avoid some of the narrowing of the curriculum that has been prevalent since NCLB was signed into law. Greater use should also be made of multiple measures within each of the subject areas assessed by augmenting state assessment results to take into account information obtained from district benchmark assessments and classroom-based formative assessments.

Finally, the multiple-hurdle approach used to determine AYP should be replaced by a compensatory or hybrid approach. This would make the system fairer for schools that serve heterogeneous student bodies. It would also enhance the reliability of school classification.

NOTE

The work herein was partially supported under the Educational Research and Development Center Program PR/Award R305B960002, as administered by the Institute of Education Sciences, U.S. Department of Education. The findings and opinions expressed in this chapter are those of the author and do not necessarily reflect the positions or policies of the National Center for Education Research, the Institute of Education Sciences, or the U.S. Department of Education.

REFERENCES

Braswell, J. S., Lutkus, A. D., Grigg, W. S., Santapau, S. L., Tay-lim, B.S.-H., & Johnson, M. S. (2001). *The nation's report card: Mathematics 2000.* Washington, DC: National Center for Education Statistics.

Bush, J., & Bloomberg, M. R. (2006, August 13). How to help our students: Building on the "No Child Law." *Washington Post,* p. 7.

Center on Education Policy. (2006). *From the Capitol to the classroom: Year 4 of the No Child Left Behind Act.* Washington, DC: Author. Retrieved from http://www.ctredpol.org/

Elementary and Secondary Act of 1965, Public Law No. 89–10.

Glass, G. V. (1978). Standards and criteria. *Journal of Educational Measurement, 15,* 237–261.

Goals 2000: Educate America Act. (1994). 20 U.S.C. § 5801 et seq.

Hess, F. M., & Petrilli, M. J. (2006). *No Child Left Behind primer.* New York: Peter Lang.

Improving America's Schools Act of 1994, Public Law No. 103–382.

Jaeger, R. M. (1989). Certification of student competence. In R. L. Linn (Ed.), *Educational measurement* (3rd ed., pp. 485–514). New York: Macmillan.

Kim, J. S., & Sunderman, G. L. (2005). Measuring academic proficiency under the No Child Left Behind Act: Implications for educational equity. *Educational Researcher, 34*(8), 3–13.

Klein, S. P., Hamilton, L. S., McCaffrey, D. F., & Stecher, B. M. (2000). *What do test scores in Texas tell us?* Santa Monica, CA: Rand.

Koretz, D. (2003). Using multiple measures to address perverse incentives and score inflation. *Educational Measurement: Issues and Practice, 22*(2), 18–26.

Koretz, D. (2005). Alignment, high stakes, and the inflation of test scores. In J. L. Herman & E. H. Haertel (Eds.), *Uses and misuses of data in accountability testing. Yearbook of the National Society for the Study of Education, 104*(2), 99–118.

Koretz, D., & Barron, S. I. (1998). *The validity of gains on the Kentucky Instructional Results Information System (KIRIS).* Santa Monica, CA: Rand.

Koretz, D., Linn, R. L., Dunbar, S. B., & Shepard, L. A. (1991, April). *The effects of high-stakes testing on achievement: Preliminary findings about the generalization of findings across tests.* Paper presented at the annual meeting of the American Educational Research Association, Chicago.

Lee, J. (2006). *Tracking achievement gaps and assessing impact of NCLB on the gaps: An in-depth look into national and state reading and math outcome trends.* Cambridge, MA: The Civil Rights Project at Harvard University.

Lee, J., Grigg, W., & Dion, G. (2007). *The nation's report card: Mathematics 2007* (NCES 2007–494). Washington, DC: National Center for Education Statistics, Institute of Education Sciences, U.S. Department of Education.

Lee, J., Grigg, W., & Donahue, P. (2007). *The nation's report card: Reading 2007* (NCES 2007–496). Washington, DC: National Center for Education Statistics, Institute for Education Sciences, U.S. Department of Education.

Linn, R. L. (2003a). Accountability: Responsibility and reasonable expectations. *Educational Researcher, 32*(7), 3–13.

Linn, R. L. (2003b, September 1). Performance standards: Utility for different uses of assessments. *Education Policy Analysis Archives, 11*(31). Retrieved from http://epaa.asu.edu/epaa/v11n31

Linn, R. L. (2005, June 28). Conflicting demands of No Child Left Behind and state systems: Mixed messages about school performance. *Educational Policy Analysis Archives, 13*(33). Retrieved from http://epaa.asu.edu/epaa/v11n33

Linn, R. L. (2007). Performance standards: What is proficient performance? In C. E. Sleeter (Ed.), *Educating for democracy and equity in an era of accountability* (pp. 112–131). New York: Teachers College Press.

Linn, R. L., Graue, M. E., & Sanders, N. M. (1990). Comparing state and district test results to national norms: The validity of claims that "everyone is above average." *Educational Measurement: Issues and Practice, 9* (3), 5–14.

Marion, S. T., white, C., Carlson, D., Erpenbach, W. J., Rabinowitz, A., & Sheinker, J. (2002). *Making valid and reliable decisions in determining adequate yearly progress.* Washington, DC: Council of Chief State School Officers.

National Commission on Excellence in Education. (1983). *A nation at risk: The imperative for educational reform.* Washington, DC: U.S. Government Printing Office.

No Child Left Behind Act of 2001, U.S.C. 20 § 6301 et seq. (2002).

Olson, L. (2005, December 14). Room to maneuver. *Education Week,* pp. S1–S6.

Public Education Network. (2006). *Open to the public: The public speaks out on No Child Left Behind. Summary of testimony and recommendations from the public, January.* Retrieved from http://www.publiceducation.org/2006_NCLB/main/index.asp

Spellings, M. (2005, November 21). Letter to Chief State School Officers, announcing growth model pilot program, with enclosures. Retrieved from http://www.ed.gov/nclb/landing.jhtml

Spellings, M. (2006, May 17). *Secretary Spellings approves Tennessee and North Carolina growth model pilots for 2005–2006.* Retrieved from http://www.ed.gov/news/pressreleases/2006/05/05172006a.html

Sunderman, G. L., Tracey, C. A., Kim, J., & Orfield, G. (2004). *Listening to teachers: Classroom realities and No Child Left Behind.* Cambridge, MA: The Civil Rights Project at Harvard University.

Vinovskis, M. A. (1999). *The road to Charlottesville: The 1989 education summit.* Washington, DC: National Education Goals Panel.

Zieky, M. J. (1995). A historical perspective on setting standards. In *Proceedings of the Joint Conference on Standard Setting for Large-Scale Assessments of the National Assessment Governing Board and National Center for Education Statistics* (pp. 1–38). Washington, DC: National Assessment Governing Board and National Center for Education Statistics.

Zwick, R. (Ed.). (2002). *Rethinking the SAT: The future of standardized testing in university admissions.* New York: Routledge Falmer.

CHAPTER 7

Standards, Tests, and NCLB

What Might Come Next

Robert Schwartz

A cornerstone premise of the No Child Left Behind Act (NCLB) is that the federal government can ensure that all states adopt rigorous, broad educational standards and aligned curricula and assessment instruments. If, as I will argue, the evidence to date casts serious doubt on this proposition, what are the implications for future federal policy?

Before addressing this question, let me take up a prior question: Why does it matter if states adopt rigorous standards and well-aligned assessments? To answer this, I need to go back to first principles and articulate some core assumptions underlying the standards movement. Although I would like to believe these are by now widely understood and shared, it is easy to lose sight of them in the arguments that continue to rage over testing, accountability, and NCLB.

In its simplest terms, the standards movement attempts to apply well-established principles of effective organizational development and behavior to the K–12 sector. Effective organizations have focused missions; articulate clear, measurable, short- and long-term goals; align their financial and human resources to accomplish their goals; measure progress regularly against their goals and make mid-course corrections where necessary based on data; empower line managers with the resources and authority to direct the core work of the organization; and hold managers accountable for results.

The architects of the standards movement argued that K–12 policymakers first needed to come to agreement that the core mission is an academic one: namely, to prepare all students with the foundation of knowledge and skills required for further learning, work, and citizenship. Given the rapidly shrinking proportion of family-wage jobs available to people with only a high school education, the "further learning" part of the mission statement has come to mean preparing all students to be "college-ready"–that is, to be able to go on to post-secondary education if they choose to do so.

In 1990, the nation's governors and President George H. W. Bush adopted a first-ever set of National Education Goals, the most important of which stated that "by the year 2000, all students will leave grades 4, 8, and 12 having demonstrated competency over challenging subject matter, including English, mathematics, science, foreign languages, civics and government, economics, arts, history and geography . . ." (National Education Goals Panel, 1991). Leaving aside for a minute the grandiosity of these ambitions, this goal became, in effect, a new academically focused mission statement for public education, and the early standards-development work already undertaken by a handful of states and by the National Council of Teachers of Mathematics suggested a way to operationalize the mission statement. By the end of the 1990s, virtually all states had developed learning standards in the four core academic subjects for each level of schooling, and most had adopted assessment systems and accountability policies designed to ensure that mastery of the state's learning standards became the core goal of the enterprise.

The adoption of learning standards and assessments by the states carried very substantial equity implications. In a pre-standards world in which individual districts were free to set their own learning goals for students, and districts and schools were free to establish different learning goals for different groups of students, race and class were the primary predictors of the quality and rigor of the academic program offered to students, and English language learners and students with disabilities were almost universally exposed to less challenging academic content. The persistence today of widespread achievement gaps between white and non-white students, and between "regular" education students and English language learners (ELLs) and special needs students, only confirms the obvious point: The adoption of common, rigorous learning standards for all students is but a starting point, necessary but by no means sufficient to meet the goal of enabling all students to achieve at high levels. But the creation of common learning standards that all students are expected to meet by the end of high school offers the most powerful lever yet available to equity advocates to assert the state's obligation to provide adequate learning opportunities for all students, as the Campaign for Fiscal Equity has demonstrated in its successful litigation against the state of New York. It is for this reason that some standards advocates describe the movement as having created a new "civil right"–the right to be taught to common high standards–for those who have historically been least well served by our schools.

THE QUEST FOR RIGOROUS STANDARDS AND ALIGNED TESTS

Virtually from the moment that the governors and President Bush adopted the National Education Goals, the question of how best to pursue national goals in the context of a highly decentralized, state-based education system has been on the table. Within a year after the adoption of national goals, then–Secretary of Education Lamar Alexander worked with congressional leaders to establish the National Council on Education Standards and Testing (NCEST), a bipartisan group charged with reporting back to Congress on the desirability and feasibility of establishing national standards and assessments. NCEST members struggled to find the appropriate balance between the need for a more national framework within which the country could pursue the attainment of the very ambitious national goals that had just been set, and the need to respect the sovereignty of states in setting educational policy. In its 1992 report, NCEST endorsed the need for national standards, emphasizing that they should be voluntary and national (as distinct from federal), but backed away from the Bush administration's proposal for a single national test, calling instead for a *system* of national tests from which states might choose, depending on the nature of their curriculum (National Council on Education Standards and Testing, 1992). This convoluted, Rube Goldberg–like solution to the challenge of providing national guidance without federal control foreshadowed the political difficulties that befell subsequent efforts over the next 15 years to impose some form of national quality control over the standards and assessment development work of states.

It is important to remind ourselves that the goal of ensuring that "all states adopt rigorous, broad educational standards and aligned curricula and assessment instruments" has been federal policy since 1994, when a provision to this effect was written into that year's reauthorization of the Elementary and Secondary Education Act (called the Improving America's Schools Act). States were given a date by which such standards and aligned assessments were to be in place: Failure to comply meant jeopardizing federal aid. Similar language was carried over into the No Child Left Behind Act (2002). To the best of my knowledge, no state has yet been penalized for being out of compliance with this provision, and yet by the testimony of the three national organizations that have been reviewing and analyzing state standards and tests over this period, there continues to be enormous variation in the quality and rigor of state standards, and in the degree to which state assessments measure the full range and depth of those standards.

The American Federation of Teachers (AFT) and the Thomas B. Fordham Foundation have been reviewing the quality of state standards since the late 1990s, with similar stated criteria. Both favor standards that are grounded in the core disciplines, focus on essential knowledge, are clear and specific, and make difficult choices about what to leave out as well as what to put in. Both organizations revisited the quality of state standards for the first time in several years in 2006. In 2000, Fordham's average state grade across all subjects was C-. Six years later, their average grade remained the same, despite the fact that 37 states made revisions in at least one set of standards during this period. While Fordham reviewers credit some states, including New York, with having made significant improvements during this period, in Fordham's view, others have gone backwards. Fordham's bottom line is that only three states deserve an A for the quality of their standards–California, Indiana, and Massachusetts; six more (including New York) deserve some form of B; the rest–more than half–get Ds and Fs (Finn, Julian, & Petrilli, 2006).

It should be no surprise that the AFT's grading scale is a bit more lenient, and that the teachers' organization gives the states more credit for progress than does Fordham. In its 2006 report, the AFT focused on alignment, looking for states that, in its judgment, had both strong content standards and tests that were well aligned with those standards (American Federation of Teachers, 2006). The AFT credits 11 states with meeting these criteria. Four of them–California, Indiana, New York, and Virginia–are Fordham A or B states; but two of AFT's other stars–Ohio and Washington–rate no better than D by Fordham's criteria. At the bottom of both lists are states such as Arkansas, Hawaii, Montana, North Dakota, and Wyoming, along with one very surprising anomaly: Connecticut, a state that normally shows up on lists of high performers. This suggests an important caution about the degree of weight to place on quality of standards in evaluating the overall quality of a state's improvement strategy, a point to which I will return below.

The third organization that has issued reports on the quality of state standards and tests, Achieve, was established in 1997 by a bipartisan group of governors and corporate CEOs, principally to provide advice and assistance to states as they were developing their standards, assessments, and accountability systems (I served as its first president from 1997 to 2002). In its first several years, Achieve's core activity was its Benchmarking Initiative, a process designed to provide in-depth analyses of standards and tests for interested states. Achieve did not rank or rate states, but rather provided them with the results of a very close analysis of the quality of their standards benchmarked against the very strongest U.S. and international standards, followed by a careful review of the state tests. While crediting most states with moving away from a reliance solely on multiple-choice questions and adopting a better mix of test formats, Achieve found that, in general, most state assessments did a much better job of measuring student performance on the low end of state standards (i.e., basic skills and knowledge) than assessing the more ambitious kind of reasoning, problem-solving, and analytic skills that are called for in most state standards documents.

While it may not be realistic to expect a federal review process to be able to undertake the kind of in-depth alignment analysis that Achieve was able to conduct at the request of states, it is important at least to understand the big questions that a serious alignment analysis is designed to answer. Achieve's alignment review began with a close examination of the test blueprint, attempting to map each test question against at least one standard. Then Achieve's reviewers examined each item along three dimensions: "content centrality" (i.e., does the content of the question match the content of the standard?); "performance centrality" (i.e., does the type of performance presented by the item match the type of performance described in the corresponding standard?); and "challenge" (i.e., does the level of challenge of the set of items related to a particular standard represent an appropriate range of difficulty for the particular grade level?). Finally, the reviewers looked at "balance and range," asking whether the test taken as a whole gauges the depth and breadth of the standards. The bottom line from Achieve's Benchmarking Initiative, at least at the time I left the organization at the end of 2002, was that, of the 14 states for which we had undertaken such an analysis, only one—Massachusetts— in our judgment had rigorous, high-quality standards and high-quality tests that were carefully aligned with its standards. Achieve's benchmarking work has shifted focus in the last several years, as I will explain below, but it is important to point out that several states, most notably Indiana, acted on the results of Achieve's early analyses to significantly strengthen their standards and tests, which was the point of the Benchmarking Initiative.

Before returning to the core question of the feasibility of expecting the federal government to "ensure" rigorous, well-aligned state standards and tests, I want to stand back a bit from the review processes and findings of Achieve, AFT, and Fordham and make some more general observations about the quality of standards and tests. In 2002, Marshall Smith and I wrote a piece entitled "Staying the Course with Standards-Based Reform: What It Will Take" (Schwartz & Smith, 2002). This was part of an edited volume of reflections from several members of the Pew Forum on Standards-Based Reform, a floating seminar that brought together leading policymakers, researchers, and practitioners to analyze (and, to some degree, help shape) the standards movement as it was developing during the 1990s. Smith and I outlined three sets of questions that we thought state policymakers should be asking about their standards, based on our own observations in schools as well as the analyses of the three reviewing organizations. These questions seem as pertinent today as they did then.

- Do the knowledge and skills we are asking students to master reflect the most essential concepts in this field—what all students really need to know and be able to do—or do they reflect the collective wish lists of subject-matter specialists?
- Are these standards grounded in the real-world requirements for effective citizenship, employability in a changing economy, and post-secondary education?

- Are these standards, taken as a package, manageable in the classroom? Could, for example, a conscientious, well-prepared elementary school faculty, working within the constraints of the normal school calendar, be expected to enable virtually all of its students, however diverse their abilities, to master the material embodied in the standards by the end of grade 5? If so, would there still be room for the teachers to include some topics of their own choosing that might fall outside these standards? (Schwartz & Smith, 2002, pp. 20–21)

On tests, Smith and I warned against the continuing practice in some states of using off-the-shelf tests to measure student progress on state standards, but we also encouraged states to work with districts to help them develop more instructionally useful assessments to supplement the state tests. In this regard, there has been substantial progress in recent years, as districts have begun to invest in the development of formative assessments and teachers have begun to see the benefits of having access to timelier and more instructionally sensitive information about skills and concepts students are struggling with as well as those they are mastering.

PREVIOUS FEDERAL ATTEMPTS AT QUALITY CONTROL

It is important to remind ourselves that, at the outset of the standards movement, the hope was that we could forge enough of a political consensus around national standards so that, even if they were voluntary, virtually all states would use them as guideposts in the development of their own standards. In fact, this is what happened in mathematics where, at least until the outbreak of the math wars in California, virtually all states adopted nearly *in toto* the standards developed by the National Council of Teachers of Mathematics. Unfortunately, the well-intentioned efforts on the part of the first Bush administration to encourage the development of similar standards in English and history backfired, leading to an environment for the next decade in which it was nearly impossible for elected officials to utter the words *national* and *standards* in the same sentence. Consequently, the Clinton and second Bush administrations had to resort to much more indirect strategies to address the challenge of bringing some measure of national quality control to the standards and assessment development work of states.

The first attempt to address the quality and comparability of state standards was a now-forgotten provision in the Goals 2000 Act (1994) that called for the creation of a national council to which states could voluntarily bring their standards and tests for review and comment. The National Education Standards and Improvement Council (NESIC), whose members were to be appointed by the president and Congress, was designed to help ensure that the standards and tests being developed by the states with Goals 2000 funding were of high quality. Governors such as Roy Romer (CO) and John Engler (MI) spoke at the time of how useful it would be for them to have access to an external review process in order to verify the claims being made to them by their education leaders that the standards under development in their states were, in fact, "world class."

Unfortunately, the proposed council was an early casualty of the Republican takeover of Congress in 1995. Conservative critics attacked NESIC as an attempt to create a national school board. Consequently, the Clinton administration never bothered to submit its proposed slate of nominees to the council, and this provision of Goals 2000 was quietly repealed. The desire of governors such as Romer and Engler for such a review service did not go away, however, and a year later, they and other governors and corporate leaders decided to create an independent, nonprofit organization to carry out this function, which explains how and why Achieve came into existence.

The next federal attempt to address the quality and comparability of state standards came at the beginning of Clinton's second term, when the president proposed the development of voluntary national tests in reading in grade 4 and math in grade 8. The unstated premise behind this proposal was that, even though these exams were to be voluntary and have no stakes attached, parents would be motivated to take action if the information they received about their child's achievement from the national test was wildly at variance with what they were told from the state test. Under the most optimistic scenario, the voluntary national tests would acquire sufficient political salience to motivate states to use them as benchmarks against which to align their own standards and tests. Again, however, a Republican-controlled Congress opposed the Clinton proposal as an undue expansion of the federal role, and the program died for lack of congressional authorization.

The most recent attempt to address the quality control problem is the provision in NCLB requiring states to participate in the National Assessment of Educational Progress (NAEP). The premise underlying this strategy is similar to that behind the proposed voluntary national test: namely, that undue discrepancies between performance on state tests and NAEP would motivate parents to take action to raise standards. Because NAEP is administered on a sampling basis and does not yield individual student scores, it is hard to see how this strategy will have the desired political effect. Thanks to a widely circulated article by Mark Musick of the Southern Regional Education Board, the disparities in many states between the proportion of students deemed proficient on NAEP tests versus those deemed proficient on state tests have been known for many years, and recent reports from the Fordham Foundation and Policy Analysis for California Education (PACE) have documented the continuing disparity between state and national assessment results (Cronin, Dahlin, Adkins, & Kingsbury, 2007; Fuller & Wright, 2007).

These reports have had virtually no political effect to date, which suggests that, absent information to parents about their own child's or school's performance on NAEP, NAEP results are highly unlikely to serve as a goad to state action to raise standards. In summary, then, the evidence to date is that, 14 years after federal law first required states to adopt rigorous standards and aligned assessments, we are still very far from that goal.

RETHINKING NCLB TO FOCUS ON STATE ACCOUNTABILITY

For all its problems, NCLB has accomplished one extremely important objective: It has forced states to redefine a successful school from one in which *on average* students are learning well, to one in which *all groups of students* are learning well. This was an intended consequence of the law, and whatever else may change in the next reauthorization of ESEA, the disaggregated reporting requirements of NCLB must be retained.

An important unintended consequence of NCLB has been to bring back on the table for public discussion the case for national standards. The "adequate yearly progress" provisions of the law have brought to the surface the absurdity of attempting to impose a federal accountability template on 50 states after each state has developed its own standards, adopted its own assessments, and set its own definition of proficiency. This has created incentives for states to game the system by lowering the bar, and it has led to a situation in which states with weak standards, low-level tests, and mediocre student performance are deemed successful (i.e., they have few failing schools or districts), while states with more rigorous standards and higher levels of student achievement have much larger proportions of schools deemed to be failing under NCLB.

A recent analysis by staff at the Northwest Evaluation Association (NWEA) has documented what it calls "the proficiency illusion" by comparing the proficiency cut scores on state assessments in 26 states with a normed test developed by NWEA and used in those same states. This analysis documented huge disparities among states, with 8th graders in Wisconsin, for example, being deemed proficient readers while scoring at the 14th percentile on the NWEA test while 8th graders in Massachusetts needed to reach the 77th percentile in order to be called proficient (Cronin et al, 2007; Fuller & Wright, 2007).

Before taking up the issue of national standards, let me make a modest proposal for the next round of NCLB discussions. The current NAEP requirements may not be working as the drafters hoped to shame states with low standards into strengthening them, but what if performance on NAEP

were to be the principal accountability measure for states? If states were required to show progress every 2 years on NAEP, it might have the effect
of motivating states to bring their own state assessment systems more into
alignment with NAEP. I realize that this is not how NAEP was intended to be
used, but NAEP tests have broad legitimacy among education policy leaders,
and at least a handful of states have already seen the virtue of aligning their
state tests with NAEP.

In addition to the general concern about using NAEP for accountability
purposes, I can anticipate at least two additional concerns that critics might
raise about this proposal. The first has to do with NAEP's performance levels, more specifically its overly ambitious definition of proficiency. This concern is at the heart of Richard Rothstein's contribution to this volume. My
proposal would require the establishment of biannual improvement targets
on NAEP that would be derived from each state's baseline performance and,
following Robert Linn's suggestion, from a careful analysis of the actual improvement rates of benchmark states, not on some artificial target rate that
no state or nation has ever achieved. With Rothstein, I would abandon the
fiction of a 100% proficiency goal, especially if we are using the NAEP measure of proficiency.

The second concern has to do with the design of NAEP tests, which are
based on a sampling technique that provides information at the state level
but does not produce scores for individual districts, schools, or students. If
NAEP is now to be used to hold states accountable for performance, how
will states persuade districts and schools to motivate students to take the test
seriously when the results don't really count for them? This may not be a
problem for elementary or middle school students, but I think there is good
reason to be nervous about attaching state accountability to a test that high
school students have no reason to take seriously. I think we need a separate
strategy for holding states accountable for high school improvement, as I will
outline below in my discussion of the American Diploma Project.

Just to be clear, I am proposing that federal AYP requirements ought to
apply only to states, not to districts or schools. NCLB should continue to require states to have their own accountability systems and adequate progress
requirements, but we should end the public confusion of publishing separate (and often conflicting) state and federal ratings of schools. For better or
worse, we have a state-based education system. The challenge in our system
for each level of government is to craft a set of policies that combine the right
mix of guidance, pressure, and support to induce the level just below it to
do the right thing. The federal focus ought to be on helping states strengthen
their capacity to provide appropriate guidance, pressure, and support to districts, and to monitor the performance of states to ensure that all groups of
students are making progress.

THE NEED FOR NATIONAL, NOT FEDERAL, STRATEGIES

Beyond NCLB, what might we do to create a more national set of strategies to ensure all students the right to be taught to comparably high standards? In 2006, the Fordham Foundation released a report outlining four possible approaches to the problem (Finn, Julian, & Petrilli, 2006).

One approach would have the federal government create national standards and tests. In my view, this would be bad policy as well as bad politics, and as a practical matter, there is virtually no likelihood that the public would entrust the federal government with this responsibility. The tradition of state and local control, however weakened by NCLB, is still strongly enough entrenched in our culture to prevent such an assertion of federal power in determining the content of what gets taught in our schools.

Another approach would involve "sunshine and shame," that is, using NAEP to embarrass states with low standards into raising them. As I argued earlier, I see no evidence that this approach will work. Their other two suggested approaches, voluntary national standards and voluntary consortia of states, strike me as having more promise, so let me outline some ways in which these strategies might work.

One way to address the problem of national standards is to encourage, with or without federal support, national organizations such as Fordham, AFT, and Achieve to come forward with proposed sets of model national standards. These organizations have well-developed views about what good standards look like, and states would likely pay attention to their proposals. If performance on NAEP were to become the accountability measure for state progress, such standards would need to be aligned with NAEP in order to be taken seriously by states.

A second, related strategy is to encourage organizations with curriculum and assessment development capacity to come forward with a broad instructional guidance package that would include standards, aligned curriculum, and formative and summative assessments. The College Board is one such organization that is already in this business; the National Center on Education and the Economy, which in partnership with the University of Pittsburgh's Learning Research and Development Center produced the best set of voluntary national standards in the 1990s, is another such candidate. The argument for encouraging organizations like these two, or the three mentioned just above, to take on the task of standards development is that they are independent, nongovernmental organizations with a clear point of view. Consequently, they are much likelier than states or the national subject-matter organizations to come up with standards that are coherent across content areas, focus on essentials, and are manageable in the classroom. While this strategy of encouraging a limited number of national organizations to offer aligned systems of standards, tests, and curricula might seem less ideal than the more unified national approach that characterizes most high-performing countries, we are a big, diverse nation, and having three or four optional systems of standards from which states may choose is clearly preferable to the current 50 states/50 sets of standards arrangement.

The most promising example of the voluntary state consortium approach is the American Diploma Project (ADP). ADP was launched in 2002 by Achieve, the Education Trust, and the Thomas B. Fordham Foundation. The initial goal of the project was to help states align their high school exit standards and graduation requirements with the expectations of higher education institutions and high-performance employers. Although one might have reasonably inferred that the standards development process in most states would have begun by asking, "What must all students know and be able to do upon leaving high school?" and then mapped backward to ensure that the standards at key grade levels would ensure that students were on track to meet those end goals, there is very little evidence that most states proceeded in this fashion. Consequently, ADP began by working with higher education officials and K–12 leaders in five states to analyze the alignment between high school graduation requirements and college admissions and placement standards in those states, as reflected in the assessment instruments used for these purposes by each system. Simultaneously, ADP launched a national study of a cross-section of high-performance worksites to ascertain the kinds of reading, writing, and math skills employers expected their entry-level hires to possess. Working from these two sets of data, ADP staff developed a set of benchmark standards against which states might measure the rigor and appropriateness of their own high school standards and exit requirements.

The work of ADP has helped raise consciousness among state policy-makers about the "expectations gap" between high school exit standards and college and workplace readiness requirements. In the wake of the high-profile 2005 National Summit on High Schools cosponsored by Achieve and keynoted by Microsoft Founder Bill Gates, 33 states have now joined with Achieve to form the ADP Network. These states have agreed to work together to take advantage of the ADP benchmark standards to align their high school standards, assessments, graduation requirements, and accountability systems with the demands of higher education and the workplace.

In 2008, Achieve updated a 2005 baseline survey of all 50 states on the four commitments required to join the ADP Network. On the first, aligning high school standards with the ADP benchmark standards, 19 states (up from five) reported having completed the process, with another 22 reporting movement in that direction. On the use of state test results for college admission or placement purposes, nine states (up from six) reported that they are currently doing this, with 23 more planning to do so. On the alignment of high school graduation requirements with the expectations of colleges and employers, 18 states (up from eight) met Achieve's criteria, which require all students to complete 4 years of rigorous English courses and a sequence of math courses that includes Algebra II; another 12 states plan to adopt such graduation requirements in the future. Finally, on the fourth commitment, building college and career-ready measures into high school assessment systems, nine states (up from four) said they have such policies in place, and 23 more plan to do so. An important prerequisite of this last commitment is the creation of a unified P-20 longitudinal data system that allows the tracking of students into post-secondary education. Only nine states currently have such a system in place, but 37 reported that they were in the process of either linking their two data systems or creating a unified new system (Achieve, 2008).

The ADP Network is potentially important for three reasons. First, it focuses the attention of state policymakers on the right goal: graduating all kids college-ready. Second, it encourages states to think in a more unified way about aligning their secondary and post-secondary systems, and to use student performance data from the post-secondary system to continuously improve the quality and rigor of their high school programs. Third, it is already prompting some states to consider investing together in the development of common end-of-course high school tests to help ensure that all students taking courses with the same label are, in fact, getting comparably challenging content. Fourteen states have banded together to jointly sponsor the development of an Algebra II test that all will use. If this initiative is successful, other states and other subjects will follow.

The ADP Network points us toward an alternative set of measures for holding states accountable for the performance of high schools, given the problem cited earlier with NAEP. If the target for high schools should be all students graduating college-ready, then the relevant measures for gauging biannual improvement should include factors such as the proportion of students completing a college-ready curriculum, pass rates on state end-of-course or other college-aligned tests, high school graduation rates, and post-secondary enrollment and success rates. It may seem utopian to imagine federal accountability requirements for states that would bridge into their post-secondary systems, but given the rising pressure on higher education to become more accountable for results, the time may be right to at least introduce the idea of an aligned K–16 approach to responsibility for student success.

CONCLUDING THOUGHTS

The big achievement of the standards movement over the past 15 years has been to remind us that the core mission of our schools is an academic one, and to redefine the core goal as one of enabling all students to leave high school with a solid foundation of college- and work-ready knowledge and skills. The main achievement to date of NCLB has been to cast a spotlight on the performance of key subgroups of students and to compel educators to pay special attention to those groups of students who have historically been least well served by our schools. If one has any doubt about the equity consequences of these shifts in focus and priorities of public policy toward the schools, think about the performance and public standing in the early 1990s of major urban districts such as New York, Chicago, San Francisco, and Boston, compared with the performance and public perception of these districts today. These districts now have rates of improvement in student performance that typically exceed their state averages, and they are seen increasingly by education leaders as sources of innovation rather than bureaucratic quagmires. Large-scale improvement in districts like these stems from many factors, not the least of which are changed governance arrangements and stable, highly skilled leadership. But the standards movement also played an important role; it has created an accountability environment that has encouraged policymakers to shift attention and resources to the districts and schools serving the neediest students, and it has provided incentives and leverage for bold district leaders to pursue an aggressive reform agenda.

The challenge for the next 15 years is to recalibrate the balance between top-down and bottom-up reform strategies, to strengthen the role of professional judgment and reduce our reliance on prescription, and to think more about carrots and less about sticks. The steps I have proposed—making *state* accountability the focus of NCLB by using NAEP as the measure of adequate progress; encouraging independent national organizations to come forward with proposed sets of national standards aligned with NAEP; supporting the development of consortia of states that are committed to the goal of college readiness for all—might free up space for state and local leaders to pay more attention to capacity building, and especially to strategies to support the professionalization of teaching. This brings me back to Connecticut, the anomalous state with weak standards but good performance. Connecticut is one of two states in the country that has placed teacher policy at the center of its reform strategy and has paid sustained attention to attracting, developing, and retaining a quality teaching force. Obviously, I am not encouraging states to choose investing in teachers over investing in high-quality standards: we need both. But the Connecticut story is an important reminder that good teachers are the heart of the enterprise and that high-quality standards and aligned tests are necessary but hardly sufficient elements in a comprehensive state improvement strategy.

REFERENCES

Achieve, Inc. (2008). *Closing the expectations gap 2008*. Washington, DC: Author.

American Federation of Teachers. (2006, July). *Smart testing: Let's get it right. Policy brief 19*. Washington, DC: Author.

Cronin, J., Dahlin, M., Adkins, D., & Kingsbury, J. (2007). *The proficiency illusion*. Washington, DC: The Thomas B. Fordham Institute.

Finn, C., Julian, L., & Petrilli, M. (2006). *To dream the impossible dream: Four approaches to national standards and tests for America's schools*. Washington, DC: The Thomas B. Fordham Institute.

Fuller, B., & Wright, J. (2007). *Diminishing returns? Gauging the achievement effects of centralized school accountability*. Berkeley, CA: Policy Analysis for California Education.

National Council on Education Standards and Testing. (1992). *Raising standards for American education. A report to Congress, the Secretary of Education, the National Education Goals Panel, and the American people*. Washington, DC: U.S. Government Printing Office.

National Education Goals Panel. (1991). *The National Education Goals report*. Washington, DC: Author.

No Child Left Behind Act of 2001, 20 U.S.C. sec. 6301 et seq. (2002).

Schwartz, R., & Smith, M. (2002). Staying the course with standards-based reform: What it will take? In Pew Forum on Standards-Based Reform, *Miles to go . . . Reflections on mid-course corrections for standards-based reform* (pp. 17–30). Bethesda, MD: Education Week Press.

CHAPTER 8

A Federal Foray into Teacher Certification

Assessing the "Highly Qualified Teacher" Provision of NCLB

Susanna Loeb and Luke C. Miller

The No Child Left Behind Act of 2001 (NCLB, 2002) requires that all students be taught by "highly qualified" teachers, defined as having a bachelor's degree and full state certification and having demonstrated subject-matter competency. States were given substantial flexibility in defining teacher standards and, yet, no state reached the goal of 100% highly qualified teachers (HQT) by the law's initial deadline at the end of the 2005–2006 school year. Even before this first deadline passed, the federal government established a new deadline: the end of the 2006–2007 school year.

Questions remain about why the original well-publicized statutory deadline was missed, whether the new deadline was met (data necessary to make this judgment were not yet available as we went to press), and whether the requirement itself is worthwhile. This chapter provides a set of answers to these three questions. The cause of many of the implementation difficulties can be traced to a key aspect of the law's design—a duality between federal standards and accountability on one hand and state flexibility and local control on the other. In contrast with the student performance provisions, states were initially given wide berth to implement the HQT provision. Consequently, the first 2005–2006 deadline was missed because of early state abuses of this flexibility and far too little initial oversight by the U.S. Department of Education (USDOE). We predict the new deadline was also missed not solely because stepped-up USDOE oversight came too late, but also because states have encountered substantial hurdles in compiling the data necessary to assess their performance accurately. However, despite these missteps, many of which could have been foreseen and avoided, we see merit in the HQT provision, particularly for new teachers, and argue for continued commitment to a quality teacher workforce.

Overall, evidence from the past 5 years suggests that it is possible to *reduce* teacher quality gaps across schools. The importance of this should not be understated. However, while many states are on the road to having a substantial majority of HQTs in all schools, it will take several more years until states arrive at that road's terminus, and then only if the federal government continues actively to oversee implementation efforts. As it turns out, a handful of states may, in fact, have met the new deadline, but most will need at least until the end of the 2007–2008 or 2008–2009 school years. States submitted HQT data for school year 2006–2007 in December 2007; however, these data were not publicly available as this book went to press. More important, while states are making progress in meeting the HQT requirements, actually improving teaching quality and eliminating differences across schools will require more than NCLB's HQT provision. It will require substantial structural changes so that traditionally difficult-to-staff schools are more attractive to teachers and less hindered by institutional constraints on the hiring, transfer, and dismissal of teachers.

The remainder of this chapter is presented in four sections. After a brief review of the original intent of the law, we follow the evolution of states' implementation efforts and the oversight activities of the department. The department's oversight shifted from reactive to proactive as evidence mounted that states were abusing the flexibility of the law. As the department became more active in overseeing implementation efforts, it increasingly relied on a variety of accountability measures authorized by the law. We review these accountability measures and states' reactions in the third section. Having looked back at the last 5 years, we turn our attention to the road ahead and to indicators of how the new requirements have affected and will continue to affect the teacher workforce.

INTENT OF THE "HIGHLY QUALIFIED TEACHER" PROVISION

It is indisputable that effective policies to raise student achievement rely on the skills of teachers. Teachers are the link between policy and students. The intent of NCLB's "highly qualified teacher" provision was to improve teaching and to encourage equity in teacher quality across all classrooms, while giving states flexibility in determining how to implement the provision.

NCLB seeks to accomplish these goals by establishing minimum credentials for teachers. It defines a highly qualified teacher as a fully state-certified teacher who holds a bachelor's degree and demonstrates competency in the core academic subject or subjects he or she teaches. In order to be fully state-certified, according to the standards set by NCLB, the teacher must obtain a certificate appropriate to his or her level of experience and must not be in a position where certification or licensure requirements are waived on an emergency, temporary, or provisional basis.

As we detail later, subject-matter competency proved the largest stumbling block for states. The law provides multiple options for teachers to demonstrate subject-matter competency. These options vary across four groups of teachers: new elementary teachers, veteran elementary teachers, new middle and secondary teachers, and veteran middle and secondary teachers. All teachers have the option of passing a state exam, while middle and secondary teachers also may demonstrate competency by completing an undergraduate or graduate degree in their field or through obtaining an advanced certification or credential offered by their state.

All veteran teachers also had the option of completing a High Objective Uniform State Standard of Evaluation (HOUSSE) in order to fulfill the subject-matter competency requirement. The legislation's guidance to states regarding acceptable HOUSSE designs consisted of a list of seven design elements, two of which in particular were most salient in the initial set of HOUSSE procedures. These elements directed the states to consider "multiple, objective measures of teacher competency" and authorized states to include teaching experience as one such measure. The HOUSSE option was intended to give states flexibility in deeming their veteran teachers highly qualified. As we demonstrate later, states took full advantage of that flexibility (and some abused it) in designing their HOUSSE procedures. The department required many states to revise their HOUSSE procedures to bring them into compliance with the law.

Significant criticism has been directed at NCLB's definition of quality teachers, attacking it as too focused on inputs at the expense of what really defines a good teacher—their actions within the classroom. Lee Shulman (2007), a key researcher in this area, believes a good teacher must simultaneously operate on four dimensions: intellectual, practical, emotional, and moral. He describes good teaching as that which engages students' intellectual curiosity and sees them employing practical thinking and problem-solving skills. Good teaching involves students emotionally in the learning process and affects their "values, commitments and identities" (p. 7). Here, good teaching is a description of the interaction between teacher and student. There is no mention of the student in the NCLB definition. Instead the law focuses on what teachers need to bring to the classroom to make good teaching happen.

Common sense identifies at least four traits that all teachers should possess. They must (1) be driven by the desire to educate and help their students learn. They must (2) have mastery of the subject matter they teach, and they must (3) have at least general knowledge of other subjects to help student draw connections across subjects and to the outside world. Teachers must also (4) possess pedagogical knowledge so they have a vehicle to convey their knowledge to students and a toolkit to access their learning progress. These traits are complements, not substitutes. For good teaching to occur, teachers must operate on all four dimensions, and this requires that they have all four traits.

The three components of the HQT definition can be mapped onto these four traits. The law is strongest in ensuring teachers have subject-matter knowledge. It requires knowledge demonstration that was already mandated by many states (Loeb & Miller, 2006). With regard to the other three common-sense traits of good teachers, the law, acknowledging the varying state teacher policy environments, relies on easily observed signals. Requiring a bachelor's degree helps ensure that teachers have some general knowledge of the core academic subjects. The process of earning a full state certification varies considerably across states (Loeb & Miller, 2006); however, all require candidates to expend substantial time and effort, be it as part of a traditional or alternative-route preparation program. Successful completion of these programs likely signals that candidates possess a desire to educate students and have had some training in pedagogical strategies and techniques, including some form of clinical experience (Loeb & Miller, 2006).

The available evidence is inconclusive about the extent to which the specific components of the HQT requirements—college degree, state certification, and subject knowledge—are important for student learning. It is difficult, if not completely unnecessary, to test for differences in teacher quality of those with or without a bachelor's degree, because almost all teachers have at least a bachelor's. Moreover, while there is a large literature testing the relationship between certification and teacher quality, certification means something different in each state. In addition, studies of the effect of certification vary widely in both their methodological rigor and analytical conclusions. In all studies, the comparison group of teachers is those teachers who are not certified in the current system, not those who would be teaching if certification were not required. Yet it is this unstudied group that is most relevant for the policy comparison. The inappropriate comparison between certified and noncertified teachers in the current system draws into question the relevance of the available research. Nonetheless, two state-specific studies in New York and Florida suggest that, on average, both traditionally and alternatively certified teachers add more to student learning than uncertified teachers (Boyd, Lankford, Loeb, Rockoff, & Wyckoff, 2008; Clotfelter, Ladd, & Vigdor, 2007). There is still plenty of room for debate about the extent to which certification reflects quality, as a similar study in Florida shows no relationship between certification and a teacher's value-added to student test-score gains (Harris & Sass, 2006). Similarly, while a group of studies has shown that high school students perform at higher levels in mathematics when taught by teachers with majors in that subject, we don't know the importance of content knowledge in other areas (see Brewer & Goldhaber, 2000; Monk, 1994; Monk & King, 1994; Rowan, Chiang, & Miller, 1997). Most studies of National Board for Professional Teaching Standards (NBPTS) certification do show that NBPTS-certified teachers have slightly greater value added to student learning, though completing the process of NBPTS certification in itself does not appear to improve teaching in most cases (Goldhaber, Anthony, & Perry, 2004).

While not overwhelmingly recommended by the inconclusive scientific literature, NCLB's three components of "highly qualified" can be justified from a pragmatic point of view, especially as they were selected through a combination of common sense and professional consensus. In addition, each of these teacher characteristics can be manipulated through carefully designed and appropriately implemented policies. In time, consideration ought to be given to new means of measuring "good teaching," including measures of student learning. The litmus test for any new component of the HQT definition needs to be whether it can be measured objectively and whether it can be implemented on a broad national level. Passing this test will be a substantial challenge. For now, the current definition is defensible. Its components signal traits that quality teachers need to have. As we will show in the next section, there have been several implementation missteps with implications for the potential effects of the highly qualified teacher provision.

STATE IMPLEMENTATION EFFORTS
AND THE DEPARTMENT OF EDUCATION'S OVERSIGHT

The implementation of the HQT provision is a tale of the struggle over how best to balance Department of Education oversight and state flexibility. States failed to ensure a highly qualified teacher for every classroom by the end of the 2005–2006 school year because the correct balance was never achieved. The first 2 years of implementation were characterized by near-complete state flexibility with the department oversight confined to releasing nonregulatory guidance and responding to specific questions posed by states. However, by March 2004, as evidence mounted of widespread noncompliant state definitions of highly qualified teachers, the department adopted a policy of more proactive oversight. A series of monitoring reports and reviews had the effect of reining the states in to ensure that the flexibility they exercised did not exceed that authorized by the law.

The state-federal struggle is a consequence of the intention of the provision to leave much of the responsibility for implementation to individual states. Universal primary and secondary education developed in this country as a state-level issue. This interest in states' rights was one driving force in giving states such flexibility. Many of the provision's key aspects required further detailing and defining by the states. For example, each state had to decide what types of state licensure and certification qualify as "full state certification" and which subject-matter tests to require and what cut scores to establish. States had to determine how much coursework is equivalent to an academic major and what elements should and should not be included in a HOUSSE procedure as evidence of subject-matter competency.

This emphasis on state flexibility makes sense from a practical as well as philosophical or political standpoint. The states have some of the infrastructure necessary to carry out such a requirement, while the federal government does not. Plus, states differ substantially in their teacher policies (Loeb & Miller, 2006). Therefore, even if federal officials wanted to establish a concrete national approach to teacher quality, the political and structural reality necessitates that the individual states provide much of the implementation detail and bear responsibility for most of the effort.

NCLB does, however, delineate a framework within which states' implementation efforts are to occur, necessitating some degree of department oversight. Delegating the detail to the individual states and the District of Columbia resulted in 51 unique approaches guided by 51 different interpretations of the law's intent and requirements. Crafters of the law, foreseeing this result, required states to establish a plan for all students to be taught by a highly qualified teacher by the end of the 2005–2006 school year. The department's initial decision not to require these plans to be officially reviewed and approved was the first signal that the 2005–2006 goal would not be met.

The department's initial reluctance to conduct rigorous oversight may have been the result of a lack of appreciation for the changes that states would need to make and the challenges they would face in traversing the distance between where they were in January 2002 and where the law required them to be by June 2006. At the signing of NCLB, there were significant differences across the states in their testing and coursework requirements for teacher licensure (*Improving Teacher Quality*, 2003). Only 23 states required teachers to pass an exam of both subject knowledge and subject-specific pedagogy prior to receiving a beginning teacher license. Another 11 states required candidates to pass a subject-knowledge exam but not a test of subject-specific pedagogy. Only 26 states required high school teacher candidates to hold a major in the subject taught. Only five states required the same of middle school teacher candidates. It ought to have been clear from the beginning that the department's oversight would be pivotal in determining the extent to which states would achieve the goal of the highly qualified teacher provision.

Reactive Oversight

The department explicitly downplayed its oversight role in its Title II nonregulatory guidance issued on December 19, 2002. For example, the law states that new elementary teachers can only demonstrate subject-matter competency by passing a rigorous test of content knowledge and teaching skills. However, the department informed states that they would not be required to submit these tests for review and approval by the department: "While the Department is always willing to respond to inquiries from States, it is the responsibility of the [State Educational Agency] to identify and approve such tests" (p. 19). Nearly identical language described subject-knowledge tests for middle and secondary teachers and state HOUSSE procedures. Review and approval would not be required. Essentially, the department took a hands-off approach to the NCLB-required state highly qualified teacher plans.

This approach to oversight stands in stark contrast to the department's actions regarding NCLB's student achievement goals. In order to ensure that states were complying with the law, each state was required to submit an accountability plan to the department for approval as a prerequisite for receiving funding under the law. The plans were to detail how the state would guarantee that 100% of students would meet state performance standards by 2014. To assist the states in their efforts, the department provided a template that laid out the 10 principles and their associated critical elements that each plan needed to address. As a result, every state submitted an initial plan by the January 31, 2003, deadline. The department's press release (February 3, 2003) declared, "Another important milestone reached in the implementation of historic law." Based on documents available on the department's website, it appears that they carefully reviewed each plan, paying close attention to the validity of baseline achievement data as well as how graduation rates were calculated and which students were excluded from the accountability system. Secretary Paige approved the last group of state accountability plans on June 10, 2003; however, the department's reviews continued as they requested additional information from states. Furthermore, every state has amended its plan multiple times since receiving initial department approval.

While the plans for increasing student achievement are noteworthy for the details they did include, the plans did not include strategies for ensuring highly qualified teachers. Section 1119(a)(2) clearly states that the highly qualified teacher plans were to be part of these accountability plans:

> As part of the plan described in section 1111 [the accountability plans], each State educational agency receiving assistance under this part shall develop a plan to ensure that all teachers teaching in core academic subjects within the State are highly qualified not later than the end of the 2005–2006 school year.

Yet, none of the 10 principles or their associated critical elements included in the department's template for plans addressing student achievement directly asks states about the details of their HQT plans. Initially, the department assumed a hands-off approach to states' implementation efforts.

Only a few months after President George W. Bush signed NCLB into law, one of the law's key sponsors, Senator Edward Kennedy (D-MA), along with Senator Jeff Bingaman (D-NM), submitted a request to the U.S. General Accounting Office (GAO) for information on what states were doing to ensure all teachers were highly qualified. The GAO report (U.S. General Accounting Office, 2003) was released on July 17, 2003 (18 months after NCLB was signed into law), and highlights the states' trepidation at revamping their certification and data collection systems in order to align them with NCLB without clearer and more detailed guidance from the department. States were well aware of the 2005–2006 deadline, yet they were concerned that they might complete a costly and energy-intensive revamping of their systems, only to have the department inform them that those changes were either unnecessary or that their systems continue to be non-NCLB compliant. GAO recommended that the department provide more information to states, especially regarding methods of evaluating teachers' subject-matter competency.

The department's response to the GAO report summarizes its early oversight efforts regarding teacher quality. Under Secretary Eugene W. Hickok points out the following aspect of NCLB:

> The law sets forth basic requirements for teachers, but provides States considerable flexibility in such areas as determining what constitutes full State certification and what is a "high objective uniform State standard of evaluation" of teacher competence. We recognize it is important to provide timely and informative guidance, while respecting each State's ability to develop its own systems for implementing the law. (U.S. General Accounting Office, 2003, p. 40)

A criticism of the law from the beginning was that NCLB forced a single national system upon the states. However, President Bush emphasized that flexibility was one of the law's four principles in his speech the day he signed the law. (Accountability, parental involvement, and greater funding were the other three.) The department had decided to use its lack of oversight of state progress on teacher quality as a means to emphasize the flexibility given to states and local education agencies under the law.

At the same time that the department was praising the flexibility given to states and many states had more flexibility than they knew what to do with, the grumblings of discontent and demands for still greater flexibility from educators and politicians in rural America were growing louder. They argued that key, unique characteristics of rural schools were overlooked when the HQT provision was crafted. For example, rural schools tend to be smaller than their urban counterparts and, thus, their rural teachers are more likely to be expected to teach multiple subjects to multiple grades (Stern, 1994). In an October 2003 letter to the U.S. Secretary of Education, asking for more flexibility for rural schools under NCLB, the governors of two rural states explained:

> A rural school with fewer than 100 students lacks similarity to Los Angeles Unified School District. NCLB attempts to treat them the same; they are not. As a result, many rural states and their schools feel as though they have not been considered in NCLB. (Rural Concerns, 2003)

By the end of 2003, the initial balance that the department sought to strike between oversight to ensure NCLB compliance and state flexibility was shown to be ineffective. It was clear that rural schools needed additional flexibility (which they received in March 2004); yet, a review of initial state HQT data highlighting mass noncompliance issues stressed the need for greater oversight.

Abuses of State Flexibility

When the first state data on the highly qualified status of teachers were due in September 2003, it became clear that states were not moving toward compliance. Seven states failed to provide any data at all. The Education Trust released an analysis in December 2003 that identified only a handful of states whose data might be considered an accurate description of teacher quality. Instead, most states reported data that did not comply with the federal definition. Some states claimed teachers were highly qualified on account of being certified, even though certification is just one component of the federal definition. About a dozen states submitted data that were not based on the HQT definitions that they had developed. Perhaps the most troubling findings of the analysis were the abuses of the HOUSSE provision for veteran teachers to demonstrate subject-matter competency.

These abuses were given even more scrutiny in reports released the following year by the National Center for Teacher Quality (NCTQ). These two reports highlighted abuses of the law's flexibility—particularly in the nontest, nonacademic degree options for veteran teachers to demonstrate subject-matter competency—and emphasized the need for improved department oversight (Tracy & Walsh, 2004; Walsh & Snyder, 2004). They found that seven states had equated subject-matter competency with only a successful performance evaluation, and 11 states considered their certification system as a sufficient indicator of content knowledge. Two states (Colorado and Oregon) had developed no HOUSSE procedure. Both reports recommend that the HOUSSE provision be discarded.

The Department's Switch to Proactive Oversight

With evidence of noncompliance mounting, the department stepped up its oversight activities in mid-2004 by sending monitoring teams to each state to review their progress. This marked the department's first commitment to reviewing and approving each state's highly qualified teacher definitions and plans for meeting the 2005–2006 goal. While the monitoring reports provide useful information on the progress states were making and the difficulties they were encountering, the timing of the visits and the formats of the reports make across-state comparisons more difficult.

As shown in Table 8.1, the department took almost 2 full years to complete visits to all 50 states, the District of Columbia, Puerto Rico, and the Bureau of Indian Affairs. This meant that states were visited between 30 and 52 months after President Bush signed NCLB into law. Observed variation in implementation progress is confounded with some states having more time to make progress prior to the monitoring team's visit than others.

In addition, states were not all evaluated using the same monitoring protocol. During the course of the visits, the structure of the reports issued to the states went through three revisions. Nevada was the first state visited (June 22–24, 2004), and its report is all text and lists no critical elements on which the state's progress was assessed. The reports for Vermont through Arkansas rated the states on 23 critical elements grouped into four areas: highly qualified teacher systems and procedures; administration of ESEA Title II, Part A; state activities; and activities of the state agency responsible for higher education. In the third version of the report (used for Louisiana through California), the critical elements for the first area were completely changed and substantial changes were made to the second area. The final revision was much less dramatic. The only change was the addition of two new critical elements to the second area.

Reports for all states (except Nevada) indicate whether or not the state had NCLB-compliant definitions for the subject-matter competency of the four groups of teachers identified in the law—new and veteran elementary teachers and new and veteran middle and secondary teachers. Only four states had acceptable definitions for all four groups. Sixteen states had yet to implement an NCLB-compliant definition for any group (see Appendices 8.A and 8.B).

Table 8.1. Timeline of the U.S. Department of Education Monitoring Teams Visits to States, June 2004–April 2006

Quarter	Months Since *NCLB* Signed	Frequency	States (in order of visit during quarter)
June 2004	30	1	NV
July 2004–September 2004	31–33	2	VT, DE
October 2004–December 2004	34–36	7	HI, NM, SD, UT, ND, NC, MT
January 2005–March 2005	37–39	9	IA, NE, AR, LA, ME, IL, MS, DC, OH
April 2005–June 2005	40–42	10	NJ, AZ, GA, WY, TN, WA, NH, AK, CA, SC
July 2005–September 2005	43–45	3	OR, MI, ID
October 2005–December 2005	46–48	8	MO, FL, MN, NY, AL, PA, KS, MD
January 2006–March 2006	49–51	9	CT, CO, IN, TX, KY, VA, OK, WV, RI
April 2006	52	2	WI, MA

Source: U.S. Department of Education, *Highly Qualified Teachers and Improving Teacher Quality State Grants (ESEA Title II, Part A): Monitoring Reports*, available at www.ed.gov/programs/teacherqual/hqt.html

With respect to new teachers, 29 states had compliant definitions for elementary teachers, but only 12 states could say the same for middle and secondary teachers. State definitions for veteran teachers met with no more success. Only 19 states had compliant definitions for veteran elementary teachers, while 14 had acceptable definitions for middle and secondary teachers. An appropriate definition is just a first step in ensuring that teachers are subject-matter competent, so these numbers show major problems in implementation of the reform (see Appendices 8.A and 8.B).

Determining the highly qualified status of middle and secondary social studies teachers proved particularly problematic for most states, and there were similar problems with special education teachers. Neither social studies nor special education appears as one of the core academic subjects identified in NCLB. However, both social studies and special education teachers teach in multiple areas that are identified as core academic subjects, and thus, they must be highly qualified in each of those subjects. In many states, such teachers were deemed highly qualified without demonstrating subject-matter competency in *each* of the disciplines they taught.

While this confusion can be partially attributed to inaccurate interpretations of the law, the same cannot be said for how new and veteran elementary teachers were allowed to demonstrate subject-matter competency. NCLB clearly says that new elementary teachers must pass a rigorous test; however, 10 states still had no testing requirement for new teachers at the time of their evaluation. Of these 10, four states had adopted a test but were not yet requiring it. Wyoming required a test, but because it had not yet established a cut score, it was considering all teachers highly qualified on the basis of having taken, rather than passed, the test. The remaining five states had not yet adopted a test, but three were either in the process of piloting or validating a test for possible adoption.

Similarly, the law clearly states that veteran elementary teachers must either pass a rigorous test or complete a HOUSSE procedure. Despite this, 14 states deemed them highly qualified if they had an undergraduate major (i.e., elementary education), coursework equivalent to a major, or a graduate degree. Another eight were not requiring teachers who were certified prior to the state's testing requirements to complete a HOUSSE procedure. Three states deemed them highly qualified on the basis of holding an elementary education degree. Pennsylvania only required that they be certified in elementary education, while Indiana also required them to hold a master's degree.

Moving Forward, the May 2006 Progress Report

The department required states that failed to implement sufficient HQT processes to submit plans detailing the corrective actions they would undertake to address the monitoring teams' findings. While no due date was established, all plans and documentation that were submitted and all subsequent communication between the state and the department were taken into account in the next stage of the department's oversight process. In May 2006, the department released progress reports for each state, entitled *Assessing State Progress in Meeting the Highly Qualified Teacher (HQT) Goals*. These reports marked the first time that all states were assessed using the same rubric over a reasonably short period of time. The department compiled these reports after the 2004–2005 *Consolidated State Progress Reports*, which showed that no state was likely to achieve 100% HQT by the end of the 2005–2006 school year. The data provided by the states also showed persistent gaps in teacher quality between high- and low-poverty schools.

The 2006 reports assessed each state on four requirements (see Appendix 8.C). The first requirement was that the state had developed *and* implemented appropriate HQT definitions. Despite more than 4 years of implementation efforts, only two states had fully NCLB-compliant HQT definitions, while definitions in 16 states failed to be even partially compliant. However, many states had made significant progress since the previous assessment. It should be noted that the monitoring team visits to some states had occurred only months before the *Assessing State Progress* reports were released. This could explain why some of the definitions remained out of compliance, since some states had not had time to complete the required corrective actions.

State Equity Plans

The *Assessing State Progress* reports also marked the first time that all states were assessed on their equity plans. State equity plans are supposed to detail the activities that a state will undertake to ensure that poor and non-white children are not taught at higher rates than other children by inexperienced, unqualified, and/or out-of-field teachers. This component of NCLB had been given little attention by the Department of Education in the early years. The first evidence of the department's intention to ensure compliance with this component of the law was the inclusion of a critical element in the monitoring reports for the final 38 states visited (i.e., starting in February 2005). At that time, the department was content if the states had policies and programs in place to address teacher-quality equity, and 23 states met this requirement. By May 2006, the department required states to have *detailed written* equity plans in order to demonstrate a coherent approach to ensuring an equitable distribution of teacher quality. Only three states were said to have written plans, but all of them lacked sufficient detail in the department's judgment.

An Extension and New State Plans

Following the department's review, as summarized in Appendix 8.C, federal government officials acknowledged that no state was likely to achieve 100% HQT by the end of the 2005–2006 school year. As a result, the department established a new deadline—the end of the 2006–2007 school year—and required every state to submit a revised teacher-quality plan. These plans were to specify the "new innovative actions" that states and local educational agencies (LEAs) would undertake to meet the new deadline (Johnson, 2006). The states were provided a copy of the protocol that would be used to assess the revised plans. All revised plans were due at the department no later than July 7, 2006.

In late July, the department convened a group of state-level practitioners and teacher-quality experts to review each plan. Only nine state plans were deemed acceptable on all six required elements (see Appendix 8.D). State plans were particularly deficient with regard to their written equity plans for an equitable distribution of teacher quality. Only 28 states managed to submit an equity plan, and only seven were deemed acceptable. Specifically, the written plans were required to identify where the inequities existed, to delineate specific strategies for addressing the identified inequities, to provide evidence of the probable success of those strategies, and to indicate how the state would monitor LEAs with respect to the inequities. The most common criticism the reviewers expressed was the lack of data contained in the plans. Many states failed to present data that clearly showed where the inequities in teacher assignments existed between schools with high minority and low-income populations and those with low minority and high-income populations. Kentucky and New Hampshire acknowledged the insufficiency of their data to determine the equity of the distribution of teachers. A lack of data also prevented states from providing evidence of the possible success of their proposed strategies. A review of the state equity plans released by the Education Trust (2006) 1 month after the department's reviews honed in on the weak state-level data collection and management systems.

Embedded in the department's July 2006 review protocol were several elements of requiring evidence on how they would ensure that students in schools failing to make adequate yearly progress (AYP) are as likely as other students to be taught by highly qualified teachers (see Appendix 8.E). The protocol included the following elements regarding the staffing and professional development needs of schools not making AYP:

- Does the data analysis included in the plan address the staffing needs of schools not making AYP?
- In working with LEAs to meet the 2006–2007 HQT goal, will schools not making AYP be given priority in terms of state activities and funds?
- With respect to schools failing to meet the 2006–2007 HQT goal, has the state identified forms of technical assistance that it will direct at schools also failing to meet AYP?
- Has the state identified assistance or corrective actions that will be applied to schools that both fail to meet the 2006–2007 HQT goal and AYP?

The reviews' findings indicate that while some states were taking this issue seriously, others were not (see Appendix 8.E). For example, nine states provided no evidence on any of these protocol elements even though they were given the protocol when asked to revise their plans. Only 30 states showed how they would target their technical assistance to schools not meeting AYP. Even fewer states (27) identified the technical assistance or corrective actions they would direct at failing schools.

All other states were required to submit yet another plan, most by September 29, 2006, with a few given until December 29, 2006. By the end of 2006, teacher-quality plans (and their associated equity plans) were approved for all but four states. Kentucky's plan was approved in January 2007. Vermont and Wyoming received approval in February, while Hawaii's plan was not approved until May.

This discussion of the states' implementation efforts and the evolution of the nature of the department's oversight activities from reactive to proactive demonstrate that without some form of accountability, compliance with the intent of NCLB was unlikely. With each consecutive round of review, the department's oversight became more detailed and the states became more responsive. The department planned a second round of monitoring visits to the states in 2007 and 2008. Monitoring and reporting on noncompliance issues is an important accountability mechanism, but not the only one available.

HOLDING STATES ACCOUNTABLE FOR TEACHER QUALITY

Accountability is one of the hallmarks of NCLB and also its most controversial element. The requirements that states annually test students in grades 3 through 8 and that parents be allowed to transfer their children out of persistently failing public schools have created a great deal of controversy. In contrast, the mechanisms written into the law to hold states and LEAs accountable for teacher quality have proven less nettlesome, though they are not necessarily warmly embraced.

In addition to the accountability provided by the oversight activities described above, there are five accountability mechanisms authorized by NCLB that target the law's teacher quality goals. Four involve public reporting—to the federal government, the public at large, and parents. Thus far, these mechanisms have met with very little success, due to widespread problems with data quality and availability. NCLB also empowers the department to withhold the states' administrative funds should they fail to meet the law's requirements (NCLB, 2002, sec. 1111(g)(2)).

The first four accountability mechanisms, listed below, require that appropriate data be available and correct.

- Consolidated State Performance Reports (CSPR). States are required to submit data to the department on "the quality of teachers and the percentage of classes being taught by highly qualified teachers in the State, local educational agency, and school" (NCLB, 2002, sec. 1111(h)(4)(G)). The CSPR reporting requirements have asked for more detail each year.

- State Report Cards. Each year, states are required to prepare and disseminate a state report card that, among other things, provides information on (1) the professional qualifications of teachers in the state, (2) the percentage of such teachers teaching with emergency or provisional credentials, and (3) the percentage of classes in the state not taught by highly qualified teachers at both the aggregate and disaggregated by high- and low-poverty schools (NCLB, 2002, sec. 1111(h)(1)(C)).
- Local Educational Agency Report Cards. School districts must prepare and disseminate report cards for both the district and for each of its member schools that contain the same information on teacher quality as included in the state report card (NCLB, 2002, sec. 1111(h)(2)(B)).
- Parental Notification. At the beginning of each school year, each school must notify parents of their right to request and receive information about the professional qualifications of their child's teacher. Schools are also required to inform parents in a timely manner when their "child has been assigned, or has been taught for four or more consecutive weeks by, a teacher who is not highly qualified" (NCLB, 2002, sec. 1111(h)(6)).

All of these public reporting mechanisms were required to be in place no later than the 2002–2003 school year. Unfortunately, the delay in states adopting appropriate HQT definitions and in establishing the needed data collection procedures has severely undermined implementation. As of the 2004–2005 CSPR almost half the states still had not reported accurate and complete data to the department (see Appendix 8.F).

According to the department's review, only Oregon and Texas had met the requirement to submit accurate and complete data (i.e., based on NCLB-compliant HQT definitions and accurate data) since the 2002–2003 school year. Another nine states have reported complete and accurate data since 2003–2004. This means that state year-to-year progress toward meeting the HQT goal can only be assessed in these 11 states using the legislatively mandated CSPR data. Our own review of the oversight information contained in the other official department documents makes the situation look even worse. Only one state—Kentucky—not 11, as the department claims, has submitted valid data for more than 1 school year.

Most states are also failing to publish the required teacher-quality data in their state and LEA report cards. About two-thirds of the states do not have the required information on their report cards or on the LEA report cards. Although all states have annual reports for the state as a whole and for each LEA, inappropriate HQT definitions invalidate the included teacher-quality data for the purpose of NCLB (assuming any are included). Other shortcomings are failure to include data on teacher qualifications (i.e., educational attainment and experience) and failure to disaggregate the data by poverty level. The *Assessing State Progress* reports found most states complying with the law's parental notification requirements. However, given widespread problems with data availability and accuracy, the extent to which this reporting places pressure on states and schools to ensure a highly qualified teacher for every class is unclear.

When NCLB became law, much was made of the potential for funds to be withheld should states fail to meet the law's requirements. Thus far, the department has shown only the slightest hint that noncompliance with the HQT provision will result in the withholding of funds for states' administrative activities. Conditions were placed on the funding for 12 states as a result of the *Assessing State Progress* reports. These conditions specified actions that the states needed to carry out by a certain date. It appears from the departmental communication available on its website that each of these states was contacted to discuss the actions the states would need to undertake to have the condition removed. Because the required actions vary across states with the same reasons for the conditions, the required actions were determined individually for each state as a result of these discussions.

As an example, the lack of complete and accurate HQT data was the reason for the conditions in nine states. The department has required these states to submit HQT data (some preliminary, others complete and accurate) for either the 2005–2006 or 2006–2007 school years. Each state was given a different deadline. Four of these states (Arkansas, Delaware, Minnesota, and North Carolina) have since submitted preliminary HQT data for the 2005–2006 school year and had the conditions removed within a few months of receiving the department's notification. It appears from the available documentation that the other states had taken the necessary actions by the end of 2006 to have the conditions lifted.

THE EFFECTS TO DATE AND A VIEW AHEAD

The department's increased oversight of the states' implementation efforts, combined with increased attention to the law's accountability mechanisms, has yielded results. All states now have HQT definitions that are compliant with NCLB, and most, if not all, have produced at least one round of complete and accurate data on teacher quality. At the end of the 2005–2006 school year, an average 90.1% of classrooms were taught by "highly qualified" teachers (*Comprehensive State Performance Report,* 2006). However, even with all states complying with the federal definitions, there is still a great deal of variation in what it means to be highly qualified.

As an example, one source of this variation across states is in the amount of coursework required for a major. Middle and secondary school teachers can demonstrate subject-matter competency with either an undergraduate major or coursework equivalent to a major. We found substantial variation across states in this regard in our previous work, with requirements ranging from only 12 credit hours in South Dakota to 46 semester hours for composite majors, such as elementary education, in Utah (Loeb & Miller, 2006). This difference represents almost 12 three-credit-hour classes.

States' HOUSSE procedures also induce a great deal of variation in what it means to be highly qualified. NCLB permits states to include teaching experience as an element in their procedures. However, states differ in the maximum weight that teaching experience carries in determining subject-matter competency, from 24% in Ohio to 60% in Illinois. The majority of states allow veteran teachers to amass up to 50% of the necessary points through experience (Loeb & Miller, 2006). However, as increasing numbers of teachers enter the labor force under the HQT rules for new teachers, this source of across-state variation will lessen.

With all this variation in implementation, it is easy to wonder whether the requirements have had any effect on teachers or teaching. There is some evidence that it has. States and districts have shifted from their reliance on emergency permits toward alternative-route certification. For example, California reduced the number of teachers not fully credentialed from more than 42,000 in 2000–2001 to around 20,000 in 2004–2005 and eliminated emergency permits altogether in July 2006. The number of University Intern Credentials (one of several alternative-route certificates that California issues) has increased 64% from roughly 3,700 in 2001–2002 to about 6,200 in 2003–2004 (Esch et al., 2005, p. 31). While both alternative routes and emergency credentials have less preservice training than traditional certification routes, there is a difference. Emergency permits do not require holders to demonstrate subject-matter competency before entering the classroom, while alternative routes do. Evidence from New York City, for example, suggests that teachers entering through the new routes have dramatically stronger academic backgrounds than the temporary-license teachers they replaced. In 2003, only 6% of newly hired teachers from these new routes failed the LAST exam (a state teacher certification exam) on their first attempt, compared with 16% of newly hired traditional-route teachers and 33% of temporarily licensed teachers (Boyd, Grossman, Lankford, Loeb, & Wyckoff, 2006).

NCLB's focus on teacher quality is broader than ensuring that every core academic class is taught by a highly qualified teacher. It also requires states to guarantee that poor and minority students are not taught at higher rates by inexperienced, unqualified, and out-of-field teachers. Our narrative tells how the department was very late in monitoring state progress with respect to their equity plans. However, there is at least some indication of changes in the distribution of teachers across schools since the passage of NCLB. Looking at the distribution of teachers across schools in New York City, Boyd, Lankford, Loeb, Rockoff, and Wyckoff (2008) found a conversion of teacher experience and test performance by student poverty concentration during the past 5 years. In 2000, there were substantially more new teachers and teachers who had failed their certification exam in schools serving the highest proportions of students in poverty than there were in other schools. By 2005, this difference, while still there, was dramatically lessened. The researchers found that both experience and passage of the certification exam predicted student achievement gains, so the convergence is likely to have directly affected student learning.

It is not easy to attribute the cause of these changes. NCLB did not develop in a vacuum. States were already implementing many of the ideas, if not the details, contained in the federal legislation. Because of this, we do not know whether the changes evident in New York City and elsewhere were the direct result of NCLB or a result of other, perhaps state-led forces, which produced both NCLB and the changes that occurred. They are clearly linked, even if the direction of cause is difficult to establish.

While we have seen substantial changes in the distribution of teachers across schools and in the workforce more generally, states are still a long way from correcting the current inequitable distribution of teacher quality whereby students in low-income, high minority, low-achieving schools are taught by less qualified teachers than other students. As noted above, the disparities across schools are likely driven both by teachers' preferences for certain working conditions and by state and district policies that restrict schools' abilities to hire and retain the best teachers available to them.

Our previous review of state teacher policies found that almost all states have funded incentive plans to recruit and retain teachers (Loeb & Miller, 2006). These incentives include tuition and fee support, loan forgiveness, salary supplements, housing benefits, or retirement bonuses. Yet, there are two weaknesses in this common approach. First, most incentives are not targeted at difficult-to-staff schools such as high-poverty, low-achieving schools, though 27 states operate at least one program that is so targeted. Additional targeting ought to help achieve a more equitable distribution of teacher quality. We intentionally say "ought to help" rather than "will help." The second weakness of the incentives approach is the lack of evaluations of its effectiveness. There are only a handful of reports that claim to evaluate specific states' policies. These available studies are more successful at highlighting the difficulties of evaluating the policies than the policies' effects. New data systems at the state and district level, if implemented well, may help with this analysis in the future, but the research base is not strong enough yet to identify key policy levers.

The changes during the past 5 years suggest that the federal government can help to increase the proportion of highly qualified teachers and reduce the disparities across schools. The nation's experiences thus far stress the need for states to avoid the temptation to game the system and artificially inflate HQT numbers and for the department to oversee states' implementation efforts proactively rather than reactively. In addition, the new information required by the law on the characteristics of teachers in each school brings to light the problems that do exist and provides a background for reform efforts. That said, teaching quality is largely in the hands of states, districts, and schools. More local efforts are needed to reduce the disparities in working conditions across schools that lead to systematic teacher sorting, to implement effective professional development programs, and to improve hiring, transfer, and firing systems so that schools are able to attract and retain the best available teachers. The highly qualified teacher provision of NCLB appears to have improved the supply of new teachers to traditionally difficult-to-staff schools. On the other hand, it appears to have had little effect on teachers who are already in the classroom. Improving teaching will likely require a shift in emphasis from the current focus on highly qualified teachers to a focus on highly effective teachers. Whether this shift can be facilitated by a federal initiative remains an unanswered question. We do not know the precise best approach for each state or locality; yet, to date, the federal government has been surprisingly able to effect change in states using monetary incentives. Such incentives could help stimulate alternative human resource policies that could go beyond the changes in entering teachers brought on by the highly qualified teachers provision of NCLB and more broadly influence the teacher workforce.

Appendix 8.A. State Progress on Implementing the Subject-Matter Competency Component of the HQT Provision for New Elementary and Middle and Secondary School Teachers, 2004–2006

Status of Implementation	Frequency	States
Elementary Teachers		
Met All Requirements	29	AR, CA, CO, CT, DC, HI, ID, KS, KY, LA, MD, MA, MI, MS, NJ, NM, NY, NC, OH, OK, OR, RI, SC, TN, TX, UT, VA, WV, WI
Failed to Meet All Requirements	21	AL, AK, AZ, DE, FL, GA, IL, IN, IA, ME, MN, MO, MT, NE, NH, ND, PA, SD, VT, WA, WY
Not Required to Pass Appropriate Test[a]	10	DE, IA, ME, MT, NE, NH, ND, SD, WA, WY
Special Education Teachers	9	AK, AZ, FL, GA, IL, MN, MO, PA, VT

Status of Implementation	Frequency	States
Alternative-Route Programs[b]	3	AL, GA, IN
Other Reasons[c]	1	GA
Middle and Secondary Teachers		
Met All Requirements	12	**CO, DE, IA, KS, KY, LA, NM, NC, SD, TN, UT, WI**
Failed to Meet All Requirements	38	**AL, AK, AZ, AR, CA, CT, DC, FL, GA, HI, ID, IL, IN, ME, MD, MA, MI, MN, MS, MO, MT, NE, NH, NJ, NY, ND, OH, OK, OR, PA, RI, SC, TX, VT, VA, WA, WV, WY**
Special Education Teachers	14	AK, AZ, GA, IL, ME, MN, MO, MT, NE, ND, VT, VA, WA, WY
Social Studies Teachers	35	AL, AL, AZ, AR, CA, CT, DC, FL, GA, HI, ID, IN, ME, MD, MA, MI, MN, MS, MO, MT, NH, NJ, NY, ND, OH, OK, OR, PA, RI, SC, TX, VA, WA, WV, WY
Middle School Teachers[d]	6	ID, NE, ND, VT, WA, WY
Alternative-Route Programs[b]	1	GA
Other Reasons [c]	3	AK, GA, MT

[a] This category includes the following cases in which states deem teachers to be highly qualified: states that require some new, but not all new teachers to take and pass a test; states that require all new elementary teachers to take a test but that have no cut score; and states that require all new elementary teachers to take a test but the test is not a sufficiently rigorous assessment of subject-matter competency.

[b] This category refers to states where teachers participating in alternative-route programs are deemed highly qualified even though they have not yet demonstrated subject-matter competency.

[c] This category includes the following cases: states' HQT definitions for out-of-state teachers may deem these teachers subject-matter competent when they have not demonstrated competency in accordance with federal statute or states where a minor equates to subject-matter competency.

[d] This category refers to states that allow middle school teachers to demonstrate subject-matter competency with coursework less than a major (i.e., minor) or states that deem middle school teachers highly qualified who have demonstrated subject-matter competency at the elementary level even though they teach upper-level courses (such as algebra).

Note: Monitoring Report for Nevada does not provide comparable information to facilitate inclusion in this table.

Source: U.S. Department of Education, *Highly Qualified Teachers and Improving Teacher Quality State Grants (ESEA Title II, Part A): Monitoring Reports*, available at www.ed.gov/programs/teacherqual/hqt.html

Appendix 8.B. State Progress on Implementing the Subject-Matter Competency Component of the HQT Provision for Veteran Elementary and Middle and Secondary School Teachers, 2004–2006

Status of Implementation	Frequency	States
Elementary Teachers		
Met All Requirements	19	CA, IA, KY, LA, ME, MD, MA, MS, MT, NJ, NM, NY, OH, OR, RI, SC, SD, TX, UT
Failed to Meet All Requirements	31	AL, AK, AZ, AR, CO, CT, DE, DC, FL, GA, HI, ID, IL, IN, KS, MI, MN, MO, NE, NH, NC, ND, OK, PA, TN, VT, VA, WA, WV, WI, WY
Certified Prior to State Testing[a]	8	CO, CT, DC, HI, IN, MN, MO, PA
Special Education Teachers	11	AK, AZ, FL, GA, IL, KS, NE, NC, ND, VT, WY
HOUSSE Requirements	7	AK, AR, CT, IL, MO, PA, WV
Major, Coursework, Grad Degree, Advanced Certification[b]	14	AK, AZ, DE, ID, MI, NH, ND, OK, TN, VT, VA, WA, WI, WY
Other Reasons[c]	2	AL, CO
Middle and Secondary Teachers		
Met All Requirements	14	CO, DE, IA, KS, KY, ME, MS, MT, NM, SD, TN, UT, WI
Failed to Meet All Requirements	36	AL, AK, AZ, AR, CA, CT, DC, FL, GA, HI, ID, IL, IN, MD, MA, MI, MN, NE, NH, NJ, NY, NC, ND, OH, OK, OR, PA, RI, SC, TX, VT, VA, WA, WV, WY
Special Education Teachers	10	AK, AZ, GA, MD, MO, NE, NC, ND, VT, WA
Social Studies Teachers	31	AL, AK, AR, CA, CT, DC, FL, GA, HI, ID, IN, MD, MA, MI, MN, MO, NH, NJ, NY, ND, OH, OK, OR, PA, RI, SC, TX, VA, WA, WV, WY
Middle School Teachers[d]	5	ID, NE, ND, VT, WA
HOUSSE Requirements	6	AK, AR, CT, OK, PA, VA
Other Reasons[c]	4	AR, ID, IL, WV

[a] This refers to states that deem elementary teachers certified prior to the state's implementation of required subject-matter testing highly qualified without either passing a test or satisfying HOUSSE requirements.

[b] Veteran elementary school teachers are not statutorily permitted to use these options to demonstrate subject-matter competence.

[c] This category includes the following cases: teachers can demonstrate subject-matter competency with coursework less than a major (i.e., minor) and states in which participants in alternative-route certification programs are allowed to teach without first demonstrating subject-matter competency.

[d] This category refers to states that allow middle school teachers to demonstrate subject-matter competency with coursework less than a major (i.e., minor) or states that deem middle school teachers highly qualified who have demonstrated subject-matter competency at the elementary level even though they teach upper-level courses (such as algebra).

Note: Monitoring Report for Nevada does not provide comparable information to facilitate inclusion in this table.

Source: U.S. Department of Education, *Highly Qualified Teachers and Improving Teacher Quality State Grants (ESEA Title II, Part A): Monitoring Reports,* available at www.ed.gov/programs/teacherqual/hqt.html

Appendix 8.C. Summary of *Assessing State Progress* Reports, May 2006

Finding	Frequency	States
Requirement 1: Appropriate HQT Definitions		
A state must have a definition of a "highly qualified teacher" that is consistent with the law, and it must use this definition to determine the status of all teachers, including special education teachers, who teach core academic subjects.		
Met	2	LA, UT
Partially Met	33	AL, AK, AZ, AR, CA, DE, DC, FL, GA, HI, IL, KS, KY, ME, MI, MN, MS, NV, NH, NJ, NM, NY, NC, ND, OH, OR, SC, SD, TN, TX, VT, WA, WY
Not Met	16	CO, CT, ID, IN, IA, MD, MA, MO, MT, NE, OK, PA, RI, VA, WV, WI
Requirement 2: Public Reporting of HQT Data		
A state must provide parents and the public with accurate, complete report cards on the number and percentage of classes in core academic subjects taught by highly qualified teachers. States and districts must provide these data to parents through school, district, and state report cards. Parents of students in schools receiving Title I funds must be notified that they may request information regarding the professional qualifications of their children's teachers, and they must be notified if their children have been assigned to or taught for 4 or more consecutive weeks by a teacher who is not highly qualified.		

Appendix 8.C (*continued*)

Finding	Frequency	States
Met	13	CA, FL, HI, IL, MS, NV, NH, NY, OH, OR, SD, TX, WY
Partially Met	26	AL, AK, AZ, AR, CO, DC, GA, IN, KS, KY, LA, ME, MA, MI, MN, NJ, NM, ND, RI, SC, TN, UT, VT, VA, WA, WI
Not Met	12	CT, DE, ID, IA, MD, MO, MT, NE, NC, OK, PA, WV

Requirement 3: Data Reporting to USDOE

States must submit complete and accurate data to the U.S. Secretary of Education on their implementation of the HQT requirements as part of their Consolidated State Performance Report (CSPR). In addition to reporting the number and percentage of core academic classes being taught by highly qualified teachers in all schools, states must report on the number and percentage of core academic classes being taught in high- and low-poverty schools. States must also provide additional information in the CSPR that describes, for classes taught by non-HQ teachers, the reasons that the teachers are not highly qualified.

Met	25	AL, CA, FL, DC, HI, KS, KY, LA, ME, MS, NV, NH, NJ, NM, NY, NC, ND, OH, OR, SC, SD, TN, TX, UT, WY
Partially Met	5	AZ, AR, GA, IL, VT
Not Met	21	AK, CO, CT, DE, ID, IN, IA, MD, MA, MI, MN, MO, MT, NE, OK, PA, RI, VA, WA, WV, WI

Requirement 4: Equity Plans

States must have a plan in place to ensure that poor or minority children are not taught by inexperienced, unqualified, or out-of-field teachers at higher rates than are other children.

Met	0	
Partially Met	50	AL, AK, AZ, AR, CA, CO, CT, DE, DC, FL, GA, HI, IL, IN, IA, KS, KY, LA, ME, MD, MA, MI, MN, MS, MO, MT, NE, NV, NH, NJ, NM, NY, NC, ND, OH, OK, OR, PA, RI, SC, SD, TN, TX, UT, VT, VA, WA, WV, WI, WY
Not Met	1	ID

Source: U.S. Department of Education, *Reviewing Revised State Plans: Meeting the Highly Qualified Teacher (HQT) Goal*, available at www.ed.gov/programs/teacherqual/hqt.html

Appendix 8.D. Summary of *Reviewing Plans* Reports, August 2006

Finding	Frequency	States
Overall Rating		
Acceptable	9	KS, LA, MD, NV, NJ, NM, OH, SC, SD
Deficient	42	AL, AK, AZ, AR, CA, CO, CT, DE, DC, FL, GA, HI, ID, IL, IN, IA, KY, ME, MA, MI, MN, MS, MO, MT, NE, NH, NY, NC, ND, OK, OR, PA, RI, TN, TX, UT, VT, VA, WA, WV, WI, WY

Requirement 1: Plan Must Have Detailed Analysis of Core Academic Subject Classes Not Taught by an HQT

The revised plan must provide a detailed analysis of the core academic subject classes in the state that are currently *not* being taught by highly qualified teachers. The analysis must, in particular, address schools that are not making adequate yearly progress and whether or not these schools have more acute needs than do other schools in attracting highly qualified teachers. The analysis must also identify the districts and schools around the state where significant numbers of teachers do not meet HQT standards, and examine whether or not there are particular hard-to-staff courses frequently taught by non–highly qualified teachers.[a]

Met	19	AL, AK, DC, GA, KS, LA, MD, MI, MT, NV, NJ, NM, NC, OH, PA, SC, SD, VA, WV
Partially Met	15	CO, CT, DE, IL, IN, IA, KY, ME, NH, NY, OK, RI, VT, WA, WY
Not Met	16	AZ, AR, CA, FL, HI, ID, MA, MN, MO, NE, ND, OR, TN, TX, UT, WI

Requirement 2: Plan Must Track LEA Progress and the Steps to Be Taken to Help Teachers Attain HQT Status

The revised plan must provide information on HQT status in each LEA and the steps the SEA will take to ensure that each LEA has plans in place to assist teachers who are not highly qualified to attain HQT status as quickly as possible.

Met	21	AL, DC, IN, KS, LA, ME, MD, MS, NE, NV, NJ, NM, NY, OH, PA, RI, SC, SD, VA, WA, WV
Partially Met	14	AK, AZ, CA, CT, DE, GA, IL, KY, MN, MT, NC, TX, VT, WY
Not Met	16	FL, HI, ID, IA, MA, MI, MO, NH, ND, OK, OR, TN, UT, WI

Appendix 8.D (*continued*)

Finding	Frequency	States

Requirement 3: Plan Must Detail State Activities to Help LEAs Complete Their HQT Plans

The revised plan must include information on the technical assistance, programs, and services that the SEA will offer to assist LEAs in successfully completing their HQT plans, particularly where large groups of teachers are not highly qualified, and the resources the LEAs will use to meet their HQT goals.

Finding	Frequency	States
Met	20	AL, AZ, CO, CT, DC, KS, LA, MD, MS, MT, NE, NJ, NM, OH, PA, SC, SD, VA, WV, WY
Partially Met	18	AK, AR, GA, ID, IL, IN, KY, ME, MI, MN, NV, NH, NY, NC, ND, RI, TX, WA
Not Met	13	CA, DE, FL, HI, IA, MA, MO, OK, OR, TN, UT, VT, WI

Requirement 4: Plan Must Detail How State Will Work with LEAs That Do Not Meet 2006–07 HQT Goal

The revised plan must describe how the SEA will work with LEAs that fail to reach the 100% HQT goal by the end of the 2006–07 school year.

Finding	Frequency	States
Met	19	AL, CO, DC, IL, IN, LA, ME, MD, MS, NE, NJ, NM, NY, OH, PA, SC, SD, VA, WV
Partially Met	17	AK, AR, CA, CT, GA, KS, KY, MT, NV, NC, ND, OK, RI, TX, WA, WY
Not Met	15	AZ, DE, FL, HI, ID, IA, MA, MI, MN, MO, NH, OR, TN, UT, WI

Requirement 5: Plan Must Detail How State Will Complete HOUSSE Process for Veteran Teachers

The revised plan must explain how and when the SEA will complete the HOUSSE process for teachers not new to the profession who were hired prior to the end of the 2005–2006 school year, and how the SEA will limit the use of HOUSSE procedures for teachers hired after the end of the 2005–2006 school year to multisubject secondary teachers in rural schools eligible for additional flexibility, and multisubject special education teachers who are highly qualified in language arts, mathematics, or science at the time of hire.

Finding	Frequency	States
Met	20	AL, AK, CO, CT, FL, LA, ME, MA, MI, MN, NV, NJ, NM, NC, ND, OH, OK, SC, SD, WY
Partially Met	16	CA, DE, DC, ID, IL, IA, KS, MD, MS, MT, NE, NY, OR, RI, TX, WV
Not Met	15	AZ, AR, GA, HI, IN, KY, MO, NH, PA, TN, UT, VT, VA, WA, WI

Finding	Frequency	States
Requirement 6: Plan Must Include State's Written "Equity Plan"		

The revised plan must include a copy of the state's written "equity plan" for ensuring that poor or minority children are not taught by inexperienced, unqualified, or out-of-field teachers at higher rates than are other children.

Finding	Frequency	States
Met	7	IN, KS, NV, NJ, OH, SC, SD
Partially Met	14	AK, FL, IL, LA, MD, MS, NH, NM, NY, OK, RI, TN, VA, WV
Not Met	30	AL, AZ, AR, CA, CO, CT, DE, DC, GA, HI, ID, IA, KY, ME, MA, MI, MN, MO, MT, NE, NC, ND, OR, PA, TX, UT, VT, WA, WI, WY

[a] The department requested additional information from Mississippi and therefore did not issue a finding with respect to the first requirement.

Source: U.S. Department of Education, *Reviewing Revised State Plans: Meeting the Highly Qualified Teacher (HQT) Goal,* available at www.ed.gov/programs/teacherqual/hqt.html

Appendix 8.E. AYP-Related Elements on Which State Revised HQT Plans Were Assessed, August 2006

Finding	Frequency	States
Requirement 1: Plan Must Have Detailed Analysis of Core Academic Subject Classes Not Taught by an HQT		

Required Evidence: Does the analysis focus on the staffing needs of schools that are not making AYP? Do these schools have high percentages of classes taught by teachers who are not highly qualified?

Finding	Frequency	States
Yes	28	AL, AK, CT, DC, GA, IL, IA, KS, LA, ME, MD, MI, MS, MT, NE, NV, NH, NJ, NM, NY, NC, OH, PA, SC, SD, VT, VA, WV, WY
No	23	AZ, AR, CA, CO, DE, FL, HI, ID, IN, KY, MA, MN, MO, ND, OK, OR, RI, TN, TX, UT, WA, WI

Requirement 3: Plan Must Detail State Activities to Help LEAs Complete Their HQT Plans

Required Evidence: Does the plan indicate that the staffing and professional development needs of schools that are not making AYP will be given high priority?

Appendix 8.E (*continued*)

Finding	Frequency	States
Yes	33	AL, AK, AZ, AR, CO, CT, DE, DC, ID, IL, IN, KS, LA, ME, MD, MI, MN, MS, MT, NE, NV, NH, NJ, NM, NY, OH, PA, SC, SD, TN, VA, WV, WY
No	14	GA, HI, IA, KY, MA, MO, ND, OK, OR, TX, UT, VT, WA, WI
Undecided	4	CA, FL, NC, RI

Required Evidence: Does the plan indicate that in the use of available funds priority will be given to the staffing and professional development needs of schools that are not making AYP?

Yes	25	AL, AZ, CO, CT, DC, ID, IL, KS, LA, ME, MD, MI, MS, MT, NE, NJ, NM, OH, PA, RI, SC, SD, VA, WV, WY
No	24	AK, AR, CA, DE, GA, HI, IN, IA, KY, MA, MN, MO, NV, NH, NY, ND, OK, OR, TN, TX, UT, VT, WA, WI
Undecided	2	FL, NC

Requirement 4: Plan Must Detail How State Will Work with LEAs That Do Not Meet 2006–2007 HQT Goal

Required Evidence: Does the plan show how technical assistance from the SEA to help LEAs meet the 100% HQT goal will be targeted toward LEAs and schools that are not making AYP?

Yes	30	AL, AR, CO, CT, DC, GA, IL, IN, LA, ME, MD, MI, MN, MS, MT, NE, NV, NJ, NM, NY, OH, OK, PA, RI, SC, SD, VA, WA, WV, WY
No	18	AK, AZ, DE, HI, ID, IA, KS, KY, MA, MO, NH, ND, OR, TN, TX, UT, VT, WI
Undecided	3	CA, FL, NC

Required Evidence: Does the plan include technical assistance or corrective actions that the SEA will apply if LEAs fail to meet HQT and AYP goals?

Yes	27	AL, AK, CO, CT, DC, IL, IN, KS, LA, ME, MD, MI, MS, MT, NE, NJ, NM, NY, OH, OK, PA, SC, SD, TN, VA, WA, WV
No	21	AZ, AR, DE, FL, HI, ID, IA, KY, MA, MN, MO, NV, NH, ND, OR, RI, TX, UT, VT, WI, WY
Undecided	3	CA, GA, NC

Source: U.S. Department of Education, *Reviewing Revised State Plans: Meeting the Highly Qualified Teacher (HQT) Goal*, available at www.ed.gov/programs/teacherqual/hqt.html

**Appendix 8.F. When Accurate and Complete Data on HQT Status of States'
Teacher Labor Force Was First Reported to the U.S. Department of Education,
2003–2006**

NCLB-Compliant	Frequency	States
2002–03	2	OR, TX
2003–04	9	CA, KY, ME, NM, NY, ND, OH, SC, TN
2004–05	16	AL, AZ, DC, FL[a], HI[a], IL, KS, LA, MS[a], NV, NH[a], NJ[a], SD, UT[a], VT, WY
2005–06[b]	6	AK, AR, DE, MN, NC, OK
None as of yet[c]	18	CO, CT, GA, ID, IN[d], IA, MD, MA, MI[d], MO, MT, NE, PA, RI[d], VA, WA, WV, WI

[a] The *Assessing State Progress* report for these states indicate that data for previous years may be accurate; however, changes in data collection procedures to improve data quality make it difficult to assess the accuracy of previous data.

[b] The data for the 2005–2006 school year these states (except Arkansas) are preliminary accurate and complete data that were submitted as a result of the department placing a condition on the state's funding following the *Assessing State Progress* reports. Arkansas reported 2005–2006 data in its 2004–2005 CSPR. These are the only states that have been required to submit data for 2005–2006. Data from the other states are due around March 2007 as part of the 2005–2006 CSPR.

[c] All these states have reported at least some data on the highly qualified status of teachers. However, the reported data are inaccurate because they are based on HQT definitions that are not NCLB-compliant.

[d] Other problems with state data include (1) Indiana's data for the both the 2003–2004 and 2004–2005 were based on inappropriate HQT definitions. Also, the state failed to disaggregate the 2004–2005 data by poverty level; (2) Michigan's data prior to 2004–2005 were based on FTE status of teachers, not the class; also, the state failed to disaggregate the secondary school data by poverty level; (3) Rhode Island's data for 2004–2005 were based on good definitions; however, the state was not confident in the accuracy of its data.

Source: U.S. Department of Education, *Assessing State Progress in Meeting the Highly Qualified Teacher (HQT) Goals*, available at www.ed.gov/programs/teacherqual/hqt.html

REFERENCES

Boyd, D., Grossman, P., Lankford, H., Loeb, S., & Wyckoff, J. (2006). How changes in entry requirements alter the teacher workforce and affect student achievement. *Education Finance and Policy, 1*(2), 176–216.

Boyd, D., Lankford, H., Loeb, S., Rockoff, J., & Wyckoff, J. (2008, May). *The narrowing gap in New York City teacher qualifications and its implications for student achievement in high-poverty schools* [Working paper 14021]. Cambridge, MA: National Bureau of Economic Research.

Brewer, D. J., & Goldhaber, D. D. (2000). Improving longitudinal data on student achievement: Some lessons from recent research using NELS:88. In D. W. Grissmer & J. M. Ross (Eds.), *Analytic issues in the assessment of student achievement* (pp. 169–188). Washington, DC: U.S. Department of Education.

Clotfelter, C. T., Ladd, H. F., & Vigdor, J. L. (2007, January). *How and why do teacher credentials matter for student achievement?* Cambridge, MA: National Bureau of Economic Research.

Comprehensive State Performance Report: Part I. (2006, December 1). Washington, DC: U.S. Department of Education. Individual state reports retrieved January 18, 2008, from http://www.ed.gov/admins/lead/account/consolidated/sy05–06/index.html

The Education Trust. (2003). *Telling the whole truth (or not) about highly qualified teachers: New state data.* Washington, DC: Author.

The Education Trust. (2006). *Missing the mark: An Education Trust analysis of teacher-equity plans.* Washington, DC: Author.

Esch, C. E., Chang-Ross, C. M., Guha, R., Humphrey, D. C., Shields, P. M., Tiffany-Morales, J. D., Wechsler, M. E., & Woodworth, K. R. (2005). *The status of the teaching profession 2005.* Santa Cruz, CA: The Center for the Future of Teaching and Learning.

Goldhaber, D., Anthony, E., & Perry, D. (2004). NBPTS certification: Who applies and what factors are associated with success? *Educational Evaluation and Policy Analysis, 26*(4), 259–280.

Harris, D., & Sass, T. (2006). *Teacher training and teacher productivity.* Unpublished manuscript.

Improving teacher quality. (2003, January 9). Quality counts 2003. If I can't learn from you: Ensuring a highly qualified teacher for every classroom. *Education Week, 22*(17), 90–91.

Johnson, H. L. (2006, May 12). Letters to each chief state school officer. Washington, DC: U.S. Department of Education, Office of Elementary and Secondary Education.

Loeb, S., & Miller, L. C. (2006). *State teacher policies: What are they, what are their effects, and what are the implications for school finance?* Stanford, CA: Institute for Research on Education Policy & Practice.

Monk, D. H. (1994). Subject area preparation of secondary mathematics and science teachers and student achievement. *Economics of Education Review, 13,* 125–145.

Monk, D., & King, J. (1994). Multilevel teacher resource effects on pupil performance in secondary mathematics and science: The case of teacher subject-matter preparation. In R. G. Ehrenberg (Ed.), *Choices and consequences* (pp. 29–58). Ithaca, NY: ILR Press.

No Child Left Behind Act of 2001, 20 U.S.C. § 6301 et seq. (2002).

Richardson, B., & Martz, J. (2003, October 6). *Letter to Honorable Rod Paige, U.S. Department of Education.*

Rowan, B., Chiang, F. S., & Miller, R. J. (1997). Using research on employee's performance to study the effects of teacher on students' achievement. *Sociology of Education, 70,* 256–284.

Rural concerns. (2003, October 22). *Education Week.* Retrieved December 3, 2008, from http://www.edweek.org/ew/articles/2003/10/22/08rural-b1.h23.html

Shulman, L. (2007). Good teaching. *The Future of Children, 17*(1), 6–7.

Stern, J. (1994). *The condition of education in rural schools.* Washington, DC: U.S. Department of Education, Office of Educational Research and Improvement.

Tracy, C. O., & Walsh, K. (2004, Spring). *Necessary and insufficient: Resisting a full measure of teacher quality.* Washington, DC: National Council on Teacher Quality.

U.S. Department of Education. (2002, June 6). *Improving teacher quality state grants: Title II, Part A non-regulatory draft guidance.* Washington, DC: Academic Improvement and Teacher Quality Programs, Office of Elementary and Secondary Education.

U.S. Department of Education. (2002, December 19). *Improving teacher quality state grants: Title II, Part A non-regulatory draft guidance.* Washington, DC: Academic Improvement and Teacher Quality Programs, Office of Elementary and Secondary Education.

U.S. Department of Education. (2003, February 3). *Paige announces that all states are on track by submitting No Child Left Behind accountability plans on time.* Retrieved December 3, 2008, from http://www.ed.gov/news/pressreleases/2003/02/02032003b.html

U.S. Department of Education. (2003, September 12). *Improving teacher quality: Non-regulatory guidance.* Washington, DC: Academic Improvement and Teacher Quality Programs, Office of Elementary and Secondary Education.

U.S. Department of Education. (2004, June 22–24 through 2006, April 25–27). *Highly qualified teachers and improving teacher quality state grants (ESEA Title II, Part A): Monitoring reports.* Washington, DC: Academic Improvement and Teacher Quality Programs, Office of Elementary and Secondary Education.

U.S. Department of Education. (2005, August 3). *Highly qualified teachers: Improving teacher quality state grants ESEA Title II, Part A, non-regulatory guidance.* Washington, DC: Academic Improvement and Teacher Quality Programs, Office of Elementary and Secondary Education.

U.S. Department of Education. (2006, April 17–May 9). *Assessing state progress in meeting the highly qualified teacher (HQT) goals.* Washington, DC: Academic Improvement and Teacher Quality Programs, Office of Elementary and Secondary Education.

U.S. Department of Education. (2006, July 25–27). *Reviewing revised state plans: Meeting the highly qualified teacher (HQT) goal.* Washington, DC: Academic Improvement and Teacher Quality Programs, Office of Elementary and Secondary Education.

U.S. General Accounting Office. (2003, July 17). *No Child Left Behind Act: More information would help states determine which teachers are highly qualified.* GAO-03-631. Washington, DC: Author.

Walsh, K., & Snyder, E. (2004, December). *Searching the attic: How states are responding to the nation's goal of placing a highly qualified teacher in every classroom.* Washington, DC: National Council on Teacher Quality.

CHAPTER 9

The Problem of Capacity in the (Re)Design of Educational Accountability Systems

Richard F. Elmore

Accountability in education requires a complex mix of pressure and support. On the pressure side, accountability systems operate by surrounding schools with systems of standards, measures, targets, and sanctions designed to move performance in a particular direction. On the support side, accountability systems succeed to the degree that they stimulate demand for new knowledge about how to meet performance targets and generate the supply of knowledge that meets that demand. In this sense, educational accountability systems are a special case of the more general class of regulatory policies. In general, regulatory policies try to get individuals or institutions to do something they might not otherwise do in the absence of external pressure or coercion. Such is the case with educational accountability systems, but with an important difference: that educational accountability systems are often—one might say usually—asking schools to do things they do not know how to do. That is, in order to meet the performance targets specified by accountability systems, schools and school systems must engage in classroom practices, develop organizational structures and routines, and manage resources in ways that are unfamiliar to them and that require significant investments in learning. Sometimes the knowledge and skill necessary to meet performance targets are resident in the organization, or are easily acquired using the existing knowledge and skill of people in the organization. More often, educational accountability systems require a level of knowledge and skill that is not embedded in the organization, and the pressure of accountability activates a demand for new knowledge that may or may not be met by the environment in which schools operate. If accountability in education were simply a matter of compliance, then strong enforcement would produce performance. But accountability is also a matter of knowledge, which means that enforcement has to be counterbalanced with support. In Thomas Schelling's (1974) terms, this is the difference between "doing the right thing," and "knowing the right thing to do."

This chapter is about the relationship between pressure and support—regulatory coercion and knowledge—in educational accountability systems. It provides a framework for understanding how accountability policies work, and a critique of existing policies, with special attention to No Child Left Behind (NCLB). It focuses, in particular, on two meanings of the term *capacity* in educational accountability policies. The first is the *capacity to enforce*. Whatever the rhetoric that surrounds accountability policy, the underlying theory is that one level of government has the power to force another level of government (or a private firm) to do something that it would not otherwise do, or would not do in the same way, by administering sanctions, or withholding valued resources. The credibility of regulatory force depends on at least three factors: (1) the capacity of the regulatory agency to enforce; (2) the feasibility of the actions required by the regulations; and (3) the consent of the targets of regulations to be regulated. We will see that federal education policy in general, and NCLB in particular, presents an unusual set of problems around regulatory capacity.

The second meaning of capacity in accountability policy is the *capacity to perform*. Educational accountability policies require schools and schools systems not just to comply with regulatory requirements—of which there are many—but also to *produce performance* of a particular kind, according to a particular metric, over a specified period of time. No Child Left Behind requires schools and school systems to improve the performance of students across grade levels in core academic subjects against a state-specified standard in such a way that all students meet a standard of proficiency by the year 2014. The capacity to produce performance is definitely not the same thing as the capacity to comply. Producing performance, as noted above, requires the development and deployment of knowledge and skill. What this capacity looks like and how it are formed are factors critical to the success of accountability policies.

THE CAPACITY TO ENFORCE ACCOUNTABILITY

Federal Policy: Borrowing Capacity and Regulatory Drift

NCLB signals a major break with past federal policy. It constitutes a federal preemption of accountability policy, which had previously been, for all practical purposes, entirely a state function. Prior to NCLB, the federal government's role in accountability was marginal at best. The 1997 amendments to the Elementary and Secondary Education Act, which were designed to situate the federal government in a more powerful position around state and local accountability systems, had failed to produce their intended effect. Governors and state legislatures had taken the initiative in forming accountability policy. All 50 states had developed and implemented accountability systems in collaboration with each other, and these systems, as is usually the case with the "laboratory of federalism," embodied wide variations around the central elements of accountability policy. States used a variety of different types of tests, sanctions varied widely, stakes were distributed among key actors differently, and success and failure were defined in different ways. NCLB, in effect, preempted the states' initiative. While the rhetoric around NCLB carefully asserts the primary role of states in accountability policy, the reality is considerably different. NCLB sets fixed parameters on state accountability systems that previously did not exist in federal policy. These requirements dramatically reduce the range of variation among state policy that previously existed: Annual testing at fixed grade levels, for example, limits the type of tests that can be used—more ambitious, criterion-referenced tests are too expensive to administer and score for every student on an annual basis. The fixed schedule of sanctions under NCLB—schools progress through uniform stages of sanctions, on a uniform schedule, as they fail to meet performance standards—limits states' and localities' flexibility in identifying failing schools and crafting remedies for them. The schedule of performance gains prescribed by the law—every student at proficiency by 2014—requires all states to define the required rate of improvement in the same way, and introduces strong incentives for states to lower their definitions of proficiency. The requirement that parents receive notification of low performance in their schools and access to alternative services prescribes the same remedy for low performance in all instances, limiting flexibility in responding to differences among schools. The requirement that every child should have a "highly qualified" teacher attempts to create uniformity in what is by definition a widely varying patchwork of regional labor markets, each with its own particular characteristics of supply and demand. Each of these elements, and many more, in NCLB is part of a dance of federalism, in which the federal government effectively preempts state and local accountability policy, while at the same time arguing that what it is actually doing is participating in a partnership in which states and localities exercise control over the specifics of their accountability systems. However one characterizes this dance, it represents a dramatic shift in the relationship among the federal government, states, and localities in the governance and control of education.

Underlying this dance of federalism is a long-term, very stable reality: The federal government has little independent capacity to produce educational outcomes at the state and local level. Its power is effectively limited to its ability to capture and redirect state and local capacity. The federal government's operating budget–as opposed to its grant-in-aid budget–is small relative to state and local operating budgets. Hence, its capacity to engage in direct oversight and enforcement of regulatory requirements is severely limited. Federal expenditures in the K–12 sector are a tiny fraction of total expenditures in the sector. Hence, federal capacity to exercise influence over state and local decisions directly, through the use of financial controls, is limited. The way federal influence works is highly specialized. While federal expenditures are a small proportion of education expenditures in general, they are a significantly larger proportion of expenditures in urban school systems, and in suburban systems with increasingly diversifying populations. Federal funds also constitute the major source of funding for most state educational agencies, which are, in effect if not in principle, wholly owned subsidiaries of the federal government. Federal, state, and local relations in the K–12 sector, then, are characterized by a long-term dynamic that Paul Manna (2006) calls "borrowing strength"–what I will call "borrowing capacity."

Manna's framework predicts that policy relations between the federal government and the states hinge on three factors: (1) the presence of *policy entrepreneurs* who capitalize on latent issues and turn them into policy problems; (2) the *license to act,* or the presence of a statutory or constitutional rationale for intervention; and (3) the *capacity to act,* or the "human, budgetary, and institutional resources" to implement its claim to license to act (Manna, 2006, pp. 28–33, 31). When policy entrepreneurs operate in a policy domain where the federal government has high license and high capacity, they are likely to intervene without regard the capacity of states or localities. Lacking high license and capacity, federal policy entrepreneurs are likely to borrow strength from states and localities. Having made the decision to borrow strength, the success of federal policy depends on the accuracy of policy entrepreneurs' assessment of the license and capacity of state and local agencies in the domain where they have chosen to act. As the limits of state and local license and capacity become apparent, Manna's theory predicts, the federal government will negotiate with states and localities to modify the demands of federal policy (Manna, 2006).

What does "borrowing strength" or "borrowing capacity" actually look like? First, federal revenue constitutes a very large share of the operating revenue of state departments of education–anywhere from 10% to 50%, depending on the composition of the student population and the mix of federal programs in which states are involved. The combination of federal revenue and the regulatory load of federal policy means that state departments of education in states with large populations of children in poverty are, as I have mentioned, close to being wholly owned subsidiaries of the federal government, at least for accountability purposes. It also means that state department organization and state capacity tends to mirror federal organization and capacity, heavily driven in the direction of regulatory oversight and away from investments in knowledge and skill at the local level (Manna, 2006). In California, for example, federal revenue in the 2006–2007 fiscal year from all sources accounts for about $7.5 billion of a $66 billion K–12 budget. About $41 billion of funding for elementary and secondary schools comes from the state general fund, about $13 billion from local property taxes. So, in effect, federal regulatory leverage in California operates on about 9% of the state's total educational expenditures. But it capitalizes on the fact that the state provides about 76% of local revenues for education. In Los Angeles, Title I accounts for about $820 million of a $13 billion education budget (all federal programs account for about $1.2 billion). So federal regulatory leverage in Los Angeles operates on a ratio of about 6% (Los Angeles Unified School District, 2006; State of California, n.d.). These ratios will vary across states, but the underlying principle is clear: Federal policy operates on a relatively small margin, using its regulatory power to influence the use of large amounts of state and local capacity, relying on influencing the flow of revenue from state and local sources as a means of control.

Within the K–12 domain, the federal government lacks both the financial and operational capacity to enact its policy goals independently; federal policy works, insofar as it works at all, by the federal government using its limited leverage in a concentrated way to "borrow" the capacity of states and localities for its own ends. The limited fiscal and operational capacity of the federal government means that borrowing capacity has to be, of necessity, a primarily regulatory activity. That is, the federal government can transfer money to states and localities, but the amount of money it has at its disposal is not, in itself, large enough to influence state and local decisions, much less to fill the gap in organizational and individual capacity within schools required to meet its goals. Its influence depends on its capacity to use money as the basis for a regulatory control. Federal influence depends heavily on the capacity of the federal government to use the threat of regulatory enforcement to cause states and localities to do what it wants them to do. Whether it wants to or not, whether its rhetoric says so or not, the federal government's influence is solely a function of its regulatory authority.

Whatever the intent of federal policy, then, its *effect* will always be primarily regulatory. I call this tendency "regulatory drift." The broad goals of No Child Left Behind may be described in terms of improvements in the quality of learning for children, or, by a more or less calculated appropriation of civil rights rhetoric, as providing equal access to quality education for poor children and children of color. In effect, though, given the realities of federal influence, these broad goals are only as good as the force of regulatory authority that the federal government exercises over state and local decisions.

Of the fiscal year 2007 U.S. Department of Education budget of about $7 billion for NCLB and related programs, about $5 billion is in formula grants to states and localities through various provisions in Title I. Of the remaining $2 billion or so, the largest share–a little over $1 billion–is in Reading First, a highly regulated categorical grant program, in which the federal government determines which reading curricula will be used by grantees (U.S. Department of Education, 2006). The vast majority of funds that flow from the federal level to states and localities are subject to the regulatory regime of NCLB. The federal government makes minimal investment outside the regulatory structure in raising the level of capacity of state and local agencies to meet the regulatory requirements, and when it does–as in the case of Reading First–it essentially runs a capacity-building program as a highly regulatory activity.

In mid-2006, USDOE Secretary Margaret Spellings released a set of proposals designed to respond to critics of NCLB, noting how important it was for policymakers to "listen carefully to the feedback from those on the ground so that they can better understand how the law translates from paper into action" and acknowledging "the need to give states some alternatives in implementation" of NCLB. The ensuing proposals deal exclusively with modifications of the testing provisions of NCLB, allowing states to modify the adequate yearly progress (AYP) requirements for students with "persistent academic disabilities." The secretary directed that $14 million be reprogrammed to deal exclusively with the assessment issues stemming from this change in policy, another $3 million in grants to states to improve state assessments for students with "persistent academic disabilities," and another $6 million to "improve accountability" and "track changes" in the effects of assessment shifts on students (USDOE, n.d.). Improvements in NCLB, from the federal perspective, are clearly equated with changes in testing, not with resources directed at improvement of instructional practice.

Regulatory drift is not solely a characteristic of federal policy. It occurs, as Manna's theory suggests, wherever the goals of governmental institutions, and the entrepreneurial actions of individual policymakers, exceed their capacity to meet those goals. In accountability policy, the dynamic of regulatory drift is played out across all levels of government. Federal policy drifts toward regulatory control of state and local agencies. State administration of federal policy drifts toward regulatory control of local agencies. Local administration of federal and state policy drifts toward regulatory control of schools. In each instance, agencies think they are acting in the interests of their clients–the children. In each instance, they think they are adding value to the service–quality teaching and learning. In each instance, the drift toward reliance on regulatory control stems from the fact that agencies are *doing what they know how to do*. Bureaucracies know how to make and enforce rules.

They have great difficulty doing anything else. While it is not impossible for them to engage in other kinds of activities, nonregulatory activities require them to move out of the regulatory zone and, in doing so, to do things they fundamentally don't know how to do, or don't know how to do well.

One thing educational bureaucracies know how to do well is administer tests. Testing is relatively cheap as an instrument of regulatory control. Procedures for test administration and for compiling and disseminating test results can be stated in relatively clear regulatory language and implemented with relatively clear procedural controls. The process of testing can be run using familiar regulatory routines—oversight, inspection, enforcement, and sanctions. Since bureaucracies tend to do more of what they know how to do, and they tend to avoid doing those things they do not do well, it is not surprising that accountability has increasingly come to be equated with testing. State and local educational agencies are thought to be "accountable" when they are administering tests, publicizing test results, analyzing test scores, developing and administering their own tests, helping school personnel analyze and use test results, and so on. In education, then, regulatory drift is synonymous with a drift toward increasing use of tests as instruments of control.

Regulatory Enforcement as Strategic Interaction

Every regulatory system involves a critical trade-off between standards and enforcement: The more stringent the standard relative to existing performance, the greater the likelihood of failure to meet the standard, and the greater the cost to the regulatory agency of inducing compliance or performance. The lower the standard is relative to existing performance, the greater the likelihood of compliance, and the lower the costs of enforcement. In real life, regulatory agencies play this game in a more or less deliberately deceptive way: They tend to set standards well above the level they know they can enforce and bet that by skillful use of enforcement—for example, by calling attention to "worst cases"—they can induce a higher level of compliance than they actually have the resources to manage. This problem is known in the regulatory theory literature as "optimal standards with incomplete enforcement" (Jones, 1989; Viscusi & Zeckhauser, 1978).

The regulatory regime of No Child Left Behind creates a framework for identifying low-performing schools that applies to all states and localities. Schools that fail to meet the increment of performance required by adequate yearly progress (AYP) advance through three distinct stages of regulatory sanctions: school improvement, corrective action, and restructuring. Each stage carries with it a particular set of required actions, at the school and school system levels, and a specific period of time, typically 2 years, within which the actions have to be completed and the next level of performance under AYP has to be met. States can choose how they define progress within the AYP framework, providing that all students reach the "proficient" level by 2014. (On the feasibility of this requirement, see Richard Rothstein's chapter in this volume.) The performance standard required for AYP must be met by all students in a federally prescribed set of categories—limited English-speaking, special education, low-income, and so on. At each stage, the sanctions that apply to schools for failing to meet AYP are exclusively procedural: school planning, notification of parents, provision of funding for access by students to externally provided supplemental services, restructuring the school's organization, closing the school and reopening it under different auspices. What schools need to know in order to improve, and who is responsible for ensuring that knowledge is present, is not specified in the law.

From a regulatory perspective, there are a number of notable features of NCLB. First, there is no empirical basis for the AYP requirement. There is no body of evidence, for example, that tells us what a reasonable period of time might be for a school to progress from one level of performance to another. Nor do we know, within schools, what the expected increment of progress might be for different groups of students over a given period of time. There was no evidentiary basis for the sanctions prescribed by NCLB, or the schedule of progressive sanctions. Standard-setting and enforcement schedules in environmental policy, for example, involve vigorous debate around the evidence, with contending parties offering differing interpretations and regulators accepting some obligation to base their final decisions on a body of evidence about the benefits and costs of the regulations to the various parties and feasible compliance schedules. No such debate has occurred with NCLB. No evidentiary basis exists yet for such a debate.

Because there is no evidentiary basis for the AYP requirement, there is no mechanism in the law, or in the regulatory structure following from the law, for adjusting the number of schools identified as failing to the resources available to remediate their failure, or to administer sanctions for that matter. In other words, there is no basis for making a strategic judgment, at any level of the system, relating the level of resources available for enforcement or remediation of performance to the actual caseload of schools that are in need of improvement under AYP. States can adjust their proficiency standards downward, at the risk of incurring federal sanctions, but otherwise, there is no mechanism in the policy to equilibrate the regulatory load produced by AYP to the resources available for school improvement.

If success in AYP were simply a matter of compliance—doing something people already know how to do but might choose not to do when they consider the costs of doing it—this condition would not be a serious matter. Federal and state regulators would simply do what rational regulators normally do under these circumstances: They would engage in strategically calculated, high-visibility, selective enforcement, designed to signal to schools and districts that they run the risk of sanctions for failure to comply. This strategy keeps enforcement costs under control and compliance at an optimal level. Schools and districts would then calculate the probability of getting caught and come to their own conclusions about whether and how to comply—just like polluting firms in environmental regulation.

But AYP poses a different kind of problem of regulatory compliance. Most schools get classified as failing under AYP because *they don't know what to do to get better*. No amount of regulatory enforcement, however cleverly contrived, will rectify this condition. Surrounding failing schools with procedural requirements, as NCLB does, doesn't solve the knowledge problem and, indeed, can make it worse, by focusing failing schools on compliance rituals—planning, consulting, issuing notices, filing reports—rather than addressing the lack of knowledge and skill that produced the problem in the first place. Furthermore, failing schools will not get better simply by pulling up their socks and doing what they are supposed to do. They can pull up their socks, but what they will probably do is a more systematic version of what they are already doing. Schools get better as a consequence of bringing new knowledge and skill into their practice—individually and collectively—not by doing what other people tell them to do. Furthermore, as accountability systems mature and as regulatory drift progresses, regulators focus more and more on tested performance, and less and less on the instructional conditions that produce that performance.

Studies of the effect of regulatory sanctions on low-performing schools have produced uniformly negative and cautionary findings. Teachers and principals generally acknowledge and internalize the negative signals the accountability system is sending them about their performance. That is, they *know* they are low-performing. The regulatory sanctions themselves generally have either very weak or nonexistent effects on the ability of schools, or the individuals who work in them, to improve their performance, even in circumstances where there are well-developed intervention strategies to improve failing schools. Under the pressure of sanctions, teachers tended to do what they knew how to do—largely to teach basic skills-oriented content with low-level pedagogy—and what they knew how to do was generally mismatched with the requirements of the accountability systems in which they were operating. The accountability systems demanded that "teachers [become] motivated to learn and become proactive. In the observed classrooms, however, such learning was widely absent, and instructional change stalled" (Mintrop, 2004, p. 143; see also Elmore & Skogvold Isaksen, 2007; O'Day, 2003).

This combination of circumstances—a regulatory regime that is disconnected from actual evidence of the problem it is trying to solve, the lack of a mechanism for equilibrating the number of failing schools with the resources available to deal with them, and the lack of fit between procedural remedies and the causes of failure in schools–creates our current situation. The number of schools that are in various stages of sanction under NCLB bears no relationship to the capacity of the federal, state, or local officials to remedy their performance. And the requirements for the remedy, as well as the resources entailed in the remedy, are largely opaque and inscrutable to those who are responsible for it.

In the best of all worlds, this problem would be self-correcting. The federal government would revisit AYP and try to establish a reasonable basis for its regulatory requirements. The states would revisit their responses to the AYP requirement based on their capacity, and the capacity of local districts to assist schools in meeting performance requirements, and so forth. But the particular incentive structure of NCLB makes this kind of self-correction unlikely. The federal government has no incentive to address the underlying conditions that produce the number of failing schools under AYP, because *the federal government does not have to bear directly any of the costs of failure.* Under the borrowing capacity theory, the federal government simply transfers money from one level of government to another, creates the regulatory regime that produces failing schools, and passes the costs of rectifying failure along with the responsibility for regulatory enforcement on to states and localities. Likewise, states take a primarily regulatory posture toward school failure, and pass along the costs to districts and schools. Some districts recognize that they are bearing the costs of performance; some don't. In either situation, district and school people end up with the knowledge and skill problem in their laps, surrounded by a regulatory policy that does nothing to address the fundamental gap in knowledge and skill that created the performance problem in the first place. So, a critical part of the feedback loop that would lead to self-correction is missing. Furthermore, the political calculus at the federal level does not lead to self-correction. If NCLB succeeds in raising student performance and reducing the number of failing schools, then federal policymakers will generate electoral credit by claiming responsibility for success. If NCLB results in no change in student performance and the number of failing schools, or an increase in failing students and schools, federal policymakers claim electoral credit by blaming the system that produces this result. (For an account of the specific political process that produces this result, see Debray, 2006.)

In Massachusetts, the total number of schools identified for improvement under various stages of NCLB in 2006 was 617 (316 for aggregate performance, 301 for subgroup performance), up from 420 in 2005. Among the newly identified schools, 57 are in the most severe category–restructuring, based on aggregate performance–up from 30 the year before. Between 2005 and 2006, 45 schools were removed from the list of schools needing improvement. Ninety of Boston's 145 schools are identified for improvement under NCLB—13 in restructuring. Of the 115 lowest-performing schools, 80% are in eight urban districts. This pattern—dramatic increases in schools entering various stages of improvement under NCLB, slow progress in schools leaving, and disproportionate numbers of school in need of improvement in the most populous urban areas—is consistent across the country. The state of Massachusetts allocates about $5 million for a program designed to provide regulatory oversight, intervention, and support to failing schools. Mass-Insight, a nonpartisan, not-for-profit, nongovernmental organization that also provides support to failing schools, estimated in 2005, when there were 400-plus schools in need of improvement, that the state should be spending at least $15 million—proportionately increased to meet the 2006 demand, that number would be over $20 million (Kim & Sunderman, 2004; Massachusetts Department of Education, 2007). Clearly, there is no relationship between the regulatory caseload spun off by the AYP requirement and the capacity of states and localities to meet the demand for support for failing schools. Equally clearly, there is no mechanism in either the policy or politics of NCLB for equilibrating capacity and demand.

The characteristic that distinguishes NCLB from a straightforward regulatory policy is that it is a regulatory policy nested within a grant-in-aid policy. The federal government transfers money to states and localities on the expectation that it will be used to benefit children, and, more important, that it will be used to drive state and local accountability policy in a given direction according to certain parameters set down in the policy. The costs of compliance at the state and local levels can be transferred to the grant-in-aid program, they can be borne out of general revenue by states and localities, or they can be met by some combination of the two. Federal and state bureaucrats tend to see the use of money for regulatory compliance purposes, from whatever source, as part of the process of holding schools accountable for performance. People in schools, and some people in local districts, tend to view the use of money for compliance purposes as a dead-weight loss—that is, money used for compliance is money that is not available for use in schools and classrooms to improve instruction. One of the problems with NCLB as a regulatory policy is that it is never clear how much of the grant-in-aid money is used for compliance, how much it actually costs state and local agencies out of general revenue to meet the regulatory requirements of NCLB, and how much federal revenue actually goes to support improvement of instruction in classrooms for children.

Such is the consequence of borrowed capacity. It is in the interest of the federal government to bury enforcement and compliance costs in the transfer of revenue from one level of government to another, and to avoid acknowledging the compliance costs to state and local jurisdictions out of their own revenue sources, in order to make it difficult for states and localities to judge whether the benefits of federal grant-in-aid money actually exceed the costs.

Moral Suasion, or "The Devil Made Me Do It"

One of the chief functions of regulation is to force us to do things we might not otherwise be inclined to do, whether we want to do them or not. This is the "doing the right thing" half of Schelling's formula. This view of policy lies behind the appropriation of civil rights rhetoric to justify the regulatory role of the federal government in NCLB. Putting the federal government in a regulatory role not only nationalizes educational policy in an arena that had previously been the primary preserve of states and localities, but it creates an economy of blame that allows state and local administrators to minimize their own role, and their accountability to state and local institutions, by transferring blame to the federal government. This is the reciprocal side of the blame shifting that occurs when federal policymakers blame the lack of success of the law on the failure of local institutions, rather than on defects in the law itself, and their own accountability for those defects. The superintendent of an urban school system said to me, "There are parts of this law that are killing us on the ground and making our work much more difficult. But I don't want the law changed on my watch because it provides leverage that I wouldn't otherwise have over schools. Wait another couple of years and then fix it." Many superintendents of high-impact school systems are, not surprisingly, unwilling to express opposition to the law, even when they feel it is dysfunctional, because they do not want to be seen as being on the wrong side of a civil rights issue, and because the law provides them with a ready-made pretext for decisions at the local level that they might otherwise not have the stamina or the political support to make. "The devil made me do it" is a useful tactic for bolstering leadership when the demands of the work exceed the skill and commitment of people on the ground.

The devil-made-me-do-it tactic works best when the person using it is predisposed to do what the policy requires and is looking for an external pretext to do it. Advocates of NCLB point to the support of leading superintendents and principals as evidence that the law "works," strategically avoiding the population of school leaders who are unconvinced of the merits of the law or, more likely, are simply unprepared to translate the law into any coherent improvement strategy in their schools or districts. By definition, these leaders constitute the vast majority of people responding to NCLB.

When I work in the rarified atmosphere of school leaders who are committed to the values behind NCLB, our discussions operate at a relatively sophisticated strategic and tactical level. These practitioners understand how to use external policy as a lever to improve schools. The problems of school improvement at scale are difficult enough under these circumstances, but at least one can assume some level of knowledge about how accountability can work to reinforce school improvement. When I occasionally wander outside this rarified atmosphere of committed school leaders into a more random sample of practitioners, the absence of understanding of the relationship between the regulatory regime of NCLB and the work of school improvement is shocking and depressing. These administrators understand NCLB, insofar as they understand it at all, solely as a regulatory game, and their role as purely bureaucratic. If the feds beat on the state, and the state beats on them, then their role is to beat on people in schools. "The test" is something that exists to be beaten, and any tactic that allows it to be beaten is a good one. People who work in schools generally have little or no control over the learning of students, since learning is largely determined by factors in the lives of children outside of school. Therefore, the best tactic is to do the minimum necessary to comply with the regulatory requirements of the law until the system acknowledges that the accountability structure doesn't work. In these situations, NCLB, not surprisingly, has little discernible effect on the attitudes and practices of administrators, and generally reinforces negative stereotypes of the effect of external policies on schools and classrooms.

The literature on bureaucratic responses to policy predicts that "bureaucrats"–defined as anyone in a position to exercise discretion in the implementation of a policy–can choose (1) to respond in the way they are supposed to ("work"), (2) to deflect the requirements of the policy and continue to do what they were doing ("shirk"), or (3) actively to undermine the policy in accord with their own interests ("sabotage") (Bardach & Kagan, 2002; Brehm & Gates, 1999). The evidence of empirical research suggests that the factors that most influence the tendency of bureaucrats to "work" are the consistency of the policy's requirements with the preferences and skills of the individual ("functional" incentives) and the preferences and skills of the individual's peer group ("solidary" incentives). The factor that is consistently *least* likely to affect a preference for "work" is hierarchical supervision (Brehm & Gates, 1999, pp. 191). In other words, vertical sanctions are relatively weak in structuring the discretion of bureaucrats as compared with their own preferences and skills and those of their peers. Leverage over the performance of organizations is most likely to be effective when it focuses on shaping the knowledge, skill, and values of agents, rather than on strengthening the command and control functions of the system.

Much of the rhetoric of NCLB focuses on "doing the right thing" by children at risk of failure in school. The primary policy instrument is regulation of performance. The underlying theory of action is that educators will change their values in response to changes in external rewards and sanctions, and vertical controls, and that this change in values will result in changes in practice that, in turn, result in changes in performance. Regulation is predicated on the belief that people can be encouraged, persuaded, or shamed into doing the right thing by changing the external rewards and sanctions under which they operate. Performance-based regulation is designed to make the consequences of peoples' actions visible, therefore subject to public scrutiny, and useable as a source of encouragement, persuasion, or shame.

As with most regulatory regimes, there is a kind of proceduralism that underlies this theory of action. If people behave according to the procedures prescribed by the policy and incorporate the goals behind the policy into their belief systems, then they will learn to do the "right thing," and, having learned to do the right thing, they will have the intended effect on student performance.

The main problem with this theory, as with most regulatory theories, is that the procedures embedded in the policy carry large capacity requirements for their successful implementation and do not operate in the same way on every organization. In schools and school systems that, for whatever reason, have acknowledged disparities in access and performance among students, and among schools with a system, making them go through the process of measuring and reporting performance creates a stimulus to examine their organization and practice. In schools and school systems with little or no awareness of disparities in student access and performance, and with little understanding of how their organization and practice have produced these disparities, the process of measuring performance has little effect. One of the first things that people report who work with schools on the use of data is how little the availability of data on student performance is related to its use, and how little the examination of student data leads directly to changes in practice (Boudett, City, & Murnane, 2005; Elmore & Skogvold Isaksen, 2007). Performance-based accountability systems produce mountains of student performance data, most of which are never examined in any systematic way by people working in schools. The regulatory procedure can create the evidence, but it cannot create the predisposition or the capacity to use it, much less the knowledge of assessment necessary to account for its limitations.

So, while regulatory policy can operate in powerful ways as a pretext for strategic action in systems that are inclined to act in accord with the goals of the policy, it is relatively powerless to create action where the predisposition doesn't exist. Furthermore, as we shall see later, the idea that people internalize the goals of a policy and then behave consistently with those goals is, at the very least, somewhat suspect. Moral suasion, whatever its attractiveness in principle, has limited traction on the ground.

THE CAPACITY TO PERFORM

Accountability as Institutional Response: Internal and External Accountability

If external pressure alone could produce performance in schools, then testing and sanctions would produce a more or less uniform, positive effect on student performance across all schools. In reality, the response is anything but uniform or positive. Uniform systems of testing and sanctions produce widely varying results across schools and school systems. Accountability, it seems, is not a matter of compliance; it is largely a matter of institutional response.

Institutional response (Abelmann, Elmore, Even, Kenyon, & Marshall, 2004), as a theoretical position, holds that organizations of all types, and schools in particular, vary along a number of dimensions that affect their responses to external forces in their environment: Some of these factors are objective—experience and expertise of teachers, material resources in classrooms, demographic characteristics of students, prior performance, mobility of student and teacher populations, and so on. Some of these factors are less tangible, but at least as important—beliefs and expectations about students' capacities to learn, knowledge of pedagogy and content, norms of individualism and collective work, skills in organizing and managing resources and people, and the like. Institutional response theory posits that the effect of an external force on an organization, like a school, is a *product* of the rewards and sanctions embodied in that force and the internal features of the organization. Hence, application of a uniform set of regulatory rules and sanctions to a highly variable population of organizations produces a highly variable organizational response. This is how policies that are designed to produce greater uniformity in performance, like NCLB, often produce greater inequality, at least in the short term.

The regulatory mindset sees the world as a collection of organizations in various stages of compliance with the requirements of the law, and sees the purpose of policy as producing a more or less uniform response to a set of prescriptions. The institutional response perspective sees the world as a collection of organizations with widely varying characteristics affecting their ability to understand, interpret, and act on external pressures, and views policy as one of many external forces operating on organizations. The regulatory mindset sees the organization as a receptacle for the demands of policymakers; the institutional response perspective sees organizations as active agents in determining their responses to various external demands, including specific policies. The regulatory mindset sees a single policy—a single set of rules and sanctions—as the central driver of organizational behavior;

the institutional response perspective sees the effect of any given policy as determined by a signal-to-noise ratio of that policy among the other competing demands operating on the organization.

Advocates of NCLB regularly employ the conceit that, before NCLB, schools were "not accountable," and with the advent of NCLB schools are now finally "accountable." Policymakers and policy geeks generally like to imagine that the world begins (and possibly will end) with their ideas. This conceit contains two serious misconceptions. The first is a simple matter of history: Performance-based accountability in public education was a state and local invention, not a federal invention; NCLB preempted and nationalized a particular model of performance-based accountability, it did not invent the idea. The second misconception is more germane to the issue at hand. Institutional response theory does not assume that accountability begins with policy. In fact, all organizations, regardless of the policy environment in which they operate, have to solve the accountability problem–they have to decide to whom they are accountable for what, and how. Schools, consciously or not, have a solution to the accountability problem embedded in their organizational structures, routines, and cultures that antedates the introduction of performance-based accountability in their external environment. So, policy does not "introduce" or "create" accountability where none existed before; policy complicates, interacts with, and attempts to alter an existing accountability system.

A brief example will illustrate: The Cambridge Public Schools, in Cambridge, Massachusetts, with which I am currently working as a consultant, have, for the past 30 years or so, had a "controlled choice" enrollment plan. Under the plan, parents were allowed to express a preference for any elementary school in the city, and places in schools were allocated based on a complex system. This plan introduced relatively tight relationships between parents–at least those who were active choosers–and school personnel; the plan also introduced significant competitive incentives among schools. Each school thought of itself as embodying a particular point of view about instruction and a particular set of relationships with parents and students. In other words, the plan created a very specific accountability structure. The advent of performance-based accountability in Massachusetts, in 1993, created serious conflicts with this embedded accountability system. It introduced sobering data about student performance in schools. It forced a common metric for measurement of student performance. And it eventually forced the district to develop a systemwide strategy for instructional improvement. Whatever one thinks about the merits of either accountability structure, it is important to acknowledge that the problem for Cambridge educators is *not* how to implement performance-based accountability. It is how to *displace* a deeply seated existing accountability system that served certain interests extremely well with another accountability system, mandated by an external authority with very little legitimacy in the community. The problem was not how to *make* schools accountable. The problem was how to make them accountable for different things in a different way. Every school in Cambridge has had to go through this process; some have done it more expeditiously and gracefully than others.

A principle of institutional response theory, then, is that *uniform policies produce differential responses* and *producing more uniform results requires differential treatment.* What determines the effect of an accountability system at the school level is not the policy itself but the interaction of the policy with the specific conditions inside the school. The same policy produces different responses in different settings. If the intent of policy is to produce greater uniformity in effects—this is called "equity" in the jargon of NCLB—then different organizations have to be treated differently. It is at this point that regulation loses its traction as a policy instrument. Regulatory policy is good at setting uniform standards for different organizations, not at adjusting the demands of policy to different settings. In fact, most of the dysfunctions of regulation arise from its incapacity to adjust to differences among organizations.

Our research on the specific conditions that determine a school's response to external accountability pressure has focused on a construct we call *internal accountability* (Abelmann et al., 2004). Briefly stated, internal accountability is the convergence between what individuals think they are *responsible* for, the *expectations* within the organization that express common norms and values, and the *processes and structures* by which people inside the organization account for their work. An organization with low internal accountability is one in which individual preferences account for most of what happens in the organization, collective norms and values exercise limited influence over individuals' work, and the processes by which people account for what they do are weak and infrequent. We call these organizations relatively *atomized.* An organization with high internal accountability has a high convergence between what individuals say they are responsible and for what the organization as a whole espouses as its values, and there are regular, visible processes by which people account for their work. We call these organizations relatively *coherent.*

Pushing hard with an external force—such as testing and sanctions—on an atomized organization, our research suggests, does not make it a more coherent organization, at least in the short term. In fact, it often makes the organization more atomized and dysfunctional because people continue to do what they know how to do, which is exactly what produced the performance that got them in trouble in the first place. Pushing hard on a coherent organization, on the other hand, often makes it more coherent, at least in ways that respond to the external force. Another way of saying this is that schools generally respond to external pressure by doing what they already know how to do, or some modest extension of what they know how to do.

Schools with low internal accountability mostly know how to manage around the edges of instructional practice, preserving an essentially atomized organization. So they generally adopt responses that least challenge established instructional practice and that stress compliance with external directives (Mintrop, 2004; O'Day, 2003) Teaching test items is one standard response. Teaching test items is something everyone can do, without incorporating any new knowledge into their practice, and it demonstrates compliance in a visible way. But teaching test items doesn't make the school a more coherent or effective organization around instructional practice. It is simply an accommodation to external pressure that leaves as much as possible of the existing organization intact.

Schools with high internal accountability generally have norms about what good teaching and learning look like. These norms may or may not be consistent with the messages they are getting from external tests and sanctions. Surprisingly, we did not find that it mattered a great deal whether instruction in high internal accountability schools was consistent or inconsistent with the norms embodied in the test. Because they knew how to manage instruction, these schools generally did well on the tests with a minimum of disruption to their internal processes. Their most visible accommodation to the testing regime was to spend a significant amount of time preparing students for the form of the questions, assuming that the students would know enough from their experience in school to handle the content. At the most, these schools would sometimes move the sequence of the content around to correspond more closely to the content of the test, but they did very little else to change their internal practices in response to the test.

In addition, for many nominally high-performing schools with students of relatively high socioeconomic status, the external test is not a serious accountability mechanism at all (Elmore, 2005, 2009). These schools operate in a parallel accountability environment that stresses attainment, not performance on the state accountability test. That is, parents and school personnel focus on practices that situate their students favorably in a competitive attainment structure, leading to access to competitive institutions of higher education. This process begins early–typically in 4th or 5th grade–when school personnel begin to make decisions about selective admission to high-track academic courses: "advanced" math, "honors" English, and so forth. There is usually no pedagogical rationale for these decisions, since privileged children can usually handle demanding academic work with skillful teaching. The main basis for these decisions is to signal to parents, and to their main accountability structure–institutions of higher education–that their schools are serious about academic work and that not everyone can succeed at "serious" academic work. For these schools, performance-based accountability is a purely prophylactic activity. They need to demonstrate a certain level of performance on the test in order to avoid public displeasure, and to justify the real estate prices that families have to bear in order to participate in the school system. The "real" accountability system in these schools, however, is not the performance-based one; it is the competitive attainment structure that they themselves design in response to the increasingly complex regime of competitive college admissions. It is not surprising that the accountability structure of attainment-oriented schools stresses access to high-level content–numbers of advanced courses offered, for example–and success in college placement, *not* performance under the external accountability system. The challenge for attainment-oriented schools is how to create an internal accountability system that mirrors the competitive market for college admissions, *not* how to produce performance in the regulatory system.

Internal accountability, then, plays a key role in determining schools' responses to external testing and sanctions. Given this reality, it is easy to see how (1) the initial response within school *systems* to performance-based accountability systems might be to *increase* inequalities in performance among schools rather than to decrease them, and (2) how increasing the performance of school systems necessarily entails treating schools *differently* rather than engaging in equal enforcement of testing and sanctions. External accountability systems produce a *range* of responses, depending on the internal accountability of individual schools. Improving performance across a range of schools, each with a somewhat different internal accountability structure, requires differential treatment, rather than uniform enforcement. It is at this point that the incapacity of regulatory systems to produce uniform improvements in performance usually becomes obvious. Telling people to do the right thing doesn't help them learn the right thing to do.

Institutional Capacity as Social Capital

I have often thought how different our accountability systems would be if policymakers, and policy analysts, were required to spend an entire day working in a school for every day they spend making policy for schools or pontificating about how to fix what is wrong with schools. Observing classrooms, and the organizational and managerial work that surrounds them, is a sobering and disorienting experience. Hard-edged preconceptions about what is wrong with schools and how to fix them evaporate into a haze of difficult questions. It is much easier to prescribe from a distance. Lessons from research and from "best practice" that seem to fit perfectly in some settings collapse in a heap of steaming rubble in others. Improvement strategies that seem robust initially run out of steam and stall after a period of time. What seem like great ideas at the outset become hopelessly superficial as the work progresses. Accountability systems are based on the premise that, with the proper system of incentives and sanctions, people in schools will somehow learn to do the work more effectively, *and* that they will learn to do it in a progressively more powerful way over time. Yet accountability systems as they are currently constructed do little or nothing to support the learning that is critical to their success. This learning is assumed to be part of the capacity that is borrowed when one level of government uses policy to make another level do something it might not otherwise do.

There are some tentative lessons from the work of improving schools and school systems that help us to understand the role of learning in accountability. The most basic of these, which sounds obvious, but is hardly ever acknowledged in the design or implementation of accountability systems, is that learning takes time. Accountability systems operate in "policy time," constructed around the regularities of political authorization cycles, electoral cycles, budget cycles, and the like. Learning in schools operates in what might be called "practice time." Even when people are highly motivated to find solutions to problems of instructional practice—which often they are not—it takes time to get those solutions translated into instructional and managerial practice, it takes time to get those practices introduced into classrooms and schools, it takes time for the practices to result in differences in student performance, and it takes time to discover the limits of those practices and to invent the next level of practice. With practice, schools and school systems become more efficient at these processes, and they learn to do work that used to take them an entire school year in a few weeks or months. It is important to acknowledge, however, that policy time and practice time *have no necessary relationship to each other.* Solutions that are crafted in policy time—like the AYP requirement of No Child Left Behind—bear no relationship to the actual time it actually takes schools and school systems to develop, introduce, nurture, test, and redevelop new practices.

A common complaint by policy operatives and senior administrators toward school people is that they lack a "sense of urgency" about the need to improve student performance. To be sure, teachers and principals vary considerably in their sense of urgency around the work. But what policy operatives and senior administrators usually fail to understand is that they have no basis for judging how long the work will take because there is no empirical basis for the regulatory requirements that accountability systems contain. You can't say that things aren't moving fast enough when you have no empirically based standard for judging how fast they can move. For this reason, people who *do* share a sense of urgency about the work, and who *are* actually moving at a rate close to the maximum feasible, often feel that policy operative and senior administrators live in a parallel universe with no understanding whatsoever of the work.

The second lesson about learning in accountability systems is that improvement in performance is never constant and linear. Improvements in performance often—one might say usually—lag behind improvements in capacity and quality; that is, one sees significant changes in classroom practice well before one sees their results in student test scores. It takes time for new practices to become seated in the culture and organization of schools, and it takes time for those practices to develop to a level that can be seen in student performance. As schools improve, they pass through various levels in the development of their internal capacity to make changes in instructional practice; they get better at the improvement process as they improve. In my experience, many schools—indeed, most—get "stuck" at levels and can't find the next set of practices that pull them to the next level of performance. Most school systems—most states—manifest similar patterns. All of these are common patterns in developmental processes in the public and private sector organizations. Accountability problems develop when the system of incentives and sanctions is not congruent with the underlying developmental processes of the organizations it attempts to regulate.

The third lesson is that learning is social. New knowledge doesn't materialize out of nowhere and spontaneously find its way into classroom practice. Knowledge travels through social relationships. Social relationships have to be constructed intentionally, and managed intentionally, in order to produce improvements in performance over time. Teaching is complex, interactive work. We who teach learn the hard way that we are usually not accurate reporters on our own teaching practice. Learning new practices requires exposing one's practice to external scrutiny, anchoring that practice in an external body of knowledge, and making judgments about practice based on its effects. All of these activities are *social practices*. They have to be learned just like any other practice. Schools have, in the past, not been places that easily accommodate such learning. So introducing new norms for adult learning requires changing the organization and culture of schools: Schedules have to be changed to accommodate group work around practice, teachers and administrators have to be introduced to more systematic ways of talking to one another about their practice, new roles have to be developed to bring new knowledge into the classroom (mentor, coach, professional developer), people have to learn new skills for analyzing evidence of student learning and converting that knowledge into new practice. To the degree that you try to improve student learning without developing these practices, you put impossible pressure on individual members of the organization to do all the required learning themselves. You are literally asking them to do something that they cannot do by, or for, themselves. Teachers are used to being asked to do impossible work. But this particular kind of impossible work has a mean and unforgiving nature. It makes the individual teacher responsible for something that only the organization can do. A rational person would not agree to work in such a setting.

It is now commonplace to conceptualize learning and improvement in school systems as a kind of Chinese box problem, or a problem of "nested learning communities" (Resnick & Glennan, 2002; see also Cohen, Raudenbush, & Ball, 2003). Learning that is instrumental to improvement occurs at the individual level, at the group level within schools, at the school level, and at the system level; each level of learning is required to support the others; learning at each level is the reciprocal of learning at all other levels. So learning at the individual level—teachers and principals, for example— is instrumental to improving learning of students, but students provide the feedback that is necessary for adults to learn. Learning at the group level within schools is necessary to generate broad-scale learning at the individual level, but learning strategies at the school level are dependent on feedback from the individual and group level. Learning at the system level is necessary to induce learning at the school, group, and individual level, but learning at these levels is necessary to inform learning at the system level.

Think about a typical strategy of improvement that many school systems adopt: curriculum-driven improvement. Systems adopt ambitious new reading and mathematics curricula that are designed to produce instructional practice in classrooms that will lead to improved student performance. If the curricula are not simply restatements of what teachers are already doing, they require significant new learning on the part of teachers, and significant new learning on the part of students, both of the new content and typically of what it means to be a student. The learning required of teachers has to be supported at the group, school, and system levels. The learning of teachers is also heavily informed by what they see as students' responses to the new content and to their teaching of it. The kinds of problems that present in the classroom—the most typical of which is that some students simply don't respond in the predicted way to new content and pedagogy—inform the kinds of knowledge and support required at other levels if the strategy is to succeed. Strategies of improvement at the school and system levels also have a logic of their own: they are predicated on problems of scale that do not occur, or do not occur in the same way, at the classroom level. The choice of curriculum, professional development, and accountability strategies has to be based on judgments of cost and administrative feasibility that would not necessarily figure in classroom decisions. In the real world of school- and system-level improvement strategies, there is a constant interplay of roles around these issues of knowledge and feasibility. If the purpose of an accountability system is to incite improvement, it has to be sensitive to the actual requirements of improvement processes as they occur on the ground.

Successful school improvement, then, requires very high levels of social capital: heavy investments in learning at various levels, structures and processes that link people at various levels with one another and create channels of feedback across levels, and investments in external supports and connections to sources of new knowledge. Most school- and system-level administrators have no idea what the required level of investment in social capital will be to support the level improvement that they are trying to achieve. This may be a good thing, since, if they knew, they might not undertake the task in the first place (see Hirschman, 1967).

Improvement in performance requires progressively greater investments in social capital, scaled to the demands of increasing performance. This is not a point of view that is well adapted to traditional forms of school organization. School systems have traditionally operated on the principle of *extracting* knowledge from individuals, rather than *developing* it. The idea was that individuals came to the organization "qualified" in one way or another for the work and the organization "used" their talents in the service of collective ends. Improvement requires a shift to a human investment view: Individuals come to the organization with a base level of knowledge and skill, and it is the job of the organization to build on that base over the course of the individual's career to make it consistent with the demands of the work. School systems have traditionally operated on the principle that the work of teachers is isolated and autonomous; improvement requires a definition of work that is collective and cumulative over time. The structures of schools and school systems, and the human resource management systems, are all built on the old model—rewarding individual work with a standardized definition of expertise, rather than a differentiated career structure that acknowledges large differences in knowledge and skill that may not correspond to differences in experience. The form of organization required for improvement is not the one that schools and school systems have.

Getting from one form of organization to another is never graceful or easy. It requires the application of knowledge and skill over time. The first stage of this process is knowing what you don't know. A very large proportion of school administrators have not yet reached this stage. Getting them there is another problem of building social capital.

How Systems Learn

The Boston Public Schools, like many other urban school systems, have a well-developed strategy for school improvement. The strategy was developed in a more or less cumulative way over the tenure of outgoing superintendent Tom Payzant, and continues with the current superintendent, Carol Johnson. The strategy represents most of the principles of improvement outlined above: heavy investments in individual knowledge and skill at all levels of the system, creation of new roles and relationships organized around bringing new knowledge of instructional practice into classrooms and schools, development of new career structures and new ways of developing leadership in the system, increased focus on reciprocal accountability relationships between system-level and school-level personnel, and significant infusions of new knowledge from outside the organization. Boston is a system that currently has more than 90 schools out of a total of 145 in various stages of sanction under No Child Left Behind. The definition of a good accountability system would be one that helps Boston get better, not one that makes it more difficult for Boston to do the work it is committed to doing.

At the school level, within the system, one can see dramatically different responses across individual schools to the district's overall improvement strategy. A handful of schools are exemplars—you can see every element of the improvement strategy represented in more or less exactly the form it was envisioned by the district, having the predicted effect on student performance. In a significant number of schools, you can see every element of the strategy faithfully represented and almost no discernible effect on student performance. In these schools, the strategy is a disconnected collection of events glued onto an atomized organization with no observable connection to classroom practice. In another collection of schools, you can see what you would expect to happen in a system predicated on organizational learning: Teachers and administrators are struggling to figure out how to use the resources that come with the strategy to support their work, they are seeing changes in the quality of instruction and student performance but not always in a consistent or robust direction over time, and they are seriously engaged in trying to learn how to do the work more effectively.

This is what learning looks like in a complex system. Well-crafted system-level strategies have differential school-level effects. In general, one can see trends in performance over time that provide guidance for what is working and what isn't. But the effects of the strategy are never uniform and never completely predictable. Large systems learn by managing diversity, not by creating uniformity. The strategy provides the base-level consistency that creates expectations for performance and assurances of support for the learning required to meet these expectations. The actual work is about responding to the wide range of differential responses that schools, and the people who work in them, have to the base-level elements of the strategy. System-level administrators are constantly trying to understand and correct for the responses that their strategies generate. School-level administrators have a similar problem at a lower level: understanding and correcting for differential responses among teachers and students to a common strategy of improvement. And teachers have a similar problem in the classroom: understanding and adjusting for differential responses among students to an overall plan of instructional practice.

An effective accountability system is one that generates pressure for performance and provides support for the development of knowledge and skill required to meet those expectations. Learning in an accountability structure is most successful when it is directed at taking general expectations and adapting them to local settings, when it creates the capacity to respond to differential effects of a common set of expectations. Sustained learning over time is what makes accountability systems work.

REDESIGNING ACCOUNTABILITY SYSTEMS

The basic problem with No Child Left Behind is that it is a regulatory policy completely divorced from both the enforcement capacity and the basic investments in social capital required to make it work. It is a regulatory strategy predicated on the assumption of borrowing capacity at the state and local levels that doesn't exist, or at the very least doesn't exist in anything like the quantity or distribution that would be required for the policy to work. The current situation has been created by a major failure of political accountability in which policymakers at the federal and state levels have been allowed to engage in unchecked regulatory drift with no countervailing pressure to take responsibility for the capacity problems they have created. The design problem that flows from the political problem is how to create some reasonable equilibrium between pressure and support so that schools have to respond to external pressure for performance, but, at the same time, policymakers have to submit to the discipline of providing the capacity necessary to produce the performance.

The most basic design principle is one I have developed in other places: *the principle of reciprocity.* Simply put, the principle of reciprocity says that for every unit of performance I demand of you, I have an equal responsibility to provide you with a unit of capacity to produce that performance. Under this principle, no accountability policy would be allowed to exist at any level of government that did not explicitly calibrate demands for performance with the provision of support, and that did not have at least a plausible empirical basis for its performance requirements. So, the federal government would not be able to enforce regulations preempting the design of state and local accountability systems without saying explicitly what the human investment consequences of those regulatory decisions would be and without saying explicitly who was going to pay for those consequences—likewise for states, and likewise for local districts vis à vis schools. The practice of borrowing capacity that does, in fact, exist is a deliberate way of shifting the cost of human investment down in the system as far as it will go until someone has to take responsibility for it. In the case of NCLB, it shifts the cost of human invest-ment to the classroom level, which is the level least capable of bearing it. If government agencies are allowed to initiate policies without regard to the capacity requirements they impose on other levels of the system, they have no reason to take these costs into account when they make policy decisions. Under these circumstances, accountability decisions become "free goods," subject to no countervailing considerations of cost or feasibility. This is the situation in which we currently find ourselves.

No Child Left Behind is a regulatory regime connected to a grant-in-aid program. This raises the question of whether the grant-in-aid compensates for the capacity costs of the accountability regulations. The problem here is that, in the case of NCLB, the federal government is not only regulating the costs incurred in implementing the grant. It is also regulating the entire accountability structure of public education in the country using the lever-age of the grant. The right metric here for determining whether the federal government has met its responsibility for reciprocity is not the amount of the grant-in-aid. It is the capacity costs to the entire system for meeting the ac-countability requirements of the law. By this standard, the money that flows from NCLB is a fraction of what would be required to meet the reciprocity requirement. A federal role in accountability that is scaled to current expen-ditures through NCLB would require an alteration of both the substance of the law and the purpose of expenditures—a shift away from issuing regula-tions that it has neither the capacity to enforce nor the resources to support, toward one of providing a common metric for state and local accountability systems and supporting investments in research, knowledge development, and implementation for which it has a comparative advantage.

The second principle of redesign is that performance standards and sanc-tions under accountability systems should have to meet a test of empirical va-lidity. This is a simple principle of regulatory policy that applies everywhere except in education. When we regulate air pollution or product safety, the standards that are set are always subject to empirical testing, and the regulato-ry standards are evaluated in terms of their impact on both the organizations that are subject to regulation and the public at large. The requirement for empirical testing sets up a system of political incentives that requires the many parties to regulatory policy to present evidence to support their point of view on what the appropriate standards are, and that requires a regulatory body to justify their decision based on evidence. The current AYP requirement has no basis in empirical evidence, and so it is completely divorced from any reality about the rate of improvement possible under prevailing resource constraints and the human investment costs required to meet certain performance tar-gets. Hence, AYP produces a regulatory caseload that does not correspond to the capacity of any agency responsible for its implementation–local, state, or federal. It creates arbitrary performance targets that do not correspond to anything that anyone knows on the ground about how to improve performance; the performance standards are completely divorced from the knowledge base of the people who are responsible for meeting them. There is no public, self-correcting mechanism for the performance standards that affect schools in which standard-setting agencies are required to justify their decisions against any criterion other than their own intuition. AYP reminds one of the sayings during the late days of the Soviet empire: "We pretend to work; they pretend to pay us."

Subjecting performance standards to a requirement of empirical justification would shift resources away from enforcement and toward a more systematic study of the processes of school improvement underlying accountability systems, and force a more direct discussion of the human investment requirements of meeting performance targets. There should be open study and debate about the feasibility of standards and about the conditions required to meet them.

The third principle of redesign should be an explicit reckoning with the institutional comparative advantage of governments at various levels. The federal government is currently in a position of regulating a sector for which it has no comparative advantage, and never has. There are reasons why we have never nationalized public schooling in American, and they are becoming progressively more obvious every day that NCLB is in effect. The states are very weak partners in the federalization of education policy, and they are complicit in the movement toward overregulation and underinvestment in human resources. Right now, those local agencies that choose to take accountability seriously are bearing the major share of the costs of both compliance and human investment, with no reciprocal recognition of what those costs are. No one is taking responsibility for the research and development function that would be necessary to create strong, empirically based performance standards and a human investment strategy that would make it possible to achieve them.

A well-designed accountability structure would pull the federal government out of its current role as all-purpose enforcement officer and regulator of state and local accountability systems and put it in a role for which it has some comparative advantage. Basic issues in the design and development of instructional systems, in the technical and practical consequences of testing systems, in the development and use of professional learning systems, and in the monitoring and calibration of state and local assessment systems against international standards are obvious roles for the federal government to play. These are issues in which it is more or less inefficient to develop knowledge exclusively at the state and local levels. They are also issues that are consistent with the federal government's limited organizational capacity and its limited knowledge of the details of school improvement. States would take the major role in developing and implementing accountability systems, consistent with the principle of reciprocity, and within the context of a well-developed federal framework for what constitutes high-level standards, high-quality testing, and state-of-the-art instruction and professional development. States also have a comparative advantage in creating social capital in the form of networks that span district boundaries for the development and dissemination of effective practice. Localities would take major responsibility for the management of school improvement and the development of school improvement strategies. And schools would take the major responsibility for delivering high-quality instruction, informed by performance standards and existing knowledge.

The existing accountability structure is massively overinvested in testing and enforcement and massively underinvested in capacity and social capital. The situation has come about largely as a result of unchecked regulatory drift, in which the federal government and its state agents have used the principle of borrowing capacity to consolidate and exercise regulatory authority and to push the responsibility and costs of school improvement down in the system as far as they will go without any countervailing discipline to control or compensate for the regulatory load or the human investment costs that the policy entails. This drift has created a situation in which the human and organizational requirements for improving student learning and performance have been superseded by regulatory politics among levels of government. The result is a preoccupation with test scores among policymakers, based on no understanding whatsoever of the conditions that create performance, and a more or less constant practice of blame shifting among levels of government to try to make the performance of schools someone else's problem. This is an accountability system that is designed to do many things, the least of which is to improve schools.

The implications for redesign of accountability systems that follow from these design principles are as follows: First, the AYP requirement should be suspended until the federal government and the states can provide an empirical justification for the regulatory regime imposed by the requirement. This action would be holding the education policy establishment to the same standard of regulatory policy design that is required of the Environmental Protection Agency and the Federal Highway Safety Administration: no regulatory requirements without corresponding evidence of the rate at which school and systems should be expected to improve and the incremental costs of the improvement. The debates around AYP should be about the feasibility of the requirement, its regulatory burden, and how the costs and benefits are distributed, not about abstractions and blame shifting.

Second, for every policy that requires an increment of performance, policymakers should have to provide an estimate of the cost of additional capacity to meet that requirement and to say where the resources will come from to meet the costs. The system currently operates by shifting the costs of meeting performance requirements away from the level of government that initiates the policy and toward the level of governments responsible for running the schools—from the federal government to the states, from the states to the localities, from the localities to the schools. Under the current allocation of incentives, there is apparently no limit to the regulatory load that the federal government can impose on lower levels, and little or no limit on the load that states can impose on schools and school systems. This is, in part, a problem of political incentives. Federal policymakers can take credit for the success of the policy whether it improves schools or not. If schools fail to meet the standard, policymakers take credit for calling attention to the dreadful quality of schools. If schools meet the standard, policymakers take credit for whatever improvement occurs. The only way to begin to solve this problem is to put some share of the burden for accounting for the costs in the lap of the initiating government.

Third, there should be no regulation without investments in an infrastructure for building knowledge and skill. The current system for making investments in human capital in the education sector is a haphazard collection of opportunistic institutions with no direct or systematic relationship to the core problems of improving schooling. People in classrooms and schools have very little access to the knowledge and skills required to meet the demands of the policies under which they work. They are expected, somehow, spontaneously to invent the new ideas and practices that will fuel performance, or to translate policy requirements into actions that make sense in the classroom. The fundamental problem with accountability policy is that people are being asked to do something they do not know how to do. And they are being asked to do it in organizations that are not built to do what they are required to do. Human investment, not regulatory control, is at the heart of school improvement.

Finally, governmental institutions need to work out a more explicit theory of comparative advantage around the intergovernmental division of labor in accountability policy. The federal government has worked its way into a regulatory role for which is completely unsuited. The costs of the rest of the system for this huge strategic error are enormous, and the politics of blame shifting are mean and corrosive. The states, operating as subsidiaries of the federal government, are forced by the ground rules of borrowing capacity to act as if they know what they are doing and to assume a regulatory role that they, too, are incompetent to execute. Meanwhile, the caseload of schools classified as in need of improvement continues to grow because the policy makes no accommodation between the level of enforcement and resources available to remedy school failure.

The federal government's comparative advantage is most explicitly *not* the regulation of school performance by remote control through state agencies. The comparative advantage of states is probably not running a regulatory system that has no controls on the number of cases it creates. Both levels of government *do* have a natural comparative advantage in building the infrastructure required to bring new knowledge and skill into schools. There are economies of scale in the development of knowledge and practice and the deployment of expertise at the federal and state levels that do not exist at the district and school level. At the moment, no one is paying attention to the human investment problems created by education accountability policy. The federal government should try to do something it can be good at instead of doing something that progressively demonstrates its institutional incompetence.

A more reasonable intergovernmental division of labor would be one more like that of environmental policy or highways. The federal government takes responsibility for a large part of the investment in research and development around the technical side of instructional practice, coupled with a monitoring system that keeps track of the overall performance of schools, localities, and states against a set of international standards for what students should know and be able to do. The federal government would set standards for what a good accountability system would look like and regularly publish assessments of the state of policy design and implementation at the state level. The states would take major responsibility for policy design and would be given broad latitude to stretch the parameters of accountability policy—trading off the frequency of assessment, for example, for the depth of what assessments measure, investing more in formative assessments that can be used at the school level, rather than focusing exclusively on summative assessments. States would scale back the reach of accountability policy to match the level of resources that have to enforce compliance, and stop playing the blame-shifting game with localities. States would regularly collect and publish performance data on schools and would make the data available to the public in accessible, user-friendly human investment infrastructure within their boundaries that would support the work of improvement in schools. In some instances, where the scale made it feasible, large districts would take responsibility for building and maintaining their own infrastructure. Over the longer run, policy would shift from an emphasis on enforcement of regulatory requirements to investment in human capital. The education sector would become—as it is in many industrialized countries—a model for the rest of the society of how to build human capital in a sensible way.

NOTE

Some of the research for this chapter was supported by the Consortium for Policy Research in Education under a grant from the U.S. Department of Education.

REFERENCES

Abelmann, C., Elmore, R., Even, J., Kenyon, S., & Marshall, J. (2004). When accountability knocks will anyone answer? In R. Elmore (Ed.), *School reform from the inside out* (pp. 133–199). Cambridge, MA: Harvard Education Press.

Bardach, E., & Kagan, R. (2002). *Going by the book: The problem of regulatory unreasonableness.* New Brunswick, NJ: Transaction.

Boudett, K., City, E., & Murnane, R. (2005). *DataWise: A step-by-step guide to using assessment results to improve teaching and learning.* Cambridge, MA: Harvard Education Press.

Brehm, J., & Gates, S. (1999). *Working, shirking, and sabotage: Bureaucratic response to a democratic public.* Ann Arbor: University of Michigan Press.

Cohen, D., Raudenbush, S., & Ball, D. L. (2003). Resources, instruction, and research. *Education Evaluation and Policy Analysis, 25*(2), 119–142.

DeBray, E. (2006). *Politics, ideology, and education: Federal policy during the Clinton and Bush administrations.* New York: Teachers College Press.

Elmore, R. (2005, September/October). What (so-called) low performing schools can teach (so-called) high performing schools. Harvard Education Letter.

Elmore, R. (2009). Schooling adolescents. In R. M. Lerner & L. Steinberg (Eds.), *Handbook on adolescent psychology* (3rd ed.). New York: Wiley.

Elmore, R., & Skogvold Isaksen, L. (2007). How accountability fails schools. *Strategic Education Research Project.* Cambridge, MA: Harvard Graduate School of Education.

Hirschman, A. (1967). *The principle of the hiding hand.* Washington, DC: Brookings Institution.

Jones, C. A. (1989). Standard setting with incomplete enforcement revisited. *Journal of Policy Analysis and Management, 8*(1), 72–87.

Kim, J., & Sunderman, G. (2004, February). *Large mandates and limited resources: State responses to the No Child Left Behind Act and implications for accountability.* Cambridge, MA: Harvard Civil Rights Project.

Los Angeles Unified School District. (August 2006). *Superintendent's 2006–07 final budget.* Los Angeles: Los Angeles Board of Education.

Manna, P. (2006). *School's in: Federalism and the national education agenda.* Washington, DC: Georgetown University Press.

Massachusetts Department of Education. (2007). State report card. Retrieved from http://profiles.doe.mass.edu/staterc/part3.asp

Mintrop, H. (2004). *Schools on probation: How accountability works (and doesn't work).* New York: Teachers College Press.

O'Day, J. (2003). Complexity, accountability, and school improvement. In S. Fuhrman & R. Elmore (Eds.), *Redesigning accountability systems* (pp. 15–46). New York: Teachers College Press.

Resnick, L., & Glennan, T. (2002). Leadership for learning: A theory of action for urban school districts. In A. M. Hightower, M. S. Knapp, J. A. Marsh, & M. W. McLaughlin (Eds.), *School districts and instructional renewal* (pp. 160–172). New York: Teachers College Press.

Schelling, T. C. (1974). Command and control. In J. McKie (Ed.), *Social responsibility and the business predicament* (pp. 79–108). Washington, DC: Brookings.

State of California. (n.d.). *State budget 2006–2007.* Sacramento, CA: Author.

U.S. Department of Education. (2006, July 24). *Fiscal year 2006 budget and congressional action on 2007 budget.* Washington, DC: Author.

U.S. Department of Education. (n.d.). *NCLB update: A new path for No Child Left Behind.* Washington, DC: Author.

Viscusi, W. K., & Zeckhauser, R. (1978). Optimal standards with incomplete enforcement. *Public Policy, 27*(4), 437–456.

CHAPTER 10

A Viable and Vital Agenda for NCLB Reauthorization

Michael A. Rebell and Jessica R. Wolff

NCLB is a highly flawed statute. In pursuing its worthy goal of closing our country's achievement gaps, the law imposes an unrealistic 100% proficiency mandate that requires unachievable annual progress targets and motivates states to lower their academic proficiency standards. The law also fails to ensure that all students are taught by truly qualified teachers and does little else to improve instructional capacity in the schools attended by most of the nation's low-achieving students. After more than 6 years of NCLB implementation, there has been little progress toward achieving its important equity goals: Average achievement levels have risen only slightly and achievement gaps have not substantially narrowed (National Center for Education Statistics, 2008).

In spite of these failings, support for NCLB within the civil rights community remains strong; this is a testament to the significant role that this major congressional initiative continues to play in advancing America's longstanding promise to provide all students equal educational opportunity. Indeed, NCLB's significance and its critical role in promoting continued national progress toward equal educational opportunity has actually increased in recent years, despite its record of minimal accomplishment. The U.S. Supreme Court has largely abandoned its own historical role in promoting school desegregation, and its most recent decision in this area, *Parents Involved v. Seattle School District* (2007), has constrained rather than enhanced school districts' abilities to pursue *Brown*'s vision of equal educational opportunity.

Importantly, the state courts have, to a large extent, replaced the federal courts as the locus of judicial enforcement of educational equity. Plaintiffs have won over 70% of litigations seeking school funding equity and educational adequacy that have been decided by the highest courts in over half the states over the past 2 decades (Rebell, in press). These state cases have blazed important paths, and they have established precedents. But, in this day and age, a child's access to educational opportunity should not be determined by the zip code into which he or she was born. As Jonathan Kozol (2005) has pointed out, "equal education ought to be regarded as a national entitlement and ought to be protected under federal law. Any notion that a child's education is essentially a state and local matter 'is increasingly so out of line with the realities of our society as to be obsolete'" (p. 253). NCLB extends and expands on Title I of the Elementary and Secondary Education Act, Congress's historic commitment to disadvantaged students that was originally enacted in 1965, during the heyday of the civil rights era. In the absence of proactive support of equal educational opportunity by the federal courts, continuing congressional commitment to Title I takes on added significance as both the symbol and the operative locus of the national commitment to equal educational opportunity.

Congress's bipartisan commitment in NCLB to closing the achievement gaps and to holding the states accountable for ensuring that economically disadvantaged students, students with disabilities, English language learners, and students from all racial and ethnic groups achieve at meaningful levels must be maintained, and the flaws in the law must be corrected. Hundreds of schools are being added to the "needs improvement" category each year, with little hope or expectation that they will really improve and provide their students meaningful educational opportunity. The advent of a new presidential administration in Washington at this time provides an important occasion to rectify the law's deficiencies, but not to abandon it.

The main problem with NCLB lies not with its core commitments to equity and accountability for results, but rather in its failure to establish a realistic theory of action and mechanism for actually achieving these important ends. Critics of all stripes agree that the law bears deep scars of political compromise and wishful thinking. As Hess and Finn (2007) describe it, NCLB, in its present form, is

> a Christmas tree of programs, incentives, and interventions that are more an assemblage of reform ideas than a coherent scheme. NCLB's remedy provisions bear all the marks of concessions to various ideologues, advocates and interest groups, with scant attention to how they fit together, the resources or authority they require, or whether they could be sensibly deployed through the available machinery. (p. 2)

A telling example of this lack of coherence is that, although NCLB proclaims a strong commitment to holding states accountable for ensuring that all of their students are proficient in challenging state standards, the law contains no mechanisms for quality control of these standards or of the tests used to assess proficiency. In homage to traditional notions of "local control," USDOE and other federal agencies are actually precluded from reviewing and regulating the standards. In the same way, this "local control" crosscurrent undermines the law's stated commitment to guaranteeing that all children will be taught by "highly qualified teachers." The NCLB definition of "highly qualified" is linked to state certification requirements, but there is no procedure for federal oversight of the substantive content of these state regulations.

Similarly, the law's focus on holding states and school districts accountable for improving failing schools, and its emphasis on parental involvement as an important mechanism for doing so, are substantially negated by inconsistent "choice" provisions. Although these transfer and tutoring provisions may benefit some individual students, these measures are counterproductive to the overall goal of ensuring a meaningful educational opportunity for *all* students. The savviest parents and the most committed students, those who have the most to contribute to a school's rejuvenation, are the ones most likely to take advantage of the transfer option. And using school resources to buy instructional services from outside vendors diffuses responsibility for student learning, jeopardizes the coherence of students' learning experience, and does nothing to help build a better climate for teaching and learning in the school.

In general, the law puts a premium on political hype, rather than on feasible implementation measures. Although elimination of achievement gaps and high achievement for all are critical and attainable goals, the law mandates that these ends must be accomplished by a certain date—the 2013–2014 school year—without any evidentiary basis for postulating that, even with maximum efforts, this is achievable. In reality, as every politician, parent, educator, and student knows, 100% proficiency by 2014 is a pipe dream. Nevertheless, the law builds its demanding adequate yearly progress (AYP) requirements, and imposes its stringent sanctions, on the basis of progress toward this unattainable mandate.

Realization of NCLB's equity and accountability goals is more critical than ever. Within the next 20 years, more than half of America's schoolchildren will be from racial and ethnic minority groups, and vast numbers of these students come from backgrounds of concentrated poverty. If our nation is to be in a position to compete in the global economy, and if it is to have the type of educated citizenry that is necessary to sustain a vibrant democracy, clearly, these students will need to be well educated.

Similar concerns, articulated 2 decades ago, led President George H. W. Bush to convene a national educational summit in Charlottesville, Virginia. This nonpartisan event, attended by all 50 governors and leading corporate CEOs—and coordinated for the National Governors Association by Bill Clinton, who headed its education committee at the time—initiated the standards-based reform movement and began the policy developments that led a dozen years later to adoption of NCLB. We think it appropriate and necessary that, early in his tenure, President Obama convene a new national educational summit to bring a range of political, educational, civic, and corporate leaders together to take stock of the status of NCLB implementation 6 years after its enactment. Because of the overriding national interest in shoring up our educational system—and of realizing the vision of equal educational opportunity more than a half century after *Brown v. Board of Education*—the leaders attending the summit should formulate a new, coherent, and realistic approach for realizing NCLB's goals and should then propose specific revisions of the present statute for its reauthorization.

These revisions should be based on the practical steps needed to achieve NCLB's core aims of overcoming achievement gaps, providing significant educational opportunities to all students, and enabling all students to reach high achievement levels. If we are to achieve meaningful results on a national scale, the conflicting values and goals that now confuse and undermine effective implementation of NCLB need to be sorted out, reconsidered, and resolved. Both liberal and conservative shibboleths will need to be set aside in this process.

The revised policy would need to focus on how to provide all children meaningful educational opportunities that can actually achieve these critical goals. We think NCLB's core purposes can be met if fundamental revisions to the law's current structure are made in the following areas: (1) establishing challenging but attainable student achievement targets, (2) recruiting and retaining highly effective teachers, (3) providing comprehensive supports to minimize the impact of poverty on student learning and achievement, (4) ensuring full and fair funding, and (5) promoting successful capacity building in low-performing schools and districts. The specific recommendations that follow were informed by the findings of the previous chapters in this book, but they and the conclusions of this chapter are our own and should not necessarily be attributed to these other authors.

ESTABLISHING
CHALLENGING BUT ATTAINABLE ACHIEVEMENT TARGETS

Much of the equity muscle in NCLB comes from its demand that positive academic results be demonstrated for all racial/ethnic, language, and economic groups. Ironically, however, this emphasis on disaggregated outcomes has become counterproductive. The AYP targets that schools must meet are calibrated from NCLB's mandate that all students—100%—be proficient in challenging state standards by 2014. This mandate requires rates of progress that no school system has ever achieved and the feasibility of which have never been demonstrated.

The 100% proficiency target is especially illusory when applied to English language learners (ELLs) and students with disabilities. Both of these categories involve students who, by definition, are not achieving at high proficiency levels, the former because they have substantial English-language deficits and the latter because their disabilities have a detrimental impact on their educational attainment. By and large, as individuals in each of these categories receive special services and acquire proficiency, they join the category of "regular" students. They are replaced by newly arrived or newly identified students who do have these deficits or disabilities. The law makes some allowances for these circumstances by continuing to count for AYP purposes successful ELLs for 2 years after they no longer have special language needs and by exempting a limited number of students with severe disabilities from the normal AYP requirements. Nevertheless, as a whole, these categories of students, which by definition are largely composed of ever-renewing groups of students defined by their inability to meet standards, cannot reach or even substantially advance toward 100% proficiency. The fundamental incongruity between the needs of these students and the law's "one-size-fits-all" proficiency requirement means that, in practice, the current 100% target can never be met.

While earlier proclamations of national goals primarily served as motivational rhetoric, NCLB's 100% proficiency objective is a legal mandate that drives the law's whole accountability scheme. Schools and districts that fail to meet the annual progress targets calibrated from this requirement suffer specific consequences. Virtually no informed parent, teacher, administrator, researcher—or legislator—thinks this mandate can be met. Senator Edward M. Kennedy, one of the congressional architects of the law, recently acknowledged that "the idea of 100 percent proficiency is, in any legislation, not achievable" (Paley, 2007, p. A1). But, as Senator Lamar Alexander noted, Americans don't want politicians to lower standards, and, as a result, no one in Congress is now pressing to modify the 2014 proficiency date. If the proficiency-for-all target were merely a motivational goal, this might be an innocuous stand. But since thousands of schools around the country are being labeled "in need of improvement"—which the public reads as "failing"—because they have proved incapable of making sufficient progress toward an impossible goal, this irrational aspect of the law is causing considerable harm. The generally recognized but unstated impossibility of meeting the law's demanding goals also means that, in practice, enforcement of the law's requirements and imposition of its stated sanctions have been limited, thus further undermining the credibility of the whole enterprise.

This situation will become increasingly unworkable as we approach 2014. By that year, almost all schools in the nation will fall far short of the AYP targets and are likely to be on the "needs improvement" list. This is because the Department of Education has allowed the states to backload their AYP requirements so that the majority of progress toward 100% proficiency can be put off until the last few years.

Unattainable though the 100% proficiency by 2014 mandate may be, both politicians and the public have been loath to give it up. To many, it serves an important purpose as inspiration and assurance of fully inclusive academic success. It expresses a firm national promise and a public compact to further the education of *all* students—and especially of blacks, Latinos, students with disabilities, and low-income students whose needs have been neglected in the past. It serves as a rallying cry that says we must overcome the impediments of poverty and racism and finally realize equal educational opportunity. Stated in these terms, "proficiency for all by 2014" is, in essence, a statement of a renewed national commitment to implement *Brown*'s vision of equal educational opportunity within the next few years.

This intensified commitment to achieving *Brown*'s vision must be maintained and thoroughgoing educational opportunity must finally be realized in practice. To do so, however, the aspirational proficiency-for-all mandate should be modified before the impetus of the act is undermined by the frustration of mounting failures and either Congress repeals the act or the USDOE totally ceases to enforce it. What should be substituted are achievement targets that are demanding, that will constitute a substantive realization of the promise of *Brown v. Board of Education,* and that, with serious national efforts and investments, can be realized.

Does this mean that NCLB must abandon its commitment to high achievement for all? We don't think so. If the true goal here is to promote maximum achievement growth for all students, we should define demanding but meaningful achievement targets and set about revising the law to be sure that all students can meet them. To do this, NCLB should specify two fundamental achievement goals. First, it should demand that the achievement curve for students from each ethnic or racial group be equivalent, with equal proportions of students from all racial, ethnic, and income groups performing at the high, middle, and low ends of the inevitable bell curve of human functioning. In other words, although student outcomes will differ, a student's racial, ethnic, or socioeconomic background should no longer predict his or her access to educational opportunity or level of achievement. (Some modification of these expectations may be required for students with disabilities, who, by the very nature of their impairments, may not be capable of achieving at the same levels as other groups; appropriate, challenging targets for improving their achievement need to be devised.)

Second, NCLB should demand that, over a reasonable time period, the average achievement range for all groups should improve to a substantial but feasible extent. This means that the average performance level of students of all racial, ethnic, and socioeconomic groups should improve by large, measurable amounts over specific time periods. These increases can be calibrated by psychometricians in terms of "effect size" increases. For example, if the target were an increase in average performance of 0.33 standard deviations over 5 years, this would mean that, at the end of that time period, average individuals (i.e., at the 50th percentile) would be performing at the level that individuals who were previously at the 63th percentile were performing 5 years earlier. Other individuals, those above and below average, would also perform at a correspondingly higher level. These effect-size increases and the exact target dates for meeting them should be set by the policymakers and psychometric experts after a realistic appraisal of the implementation mechanisms and resources that will be devoted to this task. (More detailed explanations of these concepts are set forth in Chapters 5 and 6 in this book.)

National Benchmarks for Challenging State Standards

To promote progress toward academic achievement for all, NCLB must include a mechanism to ensure consistent rigor in the state standards that define the targeted levels of achievement. Given the demands of today's competitive global economy, high interstate mobility rates, and rapid communication among all of our people, we can no longer expect or accept wide variations in the content and in the caliber of the knowledge and skills that students learn in America's schools. Indeed, many aspects of the traditional funding, curriculum, and assessment functions of local school boards have already been superseded by statewide mechanisms.

NCLB's deference to local control in the setting of state standards and proficiency levels, while asserting federal control over outcome targets and sanctions, clearly has not worked. It has created perverse incentives that have led states to lower proficiency standards, over which they have unfettered control, if their schools have difficulty meeting rigid AYP requirements, over which states have no control. Commentators from both ends of the political spectrum now agree that NCLB cannot achieve its goals unless some mechanism for ensuring real rigor in state standards is promptly adopted (Miller, 2008; Ravitch, 1995).

To ensure such consistency, the Aspen Institute's Commission on No Child Left Behind has called for the creation, by a panel of experts, of model national content and performance standards and tests based on NAEP frameworks. We endorse the Commission's proposal that states be given a choice of (1) adopting the model national standards and tests as their own, (2) building their own assessment instruments based on the model national standards, or (3) keeping their existing standards and tests (or revamping them in response to the model national standards and tests), subject to review by the USDOE. (States using low-quality standards or setting unreasonably low proficiency requirements would then be required to adopt the model standards or bring their own standards up to a satisfactory level of quality.)

Expanding on the commission recommendations, we would call for the model standards to extend beyond the core subjects of English language arts, math, and science. A basic consensus has emerged from the state court cases on education equity and adequacy about the true breadth of knowledge and skills that students need to be prepared for competitive employment and to function productively in a democratic society:

1. sufficient ability to read, write, and speak the English language and sufficient knowledge of fundamental mathematics and physical science to enable them to function in a complex and rapidly changing society;
2. sufficient fundamental knowledge of geography, history, and basic economic and political systems to enable them to make informed choices with regard to issues that affect them personally or affect their communities, states, and nation;
3. sufficient intellectual tools to evaluate complex issues and sufficient social and communication skills to work well with others and communicate ideas to a group; and
4. sufficient academic and vocational skills to enable them to compete on an equal basis with others in further formal education or gainful employment in contemporary society. (Rebell & Wolff, 2008, p. 70)

NCLB should adopt this consensus to provide a solid floor of quality for the proficiency requirements and to guard against a narrow interpretation of the educational opportunities that schools need to provide.

We also think that standards and state examinations must properly emphasize the higher-order cognitive skills that students need to succeed in college and in the world of work. NCLB must rectify the current imbalance in subject-matter emphases between basic skills and advanced conceptual thinking by highlighting the importance of students gaining deep knowledge and skills in a broad range of subject areas by the time they graduate from high school.

Valid Assessments

The integrity of NCLB relies on fair and accurate assessment of student performance and progress. If the methods used to measure progress toward proficiency are inaccurate or subject to widespread manipulation, the validity and credibility of the entire enterprise is undermined. Unfortunately, today most state tests used to measure progress under NCLB are neither aligned with state content standards nor valid in accordance with applicable professional standards. "[P]erformance targets are made out of whole cloth" (Koretz, 2008, p. 19), and we know little about what test results really mean. An area of special concern is that virtually none of the subject-matter tests being used to measure content knowledge of students with limited English proficiency have been validated for use with this population, with the result that there are almost no accurate data on the actual proficiency of these students (Garcia, Kleifgen, & Falchi, 2008; see also Chapter 3 in this volume).

NCLB should, therefore, be revised to require each state to undergo an external review of the validity of its tests and of procedures for setting performance targets and cut scores by an USDOE-approved independent agency with expertise in this area. Given that few valid tests for English language learners exist at present, USDOE should develop model tests in all mandated subjects and grade levels in Spanish and at least five other languages most commonly used in American schools.

NCLB's narrow focus on standardized testing in a limited number of subject areas needs to be changed. State courts that have interpreted constitutional requirements for an adequate education in the 21st century have repeatedly held that schools must prepare students to be capable citizens and competent workers in a global society. These outcomes require, at the least, high school–level functioning in reading, math, and science, but they also require a solid background in social studies, foreign languages, the arts, and technology. Students should be assessed in all of these areas, and states' progress toward proficiency should be judged in these broad terms.

Such an assessment of the full range of student competencies will require multiple indicators of student achievement, including measures that assess higher-order thinking skills and understanding such as essays, projects, presentations, and portfolios, as well as surveys that reveal the competence of graduates on the job or participating in actual civic activities (Rothstein, Jacobsen, & Wilder, 2008). Although the integrity and comparability of national and statewide assessments must be maintained, validated multiple measures of student progress in all areas, and not just simple standardized tests, should be part of NCLB's assessment design. The testing burden on states, schools, and districts should also be decreased by allowing them to assess students annually in selected grades, instead of uniformly mandating testing in reading and math in grades 3–8 and high school each year. Given the importance of NAEP scores as national benchmarks for proficiency, NAEP's content and proficiency levels should be reconsidered and validated (see Chapter 5).

RECRUITING AND RETAINING HIGHLY EFFECTIVE TEACHERS

Research shows what parents and students already know, that the most essential resource a school can provide to any student is a truly effective teacher. NCLB acknowledges this, and, therefore, the law includes a requirement that every child be taught by a teacher who is "highly qualified" as its sole resource input mandate. In doing so, the act purports to set a new bar for America's teaching force. However, under the act's definition, states can and do deem teachers with only minimum competency as "highly qualified." In most state certification systems, this is the operative standard, and a teacher who meets state certification standards is, generally speaking, accepted as being "highly qualified" under NCLB. These requirements seem to have led to improvement in the availability of minimally qualified teachers, but they do little to ensure that all students will, in fact, be taught by teachers with the pedagogical skills, experience, and depth of subject-matter knowledge needed to provide the kind of instruction that will lead to proficiency in meeting challenging state standards and the development of higher-order thinking skills.

In order to provide all children with a meaningful educational opportunity to meet challenging proficiency standards, maximum efforts must be made to attract, develop, and retain teachers who truly are effective, especially in the schools attended predominantly by low-income and minority students, which historically have been hard to staff. Such efforts are complicated–and potentially hindered–by the obfuscation that NCLB now creates regarding teacher qualifications. The current labeling makes it difficult to know how many teachers are truly highly qualified and effective because all of those who are merely minimally qualified are given the same designation. Moreover, continued public support and investment in quality teaching could be jeopardized if virtually all teachers in our schools are (inaccurately) labeled "highly qualified" and student achievement does not substantially improve.

If states are to provide all of their students with teachers who are truly highly qualified, state certification requirements must be demanding and graduated. States should distinguish between initial entry-level requirements and advanced effective teaching classifications that are based on appropriate assessments. They should utilize evaluation and rating systems that consider strong learning gains for students, regular classroom observations, and feedback conducted by multiple sources, and that utilize validated evaluation rubrics. The schools of education that the states accredit should be required to emphasize curricula that are fully aligned with the state content standards, to inculcate in their students teaching skills relevant to an increasingly diverse student population, and to motivate students to prepare themselves to teach the subjects, such as math, science, and special education, and the schooling levels, such as middle schools, that now have the greatest shortages and the greatest needs

Despite widespread agreement that effective teachers make a huge difference in student achievement, there is little evidence that one can predict in advance from certification status or academic degrees which individuals will actually prove to be effective. States should, therefore, focus not only on hiring teachers with strong basic credentials, but also on working with local districts to promote effective induction, mentoring, and professional development programs that will develop a maximum number of teachers who are truly effective on the job, particularly in improving the performance of at-risk low-income and minority students.

The states should be required to provide relevant information on the rigor of their certification requirements, the accreditation standards for their schools of education, and their induction, mentoring, and professional development practices in their annual report cards to the public and in the state plans they submit to USDOE. Both the department and the interested public would then be in a position to assess the steps being taken by each state to improve and equitably distribute their teachers with the progress they are making over time in student learning outcomes. They would also have the basic information they need to compare the state's efforts and achievements in this regard with the accomplishments of other states.

Specifically, we propose that NCLB be revised to distinguish among three categories of teachers: "provisionally qualified teachers," "qualified teachers," and "highly effective teachers":

- "Provisionally qualified teachers" should be defined as teachers in training who meet the state's alternative certification requirements.
- "Qualified teachers" should be defined as those who have a college degree with a major in a field directly related to the subject area in which they are teaching, and who meet the state's entry-level certification requirements.
- "Highly effective teachers" should be defined as teachers who have deep subject-matter knowledge, a thorough understanding of state academic content standards and proficiency requirements, and a demonstrated ability to impart effectively the knowledge and skills required by state standards to students from diverse backgrounds and with diverse needs (INTASC, 1992).

NCLB's current requirements for equitable distribution of "highly qualified" teachers should be applied to all of these categories; this means that low-income and minority students should not be disproportionately assigned to teachers who are inexperienced or less than highly effective.

PROVIDING COMPREHENSIVE SUPPORTS TO MINIMIZE THE IMPACT OF POVERTY

Throughout its history, the United States has largely depended on the public school system to solve its problems of social and economic inequality. The cruel irony of the American education system is, however, that low-income and minority children who come to school with the greatest educational deficits generally have the fewest resources and least expertise devoted to their needs—and, therefore, the least opportunity to improve their futures. NCLB, though ostensibly geared to remedy this critical situation, does not sufficiently confront the impediments to learning created by the conditions of poverty.

Children who are poor experience disadvantages and hardships that profoundly influence their opportunities and ability to learn. There are a number of "pathways" through which poverty exacts its toll on children's academic achievement. Poor children are more likely than other children to lack adequate health care and, as a result, to suffer from health-related barriers to learning. Children who are poor generally lack the early experiences of linguistic enrichment and cultural stimulation, "the scaffolds for learning" (Gordon, 2005, p. 322) that are the norm for more affluent children, and these deficits account for a substantial amount of the achievement gap between low- and higher-income children entering kindergarten.

The state courts have considered in detail the specific resources that students need for a meaningful opportunity to obtain a basic quality education. By virtual consensus, they identify the following school-based resources as essential for acquiring the basic knowledge and skills students need to become capable citizens and competitive workers:

- Effective teachers, principals, and other personnel
- Appropriate class sizes
- Adequate school facilities
- A full platform of services, including guidance services, summer and weekend programming, tutoring, and additional time on task for students from poverty backgrounds
- Appropriate programs and services for English language learners and students with disabilities

- Instrumentalities of learning, including, but not limited to, up-to-date textbooks, libraries, laboratories, and computers
- A safe, orderly learning environment (Rebell & Wolff, 2008)

This list of constitutional education essentials is, of course, based on the services students need during the years and the times they are in school. To reach our national goal of improving achievement for all children and closing the achievement gaps, however, we must broaden our conception of educational essentials. In order to provide a meaningful educational opportunity to at-risk children from communities of concentrated poverty, these students must be provided, as needed, specific out-of-school educational essentials, including

- High-quality early childhood education
- Necessary levels of nutrition and physical activity
- Physical and mental health care
- Home, family, and community support for student academic achievement
- Access to arts, cultural, employment, community service, and civic experiences

NCLB should be revised to require states to submit "adequacy and equity" plans that demonstrate that appropriate resources and opportunities in all of the above-stated in school-based and out-of-school resource areas are being provided to all students. This approach would allow the states broad discretion to devise methods for identifying the most significant issues and the most cost-effective ways of meeting them. The provision of these services will also necessarily involve a variety of collaborative arrangements with community and governmental agencies; broad discretion will allow states and local school districts to devise and experiment with the most effective ways to meet the full range of children's most essential educational needs.

ENSURING FULL AND FAIR FUNDING

Although funding for elementary and secondary education programs covered by NCLB has increased since the law's passage, states and school districts have argued that this amount does not even cover the law's extra costs for testing and administration. The fiscal equity and education adequacy litigations that have been decided in dozens of states around the country in recent years have demonstrated that, to narrow or eliminate achievement gaps, substantial additional funding for essential educational resources will be required. In considering the extent of resources necessary to overcome the achievement gap, Congress has also largely ignored the reality of the impact of poverty on children's learning and the need to provide a comprehensive range of school-based and out-of-school resources to minimize it.

Although NCLB imposes a host of mandates on the states and local school districts, and it provides some additional funding, the law grossly neglects the need to ensure that *adequate* levels of funding are in place to allow students a meaningful opportunity to make solid academic progress, much less the unprecedented results that are being demanded. Accordingly, the federal government should be responsible for identifying the true costs of compliance with NCLB and determining a fair allocation of funding responsibility between the federal government and the states.

To identify the actual costs of providing all students a meaningful educational opportunity, Congress should authorize comprehensive studies of the costs to states and local districts of complying with NCLB, closing achievement gaps, and reaching achievement goals. This analysis should consider the costs not only of school-based resources but also of the out-of-school resources most important for the academic success of at-risk students. The studies should incorporate best practices to overcome achievement gaps in a cost-effective manner. Once the actual costs of providing meaningful educational opportunities are determined, schools should be provided the necessary levels of funding on a stable basis; if educational opportunity is truly a national priority, children's learning cannot be subjected to the vagaries of economic cycles.

States should be held responsible for ensuring that school districts with low tax bases and high needs receive sufficient state aid to meet the basic requirements for providing all of their students with a meaningful educational opportunity. Federal aid to the states should, at a minimum, ensure that states that lack sufficient resources to ensure the availability of essential resources and services to all of their students receive sufficient federal assistance to meet these obligations. NCLB should also require state plans to include information on present and projected funding levels and to describe states' efforts to ensure equity in funding.

FOSTERING SUCCESSFUL CAPACITY BUILDING IN LOW-PERFORMING SCHOOLS AND DISTRICTS

Although we call for a more proactive federal role in the oversight of the quality and integrity of state academic content and performance standards, we believe that the federal government has overstepped its appropriate regulatory role in its insistence on a rigid cascade of consequences for schools that are not meeting their AYP targets. To build instructional capacity in low-performing schools requires more local assistance and less federal regulation.

Like other aspects of the current law, there is no evidentiary basis for the cascade of consequences and sanctions now imposed on low-performing schools or the timetable for implementing them—there is no track record prior to or since NCLB to show that these measures help to improve student or school performance. The current cascade of consequences should, therefore, be scrapped and replaced with an effective system of state-based technical assistance and accountability for school and district capacity building.

The business of school improvement is still more art than science, requiring time, expertise, resources (both human and material), flexibility, and patience. Schools must be swiftly supplied with adequate resources for improvement, but, once these are in place, the rigid timetables that now dictate in advance how quickly schools must progress through each stage of improvement should be replaced with flexible, long-term performance goals.

NCLB should identify and disseminate best practice models and encourage states to implement these practices in all of the schools and districts that need them. Further, all state education departments must have the funding and the capacity to carry out these responsibilities. NCLB should ensure as a core requirement that productive state assistance is fully funded and actually put into effect at all schools in need of improvement. The specific forms of assistance that the state representatives provide should, however, be determined by each state, based on the needs of the particular school community and on an assessment of how best to work with the people in that community.

CONCLUSION

NCLB was a major bipartisan effort to build on the Title I legislation enacted in the 1960s and to achieve in the foreseeable future the equity vision of *Brown v. Board of Education*. Though the law's aims are exemplary, many of its specific provisions undermine real progress. In its current form, NCLB is hampered by an overemphasis on accountability and an underemphasis on ensuring the availability of the quality tools and resources needed to produce those results. NCLB needs to shift from its current focus on assessing progress toward 100% proficiency to a new focus on how to provide all students with meaningful educational opportunities.

Congress should continue to increase the federal government's financial support for NCLB's vital goals, and it should motivate the states to define meaningful educational opportunity in terms of specific categories of resources, programs, and services that are essential for children's educational progress, and should ensure these are in place by 2014. We believe that the states should retain the discretion to determine the specific resources that will be provided in each category and describe them in annual plans that are submitted to the federal authorities and in report cards that are periodically distributed to parents and the public. States must be accountable for the quantity and the quality of the resources and programs provided, and the extent to which they are, in fact, providing a meaningful educational opportunity to all of their children. States must also be accountable for ambitious but realistic growth in student outcomes.

Finally, if NCLB or any other federal education policy is to succeed in the United States today, it must also consider the barriers to learning created by poverty and create realistic means for dismantling them. Current national policies that leave the bulk of responsibility for providing equity to poor children solely to the schools are both unrealistic and insufficient. To approach the national goal of meaningful academic proficiency for all children, we must broaden our conception of the educational opportunities children must be afforded for success. We need to embrace a comprehensive approach to education that seeks strategically to integrate essential out-of-school supports and services with school-based activities in order to enhance students' abilities to succeed.

REFERENCES

Garcia, O., Kleifgen, J. A., & Falchi, L. (2008). *From English language learners to emergent bilinguals.* New York: Campaign for Educational Equity.

Gordon, E. W. (2005). The idea of supplementary education. In E. W. Gordon, B. L. Bridglall, & A. S. Meroe (Eds.), *Supplementary education: The hidden curriculum of high academic achievement* (pp. 320–334). Lanham, MD: Rowman & Littlefield.

Hess, F. M., & Finn, C. E., Jr. (2007, September). Can this law be fixed? A hard look at the No Child Left Behind remedies. *Education Outlook, 3,* 1–6.

Interstate New Teacher Assessment and Support Consortium (INTASC). (1992). *Model standards for beginning teacher licensing, assessment, and development: A resource for state dialogue.* Retrieved May 30, 2007, from http://www.ccsso.org/content/pdfs/corestrd.pdf

Koretz, D. (2008). The pending reauthorization of NCLB: An opportunity to rethink the basic strategy. In G. L. Sunderman (Ed.), *Holding NCLB accountable: Achieving accountability, equity, and school reform* (pp. 9–26). Thousand Oaks, CA: Corwin Press.

Kozol, J. (2005). *The shame of the nation: The restoration of apartheid schooling in America.* New York: Crown.

Miller, M. (2008, March). *Nationalize the schools (. . . a little)!* Washington, DC: Center for American Progress.

National Center for Education Statistics. (2008). *The condition of education 2008.* Washington, DC: U.S. Department of Education.

Paley, A. R. (2007). "No child" target is called out of reach: Goal of 100% proficiency debated as Congress weighs renewal. *Washington Post,* p. A1.

Parents Involved in Community Schools v. *Seattle School Dist. No. 1,* 551 U.S. (2007).

Ravitch, D. (1995). *National standards in American education: A citizen's guide.* Washington, DC: Brookings.

Rebell, M. A. (in press). *Courts and kids: Pursuing educational equity through the state courts.* Chicago: University of Chicago Press.

Rebell, M. A., & Wolff, J. R. (2008). *Moving every child ahead: From NCLB hype to meaningful educational opportunity.* New York: Teachers College Press.

Rothstein, R., Jacobsen, R. & Wilder, T. (2008). *Grading education: Getting accountability right.* New York: Economic Policy Institute and Teachers College Press.

About the Contributors

Richard Elmore is the Gregory R. Anrig Professor of Educational Leadership at the Harvard Graduate School of Education. His research focuses on the effects of federal, state, and local education policy on schools and classrooms. He is currently exploring how schools of different types and in different policy contexts develop a sense of accountability and a capacity to deliver high-quality instruction. Elmore is Director of the Consortium for Policy Research in Education, a group of universities engaged in research on state and local education policy, funded by the U.S. Department of Education. He has held positions with the Department of Health, Education, and Welfare and the U.S. Office of Education (1969–71), as well as several government advisory positions at the city, state, and national levels.

Eugene García is Vice President for Education Partnerships at Arizona State University's Mary Lou Fulton College of Education. Before coming to ASU in 2002, he was a professor and dean of the Graduate School of Education at the University of California, Berkeley, from 1995–2001. He served as a senior officer and director of the Office of Bilingual Education and Minority Languages Affairs in the U.S. Department of Education from 1993–1995. García is currently chairing the National Task Force on Early Childhood Education for Hispanics and conducting research in the areas of effective schooling for linguistically and culturally diverse student populations. He has published extensively in the area of language teaching and bilingual development. His most recent books include *Hispanic Education in the United States: Raíces y Alas, Understanding and Meeting the Challenge of Student Diversity*, and *Teaching and Learning in Two Languages: Bilingualism and Schooling in the United States*.

Amanda V. Hoffman is a policy and evaluation research associate at WestEd in Washington, DC. Her research focuses are on transition youth with disabilities, special education policy, quantitative research methods, and large-scale databases. She received her M.Ed. in Educational Research, Measurement and Evaluation from Boston College and her Ph.D. in Special Education Policy Studies from the University of Maryland, College Park.

Rebecca Jacobsen is an assistant professor of teacher education and education policy at Michigan State University. She was a 2006–2007 Spencer Foundation Dissertation Fellow. Her research and writing focus on the achievement gap, the democratic purposes of education, and public opinion and representation. She coauthored *The Charter School Dust-Up: Examining the Evidence on Enrollment and Achievement.* She received her Ph.D. in Politics and Education from Columbia University. Prior to completing her degree, she was a public school teacher in New York City and in Connecticut.

Robert L. Linn is Distinguished Professor Emeritus of Education at the University of Colorado at Boulder and co-director of the National Center for Research on Evaluation, Standards, and Student Testing. He is a member of the National Academy of Education. He has published over 250 journal articles and chapters in books dealing with a wide range of theoretical and applied issues in educational measurement and has received several awards for his contributions to the field, including the ETS Award for Distinguished Service to Measurement, the E. L. Thorndike Award, the E. F. Lindquist Award, the National Council on Measurement in Education Career Award, and the American Educational Research Association Award for Distinguished Contributions to Educational Research. He is a past president of the American Educational Research Association and of the National Council on Measurement in Education.

Susanna Loeb is a professor of education at Stanford University and director of the Institute for Research on Education Policy and Practice. She also co-directs Policy Analysis for California Education, an organization that aims to link academic research more closely to the policy needs at the state level. Loeb specializes in the economics of education policy, studying the relationship among schools and federal, state, and local policies. Her research focuses on teacher labor markets, looking at how teachers' preferences and teacher preparation policies affect the quality of teaching and the distribution of teachers across schools. She also studies school finance and how the structure of state finance systems affects the level and distribution of funds to districts. She is a faculty research fellow at the National Bureau for Economic Research and a member of the National Center for Analysis of Longitudinal Data in Education Research.

Margaret J. McLaughlin is a professor in the Department of Special Education and serves as the associate director of the Institute for the Study of Exceptional Children and Youth at the University of Maryland, College Park. She has been involved in special education all of her professional career, beginning as a teacher of students with serious emotional and behavior disorders. She earned her Ph.D. at the University of Virginia and has held positions at the U.S. Office of Education and the University of Washington. She has conducted a number of national research institutes and projects investigating educational reform and students with disabilities, specifically related to standards, large-scale assessments, and accountability.

Meredith A. Miceli is a doctoral candidate and fellow in the Special Education Policy Studies program at the University of Maryland, College Park. Her research interests include secondary special education, transitioning youth with disabilities, and the effects of standards-based reform on youth with disabilities. Upon completing her dissertation, she will be taking a job as an education program specialist in the Office of Special Education Programs at the U.S. Department of Education. Her work at the Department of Education will focus on the collection and analysis of state data related to the implementation of the Individuals with Disabilities Education Act.

Luke C. Miller researches education policy at the Urban Institute in Washington, DC. His research interests include state teacher policies, teacher and principal labor markets, secondary school reform, and rural education. He holds a doctorate in the economics of education from Stanford University.

Catherine M. Millett is a senior research scientist at the Policy Evaluation and Research Center at the Educational Testing Service in Princeton, NJ. Her research focuses on access, persistence, and achievement for students from various population groups at the postsecondary level. One area of her current research is on the doctoral student experience. She is the coauthor of *Three Magic Letters: Getting to Ph.D.* She served on the Technical Review Panel for the Educational Longitudinal Study 2002 as well as the Beginning Postsecondary Study 2004/06, both sponsored by the National Center for Education Statistics. Millett has been a visiting lecturer at the Woodrow Wilson School of Public and International Affairs at Princeton University.

Michael T. Nettles is senior vice president and holds the Edmund W. Gordon Chair for Policy Evaluation and Research at the Educational Testing Service in Princeton, NJ. He has a national reputation as a policy researcher on educational assessment, student performance and achievement, educational equity, and higher education finance policy. His publications reflect his broad interest in public policy, student and faculty access, opportunity, achievement, and assessment at both the K–12 and postsecondary levels. Nettles serves on the National Research Council Board on Testing and Assessment and the Board on Higher Education and the Workforce, the board of the Center on Research on Teaching and Learning, the joint advisory board for Education Research Centers in the state of Texas, the board of the Center for Enrollment Research, Policy, and Practice at the University of Southern California, the National Center for the Improvement of Educational Assessment, Inc., and the Harvard University Medical School Advisory Committee on Diversity. Nettles is also a member of the Bank Street College of Education Board of Trustees.

Hyeyoung Oh is a second-year doctoral student in sociology at the University of California-Los Angeles. She is currently on the Edwin W. Pauley Fellowship, offered to UCLA graduate students with outstanding academic records and promise of scholarly achievement. Oh received her B.A. degree in sociology from Princeton University in 2005. From 2005 to 2007 she was a research assistant in the Policy Evaluation and Research Center at the Educational Testing Service, located in Princeton, NJ.

Michael A. Rebell is executive director of the Campaign for Educational Equity and a professor of law and educational practice at Teachers College, Columbia University. He is also an adjunct professor of law at Columbia Law School. He taught for many years at the Yale Law School and last year was a visiting professor at Harvard Law School. Mr. Rebell co-founded and served as executive director and counsel for the Campaign for Fiscal Equity, which won a major constitutional ruling that entitles all children in New York State to the opportunity for a sound basic education. He is one of the nation's foremost authorities on fiscal issues in education and has pioneered the legal theory and strategy of educational adequacy. Mr. Rebell has litigated numerous class-action lawsuits on a variety of issues involving law and education, including *Jose P.* v. *Mills*, the landmark New York State case establishing the legal rights of students with disabilities. He served as special master in the Boston Special Education litigation, *Allen* v. *Parks*. He recently coauthored (with Jessica R. Wolff) *Moving Every Child Ahead: From NCLB Hype to Meaningful Educational Opportunity*. He has also coauthored two other books, *Equity and Education* and *Education Policymaking and the Courts*, and has written several dozen articles on a wide range of education issues.

Richard Rothstein is a research associate of the Economic Policy Institute and of the Campaign for Educational Equity, Teachers College, Columbia University. From 1999 to 2002 he was the national education columnist of *The New York Times*. Rothstein is coauthor (with Rebecca Jacobsen and Tamara Wilder) of *Grading Education: Getting Accountability Right*. He was a member of the national task force that drafted the statement, "A Broader, Bolder Approach to Education" (www.boldapproach.org), and is also the author of *Class and Schools: Using Social, Economic, and Educational Reform to Close the black–white Achievement Gap,* and *The Way We Were? Myths and Realities of America's Student Achievement.*

Robert Schwartz has been a faculty member at the Harvard Graduate School of Education since 1996, where he currently serves as academic dean and Bloomberg Professor of Practice. From 1997–2002 he also served as president of Achieve, Inc, a national nonprofit established by governors and corporate leaders to help states strengthen academic performance. He previously served in a variety of roles in education and government, including as a high school teacher in California and a principal in Oregon; education advisor to Boston mayor Kevin white and Massachusetts governor Michael Dukakis; executive director of the Boston Compact; and education program director at the Pew Charitable Trusts. He currently co-chairs the Aspen Institute's education program and serves on the boards of the Education Trust, the Noyce Foundation, and the Rennie Center for Education Research and Policy.

Amy Stuart Wells is a professor of sociology and education at Teachers College, Columbia University. Her work has focused broadly on issues of race and education and on educational policies, such as school desegregation, school choice, charter schools, and tracking and how they shape and constrain opportunities for students of color. Currently she is the principal investigator of the Study of Urban-Suburban School Change, which examines the role of public education in the demographic shifts occurring across and within urban and suburban boundaries in four metro areas. From 2006–08 she was the director of a research initiative for Teachers College's Campaign for Educational Equity.

She is coauthor (with Jennifer Jellison Holme, Anita Tijerina Revilla, and Awo Korantemaa Atanda) of *Both Sides Now: The Story of Desegregation's Graduates;* coeditor (with Janice Petrovich) of *Bringing Equity Back: Research for a New Era in Educational Policy Making;* editor of *Where Charter School Policy Fails: The Problems of Accountability and Equity;* author of "The 'Consequences' of School Desegregation Take Two: The Mismatch Between the Research and the Rationale" in *Hastings Constitutional Law Quarterly*; and coauthor with Robert L. Crain of *Stepping Over the Color Line: African American Students in white Suburban Schools.*

Tamara Wilder is a postdoctoral fellow with the Center for Local, State and Urban Policy (CLOSUP) at the University of Michigan's Ford School of Public Policy. Wilder is coauthor (with Richard Rothstein and Rebecca Jacobsen) of *Grading Education: Getting Accountability Right.* Her research focuses on equity issues, accountability, school choice, and parent and community involvement in schools. She received her M.A. in Quantitative Methods in the Social Sciences from Columbia University and her Ph.D. in Politics and Education from Columbia University.

Jessica R. Wolff is the policy director of the Campaign for Educational Equity at Teachers College, Columbia University, and conducts policy research in educational accountability and comprehensive approaches to educational opportunity. She served as director of policy development of the Campaign for Fiscal Equity (CFE) from 2000–2005, where she played a critical role in bringing the public voice into policy development through "Accountable Schools, Accountable Public (ASAP)," "Making the Money Matter: A Community Dialogue" and other public engagement projects. Her work with the Sound Basic Education Task Force on Accountability helped guide school funding legislation in New York State. Among other works, she is author of the series *In Evidence: Policy Reports from the CFE Trial,* and coauthor (with Michael A. Rebell) of *Moving Every Child Ahead: From NCLB Hype to Meaningful Educational Opportunity.*

Index